BUSINESS LAW
An Introduction

Second Edition

FRANK W. SHAW

american press
BOSTON, MASSACHUSETTS

Preface

This book uses a unique approach to the presentation of business law. The hornbook method presents law efficiently at the expense of providing enough examples to make the material meaningful to students with limited experience and vocabulary. The casebook method presents the law through numerous cases at the expense of efficiency by leaving synthesis to the student and requiring the review of many cases. This text covers only essential, "every day" legal concepts. The student is presented with a short set of legal principals to memorize and several examples of their application. By memorizing terse generalizations, studying the text and practicing, a business law student can acquire a comprehensive and practical first exposure to the law that governs business.

The method introduced in this text will facilitate future study of the law by providing a student with an outline of basic principals that can be elaborated upon as the need and opportunity. Essential vocabulary is presented and defined while every legal principal applied in short case scenarios. The questions at the end of the chapters can be used to monitor understanding of the key concepts discussed in the text.

The text also develops a practical approach to researching problems in business law. Sample forms are included as well as special sections on practical legal research and contract critique which can be expanded by the instructor into major classroom activities if time permits. An optional classroom activity in which students can experience first hand the use of the law in a small claims court setting is also available A test bank organized by concept is available for quick reference and convenient expansion.

This text differs in approach substantially from existing texts that present large amounts of background material, numerous rules and relatively rarely used exceptions that many students have difficulty mastering due to their limited experience in business. This text compensates for students' lack of experience by presenting fewer rules with common exceptions in the context of numerous examples. In addition, outrageous examples are often used because students find it easier to recall the humorous or bizarre.

Serious students should memorize the short, generalizations. These statements provide students with a means of focusing effort during study. They also provide students with a serviceable study tool and outline for future use in more advanced courses. Often in the study of law, the novice can become so lost in the details that sight of the overall scheme and system of the law is lost. This makes the subject unnecessarily difficult and ruins the natural pleasure that mastery of the law evokes. This problem is addressed by giving students enough, easily assimilated legal generalizations to answer practical questions and develop sound business procedures.

Acknowledgements

I would like to thank Professors Charles Rice and Robert Rhodes of the University of Notre Dame Law School for their encouragement and instruction. To a great extent, I owe my love of the law to Professor Rhodes and my methods of instruction to Professor Rice. I would also like to thank my family — Carolyn (Lyn), Frank M. Shaw, Rebecca L. Shaw, and Emily A. Shaw for their patience and love. I owe a great debt of gratitude to my parents, Doris and Frank W. Shaw. My mother's willingness to proofread the rough draft of this text went well beyond the call of duty. My father's assistance with teaching, evaluation and research has helped make the law courses I have taught relevant and practical for students of general business. I hope this text brings the user the same excitement and satisfaction the law has given to me. On a final note, I would like to express my appreciation to the students and faculty at Westminster College in Salt Lake City, Utah for their support and encouragement. Special thanks are due to Shana L. Hopperstead, a fine student of management, for assisting with the editing of the second edition.

Disclaimers

All characters and fact patterns used in this text, the instructor's manual, and the test bank are fictitious and any resemblance to actual persons, living or dead, or real events is purely coincidental. Names were chosen at random to assist with the presentation of imaginary fact patterns.

The forms used in this text were developed by the author merely for purposes of illustration and are neither intended nor fit for use in any actual transactions.

The purpose of this text is to assist a student beginning the study of business law to develop a background for future inquiry as well as an understanding of the law. The text is not designed to assist or encourage the unauthorized practice of law. Readers should always obtain competent legal assistance when the need arises.

Contents

SECTION I

THE LAW IN GENERAL, 1

SECTION II

TORTS, 19

SECTION III

CONTRACTS, 79

SECTION IV
BUSINESS ORGANIZATIONS, 175

SECTION V
UNIFORM COMMERCIAL CODE, 247

SECTION VI
MISCELLANEOUS TOPICS, 329

SECTION I
THE LAW IN GENERAL

Sources of the Law
Practical Legal Research

Chapter 1

Sources of the Law

There are three main sources of business laws: legislatures, courts and administrative agencies. Each of these governmental bodies publish their laws in different sets of books so being aware of the source of a law will enable a student to find it for reference. The complexity of the law, the frailty of human memory, and the unceasing adaptation of the law to our collective experience make an awareness of how to find the law essential. The law is changing even as you read this. A student interested in using the information gained in a business law course to manage business practices in the future must acquire both a working knowledge of basic legal principles and a practical means of updating that knowledge. Chapters one and two are devoted to developing the rationale and technique for efficiently conducting legal research.

It is advantageous to be able to access the law independent of an attorney. Since it is expensive to resort to legal counsel in the absence of a clear necessity, the ability to conduct preliminary research can ultimately contribute to the more efficient use of a company's legal consultants. When the need for counsel is not obvious, an examination of the law will often help clarify the issues and the consequences of a business decision. When it is appropriate to purchase the assistance of legal counsel, an independent knowledge of the law will contribute to using those services more efficiently as well as making informed decisions during the course of the work.

I. LEGISLATIVE LAW

Legislative laws consist of constitutions with their amendments and statutes that are printed in state codes and the United States Code.

Each state government as well as the federal government has a legislature which is composed of elected representatives of the people. These elected representatives pass laws that impact every aspect of business. A "law" is a rule the government will enforce. "Legislative laws" are the laws enacted by the various state legislatures and the United States Congress. Legislative laws can be classified as constitutional laws and statutes. Without going into great detail, it can be said that the state and federal "constitutional laws" consist of constitutions with their amendments. They require, among other things, a two-thirds majority to enact. This type of law is best used to establish and limit the power of the government. Constitutional laws are not normally used to control the actions of private individuals and companies. Due to the larger majority required to pass and amend them, they are generally too cumbersome for use in the regulation of business. The rapidly changing relationships characteristic of modern business require relatively frequent adjustments of the law that would be very difficult to accomplish by repeated constitutional amendments. For this reason, constitutional provisions are generally used to limit the power of the government rather than to control the people.

"Statutes", on the other hand, are legislative laws used to control both the government and the people. They require only a majority vote to enact, and are, therefore, a better tool for governance because they are more easily amended as ways are found to improve them. Legislative laws are published in codes. A "code" is an orderly arrangement of laws organized according to subject matter. State constitutional provisions and statutes are printed by each state in their respective "state codes." For example, the legislative laws enacted by the Utah State Legislature are published in Utah's state code which is called the "Utah Code." The legislative laws enacted by the United States Congress are published in the federal code referred to as the "United States Code" or, simply, the "U. S. Code."

Essential Vocabulary

1. law
2. legislative law
3. constitutional law
4. statute
5. code
6. state code
7. U.S. Code

II. JUDICIAL LAW

Judicial law consists of reported case decisions and is summarized in legal encyclopedias.

Judicial law, or case law, is essentially the interpretation of the law made by the courts. Courts attempt to be consistent and decide similar cases in the same way. Their decisions, therefore, become "precedents." A precedent is a case decision which the courts will follow in the future when similar situations present themselves. Case decisions are reported through an extensive system of state, regional and national reporter systems. However, the legal encyclopedias remain the most efficient research tools for people who have not completed law school. One such legal encyclopedia is [American Jurisprudence 2nd, or Am. Jur. 2nd.] This encyclopedia consists of many volumes and is very well indexed. The articles contained in it summarize state and federal case law and are well organized and clearly written.

Sometimes, courts actually produce laws as they interpret the law. In addition, the courts are the primary authority on the "common law." When William the Conqueror took over England in 1066, English law was quite variable from area to area throughout the country. To unify the country, English monarchs adopted the policy of establishing and enforcing a uniform, or "common," set of laws that would be followed in every jurisdiction in England. The "English Common Law" became the body of law that was common to all parts of England. When the English colonized America they brought their Common Law with them. Prior to the American Revolutionary War, the English Common Law was in force in each of the colonies. At the close of the revolutionary war, the colonies still needed a system of laws so they continued to enforce the English Common Law through their courts until their legislatures had the time and need to alter it.

The English Common Law continued to be a part of the judicial law of the United States and, to the extent that the state legislatures and the United States Congress have not altered it, the common law is still enforced by the courts today. Judicial law is often referred to as "common law" because of this. Much law that affects business in the areas of torts, contract law and property law is primarily judicial law because it originated in the courts' interpretations of the common law.

Essential Vocabulary

1. judicial law
2. common law
3. precedent
4. legal encyclopedia
5. Am. Jur. 2nd

III. ADMINISTRATIVE REGULATIONS

Administrative regulations are rules made by administrative agencies which are printed in state codes of [administrative regulations] and the [Code of Federal Regulations].

"Administrative agencies" are governmental units [created by state legislatures and Congress] to regulate areas of the law [requiring special expertise] and [constant vigilance]. State agencies consist of such organizations as the State Tax Commissions, the State Highway Commissions, the State Offices of Education, the State Departments of Securities, Social Services, Health, and Employment, etc/Federal agencies consist of such agencies as the Internal Revenue Service, the Securities Exchange Commission, the Federal Communications Commission, the Federal Aviation Administration, and the Securities Exchange Commission, etc/ These agencies regulate business along with the legislatures and the courts/Regulations are arranged according to subject matter and grouped with other regulations formulated by the same agency/The regulations of all state agencies are published in a "state codes of administrative regulations."/The regulations of all federal agencies are published in the "Code of Federal Regulations," or "CFR./ Local counties and municipalities also have regulations that apply to their respective areas which are published in codes available at the county or city offices. Unlike the state and federal administrative agencies mentioned above, the city and county ordinances do not generally need to be researched unless a specific need is apparent.

/Administrative agencies are created by statutes called "enabling acts."/These statutes give agencies authority to regulate various aspects of governmental activities/Agencies may not exceed their authority in developing administrative regulations needed to carry out their missions./The courts protect the people from state and federal agencies' exceeding their authority by stopping them from enforcing offending regulations/

For example, Andre ran a motel and provided access to the units by means of a narrow, paved roadway which he owned and maintained. Only Andre's guests used the roadway. After three accidents involving vehicles and pedestrians, the State Highway Commission posted a 10 mile per hour speed sign on the roadway. In its enabling act, the State Highway Commission was directed to "establish safe speed limits on all public streets and roadways." The Commission probably exceeded its authority in this example because the roadway was not a public street or roadway. If the enabling act had given the Commission the power to regulate all motor vehicle traffic, it would have been able to control Andre's private access road.

Essential Vocabulary

1. administrative agency
2. administrative regulation
3. state code of administrative regulations
4. Code of Federal Regulations
5. CFR
6. enabling acts

IV. PRIORITY OF LAWS

/Laws are accorded priority in the following order: constitutional provisions, statutes, judicial law, and administrative regulations/

To remember the basic structure of our legal system, it helps to understand the basic "priority of the laws." The priority of a law is its relative strength compared to laws from other sources. In the event of a direct conflict, the law with the greatest priority should be followed by the courts. At both the state and federal level, the constitutions with their amendments have the highest priority because they have the closest connection to the people. They are enacted by elected representatives with a two-thirds majority and must be further approved by the public through referendums and the like. Constitutional laws are followed in priority by statutes. Statutes have the second closest connection to the public by virtue of their enactment by a majority of the elected representatives of the people. Judicial law ranks third due to the fact that these laws are developed by judges who are more difficult to remove from office than legislators and for that reason are relatively more independent of the people. Finally, administrative regulations have the lowest priority in the event of conflict. Agencies that create these regulations are more insulated from the will of the people than the legislatures and courts because they are created by legislative bodies and their directors are usually political appointees rather than elected officials.

Generally, if a state administrative regulation conflicts with a state case decision, statute, or constitutional provision, it cannot be enforced. Similarly, if a state court decision conflicts with a state statute it will be corrected on appeal and will not become part of the state judicial law. A state statute will not be enforced if it conflicts with a constitutional provision. The same is true of the federal constitutional provisions, statutes, judicial laws and administrative regulations.

V. DOCTRINE OF FEDERAL SUPREMACY

/When state and federal laws conflict, federal laws have supremacy./

It is important to remember, however, that there are two systems of law in force in every state — state laws and federal laws. When there is a conflict between state and federal laws, the federal law takes precedence by virtue of the "Doctrine of Federal Supremacy." If, for example, a state constitutional provision conflicts with a federal administrative regulation, the federal administrative regulation will generally be given precedence under the Doctrine of Federal Supremacy. This is necessary to ensure that the fifty states of the United States continue to function together as a single unit in areas that affect the national interest.

Essential Vocabulary

1. priority of laws
2. Doctrine of Federal Supremacy

VI. RESEARCH FOR BUSINESS PEOPLE

A practical research procedure for business people involves searching five sources:
 (1) the state code,
 (2) the U. S. Code,
 (3) a legal encyclopedia,
 (4) the state code of administrative regulations, and
 (5) the Code of Federal Regulations.

The great majority of laws that apply to business can be found within the five sources listed above. The state code contains the legislative law in force in the state in question while the U.S Code contains the federal legislative law. The legal encyclopedia contains well analyzed articles summarizing the state and federal judicial law in force in the state. Although there are several high quality legal encyclopedias from which to choose, *American Jurisprudence 2nd* is an excellent choice for business people. State and federal administrative regulations can be researched through their respective codes which are well indexed. These sources provide efficient access to the three basic types of law regulating business activities — legislative law, judicial law and administrative regulations.

CHECK YOUR UNDERSTANDING

DIRECTIONS: Read each of the following questions. Choose the best answer and study the discussion of the question.

1. Law is:
   a. justice.
   b. almost totally dependent upon cultural variables.
   c. synonymous with concepts of morality.
   d. a body of rules which will be enforced by the state.
   e. primarily a product of the collective cultural experience.

DISCUSSION

(d)   Laws are rules that are enforced by the power of the executive branch of government. Rules that are not enforced tend to be of little use in controlling behavior. Freeway speed limits are an excellent example of this phenomenon. When the police are present, the speed limits are observed. When they are absent, the average speed tends to increase dramatically.

Although the goal of a good law is to produce justice or a fair result, justice and law are not synonymous. Justice is the desired result of properly applying good laws. Law is not totally dependent upon cultural variables. The law tends to be based upon the collective experience of the people it governs as well as their culture. Although laws vary from culture to culture, the problems of living together in a cohesive society often result in very dissimilar cultures generating very similar solutions to the same problems. For example, stealing, killing, marriage etc. are regulated in nearly every legal code of every culture. While concepts of morality affect the details of the laws solving common problems, the human experience makes the laws of various cultures surprisingly similar.

2.   Assume you need to find out what the courts have declared to be the law governing the rights and duties of beekeepers. The best resource book to use would be:

a.   *American Jurisprudence 2nd.*
b.   the state code.
c.   a textbook on bees.
d.   advance sheets of court decisions.
e.   a good index to legal periodicals.

DISCUSSION

(a)   Court decisions are summarized by experienced lawyers in the legal encyclopedias. Unanalyzed court decisions are often not useful to business researchers without the formal legal provided in law schools. One very good reference tool for the business researcher is *American Jurisprudence 2nd*. This encyclopedia is more useful than advance sheets reporting court decisions because the articles in the encyclopedia place the decisions in perspective.

State codes contain the legislative laws of each state rather than a summary of judicial law. Textbooks dealing with bees may cover the law to some extent, but the law would not be their main focus. The advance sheets merely chronicle the decision of the court in one case at a time without providing a broad perspective of the law. An index to legal periodicals would merely allow a researcher to find legal periodicals dealing with very narrow issues of the law. Legal periodicals tend to provide highly technical discussions of very narrow legal issues rather than general discussions of the law from the broad perspective needed by researchers without formal legal training.

3. A governmental entity created by the legislative branch of the state government for the purpose of exercising judicial, executive, and legislative powers within prescribed limits of authority would probably:

    a. be illegal as an unconstitutional delegation of authority by the legislature attempting to create it.
    b. be classified as an administrative agency.
    c. be unconstitutional because it would violate the "separation of powers" safeguards of the U.S. Constitution.
    d. violate the substantive due process requirements of the 14th Amendment.
    e. not be allowed to operate because its enabling legislation would be ultra vires.

DISCUSSION

(b)   Administrative agencies are created by the state legislatures and the U. S. Congress by enabling acts. The courts have ruled that legislative bodies creating agencies do not unconstitutionally delegate their law-making powers or violate constitutional requirements of separation of powers when they form an agency if they limit the agency's rule making authority. The action of creating administrative agencies is not "ultra vires" or beyond the power of legislative bodies. Administrative agencies are frequently created by various legislative bodies to administer the law in areas considered too technical or too rapidly changing to be efficiently overseen by the legislative bodies themselves. However, administrative agencies are ultimately answerable to the legislatures that created them as well as the courts.

4. The state constitution provided that no tax could be levied on the sale of medicine to consumers. A federal taxing authority issued a regulation requiring the collection of a 2% tax on all drug sales. Which of the following is probably correct?

    a. No drug tax needs to be collected because administrative regulations are subordinate to constitutional provisions.
    b. No drug tax needs to be collected because the taxing regulation is unconstitutional.
    c. No drug tax needs to be collected until the courts resolve the ambiguity resulting from these conflicting laws.
    d. A drug tax must be collected under the Doctrine of Federal Supremacy.
    e. A drug tax must be collected under the doctrine of apparent authority.

DISCUSSION

(d)   A drug tax will need to be collected under the Doctrine of Federal Supremacy. This principle dictates that federal laws will generally be superior to state laws when they directly conflict. Since a federal administrative regulation conflicted with a state constitutional provision, the doctrine of federal supremacy would dictate that the federal law be observed. The taxing regulation would not be unconstitutional unless it violated the United States Constitution since it came from a federal agency. Generally, taxing authorities have the right to collect taxes until the courts rule that the tax law is defective. Tax payers who dispute the tax may pay the tax under protest until the courts rule on the validity of the tax. If the courts ultimately rule that the tax is improper, the taxes paid are usually returned to the tax payers when they can be identified. Apparent authority is a type of authority a private agent can acquire from his principal and will be discussed in the chapter dealing with the law of agents. It has no application here.

5.   Laws made by a state legislature to regulate business are usually called:

   a.   statutes.
   b.   constitutional amendments.
   c.   administrative regulations.
   d.   common law.
   e.   judicial law.

DISCUSSION

(a)   Legislative laws regulating business are usually statutes. State legislatures make constitutional laws and statutes. Constitutional provisions and amendments are generally used to regulate only the government. Legislatures pass enabling acts that create administrative agencies, but it is the task of administrative agencies to develop administrative regulations. The common law is part of the judicial law, and judicial law is created by the courts through their interpretation of legislative laws, administrative regulations and the common law.

Chapter 2

Practical Legal Research

Law books only summarize the law. The basic principals of the law are amazingly consistent from place to place and era to era. However, the details differ considerably due to changes in technology and other aspects of cultural experience. For this reason, no law text can effectively teach a person the law. Texts are only collections of generalizations that are true much of the time and false some of the time. The extent to which a legal generalization is true more often than it is false is the measure of the strength of the generalization. Legal encyclopedias generally have over one hundred volumes containing more than 100,000 pages of articles. Even these massive works are only summaries of the law. In a sense, they too merely present generalizations. They are more accurate summaries, however, than typical law texts because their huge volume allows for more detailed approximations of what the law is at a given time.

It is important, therefore, for business people to be able to find the law efficiently after they have completed an introductory course on the subject. Being able to find the law provides managers with access to additional and important sources of information that can be used in making decisions. Awareness of the law also facilitates the effective use of legal counsel to avoid the costly and wasteful litigation. The generalizations that follow provide a systematic approach to investigating the legal aspects of issues that may arise in business. Lawyers are generally not consulted until legal issues have been identified due to the cost involved. Managers who are aware of the legal aspects of their decisions will be better able to identify situations in which legal counsel can be useful and cost effective.

Legal research in business can be conceived as a process beginning with an investigation, progressing to research, and culminating with a memorandum of findings and recommendations. The sections that follow discuss each of these activities in detail and suggest a method for systematic research.

I. PREPARATION FOR RESEARCH

Preparation for research consists of finding facts, identifying issues, and compiling a descriptive word list.

Finding Facts

Once a legal question is tentatively identified, the facts relating to the issue need to be gathered and documented. If the matter is later submitted to an attorney, this information will save time and assist the attorney in accurately evaluating the case. A cardinal rule for conducting an investigation is whenever possible, the actual files, documents, and people involved should be consulted.

Interviews should not be threatening or adversarial. People tend to hold back important information when they become defensive. It is usually best to make notes immediately after the interview to avoid intimidating the person being interviewed unless the interview is conducted over the telephone. Often, people will not answer questions candidly when their responses are recorded in writing or electronically. People often refuse to answer questions or discuss matters when they believe litigation may be involved.

A record of the facts should be put into writing after a thorough investigation has been conducted. Although the report need not be lengthy, it should contain all versions of the facts when contrary versions are discovered along with references to the sources of the facts reported. If the research of the issue is interrupted by another project, the report should be reviewed prior to continuing after the interruption to assure that known facts are fresh in mind.

Identifying Issues

After the incident has been investigated, the legal questions or issues should be formulated for research. This is done simply by asking oneself what questions of law were raised by the investigation. These issues will be used to develop a descriptive word list for use in searching the indexes of the law books. No special wording is required, but familiarity with the law may save time and make interpretation of the texts much easier. A quick review of a good business law prior to conducting the research may save time and improve the quality of the research product.

Compiling a Descriptive Word List

The final step necessary to prepare for legal research is the development of a descriptive word list for the purpose of systematically searching the indexes to the law books. To make the list, the researcher must identify the persons, places, things and actions mentioned in the formulated issues. If the issue were, for example, "Will our company be liable for negligence if the owner loans a company truck to his daughter's minor friend for personal rather than company use?" The persons, places, things and actions suggested by the statement of the issue are as follows: company, liable, negligence, owner, loan, truck, daughter, minor, friend, personal use, and company use.

This list should be expanded to include common synonyms for these words to allow for differences in language and errors in indexing. In identifying synonyms, a thesaurus should not normally be used because it makes the list needlessly lengthy. An expanded list might look something like the following.

company	motor vehicle
proprietorship	vehicle
business	daughter
liable	child
liability	minor
negligence	child
carelessness	infant
owner	friend
proprietor	personal use
loan	private
bailment	company use
truck	business

Since the systematic search of the legal sources mentioned earlier is essential in finding the law, the indexes should not be approached without a descriptive word list. Once the list has been developed, the researcher is ready to search the indexes of the five sets of law books mentioned in the chapter describing the basic sources of business law. The same descriptive word list will be used with all five sets of books. When citations are located in the indexes, a note can be made next to the word that led to it for later use in locating the law in other books. Although most of the words will not be found in the indexes, it is important to remember that thorough descriptive word lists produce thorough research. With practice, long lists can be searched relatively quickly. The law books discussed in the following section are also available on disk and online. However, since the books themselves are usually available in public law libraries free of charge and a fee is often charged for access to computerized versions of these resources, we will concentrate on the use of books rather than computers to access the law.

II. RESEARCH

Research consists of searching indexes and copying the law from books, pocket parts and interim supplements.

Since the descriptive word list will be used five times, some method of marking one's place without obscuring it should be employed. Most of the words on the list will not be located in the index and should be marked off when they are not found. When a word is found, it will be quickly observed that much material irrelevant to the search will be listed under the heading in the index. Each item under the heading must be skimmed and relevant citations noted on the list. The most common and frustrating errors made by novice researchers are the failure to read all of the citations under the main heading when they go on for many pages in the index and the failure to go completely through the list even if promising citations are found early in the search. These errors cause researchers to miss citations critical to the issues they're investigating.

The citations are usually made to title and section numbers rather than to page numbers. A typical citation may be look something like "12-4-22." The first number, "12," is the title number. The volumes of the law books usually have the title numbers listed on their spines in print which is smaller than the volume number. The title numbers are used to locate the proper volume rather than volume numbers which are typically used only to quickly re-shelve the books. In our example, title 12, may be in volume one or two of the set. Once title 12 is located the chapter ,"4", and the section, "22", are used to locate the section needed.

Another commonly used scheme involves the use of a title word and a section number. For example, the index may present citations that look something like: "NEGLIGENCE Sec. 1243". In this case, the researcher would find the section by first finding the article on negligence in the same way as one would find an article in an encyclopedia. Once the article entitled "NEGLIGENCE" is found, Section 1243 could be located.

Law books are regularly updated by "pocket parts" that are located at the back of the volume containing the desired section and interim supplements that are usually found at the end or the beginning of the set in a separate paperback or looseleaf binding. If the section is located in the pocket part or interim supplement, the update must be copied along with the text in the main volume. If it is missing, the legal text has not been updated and may be relied upon as written in the main volume. Using a copy machine to copy the law is important. Reduced sized print often makes sections look deceptively brief and copying them by hand is not efficient. Paraphrasing a section is not useful since the exact words used in the law are of critical importance.

Remember to search the following five sets of books: the state code, the U.S. Code, a legal encyclopedia (e.g. American Jurisprudence 2nd), the state code of administrative regulations, and the Code of Federal Regulations (the "CFR").

III. MEMORANDUM

Memorandums summarize the facts, list the issues, discuss the law, and report recommendations to members of the management team.

The memorandum preserves the work of the researcher and provides helpful guidance and reference for the management team. If litigation later becomes necessary, it can be used by an attorney in conducting her own investigation. Memorandums of this type should not be sent to opponents or anyone outside of the management team because they are likely to interfere with negotiations and legal action that may later be deemed necessary. The memorandum should report all of the facts gathered. If facts are in dispute, it should fairly report all versions of the facts with their sources. Who, what, when, where and how are important. The facts most frequently omitted by students learning to conduct legal research are dates and times. The exact date of events is often critical to the application of the law in a given situation. The legal issues addressed should be clearly stated in the memorandum for quick reference.

The discussion of the law should not merely be an exact quote from a law book. It should be a well drafted and readable summary of the law along with an explicit application of the law to the situation at hand. The memorandum should contain proper citations to all law that is applicable and note that copies are attached. A copy of the entire text of the law should be attached to the memorandum for the reader's convenience. When only a portion of a statute or other law or article is relevant, the entire section should be attached to the memorandum with important parts highlighted. This is necessary to allow the careful reader to make an independent evaluation of the accuracy of the memorandum. The copies of the law should be on the same size paper as the memorandum itself so that they can be handled easily. When irrelevant material shares the pages containing the statutes, regulations, and articles cited in the memorandum, copy the entire page and merely highlight the relevant portions. It wastes time to cut out the irrelevant material. If the copies do not clearly show their citations, proper citations can be typed at the top of the copies for easy reference.

A typical memorandum might be organized somewhat like the following:

Date:

To:

From:

Re: Loaning a Truck to a Minor

  In our meeting on Sept. 1, 1993, you indicated that you are considering loaning a company truck to your friend. He would use the truck for two days to move his personal belongings to a new residence. He is now seventeen years old and living with his parents. He has been a licensed driver since he was sixteen and currently holds a valid driver's license. He has had no accidents of which you are aware. You did not know whether or not he has liability insurance.

  The issue raised is whether the company will be liable if he borrows a company truck and is involved in an accident.

  Utah Code Ann. Sec. 41-2-116 (1953) makes the owner of a motor vehicle liable along with the driver for negligence when the driver is younger than 18 years old. I have attached a copy of this statute for your convenience. The company is the owner of the motor vehicle. Since your friend is only 17 years old, the company would be liable along with him for any accident caused by his negligence.

  We should check the insurance coverage on the truck to make certain that it covers liability and damage to the truck resulting from an accident when a minor is driving on personal, rather than company, business. In light of our potential exposure to liability, it may be wise to contact our attorney before proceeding further.

SECTION II
TORTS

The Intentional Torts
Defenses to Intentional Torts
Negligence and Strict Liability
Defenses to Negligence

Chapter 3

Intentional Torts

"Torts" are wrongful actions for which the courts will grant compensation. The word, tort, comes from a Latin word meaning twisted. When a person's twisted or wrongful conduct causes another to suffer some harm, the victim acquires a "cause of action," or a right to relief from the courts. Since the cause of action belongs to a private individual or company rather than the public at large, it is referred to as a "civil action." Wrongs against the public in general are actionable by the government in "Criminal actions." Misconduct that generates tort liability often generates criminal liability also. Since each aggrieved party acquires a cause of action against the individual who harmed him, a single occurrence can result in numerous law suits by private individuals and companies as well as governmental units.

For example, a person who throws a bomb on a bus with five passengers may be sued or prosecuted a number of times for his actions. Each passenger and the driver would have a tort action against the bomber. In addition, the bus company that owned the vehicle would have an action along with motorists who were injured because of the bombing. The bomber would also be prosecuted in a criminal action since bombing violates the criminal law.

These numerous court actions would not violate the prohibition against "double jeopardy" which is the constitutional and common law prohibition against trying a person again after a first trial for the same offense because no victim would have more than one trial. Not only would the government be a victim, but each of the passengers and other persons or companies injured would be victims and, as such, have their own causes of action. The prohibitions against double jeopardy would prevent the state from prosecuting the bomber again if it lost in its first criminal prosecution. However, each of the other victims of the bombing would have the right to pursue their actions in court also.

The doctrine of "res judicata," a Latin expression that literally means that the matter is settled, is another legal doctrine that prevents an aggrieved party from taking a matter before a court more than once. This legal doctrine does not bar more than one action arising from a single occurrence because each aggrieved party has a separate legal matter to be settled in the courts. If, however, one of the victims sued and lost, she would not be able to bring another action against the bomber arising out of the same incident because she would have had her "day in court," or trial, arising out of that incident.

When torts are committed, the courts have a number of options in providing relief. They can award an "injunction," a type of court order, prohibiting the tortious conduct in the future by ordering the "tortfeasor," the person who has committed the tort, to refrain from the tortious conduct. Wrongdoers who violate injunctions can be jailed or fined for being in contempt of court. The courts may also award "damages. Damages are money awards and may be "nominal," "compensatory" or "punitive." Where there is no economic or other loss to the victim, the courts will only award nominal damages. Nominal damages are damages in name only and are usually no more than one dollar. Where the victim suffers economic or other loss, the courts may award money damages which the victim can collect from the tortfeasor. Compensatory damages are damages designed to merely cover the cost of the losses to the victim. Punitive damages are awarded in addition to compensatory damages to punish a wrongdoer or discourage him from similar conduct in the future.

The torts that are discussed in the pages that follow should be memorized by name. Even if a wrongdoer's tortious conduct results in liability for several torts, each victim can maintain only one court action for a single occurrence. Victims generally sue for all torts committed in a single action in the hope that at least one can be proven. Once the elements of a tort have been proven, a victim is entitled to recover damages or an injunction or both. It is important not to confuse torts which are civil wrongs with crimes which are public wrongs. A victim cannot recover damages in a criminal action because the action belongs to the public at large. Technically, the victim is not a party to a criminal action. Fines and other forfeitures that are imposed by the government representing society for criminal misconduct are paid to the governmental agency imposing them rather than the victim. Private victims must seek their relief from the courts in the form of civil actions for the torts discussed in the pages that follow.

Essential Vocabulary

1. tort
2. cause of action
3. civil action
4. criminal action
5. double jeopardy
6. res judicata
7. injunction
8. nominal damages
9. compensatory damages
10. punitive damages

I. BATTERY

Battery is intentionally causing the offensive touching of another.

Battery is an intentionally caused tort as are all of the torts discussed in this chapter. The intent required for the tort of battery is the intent to touch or cause the touching of another. If the person actually touched is not the intended target, the person touched can still sue for battery because the intent to touch the chosen victim would be transferred to the actual victim.

Paula decided to play a little joke on Sylvia so she bought a pie. When Sylvia walked through the doorway, Paula threw the pie into her face. If Sylvia did not see the humor in the prank and sued for battery, Paula would be liable. If Sylvia had ducked and the pie had struck Francis instead, Paula would have been liable to Francis since Paula intended to touch Sylvia.

In the case of the pie, Paula caused the touching directly. Paula would have been liable even if she had caused the touching indirectly. Consider this scenario. Paula noticed that Sylvia walked across her lawn each night to get from the car to her front door. In an attempt to break her of the habit, Paula dug a deep hole in the yard across the path and carefully replaced the sod to conceal it. When Sylvia got off work and returned home, she was injured when she fell into the hole. Paula would be liable for battery because she intended for Sylvia to be "touched" by the bottom of the hole. If someone else had fallen into the trap instead, Paula would still have been liable because the intent to touch someone was present.

The touching must be an "offensive touching". An "offensive touching" may be defined as any touching to which the victim has not given his consent. If consent is given, the resulting touching is not offensive and there is no battery.

Andrew was a milkman. Each morning, he entered Katie's home with her permission to place the milk in her refrigerator. Katie was typically asleep when Andrew delivered the milk. One morning, Andrew kissed Katie while she slept. She later found out what had occurred when she heard him bragging about the experience. Andrew is liable to Katie for battery even though she was not aware of being touched at the time it occurred. The kiss was offensive because she had not consented to it.

Consent to being touched is a defense to battery. Touching is not offensive if the people touched give their consent. A person's consent may be express or implied. Consent is "express" when it is made with words and "implied" when it is made by actions.

Bill went to his dentist to have a tooth filled. He discussed the problem with the dentist and agreed to have the tooth repaired. When the dentist told him to open his mouth, Bill complied. After the work was completed, Bill decided that he did not like the way the filling looked and sued the dentist for battery. The dentist would not be liable for battery because Bill expressly consented to the touching associated with the tooth repair.

Bill later participated in a football game at school. When the ball was snapped, one of the linemen knocked him down. Bill sued for battery because he was injured when he hit the ground. The lineman would not be liable for battery even though he intentionally knocked Bill down since Bill had given his implied consent to all forms of touching normally associated with football when he joined the game. A football player consents to all types of legal and illegal touching usually associated with the game. If the lineman had produced a baseball bat from under his jersey when the ball was snapped and used it to knock Bill down, he would have been liable to Bill for battery because the use of clubs is not normally associated with the game.

Essential Vocabulary

1. battery
2. offensive touching
3. express consent
4. implied consent

II. ASSAULT

Assault is intentionally causing apprehension of battery.

Assault is committed any time a person intends an action that causes another to suffer "apprehension" of a battery. Apprehension is defined somewhat differently for this tort than in common usage. A person suffers apprehension of battery when he expects to be touched immediately. He does not need to suffer fear, but it is essential that he does expect to be touched at that instant and not at some time in the future.

Doris intentionally pointed a pistol at Laura. Laura believed that she would be touched at that instant with a bullet. Doris would be liable to Laura for assault. It would not be a defense to an action for assault that the pistol was not loaded or that Laura was not afraid. If Laura reasonably believed that she was going to be shot at that instant, an assault was committed. There would be no assault, however, if Doris had merely threatened to shoot Laura in a few minutes without pointing the weapon at her. The element of apprehension would have been lacking since Laura did not expect to be touched at that instant. Similarly, there would be no assault if Doris had merely threatened to strike Laura with her fist while standing too far away to carry out the threat. However, if Doris had begun to walk toward Laura after making the threat to strike her, the assault would have been complete at that moment. The attack began the instant Doris started to move toward Laura while making threats. Once an attack has begun, the tort of assault is complete even if the attack is never completed.

Essential Vocabulary

1. assault
2. apprehension of battery

III. FALSE IMPRISONMENT

False imprisonment is intentionally causing confinement where the victim is aware of the confinement or harmed.

The tort of false imprisonment is committed when a person intentionally confines another without a right to do so. Imprisonment is "false," or wrongful, when it is without the consent of the victim and without a legal privilege such as the defense of people or property. "Imprisonment" is confinement. Confinement has been defined by the courts as detaining someone who is aware of being detained or injured in the process for any length of time whatsoever. The length of the confinement may only have an impact on the extent of damages that can be recovered. The confinement may itself be intended or merely be the result of other intended conduct.

During the robbery of a drug store, a robber pointed a gun at the clerk and demanded that he fill a bag with money. In addition to the tort of assault, the robber committed the tort of false imprisonment by detaining the clerk at gun point. The robber intended to rob the store and the result of detaining the clerk was a product of his conduct. Similarly, a hijacker who takes control of a plane commits the tort of false imprisonment by detaining passengers who are aware of the hijacking even if they are not injured. If the passengers were not aware of the hijacking at the time and were not injured, they could not sue successfully for false imprisonment.

Essential Vocabulary

1. false imprisonment
2. imprisonment
3. confinement

IV. INTENTIONAL INFLICTION OF EMOTIONAL DISTRESS

The intentional infliction of emotional distress is intentionally causing severe emotional distress by outrageous misconduct.

The tort of intentional infliction of "emotional distress" generally requires some type of outrageous conduct directed at the victim that causes him to suffer severe emotional trauma. To commit this tort, the perpetrator must intend the victim to suffer emotional distress or engage in intentional conduct that is substantially certain to result in the victim's distress. Emotional distress is mental suffering such as grief, fear, anger, humiliation, etc. Outrageous conduct is conduct that substantially exceeds the limits of human decency. People must be "thick skinned" enough to withstand the normal lack of manners and poor taste of others. However, where inappropriate conduct goes beyond the limits of human decency by virtue of its cruelty, disgusting nature, unreasonable duration, involvement with sex, etc. it may be outrageous enough to support this tort. Mere name calling is generally not outrageous enough to support the action.

A practical joker committed the tort of intentional infliction of emotional distress by telling the victim who was confined to a wheelchair on the third floor of a building that there was a fire and that the elevators could not be used in evacuation. The crippled victim suffered extreme emotional distress in attempting to evacuate the building using the fire stairways. The actions of the practical joker were outrageous and were likely to cause the victim to suffer severe emotional distress.

A murderer would commit this tort by shooting a woman's husband before her eyes because his intentional conduct would be substantially certain to result in her suffering emotional distress even if he did not intend to cause it directly. However, negligently running over her husband would probably not result in liability for this tort since the action would not have been intended.

Essential Vocabulary

1. emotional distress
2. outrageous conduct

V. INVASION OF PRIVACY

The invasion of privacy is intentionally causing:

    (1) appropriation of the right to publicity, or

    (2) intrusion into private places, or

    (3) public disclosure of private facts, or

    (4) placement in a false light.

Invasion of privacy can be conceived as four torts grouped together under a single title. The "appropriation" of a person's name, face, or in rare instances, voice for advertising violates their right to privacy. This tort is gradually being extended to protect people from having their rights to publicity. Appropriation can be defined as using a person's name or image without consent.

Bill cannot tell others that Sandra endorses his wine products or use a picture of her in his wine advertisements without her permission. Celebrities' images and names often have commercial value, and they charge fees for their use. People have a right to avoid unsought publicity and associations with products and services.

"Intrusion" into the private places of another can be defined as entering into the private places of another by physical, electronic or other means. Observing others or taking pictures of them while they are in their showers or going through their wallets would constitute invasion of privacy by intrusion into a private place. Intrusion by electronic means could involve listening to private phone conversations or bugging a person's home.

"Public disclosure" is the communication of information about a person to someone without a legitimate interest in the information. People who are not public figures have a right to have their private affairs remain private until they consent to the disclosure of private facts or are involved in occurrences of public interest such as crimes, elections, etc. "Private facts" are facts that people generally consider to be personal such as credit ratings, health conditions, educational records, etc. These facts can be disclosed to people with a legitimate need for the information.

Where Dan owed money to his creditors and would not pay them, the creditors would be liable for invasion of privacy by public disclosure of private facts if they were to circulate flyers to Dan's neighbors detailing his financial difficulties in an effort to embarrass him into paying his bills. The neighbors would not have a legitimate interest in Dan's financial affairs. However, if Dan attempted to obtain a loan, he would consent to the lender's obtaining a credit report detailing his financial affairs. His consent would eliminate any question of invasion of privacy. However, if the lender took the report home to enjoy it with his friends at a party, he would violate Dan's right to privacy because his friends would have no legitimate need for the information. Dan's consent extended only to the lender. If Dan had been a burglar, the disclosure of his crimes and other facts to the police would be permissible because the police have a legitimate interest in Dan's illegal activities.

Placing someone in a false light also violates his right to privacy. A person in a "false light" by creating a situation in which others are led to believe something about the person that exposes him to ridicule or contempt. This type of invasion of privacy sometimes overlaps the tort of defamation of character discussed later in this chapter.

Where a newspaper placed a picture of a beauty queen on the front page next to a story detailing the arrest of a bank robber, it may be liable to the beauty queen for placing her in a false light even though her story was told in an article on page two. In this case, the implication was that she was the bank robber.

Essential Vocabulary

1. invasion of privacy
2. appropriation
3. intrusion
4. public disclosure
5. private facts
6. false light

VI. TRESPASS TO LAND

Trespass to land is intentionally causing something to enter the land or airspace of another.

A "trespass" is an unlawful act or a lawful act done in an unlawful manner. A trespass to land requires only that the trespasser intend to enter real property belonging to another or go to that particular place. "Real property" is the land and everything attached to it in a permanent way. It is not a defense that the trespasser thought she was somewhere else or that she didn't know that the real property belonged to the victim. Where the trespasser is aware that her entry is wrongful at the time, the courts will sometimes award punitive damages in addition to any compensatory damages for actual harm to the property. Not only are trespasses to the surface of the real property actionable, but intentional and wrongful intrusions into the air space above the property and the earth below the surface are actionable. The earth below the surface at all depths and the air above the property to the altitudes used for aviation are considered part of the land.

Where Julie was hiking on what she thought was public land, she would be liable for trespass if the property was privately owned even though she did not intend to enter private property. The requirement of intent would be met because she intended to hike to that particular location. She would, however, probably not be liable for substantial damages if she did not actually damage the property. If she had cut down a tree, however, she would have been liable for its reasonable value. If she had known that the property belonged to another and that she was there without permission, she might also be liable for punitive damages.

Trespassers do not need to enter the property personally. It is enough that they cause someone or something to enter the property. When Arnold throws his garbage over the fence into his neighbor's yard, he commits the tort of trespass directly. He could also commit the tort of trespass if he trained his pet St. Bernard to relieve itself on his neighbor's lawn. Note, however, that if the dog went to the neighbor's yard without Arnold's training it or other intentional action, Arnold would not be liable for trespass to land because he would lack the required intent. Arnold would also be liable for trespass if he dug a tunnel under his neighbor's property while searching for gold ore or flew his model helicopter twelve feet off the ground over his neighbor's back yard. A person's property normally extends downward to the center of the earth and upward to the point where the government has taken an easement for private, commercial, military and scientific aviation. Even where no damage is done, a victim of repeated trespasses can usually obtain an injunction that restrains a trespasser from entering the property in the future.

Essential Vocabulary

1. real property
2. trespass to land
3. airspace

VII. PRIVATE NUISANCE

Private nuisance is intentionally causing interference with the use of privately owned land.

The tort of "private nuisance" requires the wrongdoer to intend the action or intentionally create the condition that ultimately results in interference with another's use or enjoyment of real property. A nuisance is private when it interferes with privately owned land rather than publicly owned land. Interference with publicly owned land is referred to as "public nuisance" and is usually not actionable by private individuals. Actions for public nuisance belong to the government unless a victim suffers a harm that is different from the harm suffered by the general public. No entry is required for private nuisance because the essence of the tort is the interference with the use of the land rather than wrongful entry which is the basic requirement for the tort of trespass to land.

Donald was in the habit of listening to his stereo at 2:00 a.m. When his neighbor complained, Donald told him to mind his own business. Donald committed the tort of private nuisance when he interfered with his neighbor's use of his private property as sleeping quarters. It would not be a defense that Donald merely intended to listen to the music rather than to interfere with his neighbor's sleeping. If, however, Donald had been camping at a public camp ground operated by the forest service when he played his stereo at the same early hour, he would not have been liable to other campers for creating a private nuisance since he would have interfered with the use of public rather than private property. The primary difference between trespass to land and private nuisance is that trespass to land involves some type of entry onto the land belonging to another while private nuisance does not require any entry.

Essential Vocabulary

1. private nuisance
2. public nuisance

VIII. TRESPASS TO CHATTELS

Trespass to chattels is intentionally causing interference with the chattels of another.

Trespass to chattels is intentionally interfering with the chattels of another. "Chattels" are personal property. Personal property is all property that is not land or permanently attached to land. The intent required for this tort is merely the intent to touch a particular item of personal property. The tort is committed even if the wrongdoer thought that the victim's property was his own. When a person interferes with the property of another, the measure of damages is usually the cost of repair of the item, its reasonable rental value or depreciation. Damages are designed to compensate the owner for the inconvenience resulting from the interference, and the victim retains ownership of the property after the tortfeasor pays the damages.

Warren owned a pet skunk that was in the habit of displaying its scent around the yard to mark out its territory and attract other skunks. This annoyed Stella, the next door neighbor. To deter the animal from further malodorous conduct, Stella shot the animal and wounded it. Stella would be liable to Warren for the animal's veterinary care. After she had paid the damages awarded to Warren, the skunk would still belong to him. Stella would have been liable even if she believed the skunk was merely a wild animal. It is enough that she intended to shoot it. The skunk would not have an action against Stella because only human beings have the right to bring tort actions. Stella would not have been liable to Warren for "cruelty to animals" because that is a crime and can be prosecuted only by the government. If Stella had been prosecuted and fined for the crime of cruelty to animals, the fine would go to the government rather than Warren. She would also not be liable to Warren for battery because she touched the skunk. Animals are merely property under the law and have no right to bring actions in tort. Warren's civil action must be for trespass to chattels. If the skunk had been killed, the proper action would have been for conversion which is discussed in the next section.

Essential Vocabulary

1. chattels
2. personal property
3. trespass to chattels

IX. CONVERSION

Conversion is intentionally causing the taking of the chattels of another.

As with the tort of trespass to chattels, the intent required for conversion is the intent to take a particular item of personal property. It is not a defense to an action for conversion that the wrongdoer thought that the item he took was his own or belonged to someone other than the victim. The taking of chattels can be accomplished by actually carrying the item away or merely rendering it useless while it is still in the possession of the victim.

James used Phil's toothbrush believing that he was using his own. James intended to take the property because he intended to use that particular toothbrush. He would be liable to Phil for its reasonable value. However, unlike the tort of trespass to chattels, the tort of conversion amounts to a forced sale of the chattel by the victim to the wrongdoer. After the wrongdoer has paid the damages, he becomes the owner of the converted property. In this case, James would be the owner of the toothbrush after he paid Phil for it.

Sometimes, a victim may have a choice as to which tort to use. Trespass to chattels should be used where the victim wants to retain the property after being compensated for its damage or use. If the victim does not want the property back, the tort of conversion is properly used. In the case of Warren's skunk discussed above, it is important to note that if the skunk had been killed or rendered useless by the gunshot wound, Warren could have sued for conversion. However, Stella would have become the owner of the skunk or its body after she had paid its reasonable value.

Essential Vocabulary

   1. conversion
   2. taking

X. INTENTIONAL MISREPRESENTATION

Intentional misrepresentation is intentionally misrepresenting material facts to others who justifiably rely to their detriment.

An "intentional misrepresentation" is a lie told for the purpose of motivating another to do something or refrain from doing something. The person telling the lie must intend the victim to rely on it. The victim's reliance must be reasonable and result in harm. The victim must not be negligent in relying on the misrepresentation, or reliance will not be found to be reasonable and there will be no liability. An intentional misrepresentation can be classified as "fraud in the inducement" or "fraud in the execution" or "factum." The word fraud is another word for a lie. Fraud in the inducement is lying to people to motivate them to take some action that is not in their best interest. A person "executes" a document when he signs it. Fraud in the execution, therefore, is lying to someone about what they are signing. Fraud in the may also be called "fraud in the factum." The factum of an instrument is its contents. So fraud in the factum is another term for lying to people about what they are signing.

Lois wanted to sell her business to Clark. Although the business had been losing money for five years, Lois told Clark that it had produced $40,000 of net income each year. She altered the company's records to show false income. Clark purchased the business relying upon her misrepresentations and was unable to extricate himself from it after discovering the true state of affairs until he had lost $100,000. Lois would be liable to Clark for his payment and losses because Clark had justifiably relied upon her misrepresentations to his detriment. Lois's intentional misrepresentations would have amounted to fraud in the inducement since her lies induced him to enter into the contract. If Lois had not altered the books, and Clark had purchased the business without bothering to check them, he might not have had a claim for intentional misrepresentation. If he could have discovered the true state of affairs by examining records and tax returns that Lois made available to him, his reliance on her statements would not have been reasonable. Although a party does not ordinarily need to consult outsiders to determine whether another's representations are true, he does need to take the steps commonly taken in similar circumstances to protect himself and his interests.

If Lois had concealed the signature page in a multiple copy contract for the sale of her home to Clark, and Clark had justifiably believed that he was only purchasing a home, Lois's fraud would have been a fraud in the execution. She would have tricked Clark into signing the contract to purchase her business by convincing him that he was only purchasing her home. This would have been fraud in the execution or fraud in the factum rather than fraud in the inducement.

Essential Vocabulary

1. intentional misrepresentation
2. fraud
3 justifiable reliance
4. fraud in the inducement
5. fraud in the execution (fraud in the factum)

XI. DEFAMATION OF CHARACTER

Defamation of character is intentionally publishing a false and defamatory statement about a person without a privilege to do so.

Defamation of character is commonly called "libel" if committed through written statements and "slander" if committed through verbal statements. "Intentional publication" is accomplished by communicating a defamatory statement to a person other than the victim. It is not necessary to prove that the person communicating the statement was aware that it was false. In fact, it is not a defense that the person sued for defamation of character genuinely believed the statement. The statement must be both false and "defamatory." A defamatory statement is one that subjects the victim to ridicule or contempt, i.e. it must be "bad."

George became angry with Carl and told their boss that Carl had been stealing office supplies from the company. If he was fired because of the statments, Carl would have an action for defamation of character against George provided that he had not stolen the supplies. George intentionally published a defamatory statement by telling the boss that Carl had been stealing supplies. Since being a thief is "bad," the statement was defamatory. If George had merely told Carl that he thought he was stealing supplies, there would have been no liability because the statement would not have been published. Also, George would not have been liable for defamation if Carl had actually stolen office supplies because the defamatory statement must be false to generate liability.

To be liable for defamation, a person must defame without a privilege to do so. There are several circumstances in which a person is held to have a privilege to publish a false and defamatory statement about another. We will deal only with one that is especially important in the context of business — the "conditional privilege." People have a conditional privilege to publish false, defamatory statements about others when they have reason to believe the statements are true and they communicate only with parties who have a legitimate interest in the information.

In our case above, George would not have been liable to Carl even though the statement had been false if George had reason to believe that Carl really was stealing the office supplies because George's boss would have a legitimate need to know. If George had not had reason to believe that Carl was stealing or had told someone not connected with he company, George would have been liable because he would not have met the conditions of the privilege.

Essential Vocabulary

1. defamation of character
2. libel
3   slander
4. publication
5. defamatory
6. conditional privilege

XII. INJURIOUS FALSEHOOD

Injurious falsehood is the intentional and malicious publishing of a false and derogatory statement about a person's title, property, credit, business or other property or interests.

While defamation is a cause of action for people aggrieved by false statements intentionally published about them, the tort of injurious falsehood provides a remedy for false statements maliciously published about things belonging to a person. Unlike defamation, injurious falsehood requires the publication of the false statement to be both intentional and "malicious." To be malicious, the statement must be made for an improper purpose knowing that it is false or with reckless disregard for the accuracy of the statement. It must not merely be the result of an innocent mistake or negligence.

Sue wanted to purchase a rare antique sofa under an installment contract. City Furniture ordered a credit report on her prior to extending credit. The report issued by Leslie's Credit Bureau indicated that Sue had very poor credit. City Furniture refused to sell to Sue on the basis of the credit report and subsequently sold the antique sofa to another buyer. The report was false. Sue actually had excellent credit. Leslie's Credit Bureau would not be liable to Sue for injurious falsehood unless Sue could show that Leslie or one of her employees had maliciously made the false report. If, however, Leslie had made the report knowing it to be false so she could purchase the sofa herself, she would have been liable for injurious falsehood. If she had only inadvertently made the error, her liability would have been limited to the tort of negligence which will be discussed in a later section.

Essential Vocabulary

1. injurious falsehood
2. malicious

XIII. INTERFERENCE WITH CONTRACTUAL RELATIONS

Interference with contractual relations is intentionally causing another to breach a contract.

Intentionally causing another to breach a "contract" gives rise to liability for interference with contractual relations. A contract is a promise that the courts will enforce. Intentionally causing someone to breach a contract requires that the person causing the breach know about the contract's existence. In the absence of a binding contract, wrongful interference may generate tort liability for interference with prospective advantage which is discussed below.

Paul and Miko entered into a contract in which Miko was required to sing weekly in Paul's club for three months. Rita, who was aware of the contract, told Miko that she would pay her twice what Paul was paying her if she would sing at Rita's club instead. Miko breached her contract with Paul to take advantage of Rita's offer. Not only is Miko liable to Paul for breach of contract, but Rita is liable to Paul for intentional interference with contractual relations. Rita would not have been liable if she had not been aware of the contract between Miko and Paul because her interference would not have been intentional. Also, if Rita had made her offer to Miko prior to the formation of the contract between Miko and Rita, there would have been no tort because this amounts only to lawful competition.

Essential Vocabulary

1. interference with contractual relations
2. contract

XIV. INTERFERENCE WITH PROSPECTIVE ADVANTAGE

Interference with prospective advantage is intentionally interfering with another's business for a purpose other than fair competition.

Interference with "prospective advantage" is the wrongful interference with future opportunities to earn profits from a person's business. The organization of a business enterprise gives rise to prospective advantages or opportunities to earn profits in the future. Prior to the existence of a contract, competition for business is legal and encouraged. Intentional competition is a lawful activity even though the competition results in one of the competitors losing business. If, however, the interference is for a purpose other than legitimate competition, it is wrongful and tortious. Interference for the purposes of eliminating competitors, exacting revenge, or reducing bargaining power is wrongful.

Thomas opened a barber shop in a small town that had no barber. Gary, Thomas' enemy, decided to drive Thomas out of town by destroying his business. Gary hired another barber to set up a shop in the same town and paid him to sell haircuts below cost. Soon, Thomas had to close his shop because he could not sell haircuts as cheaply as his subsidized competitor. Gary is liable for intentional interference with prospective advantage because he interfered with Thomas' business for revenge rather than for the purpose of fair competition. If the other barber had merely been competing fairly and Thomas had been driven out of business, there would have been no liability.

Essential Vocabulary

1. interference with prospective advantage
2. prospective advantage

CHECK YOUR UNDERSTANDING

DIRECTIONS: Read each of the following questions. Choose the best answer and study the discussion of the question.

1. Cathy stole Owen's stereo and destroyed it. Owen complained to the police, and Cathy was prosecuted. Upon being found guilty of the crime of theft, Cathy was fined $200. Owen will probably:

   a. be entitled to the $200 fine.
   b. be entitled to only the value of his stereo with the court retaining the excess.
   c. be entitled to the $500 less court costs and attorney's fees.
   d. need to file a separate civil action for conversion to recover any damages.
   e. be entitled to nothing because he elected to pursue a criminal action, and the rule against double jeopardy prohibits trying Cathy a second time in a civil action for damages.

DISCUSSION

(d)   Owen will need to file a civil action for conversion to recover damages for himself. Criminal actions are brought by the government to address an injury to society. Any fines imposed are normally retained by the state. Cathy's taking of the stereo injured two parties in this case: the state and Owen. Each party is entitled to a "day in court" or trial. The constitutional and common law prohibitions against double jeopardy only prohibit a party from bringing two different actions arising from the same occurrence. The doctrine of res judicata merely prevents a party from bringing a single incident before the courts twice.

2. Amy put a lethal dose of poison into Carl's drink at a party in an attempt to bring his boring and lengthy anecdotes to an early end. Carl didn't see Amy poison his drink and was so busy talking that he never got around to drinking it. However, he found out about Amy's attempt to poison him later so he sued her. Amy will probably:

   a. be liable to Carl for attempted murder.
   b. be liable to Carl for assault.
   c. be liable to Carl for battery.
   d. be liable to Carl for private nuisance.
   e. not be liable to Carl.

DISCUSSION

   (e)   Amy will probably not be civilly liable to Carl at all because no tort was committed. Attempted murder is a criminal action and as such belongs to the state rather than Carl. Amy would not be liable for assault because Carl didn't know about the poison at the time of the party. Since he was unaware that he was about to be touched he would not have suffered the apprehension of battery required for assault. Carl cannot maintain an action against Amy for battery because he didn't drink the poison. He had not been touched. A private nuisance arises when someone creates or maintains a condition that prevents another from enjoying privately owned land. This did not occur here. Carl did not acquire any cause of action listed here.

3. Arnold tried to kill MaGoo during a hunting trip in a national park by shooting and lobbing grenades at him. MaGoo, however, was uninjured and didn't notice Arnold's attempts due to unimaginable luck and being deaf. MaGoo later found out about the attacks when forest service personnel investigated the extensive damage caused by Arnold's blasting. For which of the following torts would Arnold probably be liable to MaGoo?

   a. assault
   b. battery
   c. nuisance

    d. trespass to land

    e. Arnold would not be liable to MaGoo for any of these torts.

DISCUSSION

    (e)   Arnold would not be liable to MaGoo for assault because MaGoo didn't have apprehension of being touched at the time of the attacks. Similarly, Arnold would not be liable to MaGoo for battery because he failed to touch him. The land the parties were on was public and did not belong to MaGoo so private nuisance would not be available to redress Arnold's conduct. If others had been disturbed by Arnold's activities, Arnold might have been liable for public nuisance but such an action can be brought only by the government for damages suffered by the general public. Arnold's damage to the land would not be actionable by MaGoo as a trespass to land because MaGoo did not own the land. Although Arnold's conduct would not generate any liability to MaGoo, he would undoubtedly be liable for a number of crimes for which the government would need to prosecute him in a single criminal action to avoid double jeopardy.

4.   Bill and Dave drove recreational vehicles into a remote and deserted area. As a joke, Bill took Dave's keys and told him to see how he liked "really roughing it." Dave stayed by his vehicle because the nearest road was 75 miles away. About four hours later, Bill returned and gave Dave the keys explaining that it was only a joke. Dave, who thought he might die before help arrived, was not amused so he sued Bill. Bill will probably:

    a. be liable to Dave for false imprisonment.

    b. be liable to Dave for assault.

    c. be liable to Dave for injurious falsehood.

    d. not be liable to Dave because he was not injured.

    e. not be liable to Dave because Bill was only joking.

DISCUSSION

    (a)   Bill would be liable to Dave for false imprisonment because he effectively confined Dave near his vehicle for four hours. There was no assault because Bill never caused Dave to expect an immediate battery. There was no injurious falsehood since Bill had not lied to another person about something Dave owned. Dave was injured by virtue of being aware of being stranded for four hours. If he had been asleep at the time, no false imprisonment would have occurred because the victim must be aware of the confinement or injured during it. Bill's joking would not be a defense to the tort because he intended to say what he said and drive away.

5. Hazel decided to play a joke on Ivana whom she knew had a severe fear of mice. She arranged to have a dead mouse placed in a pop bottle just after Ivana had finished her drink and convinced her that the mouse had been in the bottle while she had been drinking out of it. Ivana became irrational and had to be restrained. She was ultimately arrested and placed in a hospital ward for psychological evaluation. When Ivana was released from the hospital and learned of the prank, she sued Hazel for the cost of her hospitalization and punitive damages. Hazel is probably:

   a. liable for the intentional infliction of emotional distress.
   b. liable for battery.
   c. only liable for trespass to chattels.
   d. not liable because Ivana had an unusual fear of "mouse cola."
   e. not liable because she could not have foreseen the consequences of her prank.

DISCUSSION

   (a) Hazel's conduct was outrageous enough to support the tort of intentional infliction of emotional distress. She intended the conduct that resulted in Ivana's suffering. There would be no liability for battery because Ivana was not touched by the mouse. Hazel might have been liable to Ivana for trespass to chattels in addition to the infliction of emotional distress because she tampered with the empty pop bottle. However, Ivana's damages were not primarily the result of damage to the bottle or interference with it. Hazel would be liable to Ivana notwithstanding her unusual fear of mice and her extreme reaction to the prank because tortfeasors must take their victims as they find them. In other words, a person committing a tort takes the risk that damages may exceed what they expect.

6. A school newspaper printed a photograph of Titus without his permission next to an article on the prevalence of chronic bowel disorders on campus. Titus may have a cause of action for:

   a. conversion.
   b. invasion of privacy.
   c. disparagement.
   d. injurious falsehood.

e.   deceit, misrepresentation, or fraud if he could prove that he did not suffer
     from this condition.

DISCUSSION

(b)   The newspaper could be liable to Titus for invasion of his privacy by
placement in a false light since the article implied that he was a student with a
chronic bowel problem. Titus could probably sue the people responsible for the
publication of the photograph and perhaps the school. The school newspaper did
not take any of Titus' personal property so there would be no action for conversion. Disparagement and injurious falsehood are two names for the same tort.
This tort was not committed because no lie about Titus' property was published.
Deceit, misrepresentation and fraud are all names for the tort of intentional misrepresentation. This tort would not be actionable because Titus did not justifiably
rely to his detriment on any intentional misrepresentations made by the newspaper.

7.   Alice lived between Rambo and a vacant lot. Rambo taught a course on urban go-
     rilla tactics. In his class, he taught approximately 57 students how to use mortars
     and bazookas by having his students hide in holes in his back yard and fire their
     weapons at targets set up in the field next door to Alice. A large variety of war-
     heads passed over Alice's property each day at heights between 6 and 30 feet.
     Alice would probably:

     a.   have an action for trespass to land.
     b.   have an action only if the shells had struck her property or family members.
     c.   have an action for invasion of privacy.
     d.   have no direct legal action unless damage resulted, but she may have been
          able to force Rambo to issue combat helmets to her family and guests.
     e.   have an action for negligence even if no physical damage resulted.

DISCUSSION

(a)   Alice could bring an action for trespass to land because the missiles
passed through her airspace at altitudes below those taken by the government for
aviation. She would be entitled to damages for the interference it caused as well as
an injunction to stop the activity in the future. Punitive damages might be available as well. The tort of trespass was complete when the projectiles entered her
airspace even if no damage to the land resulted. Alice could maintain the action if
she owned the land or occupied it legally pursuant to a rental agreement. If the
shells had struck someone on the premises, additional torts of assault and battery

may have been committed. The intrusion of the shells into Alice's airspace would not constitute an invasion of privacy by intrusion into a private space. While the airspace over one's land may be considered private property, it is not private in the same way as the interior of one's home. A person's expectation to be free from the observation of others is reasonable inside the home. However, outside the home, people are usually subject to being seen and heard by others. Rambo must stop his activities rather than merely help Alice to cope with them by issuing combat helmets. An action for negligence can be maintained only when the victim suffers damage to her person or property. Negligence is discussed in a later chapter.

8. Which of the following would probably be the appropriate tort action for stopping neighbors from having parties all night involving loud music during early morning hours?

    a. invasion of privacy
    b. private nuisance
    c. trespass to land
    d. conversion
    e. disturbing the peace

DISCUSSION

(b)   There would be an actionable private nuisance because the loud noises would disturb the use of the private property for sleeping. No invasion of privacy would result from loud parties since there would be no appropriation of the right to publicity for commercial purposes, no physical intrusion into a private place or monitoring of private conversations, no public disclosure of private facts, and no placement in a false light. There would be no action for trespass to land because, unlike private nuisance, trespass to land requires an unlawful entry onto private property which did not take place. Conversion is committed only when there is an unlawful taking of private personal property. Disturbing the peace is a crime that is actionable only by the government.

9. Alice scratched a foul word into the finish of Sally's car because Sally had threatened to "box" her ears if she cheated on any more tests. Alice is probably:

    a. liable for conversion.
    b. liable for trespass to chattels.
    c. liable for criminal conversation.

d. not liable to Sally because Alice was defending herself.

e. not liable to Sally because Sally had assaulted her.

DISCUSSION

(b) An action for trespass to chattels would arise because Alice's interference with the car resulted in damage to its finish. Sally would be able to recover the cost of repair and possibly punitive damages. Alice would not be liable for conversion because the vandalism did not impair the value of the car enough to constitute the taking required. Criminal conversation is a tort allowed for adultery in some jurisdictions. Alice was not defending herself within the definition of self defense discussed in a later section of this book. People can use reasonable force to defend themselves, others and property when they are under attack. Alice damaged the property in response to Sally's threat. Sally's threat did not amount to an assault because no immediate battery was threatened.

10. Which of the following torts provides a civil remedy for theft of personal property?

a. invasion of privacy .

b. larceny

c. embezzlement

d. conversion

e. trespass to land

DISCUSSION

(d) Conversion is the tort used to recover damages for a taking of personal property. A theft is one type of taking that would satisfy this requirement of conversion. No invasion of privacy or trespass to land would be committed merely by the theft of personal property without intruding into a private place or entering on private land to take it. Larceny and embezzlement are criminal actions that belong to the government and are not actionable by private individuals.

11. Phil, a jeweler, knowingly induced Meredith to purchase a piece of colored glass from him by misrepresenting it to be a valuable gem. Meredith paid $7,000 for the gem because Phil assured her it was a two-carat emerald. When Meredith learned the truth, she wanted her money back with punitive damages. The proper tort action for Meredith would probably be:

a. theft
b. trespass to chattels
c. conversion
d. intentional misrepresentation
e. disparagement

DISCUSSION

(d)   The tort of intentional misrepresentation of material facts was committed in this case. Phil intentionally misrepresented the nature of the "gem" to Meredith. Her justifiable reliance upon his representations resulted in her paying too much for the gem. She was not required to obtain a third party evaluation of the gem prior to purchasing it. Theft is a criminal action that belongs to the government rather than Meredith. Trespass to chattels was not committed by Phil because he never interfered with Meredith's personal property. Similarly, conversion did not take place because Phil had not taken any of Meredith's personal property. The tort of disparagement was not committed because no lie was told regarding anything belonging to Meredith.

12.   For a modest fee, Randy provided a computer service to landlords in his area who wanted to screen potential renters. A landlord could enter the name and social security number of a potential renter into Randy's computer data base and receive a report regarding rent payments, treatment of the premises in past rentals and criminal history. Randy's computer had Jason listed as a vicious killer who did not pay rent on time. Randy had obtained this information from landlords but required no corroboration and had no reason to believe it was true. Although this information was not correct, no landlord would rent to Jason. Jason may have an action for:

a. conversion.
b. defamation of character.
c. trespass.
d. wrongful exclusion.
e. discrimination.

DISCUSSION

(b)   Randy committed the tort of defamation of character when he intentionally published statements which were false and defamatory. Jason could recover damages even if Randy had erred innocently because the intent required for this tort is merely the intent to publish the statement. It is not required that the tortfeasor be aware that the statement is false at the time of publication. Jason was harmed by the publication of the false statements. Randy did not have a conditional privilege to publish the defamatory information because he had no reason to believe the information. Without personal knowledge or some other corroboration of the allegations, Randy would have no basis upon which to form a belief that the statements about Jason were true. There would be no action for conversion because there had been no taking of personal property. There was no trespass because there was no entry upon real property. Wrongful exclusion is not a tort. Discrimination is not a tort. In fact, discrimination is merely the treatment of one person differently than another. This common practice that is not wrongful under the law unless people are treated differently based upon inappropriate characteristics such as race, sex, age, etc. Even when wrongful, the remedies for discrimination do not usually come from the law of torts.

13. Lyle ran advertisements indicating that Frank's Restaurant sold fish and chips cooked in motor oil. Lyle knew this was false. Some people who read the advertisements quit eating at Frank's Restaurant and patronized Lyle's Restaurant instead. Frank sued Lyle to put a stop to the advertising and to recover damages. Frank will probably:

   a. lose because Lyle has a constitutional right to free speech.
   b. lose because he didn't try to protect himself with curative advertising.
   c. lose because the advertisement was not defamatory.
   d. win in a action for defamation of character.
   e. win in an action for injurious falsehood because he intentionally published the false information.

DISCUSSION

   (e)   The false statements about Frank's products would be actionable as injurious falsehood because they were intentionally and maliciously made. The constitutional right to free speech is not unlimited. The publication of false statements is not protected. A victim of a tort is sometimes required to take steps to minimize his damages; however, failure to do so merely results in the reduction of the damages that could have been avoided rather than a bar to the action itself. In this case, Frank would not lose his cause of action for failing to resist Lyle's misrepresentations through curative advertising. Although the statements were defamatory in the sense that they were "bad," there would be no action for defamation since they were made about products rather than Frank himself.

14. Universal Broadcasting Inc. and Dick entered into a contract whereby Dick agreed to host a late night TV show for Universal for five years. After two years, North American Broadcasting, Inc. enticed Dick to work for them and breach his contract with Universal. North American promised to pay Dick a higher salary and pay his damages for breach of contract. Universal Broadcasting sued North American Broadcasting. Universal will probably:

    a. lose because North American made no false statement about Universal.
    b. lose because North American was merely exercising its right to compete in a free market economy.
    c. lose because North American was not a party to its contract with Dick.
    d. win because this constituted a tortious interference with prospective advantage.
    e. win because this constituted a tortious interference with a contract.

DISCUSSION

(e)   Universal Broadcasting would probably be successful in an action against North American Broadcasting because North American intentionally interfered with an existing contract. The right to compete is limited to competition prior to the existence of a binding contract. Once Dick entered into a contract with Universal, it had prevailed in the competition and was entitled to enjoy the benefits of its contract without interference from North American Broadcasting.

15. Phil's former brother-in-law, Ed, was in the tree trimming business. In an effort to exact revenge for Ed's divorce of his sister, Phil contacted all of Ed's customers and gave them the names and phone numbers of every tree trimming company that offered equal or better prices than Ed. Soon, Ed could not find work. Ed sued Phil. Ed probably:

    a. lost because Phil was exercising his right to free speech.
    b. lost because Phil was merely engaged in competition.
    c. won because Phil's statements, although true, constituted injurious falsehood.
    d. won because Phil's statements were defamatory.
    e. won because Phil's statements constituted a tortious interference with prospective advantage.

DISCUSSION

(e)   Ed would be liable to Phil for interference with prospective advantage because Ed was not engaged in competition. Rather, he was engaged in ruining Phil's business. The intentional interference with prospective advantage is not protected by the right to freedom of speech by virtue of its improper purpose and damaging effects. To be actionable as either injurious falsehood or defamation, the published statements must be false. In this case, the price quotations were true.

Chapter 4
Defenses to Intentional Torts

No "defense" is necessary in a "cause of action" unless the victim can prove all of the required "elements of the tort." A defense is a legally accepted reason for excusing the "defendant" from liability to the "plaintiff." The defendant is the party in a law suit who is accused of conduct that gives the plaintiff a right to recover damages or other legal relief. The plaintiff is the victim who sues the defendant. A cause of action is a legal reason for a court to award a plaintiff damages or some other legal relief. The elements of a tort are the facts that comprise its legal definition. These facts are the important parts of the definitions of the torts presented in chapter 3.

The court must dismiss an action based upon an intentional tort if any of the elements of the tort are not proved by the plaintiff. When a plaintiff fails to prove the elements of a tort, the defendant cannot be found liable so no defense is necessary. When, however, a plaintiff has proven the elements of an intentional tort, the defendant can avoid liability by pleading and proving the elements of one of the defenses to intentional torts discussed in this chapter.

The defenses that excuse liability for the intentional torts will not excuse liability for negligence. The defenses listed below are used only in actions based upon intentional torts. Essentially, a defendant admits that she has committed the tort when she asserts a defense, but she claims that legally recognized circumstances excuse the conduct that would otherwise be actionable. The rules of court procedure allow a defendant to deny the elements of the tort and raise a defense in the same action. When a defendant exercises this option, she will not need to prove her defense unless the plaintiff proves the elements of the intentional tort.

Essential Vocabulary

1. defense
2. cause of action
3. elements of a tort
4. defendant
5. plaintiff

I. CONSENT

The voluntary and informed consent of the victim is a defense to an intentional tort.

Generally, the "voluntary" and "informed" consent of a victim given prior to action that would otherwise constitute an intentional tort is a defense to liability. Voluntary consent is given when the victim has a real opportunity to withhold it. Consent is informed when the victim is aware of enough facts to make a rational decision as to whether to give or withhold consent. Consent can be express or implied. "Express consent" is consent given with words and may be written, oral or given by signs understood to be words. "Implied consent" is consent given by the actions of the victim.

Andy asked Ben if he would like to go for a 50 mile flight in Andy's private plane. Ben consented and the two began their flight. While the flight was in progress, Andy asked Ben to accompany him for an additional 300 miles to run an errand. Ben replied that he was very busy and would rather not continue the flight. Andy then told Ben to jump out with a parachute he had placed under Ben's seat or consent to accompany him on the flight. Ben still objected so Andy put the plane on auto pilot and began to drag Ben to the door. Ben suddenly said, "Oh, you're serious! I'd be happy to accompany you." When the plane finally landed, Ben sued Andy for false imprisonment, and Andy "plead" the defense of consent. A party pleads in a legal action when he formally raises a cause of action or defense. Andy would be liable for the tort because Ben's consent to continue the flight was not voluntarily made. He had no choice unless he was willing to use the parachute.

Carla's doctor told her she needed an injection and explained the desirable and undesirable effects of the drug. Carla then rolled up her sleeve and held her arm out without saying anything. Her action implied that she was consenting to the injection. Although her doctor touched her, Carla cannot later sue the doctor successfully for battery because he could assert the defense of consent. Carla could have consented verbally or in writing as well. Her consent was voluntary because she had a real opportunity to refuse the treatment. Her consent was also informed because the doctor explained the possible desirable and undesirable effects of the drug. If the doctor had failed to discuss the drug with her and her hair had fallen out, Carla's consent would not have been informed consent. Consent is not effective as a defense if the person consenting is not aware of the important facts necessary to make a decision.

Essential Vocabulary

1. voluntary consent
2. informed consent
3. express consent
4. implied consent

II. DEFENSE OF PEOPLE AND PROPERTY

Self defense, the defense of others, and the defense of property are defenses to the intentional torts.

People may use reasonable force to protect themselves, others and their property from harm or loss. Reasonable force is the minimum amount of force necessary to stop tortious or criminal action. What is reasonable in a given situation can range from merely a word of warning to lethal force. The force used can initially be minimal and later escalate as the force or threat of force being applied by the tortfeasor escalates. Potentially lethal force may not be used to protect property. It may be used only when a human being is threatened with death or serious bodily injury. However, during a robbery, a victim could justifiably begin using non-lethal force to protect his property and find it necessary to increase the force to a lethal level if the thief threatens him with death or serious bodily injury. The policeman in a bank wears a firearm to protect the people rather than the money in the bank.

Harvey heard a burglar breaking into his business one night. He could not shoot through the door and successfully defend a suit for battery brought by the burglar on the basis of defense of property because lethal force cannot be used to protect property. The least amount of force necessary might have been merely switching on the lights and calling the police. If the burglar threatened Harvey with death or serious bodily injury, Harvey would have been justified in using potentially lethal force to protect himself. Traps or animals likely to cause death or serious bodily injury may not be used to protect property.

Essential Vocabulary

1. defense of people and property
2. reasonable force

CHECK YOUR UNDERSTANDING

DIRECTIONS: Read each of the following questions. Choose the best answer and study the discussion of the question.

1. Which of the following is not normally a defense to false imprisonment?

    a. consent
    b. comparative negligence
    c. self defense
    d. defense of property
    e. defense of others

DISCUSSION

(b)   Consent, self defense, defense of property and others are defenses to the intentional torts. Comparative negligence is a defense to negligence that comes from statutory or judicial law . The defenses to the intentional torts will not excuse liability for negligence, and the defenses to negligence will not excuse liability for the intentional torts.

2. Evelyn asked her dentist to fill a decayed tooth. After he had done the job, she refused to pay him. When he sued her, she sued the dentist for battery. Evelyn will probably:

    a. lose because she consented to the procedure.
    b. lose because dentists cannot be sued for battery if their work helps rather than injures the patient.
    c. lose because the dentist had not touched her.
    d. win because the dentist failed to obtain a written release of liability from her.
    e. win if the dentist had to touch the tooth to fill it, and Evelyn found this offensive.

DISCUSSION

(a)   Although Evelyn's dentist touched her when he filled her tooth, he would not be liable for battery because Evelyn had consented to the procedure. Voluntary and informed consent is a defense to the intentional torts. In this case, no one was exercising force to pressure Evelyn into giving her consent. Her decision to ask the dentist to fill her tooth was voluntary. Since she asked for the procedure, she can be presumed to have been informed regarding its nature. Dentists can be sued for battery if their patients do not consent to their treatments even if the patients are actually helped. When patients are unconscious, medical practitioners can presume that they would consent to procedures necessary to stabilize their conditions or preserve their lives. Written consents are desirable because they make good records for future reference if a problem arises. However, consent may be express or implied, and, if express, it may be written or verbal.

3. Leah's Drugstore had been burglarized five times in two months. During the investigations, it was found that the burglar had read a stolen newspaper in the bathroom each time. Leah decided to put an end to the "Bathroom Burglar's" crime spree by wiring the toilet seat to a high voltage electrical source when the drugstore was closed. The next time the burglar struck, he sustained a high voltage electric shock. Although he survived, he sustained physical burns, brain damage, and an acute aversion to toilet seats. The burglar sued Leah. Leah is probably:

   a. not liable because she was defending her property.
   b. not liable because the burglar was not killed.
   c. liable for invasion of privacy by intrusion into a private space.
   d. liable for assault.
   e. liable for battery because she used potentially lethal force to protect property.

DISCUSSION

   (e)   Lethal force or force likely to cause serious bodily injury cannot be used to protect property. The victim of unreasonable force does not need to be killed to maintain an action. Leah would not be liable for invasion of privacy by intrusion because she had not physically intruded into the bathroom while the burglar was using it. There was no assault because the burglar never had apprehension of an immediate battery. Leah would have been liable for battery because she caused the burglar to be touched by the electricity. Leah had a right to use reasonable force to protect her property, but that did not include the right to use potentially lethal force.

Chapter 5
Negligence and Strict Liability

Negligence is a complex tort that allows victims of unintended harm to recover damages for their injuries. When a person injures another without intending to do so, the policy of the law is to require them pay for the damage they caused. Unlike actions based upon the intentional torts, only compensatory damages are awarded to victims of negligence. Punitive damages are not usually granted because punishment is not viewed as a deterrent to unintended conduct. When a person's acts or failures to act unintentionally injure another, liability for negligence generally follows. However, there are limits to this liability. People are not insurers of each other. Losses occurring without a person's failure to exercise due care are generally not actionable. The sections that follow delineate the broad limits of the tort of negligence.

Some activities and defective products are so exceptionally dangerous that the law makes people responsible for them strictly liable for any resulting damage. "Strict liability" is liability imposed without fault or negligence. People who engage in unusually dangerous activities or in selling unreasonably dangerous defective products will be liable for any damage resulting from their activities or products regardless of how careful they have been.

Essential Vocabulary

1. negligence
2. strict liability

I. NEGLIGENCE

Negligence is the breach of a duty to behave reasonably which causes foreseeable harm to foreseeable victims.

Except in relatively rare circumstances, people have a "duty" to behave reasonably so that they do not cause others to suffer harm. A duty is a legal obligation to do or refrain from doing something. The law imposes liability for the violation of one's duties.

Generally, people intuitively know the extent of their duties to others. If a person drives a car, the person should know that driving it into other people and their property must be avoided. If fireworks are used, the person using them should know that steps should be taken to avoid injuring others and starting fires.

An exception to the duty to behave reasonably towards others is the rule that there is no duty to rescue another in the absence of "contribution" or "fiduciary duty." Contribution occurs when a person provides an action or thing necessary for an occurrence in which someone is injured. Merely being present is usually not enough. There must be some additional connection between the occurrence and a contributor to the occurrence. The law imposes a duty on a person to rescue another when he contributes something to the situation that results in an injury.

If a doctor passed by an accident, would she be liable for negligence if she failed to stop and render first aid? The answer is "no" unless she somehow contributed to the accident or owed a fiduciary duty to the victim. To acquire the duty to rescue by contribution to the situation, the doctor would probably need to do more than merely be present in passing by the scene of the accident. If she was merely operating her vehicle in the accepted manner and the other driver drove off the road, there would be no legal duty to stop and render aid to the victim. However, if the victim had swerved and made contact with the doctor's vehicle before running off the road, she would have acquired a duty to rescue and render first aid by contribution. This would be the case even though she was not at fault. The contact between the doctor's vehicle and the victim's vehicle would provide the connection between the doctor and the accident necessary for contribution. The contact would give rise to the duty to stop and render assistance.

A person may also acquire a duty to rescue by being in a "fiduciary relationship" with the victim. Fiduciary relationships are relationships in which one or both of the parties have the legal right to rely upon and trust the other. These relationships are relatively rare. Some common examples are husband-wife, investor-broker, doctor-patient, priest-penitent, and principal-agent. A fiduciary relationship imposes a "fiduciary duty" on one or both of the parties involved. A fiduciary duty is a legal obligation to act in the best interests of another. The specific requirements of this duty vary to some extent with each type of fiduciary relationship. However, the requirements would generally include the duty to rescue a person to whom the fiduciary duty is owed.

Spouses must trust each other with their property so their fiduciary duties run both ways. They must each act in the best interest of each other. While investors must trust their brokers with their money, brokers do not need to entrust investors with anything. The fiduciary duty in this case is owed by the broker to the investor but not owed by the investor to the broker. Both the doctor and the priest must be entrusted with private information to make their professional relationships work, but they do not entrust anything to the people they help. As in the case of the brokers' fiduciary duties, fiduciary duties are owed by doctors and priests but not by the people they help. Applying these principles accordingly, a doctor would have a legal duty to stop and help a victim at the scene of an accident only if she had contributed to it by some sort of involvement of her property or actions or if the victim was her patient. The patient would not have a fiduciary duty to rescue her doctor arising out of their fiduciary relationship. The presence of a duty is of critical importance to the tort of negligence. If a person sees another person drowning and runs for help instead of throwing him a rope, there is no liability even if this action was unreasonable unless there had been some sort of contribution or a fiduciary relationship between the victim and the incompetent rescuer.

When the duty to behave reasonably does exist, the courts must take into consideration any special characteristics of the person with the duty and the circumstances of the incident to determine what would have been reasonable. If a person without formal medical training stopped to render first aid, he would be held to a lower standard of care than a physician due to the differences in their training and knowledge. A blind person would need to behave as a reasonable blind person under the circumstances and not like an individual with sight.

Deciding who caused an accident when a person has been negligent is not as simple as it might appear at first glance. If a driver fails to yield the right of way during a left hand turn, who caused the accident? Was it the driver who failed to yield the right of way? Was it the gas station owner who sold him the gas that morning that made it possible for him to be at the scene? Was it the automobile dealership that sold him the car in the first place? In the absence of any of these parties, there would not have been an accident. The courts require that the negligent conduct of the defendant actually cause the plaintiff's damages. In defining what is meant by causing the plaintiff's damages, the courts require that the conduct be the "proximate cause" of the victim's damages to be actionable. Proximate cause is the nearest cause of the harm. In the example cited above, the dealership's selling the car to the driver and the gas station's selling gasoline to the defendant were more distant in the causal chain leading to the accident than the driver's failure to yield the right of way so the dealership and gas station would have no liability.

This analysis can be cumbersome and complex. Over a period of time, the courts have held that a defendant's conduct is the proximate cause of the victim's damages if both the harm and the victim were foreseeable. This means that the people harmed by negligence must be members of a group we would expect to be placed in peril by the actions of the defendant and that they must suffer the type of harm that commonly comes from the type of carelessness for which the defendant was at fault.

If a person operates a motor vehicle while she is intoxicated, we would expect that she would endanger pedestrians and motorists and their passengers. Therefore, she would be liable for any damages caused to people in these classes who suffered the types of injuries commonly caused by automobile accidents. She would probably not be liable for damages to the passengers of a plane attempting an emergency landing on the road because plane passengers are not in the group foreseeably endangered.

The final element of negligence is the requirement that the plaintiff suffer "harm." Harm is damage to a victim's body or economic interests. Mental distress is not normally considered to be the type of harm for which negligence allows a recovery of damages unless it is accompanied by bodily damage or damage to property. In the absence of some type of physical or economic loss, actions for negligence cannot generally be successfully maintained.

Ivan nearly ran into Jerome while driving under the influence of alcohol. Although he successfully avoided the accident, Jerome was extremely frightened by the incident. Ivan would not be liable to Jerome for negligence because Jerome had not suffered an economic loss arising from any physical injury to his body or property.

Essential Vocabulary

1. negligence
2. duty
3. contribution
4. fiduciary duty
5. fiduciary relationship
6. proximate cause
7. harm

II. TRESPASSERS AND CONSTRUCTIVE BAILEES

The owners and possessors of property owe no duty to trespassers and constructive bailees.

The extent of the duty owed by owners and possessors of property is often determined by the status of the victim. "Trespassers" are people who enter or remain on real property without the permission of the owner or possessor. "Real property" is the land itself and fixtures. "Fixtures" are things permanently attached to the land. A person who wanders into a house without the permission of the owner would be a trespasser. The owners and possessors of real property owe no duty of care toward trespassers so they will not be liable to them for negligent conduct.

Trespassers must accept the land they trespass upon and buildings they trespass in as they find them. Owners of real property have no duty to make their property safe for people who enter without permission. If a person entered a home without permission and tripped on a skate that had been carelessly left on a stairway inside a house, he could not successfully maintain an action for negligence. Since the person entering the house without permission would be a trespasser, the owner would have no duty to keep the stairway free of skates. The owner would have been liable for battery, however, if he had intentionally left the skate on the stairway to injure people.

The law is similar when people are injured by "personal property" belonging to someone else. Personal property is all property other than land and things attached to the land such as buildings, shrubs, lights, etc. A "bailment" is a relationship that comes into existence anytime a person has possession of personal property without also having title. "Title" may be loosely defined as ownership. Since a book is not real property, it is personal property. When one has possession of a book that he owns, he has both possession and title so no bailment exists. When he loans the book to someone else, a bailment comes into existence. The person with title is called the "bailor", and the person with possession is called a "bailee." If the individual who takes the book does so without the permission of the owner, he would be a "constructive bailee." Constructive bailees are people who are in possession of the personal property of others without their permission.

If a person steals a car, he would have possession without title. A bailment would exist and the thief would be a constructive bailee because he would not have the owners permission to have possession of the car. If the thief was injured because the owner had carelessly failed to have the brakes repaired, he would not have an action for negligence against the owner because the owner had no duty to behave reasonably in protecting the constructive bailee from injury. If, however, the owner had purposely sabotaged the brakes to teach the thief a lesson, he may have incurred liability for one or more of the intentional torts, e.g. battery.

Essential Vocabulary

1. trespasser
2. real property
3. fixtures
4. personal property
5. bailment
6. title
7. bailor
8. bailee
9. constructive bailee

III. LICENSEES AND GRATUITOUS BAILEES

The owners and possessors of property have a duty to protect licensees and gratuitous bailees from known dangers.

A "licensee" is a person who enters real property with the permission of the owner. A person who has possession of another's personal property without paying for the privilege or being paid is called a "gratuitous bailee." When the person who enters real property or has possession of personal property does so with the permission or consent of the owner, the owner has a duty to behave reasonably to protect the visitor or borrower from dangers of which she is aware.

If Georgia invites Harry to dinner, Harry will be a licensee when he arrives at her home. If he is injured by a loose step of which Georgia is aware, Georgia will be liable for negligence in not taking steps to protect him from this known danger. On the other hand, Georgia would not be liable if she was not aware of the condition.

If a person loans a chain saw to a friend as a favor, there will be no liability for negligence if the borrower is injured because the saw is defective provided that the owner was not aware of the condition when he loaned the saw. If, however, the owner knew or should have known about the defect, he would be liable for negligence in loaning the chain saw since he owes a duty to the borrower or "gratuitous bailee" to protect him from known dangers.

Essential Vocabulary

1. licensee
2. gratuitous bailee

IV. BUSINESS INVITEES, MUTUAL BENEFIT BAILEES AND CHILDREN

The owners and possessors of property have a duty to inspect property and protect business invitees, mutual benefit bailees and young children from danger.

A "business invitee" is a person who enters real property with the owner's or occupier's permission to conduct business or enters the portion of business premises that are held open to the general public. A "mutual benefit bailee" is a person who takes possession of another's personal property for a price. The owner or possessor of property has a duty to actually inspect the property to protect the business invitee and mutual benefit bailee from reasonably discoverable dangers.

While a friend who loans an automobile as a favor would have no duty to inspect the vehicle for mechanical difficulties prior to loaning it, a car rental agency will have a duty to inspect the vehicle because it will be paid for the rental. The payment makes the relationship of the parties a mutual benefit bailment.

If a visitor to a person's home slips on some water that is on the floor, there will be no liability for a home owner who is unaware of this dangerous condition because there is no duty to inspect the premises to protect licensees. If, on the other hand, a person slips on water on the floor of a super market, the owner of the store will be liable if employees could have discovered the condition and taken steps to protect customers within a reasonable time because the victim is a business invitee. This would be the case whether or not the victim intendend to purchase anything.

The law also imposes a duty to inspect property and protect "young children" who may trespass from injury resulting from their meddling with real or personal property under the "attractive nuisance doctrine." The young children protected by this doctrine are typically very young. The attractive nuisance doctrine requires the possessors of property to inspect it and protect children from any dangers they could have discovered. Only children too young to appreciate the danger posed by the property are entitled to this high degree of protection under the law.

A person who owns a swimming pool must take steps to protect young children who are too young to appreciate the danger of deep water. One precaution that could be taken would be building a fence around the pool. However, the pool owner does not need to put a lid on the enclosure to keep teenagers from climbing over the fence without his permission because they are mature enough to appreciate the danger. The doctrine also requires taking precautions with personal property. A carpenter must put his skill saw away or watch it when young children who might meddle with it are in the area.

Essential Vocabulary

1. business invitee
2. mutual benefit bailee
3. young children
4. attractive nuisance doctrine

V. BAILEE LIABILITY

Bailees are liable for negligence and are strictly liable for unauthorized use and misdelivery.

Bailees must exercise reasonable care to protect bailed property in their possession. Ordinarily, they are liable only for damage to the bailed property caused by their negligence. However, the scope of their duty increases dramatically when they engage in an "unauthorized use" or "misdelivery" of the bailed property. An unauthorized use of bailed property occurs when the bailee uses the bailed property without the owners permission.

A misdelivery occurs when the bailee delivers the bailed property to the wrong person to end the bailment. When these events occur, bailees take the property for their own use and are strictly liable for conversion or trespass to chattels if the property is damaged in any way. This liability is imposed regardless of how reasonably the bailee behaved or how much care was exercised.

Connie loaned her camper to Danny for the weekend. During his camping trip, Danny forgot to roll up the windows, and the floor of the camper was ruined by snow. Danny had a duty to behave as a reasonable person. Since a reasonable person would have rolled up the an Danny failed to do so, he would be liable for negligence.

Ellis left his watch off at a shop to be repaired. The repairman, a bailee, would be liable for any damage caused by his negligence. If the repairman exercised reasonable care to protect the watch, he would not be liable if a burglar stole it from the shop at night. However, he would be strictly liable if he took the watch home to show his wife since this was not authorized by Ellis. The repairman would be liable for conversion if the watch was stolen from his home regardless of how careful he was. The fact that he intended to take the watch home would satisfy the intent requirement for conversion. If he took the watch home unintentionally, he would be liable for negligence arising from his failure to lock up the watch at night.

Bailees are also strictly liable for misdelivery of bailed property. If a delivery man delivered property to the wrong address, and the property was lost, he would be liable no matter how careful he was in trying to verify that the address was correct. If the watch repairman delivered the watch to someone other than the owner without permission, and the watch was lost, he would be liable even even if the person picking up the watch had the repair receipt.

Essential Vocabulary

1. unauthorized use
2. misdelivery

VI. UNUSUALLY DANGEROUS ACTIVITIES AND PRODUCTS

Persons engaging in unusually dangerous activities or selling unreasonably dangerous products are strictly liable for proximately caused damages.

Strict liability, or liability without fault or negligence, is imposed for dangerous activities conducted in unusual places and for the sale of defective products that are unreasonably dangerous. The rationale for this cause of action is that those parties engaging in unusually dangerous activities or selling unreasonably dangerous, defective products should bear the burden of any damage occurring rather than the victims. When damage results from this conduct, the victim is required to prove only that the defendant was engaged in a dangerous activity in an unusual place or that he sold a defective product that was unreasonably dangerous when it left his control and that the activity or product proximately caused the victim's injuries. Damages are proximately caused when both the victim and the harm are foreseeable. The plaintiff does not need to prove that the defendant breached his duty to exercise reasonable care.

Driving an automobile is a dangerous activity. As long as the driver is on a road, liability is imposed only for negligence because this is where driving normally takes place. If, however, the driver is driving around on a school playground, strict liability may be imposed because of the extreme danger resulting from the presence of young children. An injured child would only need to prove that the driver was operating a vehicle on the school grounds in the presence of children and that she suffered injuries caused by being struck by the vehicle.

Gas stations are only liable for negligence if their gas tanks explode because this is where gasoline is normally stored. However, a home owner may be strictly liable if he stores 500 gallons of gas and the tanks explode because gasoline is not normally stored in garages in quantities larger than that held by the tanks on vehicles and that used for appliances such as a lawn mower. Neighbors who lose their homes to fire caused by an explosion would need to prove only that the defendant was storing gas in unusually dangerous quantities, that they were foreseeable victims of the explosion and that they suffered foreseeable injuries such as fire or smoke damage. It would not be a defense that the person storing the gas was very careful and had not been negligent. He would probably not be liable, however, if it could be proven that someone else intentionally detonated the gas.

A soup manufacturer that allows contaminated soup to be sold to grocery stores would be strictly liable to anyone consuming it. Contaminated food is unreasonably dangerous because it is difficult for a consumer to detect prior to ingesting it. Although beer is a dangerous product even when not defective, the dangers presented by beer do not generate strict liability because consumers are familiar with the dangerous characteristics of the product. Product liability can also be based upon negligence and breach of warranty. Breach of warranty will be discussed in a later chapter.

Essential Vocabulary

1. unusually dangerous activity
2. unusually dangerous product

CHECK YOUR UNDERSTANDING

DIRECTIONS: Read each of the following questions. Choose the best answer and study the discussion of the question.

1. Which of the following torts would be committed by a custodian carelessly locking a customer in a restroom for the weekend?

    a. assault
    b. false imprisonment
    c. negligence
    d. invasion of privacy
    e. trespass to chattels

DISCUSSION

(c)   The only torts that can be committed without intent are negligence and strict liability. The custodian was negligent in carelessly locking the restroom without making sure that no one was in it. Assault requires intentional action that causes the victim to suffer apprehension of battery. False imprisonment requires intentional conduct that results in the victim being aware of or injured during confinement. Invasion of privacy requires intentional acts resulting in the appropriation of a persons name or face for commercial purposes, in the intrusion into a private place, in the public disclosure of private facts or in the placement of the victim in a false light. Trespass to chattels requires intentional interference with another's personal property.

2. A doctor passing by at the time of a car accident sees an injured stranger who could benefit from her immediate medical attention. Which of the following best describes the doctor's legal duty in the ordinary case?

    a. She must render full care to the victim.
    b. She must render reasonable care to the victim.
    c. She must call an ambulance if she declines to treat the victim.
    d. She must render first aid only until an ambulance arrives.
    e. She has no duty to treat the victim at all.

DISCUSSION

(e)   There is no duty to rescue someone unless contribution or fiduciary duty is present. A physician does not have a duty to rescue people simply because she is a health care professional. Contribution usually requires that a person's property or actions play an important role in the occurrence generating danger. Merely being present or observing someone's distress is not enough. The doctor has no fiduciary duty to rescue a stranger. There would have been a duty if the victim had been the doctor's patient, spouse, child, partner etc. If a duty to render first aid had existed, the doctor would have been required to render the standard care and treatments a reasonable doctor would have rendered in similar circumstances.

3. Peter burned trash in his backyard without any type of container. Not only was this against city ordinances, but Peter left the area while the fire burned out of control. Smoke rose to a level of 10,000 feet due to an exceptional updraft and caused Robin, an amateur stunt flyer, to crash due to lack of visibility. Robin was injured and his plane was destroyed. Which of the following elements of negligence is likely to present Robin with the most difficulty in his suit to recover damages?

    a. duty
    b. breach of duty
    c. proximate cause
    d. damages
    e. res ipsa loquitur

DISCUSSION

(c)   Proximate cause will be the most difficult element of negligence to prove in this case. Peter had a duty to exercise reasonable care in burning his trash. This would include the duty to remain in the area supervising the fire and to control it. He breached his duty when he failed to behave as a reasonable person by leaving the area. There is also no question that Robin suffered damages in this case to his person and property. The issue of probable cause is problematic because Robin would need to show that he was a member of the class foreseeably endangered by the fire and that he suffered damages that were the foreseeable result of Peter's negligent conduct. The foreseeable victims would be nearby property owners and people in the area. It is not foreseeable that someone in an airplane would be injured by a fire on the ground. The type of injury suffered by Robin is also not foreseeable because smoke and fire damage are foreseeable while airplane crashes due to poor visibility are not. "Res ipsa loquitur" is a Latin legal term which literally means "the thing itself speaks." This legal doctrine is used to assist the plaintiff with the burden of proof in cases in which the damages caused do not normally occur in the absence of negligence. It has no applicability here.

4. Todd, while intoxicated, drove about ten miles to his home. He was followed by Alan who observed Todd weaving black and forth. Alan also saw Todd nearly run into two parked cars and then run through two red lights and a stop sign at a high rate of speed. Alan sued Todd for negligence. Alan will probably:

   a. lose because Todd wasn't negligent — he was drunk.
   b. lose because he did not suffer damages.
   c. lose unless he is a police officer.
   d. win because drunken driving is negligent operation of a motor vehicle.
   e. win because such an action constitutes a civil prosecution for a crime.

DISCUSSION

(b) Todd was negligent. He had a duty to refrain from operating a motor vehicle while intoxicated. He breached that duty by failing to behave as a reasonable motorist when he drove anyway. The negligence is not actionable by Alan, however, because he did not suffer economic damages. The mental distress Alan suffered is not actionable because Todd did not intentionally engage in the conduct that caused it. A state, city or county government could prosecute Todd for driving while intoxicated but this would constitute a criminal prosecution brought by the government rather than by Todd or a police officer. Civil actions belong to private parties while criminal actions belong to governments. A private party has no standing to prosecute a criminal action.

5. Amy stole Jim's car. While she was driving it away, she was injured when the front wheels fell off the car. Jim knew that the car was in very dangerous condition before it was stolen but hadn't gotten around to making required repairs. Amy sued Jim for negligence in maintaining the car in such a dangerous state. Amy will probably:

   a. win because Jim didn't place a warning notice on the car.
   b. win because a car in such dangerous condition constitutes an attractive nuisance.
   c. lose because Amy was a constructive bailee, and Jim owed her no duty.

d. lose because Jim had a right to protect his property even with lethal force if necessary to prevent the theft.

e. lose because a thief is an "outlaw" who is technically outside the protection of the law.

DISCUSSION

(c)   Since Amy was injured while in possession of Jim's property, it is necessary to determine what type of bailment existed to determine the extent of Jim's duty to protect her from harm. Amy took the car without Jim's permission giving rise to a constructive bailment. Owners of property have no duty to protect constructive bailees from harm resulting from their unauthorized use of bailed property. Jim, therefore, had no duty to post a warning notice in the car or take any other action to protect Amy. The attractive nuisance doctrine requires owners of property to protect very young children from being injured by personal property and conditions on real property that they are too young to appreciate. Amy was not that young if she had the ability to steal Jim's car. If Jim had left the keys in the car and a very young child had been injured, he may have had liability under the attractive nuisance doctrine. Jim could not use force likely to cause death or serious bodily injury to protect his property. If he had intentionally maintained the car's condition as a trap for a thief, he would have had liability for the intentional tort of battery as well as other intentional torts. People committing crimes and torts are not "outlaws" in the old English sense of the word which meant that they were completely outside the protection of the law. Only reasonable force can be used to protect oneself, others and property.

6. George's son spilled about a pint of oil on the back porch while working on his skateboard. He didn't clean it up, and he didn't tell George. Three hours later, George invited Alice to come to dinner. That night, Alice went out on the back porch with George's permission to smoke a cigarette and was injured when she slipped on the oil. She sued George for negligence in allowing the oil to remain on the porch. The first time George had heard about the oil was when Alice fell. Alice will probably:

a. lose because she assumed the risk by going onto the back porch to smoke a cigarette.

b. lose because she was a licensee and George had no duty to inspect the premises to make them safe.

c. win because she was an invitee and George had a duty to inspect and make the premises safe.

d. win because parents are liable for the torts of their children.

e. win because homeowners are strictly liable for dangerous conditions on the premises.

DISCUSSION

(b) George's son was negligent in not cleaning up the oil he spilled on the porch and would have been liable to Alice. Alice did not assume the risk of slipping in the oil because she did not voluntarily confront a known danger. However, in the absence of a statute altering the common law, parents are not liable for the torts of their children. Alice sued George for failing to discover the oil and protect her from injury resulting from this condition. Alice was on George's property with his permission as a social guest. She would have been a licensee. George had a duty to protect her from dangers of which he was aware, but he had no duty to inspect the premises and make them safe because Alice was not there on business. Since George was not aware of the condition, he would not be liable for failing to take steps to protect Alice. A homeowner can be strictly liable for unusually dangerous activities intentionally undertaken on the premises. However, George was not engaged in any such activity.

7. The attractive nuisance doctrine is primarily concerned with:

a. the use of personal property.
b. child trespassers.
c. licensees.
d. invitees.
e. joint tortfeasors.

DISCUSSION

(b) The attractive nuisance doctrine imposes a duty upon the owners and users of real and personal property to inspect the property and take steps to protect children from foreseeable dangers. A young child tampering with chattels or committing a trespass to real property is treated like a business invitee. A humorous explanation for treating trespassing children like business invitees is that their meddling with the property of adults is viewed by the law as their business. The attractive nuisance doctrine is applied to conditions on real property as well personal property. Licensees are people on real property with the permission of the owner or occupier of the land. Invitees are people who enter on real property with the permission of the owner or occupier for the purpose of conducting business. Joint tortfeasors are people who commit a tort together and are together responsible for the resulting damages. This concept is not applicable in this case.

8. Which of the following visitors would be an invitee at your home?

    a. anyone on the premises with your permission
    b. only social guests you have specifically invited on the premises
    c. a plumber you have called to fix a leaking faucet
    d. any relative or close friend
    e. an officious intermeddler

DISCUSSION

(c) An invitee is a person who enters real property with the permission of the owner or occupier for a business purpose. Without additional facts only the plumber in this question qualifies as an invitee. Others on the premises with permission are merely licensees. Anyone entering a business open to the general public is an invitee regardless of his purpose for being there. Relatives and close friends can be trespassers, licensees or business invitees depending on the situation. An officious intermeddler is an individual who injects himself into a situation that does not concern him. The legal status of such a person would determined by the facts of a given case.

9. Dean drops his watch off at Martin's Watch Repair for cleaning. The cleaning cost is $8.50. This is an example of a:

    a. gratuitous bailment.
    b. mutual benefit bailment.
    c. constructive bailment.
    d. fixture repair.
    e. secured transaction.

DISCUSSION

(b) A bailment arose when Dean left his watch because he retained ownership while Martin had possession of the watch. Since the bailment was for a business purpose and each party benefited from it, it was a mutual benefit bailment. A gratuitous bailment is a free bailment entered into as a favor to the bailor or bailee. A constructive bailment is a bailment arising without the permission of the bailor or owner of the personal property. A fixture is property that is permanently attached to the land with the intent that it should become part it. There was no repair of fixtures involved here because the watch was not a fixture. A secured transaction is a contract allowing a creditor to repossess collateral owned by the debtor in the event of a breach of contract. Secured transactions will be discussed in a later chapter and do not apply.

10. Flee asked Bailey to drive his car from Sandy to Salt Lake City and deliver it to his mechanic for routine repairs. Bailey consented and took the car to pick up his girlfriend in Provo, a town 55 miles out of the way. While in Provo, the car was run off the road, and Bailey was ordered out of the car at gun point. The car was never seen again. Flee sued Bailey for the value of the car. Flee will probably:

    a. not recover damages because Bailey was not negligent.
    b. not recover damages because Bailey is not liable for losses arising from a gratuitous bailment.
    c. recover damages because Bailey was not using the car as authorized.
    d. recover damages because Bailey was negligent in being unarmed in Provo.
    e. recover damages because Bailey was a business invitee.

DISCUSSION

(c) Flee and Bailey entered into a gratuitous bailment because nothing was being charged by either party for the relationship. Flee was the bailor and was required to take steps to protect Bailey from any dangerous condition of which he was aware. In this case, there were none. Bailey, on the other hand, was a bailee and, as such, had a duty to take reasonable care to protect the car during the bailment. Unfortunately, he increased his liability by using the car without Flee's permission to pick up his girl friend. He became strictly liable for any harm occurring during his unauthorized use. He would be liable to Flee for conversion as would the real thief if he could be found. Flee could not recover the value of the car more than once so Bailey could recover damages from the thief if he was forced to pay Flee for the car. It is irrelevant that Bailey was not negligent when the car was stolen. Since no land was involved, the concept of business invitee does not apply.

11. Tony borrowed Pat's calculator with her permission. During an earthquake, the calculator was shaken off of the table where Tony had been using it. Just after it struck the cement floor, another student stepped on it while fleeing from the building. Tony returned the calculator casing along with its numerous, broken parts in a brown paper bag. Tony is probably:

    a. not liable to Pat at all.
    b. liable for necessary repairs.
    c. liable to Pat for the cost of the calculator, but he is entitled to the wreckage.
    d. liable to Pat for conversion.
    e. entitled to damages from Pat since the calculator did not serve him as long as originally anticipated.

DISCUSSION

(a)   When Tony borrowed Pat's calculator with her permission, a gratuitous bailment arose in which Tony had a duty to take reasonable precautions to protect it. He behaved as a reasonable person in the earthquake. Since he did not breach his duty to be careful with the calculator, he is not liable for negligence. He was not using the calculator for an unauthorized purpose, and he did not misdeliver the calculator in returning it to Pat. Therefore, Tony did not have strict liability for damage to the calculator. Pat would not be liable to Tony because there was no enforceable contract in which Pat was required to provide Tony with a calculator for any length of time.

12.   Duane was using dynamite to remove tree stumps from his back yard which was located in a crowded subdivision. During blasting, a rock was thrown by the explosion into Elsie's air cooler. The cooler was destroyed and extensive water damage resulted because water pipes had been severed. Duane could prove that he took every precaution possible to contain the blast and protect his neighbors. He was not negligent. If sued, Duane would probably:

a. not be liable because he was not negligent.
b. not be liable because the damages were not foreseeable.
c. not be liable because the victims were not foreseeable.
d. be strictly liable despite his precautions.
e. be liable fore trespass to his neighbor's airspace.

DISCUSSION

(d)   Duane was using dynamite in residential area. This would generate strict liability because the use of explosives is highly dangerous and a residential area is an unusual place for blasting. Since he would be strictly liable for any damage, the precautions he took to avoid accidents are not relevant. The only requirements for strict liability are that the defendant be engaged in an unusually dangerous activity and that the activity be the proximate cause of the plaintiff's damages. In this case, the class of foreseeable victims was the neighbors. Since she was a neighbor, Elsie was a foreseeable victim. The harm expected was harm to people and damage to property caused by flying debris and concussion. Elsie suffered damage to her home which was a foreseeable harm. Although Duane was strictly liable for damage to Elsie's home, he would not be liable for trespass to land because he did not intentionally cause the rock to enter Elsie's airspace or damage her home.

Chapter 6
Defenses to Negligence

States usually recognize either the common law defenses to negligence which are contributory negligence and assumption of the risk or a more modern defense called comparative negligence. Defenses to the intentional torts will not excuse negligence. While consent is a defense to the intentional torts, consent to negligence in advance in the form of an "exculpatory clause" is against public policy and generally not enforced by the courts. An exculpatory clause is a clause in a contract that excuses a person from liability. To the extent that these clauses purport to excuse negligence, they are not enforceable. In the same way, self defense, defense of others, and defense of property are defenses to intentional torts but not to negligence. Although a person has a right to defend herself, others or property, she must exercise that right in the same manner as the hypothetical reasonable person, or she will be liable for negligence.

Jane reasonably feared for her life while being attacked by a man on the bus. She pulled a pistol that she had recently purchased for just such an eventuality from her purse. She then began to fire it in the general direction of her attacker. Unfortunately, the bus was crowded, and she had never practiced shooting before the attack. She miraculously missed her attacker but wounded eight people hiding in their seats. Although Jane had a right to use lethal force to defend herself, she was negligent in using this type of weapon under these circumstances. Self defense is a defense to the intentional torts. However, the fact that she was defending herself would not excuse her from liability if she were sued for negligence by the wounded bystanders.

Essential Vocabulary

1. exculpatory clause

I. EXCULPATORY CLAUSES

Contractual limitations of liability for negligence are against public policy and will not be enforced.

Consent is a defense to liability for the intentional torts. Allowing such a defense for negligence is against public policy because it could remove the incentive to exercise reasonable care in situations where a party could contractually limit the extent of his liability. The courts will not enforce exculpatory clauses to excuse liability for negligence. However, they can be used to excuse liability for harm resulting from other causes and give notice of the extent of responsibility being taken for the safety of others.

Where a person signs a contract agreeing not to hold an amusement park liable for injury or harm of any kind occurring on the premises, a customer injured at the park due to the negligent failure to properly maintain the equipment would have a cause of action for negligence in spite of the waiver. In the absence of negligence on the part of the amusement park staff, however, there would be no liability.

COMMON LAW DEFENSES TO NEGLIGENCE

II. CONTRIBUTORY NEGLIGENCE

A victim of negligence cannot recover damages if the victim's own negligence contributed to the damage.

III. ASSUMPTION OF THE RISK

A victim of negligence cannot recover damages if the victim knowingly and voluntarily assumed the risk.

At common law, contributory negligence and assumption of the risk are defenses to negligence. States that still allow common law defenses to be used in negligence actions generally allow both of them. While they make a victim responsible for his own safety, they tend to produce sharp results at times because a victim is completely barred from recovery for negligence if his own failure to exercise reasonable care contributed to his injuries.

If a hunter negligently shot a person without properly identifying the target, he might not be liable if the victim was not wearing the customary red hat required for safety in the hunt. If the hunter fired toward a road and injured a motorist, there would be liability for negligence even in the absence of the red hat because reasonable motorists do not need to wear red while driving as a safety precaution even during hunting season.

A person who sees a large puddle of water and walks in it rather than around it might not be able to recover for the injuries sustained when he slipped and fell in it even if the owner of the property had negligently created the puddle. If the victim had "knowingly" and "voluntarily" encountered the puddle, he would have assumed the risks inherent in walking through it. A person knowingly assumes a risk when he is aware of or put on notice of the important facts relating to the situation. Since reasonable people are aware of the nature of puddles, the man in this case would be held to have knowingly encountered it. If, however, the owner of the land upon which the puddle was located had created a ten foot deep trench that looked like an ordinary puddle, a person walking through it would not be encountering a known danger and would, therefore, not assume the risks associated with it. A person voluntarily encounters a danger when he has other options but chooses to encounter the danger anyway. If there was no way around the puddle and the person encountering it needed to walk through it to get to a pharmacy to purchase medicine, there would be no assumption of the risk because the victim's encounter with the obstacle would not have been voluntary.

Essential Vocabulary

1. contributory negligence
2. assumption of the risk
3. knowingly
4. voluntarily

MODERN DEFENSES TO NEGLIGENCE

IV. COMPARATIVE NEGLIGENCE

Comparative negligence statutes and court decisions limit the recovery of a victim of negligence to the percentage of the damage for which the defendant was at fault.

Many states have adopted a new system of defense to negligence which is less severe than the common law system. The defense of comparative negligence replaces the common law defenses of contributory negligence and assumption of the risk by allowing the court to compare the negligence of the parties and limit the recovery of the plaintiff to that portion of his injuries caused by the negligence of the defendant.

If a person driving 30 miles over the speed limit struck a pedestrian who had darted out in front of his car without warning, the court would be able to consider the relative fault of both parties and award the pedestrian 60% of his damages if the court determined that the driver was 60% at fault. In this example, the victim would have recovered only

$6,000 if she suffered damages in the amount of $10,000. If, on the other hand, the court had determined that the victim was entirely at fault for the accident, it would have awarded nothing.

Some states have adopted a version of the comparative negligence defense described above with the addition of what is referred to as the "fifty percent rule." The fifty percent rule denies the victim recovery of any damages if the defendant is not more than 50% at fault for the accident. In our example above, the victim would have recovered $6,000 even in states that have adopted this version of comparative negligence containing the 50% rule. However, if the court had found that under the circumstances of the case the driver was 50% at fault or less, the victim would not have received any award of damages at all.

Essential Vocabulary

1. comparative negligence
2. fifty percent rule

CHECK YOUR UNDERSTANDING

DIRECTIONS: Read each of the following questions. Choose the best answer and study the discussion of the question.

1. Arnold hired Ripley to haul a load of rock from the quarry to his home. Ripley owned her own truck and required Arnold to sign an agreement in which he waived any right to sue for damages arising from the delivery. When Ripley tried to make the delivery she unintentionally backed over Arnold's car and knocked down his chimney. Angered, Arnold swore at Ripley, and, when Ripley jumped out of her truck and asked Arnold if he wanted to fight, he answered, "Yes." Ripley and Arnold slugged it out with Ripley scoring a knockout in the second round. Arnold sued Ripley for battery and negligence. He will probably:

   a. not recover anything.
   b. recover for battery but not for negligence.
   c. recover for negligence but not for battery.
   d. recover for both negligence and battery.
   e. recommend that Sam, a bigoted male supremist, hire Ripley to deliver some bricks to his home.

DISCUSSION

(c)   Arnold's agreement waiving the right to sue Ripley any damage arising from the delivery was an exculpatory clause excusing negligence. These clauses violate public policy and are generally not enforceable. Therefore, Arnold could maintain an action for negligence against Ripley for the damage to his car and chimney. When Ripley asked Arnold if he wanted to fight, and he answered in the affirmative, he may have consented to the resulting battery inflicted by Ripley. Consensual combat is handled in a variety of ways in different jurisdictions. Some jurisdictions will not recognize this type of consent because it violates public policy against fighting. Others, do recognize it. We have chosen to present the concept that consent is normally a defense to the intentional torts. The correct answer to this question is that Arnold could recover for negligence but not the battery. For the purposes of this text, we have adopted the strategy of presenting only basic rules with the idea that a student would be able to research the law when a specific case arises.

2.   During hunting season, Davis used a deer that he had shot as a blind and hid behind it while making noises that he thought would attract other deer. Although Davis was wearing a red hat, Warren shot at the carcass believing it to be a deer with some type of red cloth tied to its antlers. He failed to positively identify his target prior to firing at it. Warren missed the deer, but a bullet struck Davis. In a state recognizing contributory negligence, Warren will probably:

a.   be liable to Davis for negligence.
b.   be liable to Davis for battery.
c.   be liable to Davis on a comparative negligence theory.
d.   not be liable to Davis because his actions constituted an implied consent to negligence.
e.   not be liable to Davis because he negligently placed himself in peril.

DISCUSSION

(e)   Davis was negligent in using the deer carcass as a blind. He had the duty to take reasonable steps to protect himself from injury, and he breached that duty when he placed himself in danger by hiding behind the carcass. His using the carcass as a blind was the proximate cause of his injury because he was a foreseeable victim and his injury from a gunshot wound was a foreseeable harm. Contributory negligence is a defense to negligence in states that still recognize the common law defenses to negligence. Davis would not be able to recover damages for his injuries even though Warren was negligent in shooting at an unusual target that he had not positively identified.

States that recognize the common law defenses of contributory negligence and assumption of the risk do not recognize comparative negligence. In a comparative negligence state, Davis could have recovered the percentage of his damages caused by Warren's negligence if the court found Warren to be more than 50% at fault. If the court found him to less than 50% at fault in Davis' injury, Davis could only recover damages in states that have adopted the comparative negligence defense without the 50% rule.

3. Terry, a mechanic, forgot to tighten the lug nuts on one of the wheels of a large truck owned by Ursula. Ursula noticed this but took the truck anyway to pick up a load of oil. After the truck was loaded and being driven on the freeway by Ursula, the wheel fell off of the truck due to the improper tightening of the lug nuts. Ursula was injured and was sued for damages by other motorists and the state. She sued Terry for negligence in not tightening the lug nuts properly. In a state retaining the common law defenses to negligence, Ursula probably:

   a. lost because she assumed the risk.
   b. lost because she was comparatively more negligent than Terry.
   c. lost if she signed an exculpatory clause when she hired Terry in which she released him from all liability arising from his work.
   d. won because a reasonable truck mechanic would have tightened the lug nuts more carefully.
   e. won in an action for conversion because Terry's negligence resulted in a taking of the oil she was hauling.

DISCUSSION

(a) Terry was negligent in failing to tighten the lug nuts on one of the truck wheels, but Ursula assumed the risk because she knowingly and voluntarily took her chances. She knowingly assumed the risk because she was aware of the condition. She voluntarily assumed the risk because she could have had the nuts tightened prior to taking the truck. This would be a defense to Terry's negligence in states recognizing the common law defenses to negligence.

Comparative negligence is not recognized in states retaining the common law defenses to negligence. An exculpatory clause would not have excused Terry from negligence because consent to negligence violates public policy. Conversion is an intentional tort that is not applicable because Terry was merely negligent in forgetting to tighten the nuts.

4. When Swift got on the roller coaster, the attendant forgot to strap him into the seat. Although Swift had ridden the roller coaster many times before, he not only did not fasten the belt himself, but he stood up just as the device began going down the first hill. Swift was thrown from the ride and severely injured. In a state that has adopted comparative negligence, Swift will probably:

    a. recover only the percentage of damages caused by the attendant's negligence.
    b. recover nothing because he was partially at fault.
    c. recover all of his damages.
    d. recover half of the damages he suffered regardless of fault.
    e. recover nothing because this was an act of God.

DISCUSSION

(a) Although Swift knowingly and voluntarily assumed the risk of riding the roller coaster without using a safety belt, he can still successfully maintain an action for negligence in states recognizing comparative negligence. The attendant was negligent in forgetting to check Swift's strap, and Swift was negligent in failing to take steps to protect himself and by standing up. Swift will be able to recover the percentage of his damages caused by the attendant's negligence if the attendant was more than 50% at fault. If, however, the attendant is found to be less than 50% at fault, Swift can recover damages only in states which have not adopted the 50% rule.

SECTION III
CONTRACTS

Contract Formation
Contract Defenses
Contract Discharges
Assignment and Delegation
Remedies
Contract Critique

Chapter 7
Contract Formation

A "contract" is a promise or set of promises that the courts will require a person to keep. The person making a promise is called the "promisor." The person to whom the promise is made is called the "promisee." In every contract, one or both of the parties are making promises. Breach of contract is a wrong for which an injured party can bring a legal action. A "valid contract" is a contract enforceable by all parties. Most contracts are valid contracts. A "voidable contract" is a contract enforceable by some but not all of the parties. In a voidable contract, one or more of the parties has the power to avoid or disaffirm his contractual obligations. Under special circumstances, contracts may be voidable such as when a contract is entered into by a minor. A "void contract" is a contract that none of the parties can enforce. The promises that make up void contracts are really not contracts at all because a contract is a promise that the courts will enforce. For example, promises to commit crimes or torts are unenforceable and therefore void. Since a void contract is not enforceable, it is really not a contract at all.

Essential Vocabulary

1. contract
2. promisor
3. promisee
4. valid contract
5. voidable contract
6. void contract

I. CONTRACT

A contract is an enforceable promise created by offer, acceptance and consideration.

Just as the elements of battery were intent, offensive touching and damages, the elements of a contract are "offer," "acceptance" and "consideration." Although each of these elements will be discussed in more detail later, a brief description of each of these terms will be provided here. An offer is a proposal that the parties enter into a contract that contains all of the terms of the desired contract. An acceptance is merely an agreement to be bound by the offer. Consideration is whatever a party receives for his promise. During the Middle Ages, the courts of England decided that a promise did not have to be kept unless the party making it received something in return. What he received was called the "consideration" for his promise. If nothing was received for the promise, it was simply a promise to make a gift and would not be enforced.

Roger told Sally, "I'd like to sell my radio. Would you like to buy it for $50?" He was making an offer to Sally by proposing that they enter into a sales contract. If Sally had said, "I accept," or "O.K." or made some other response that indicated that she wanted to pay $50 for the radio, she would have accepted the offer. Once it has been determined that both an offer and an acceptance have been made, the agreement must be analyzed to determine whether or not each party received something for their promises. In this case, Roger would be receiving Sally's promise to pay the $50 price of the radio, and Sally would be receiving Roger's promise to give her the radio.

When the elements of a contract can be proved, the promises made are enforceable and become a "contract." In analyzing a set of promises to determine if the promises are an enforceable contract, one should begin the process with the element of offer. If there has been no offer, there is no power of acceptance. The second element that should be considered is the element of acceptance. If the offeree has not agreed to be bound by the terms of the offer, there is no need to look for the consideration supporting the promises made. The last element to be considered should be the element of consideration.

A breached contract is a broken promise. The legal action for enforcing a broken promise is a suit for "breach of contract." When a contract is breached, the courts will provide a variety of remedies to give the aggrieved party the benefit of the bargain.

Essential Vocabulary

1. offer
2. acceptance
3. consideration
4. breach of contract

II. EXPRESS CONTRACT AND IMPLIED CONTRACT

An express contract is made with words, and an implied contract is made with actions.

[The word "express" is used in the law to denote that words are used. An express contract is, therefore, a contract made with words.] A contract in which the offer and acceptance are formed with words is an express contract whether the words are made verbally, in writing or by signs or symbols. For example, two people could form an express contract using spoken words or even Morse code. [Express contracts can be "informal" or "formal".] [An informal contract is a contract that can be formed without the use of any particular words or format. Most express contracts are informal contracts.] [A formal contract is a contract required by law to contain certain words and follow certain rules.] A few types of express contracts are formal contracts. Negotiable commercial paper, such as checks and promissory notes, are types of formal contracts that will be discussed in the chapter on commercial paper.

[The word "implied" is used to denote legal relations arising from actions rather than words.] [An "implied contract" is a contract formed by actions rather than words when the price or consideration is known by the parties.] When a person goes into a store and puts a bottle of shampoo on the counter, the purchaser may say something like, "How are you today?" But placing the item on the counter means that the purchaser is offering to buy it at the posted price. The clerk may say, "Fine, thank you. That will be $5.43." But when the clerk accepts the purchaser's money, he is actually accepting the purchaser's offer and the sales contract is concluded. The consideration for the payment is the transfer of ownership of the shampoo from the store to the purchaser, and the consideration for the transfer of ownership is the payment.

[An essential factor in an implied contract is the fact that the price must be known to the parties.] If a person goes to the dentist to have a tooth filled, there is no express contract or implied contract if the dentist and patient do not agree on the price prior to the tooth being filled. The consideration would be indefinite. In such cases, there would be no contractual liability at all. If the dentist needed to collect for her services in court, she would need to resort to another legal theory that will be discussed later called "quasi-contract".

Essential Vocabulary

1. express
2. express contract
3. informal contract
4. formal contract
5. implied
6. implied contract

III. OFFER

An offer is an intentionally communicated set of promises specifying price, quantity and description.

[The offer contains all of the terms of the proposed contract and creates a power of acceptance in the offeree.]The person making an offer is called an "offeror," and the person to whom the offer is made is called the "offeree."] A valid offer that is capable of being accepted must be communicated intentionally and be definite enough for the court to determine what the parties intended so that the promises can be enforced.

Determining whether the offeror intended to make an offer in the first place presents an interesting problem. It is very difficult to determine what the offeror was thinking at the time the offer was made.[The courts have adopted an objective test for the presence of intent to make an offer.] If the offeror appeared to be serious about making the offer, the courts treat the offer as having been intentionally made regardless of the offeror's subjective intent.]

Doris asked Tom if he'd like to purchase her watch for $45 and Tom accepted. If a reasonable person would have thought she intended to make the offer, her offer would have been intentionally made even if she claimed that she was only joking. Consequently, she would not be able to avoid liability on the ground that she did not intend to make the offer Tom had accepted.

[The offer must be "communicated" to create the power of acceptance in the offeree. An offer is communicated when it is brought to the offeree's attention] Normally, this does not become an issue because the offeree would not try to accept an offer if she did not know about it. This does become an issue in cases where rewards are offered and someone performs the required act without knowing of the offer and later attempts to enforce the reward contract when the offer is discovered.

If Andy lost his dog and offered a reward in the paper for the return of the animal, Sam could not enforce the promise of the reward if he found and returned the dog before he learned of Andy's offer to pay the reward. This is the case because an offer must be communicated to the offeree before he can accept it.

[An offer must be "definite" to create a power of acceptance in the offeree.] A definite offer contains the "material terms" of the contract.] The word "material" means important. Material terms are terms that are essential to the enforceability of the proposed contract.] If a material term is missing, the offer is indefinite and cannot be accepted to create a contract.] The material terms of a contract are the "price," "quantity" and "description."[1] The "price" is whatever is promised as consideration for a promise or performance. It can be money, property, services or some other thing or right. The "quan-

---

[1] See page 276 (16-I) for an exception to the requirement of price in offers for the sale of goods.

tity" is essentially the term dealing with how much or how many. The "description" is a description of the property or service which is the subject of the contract. While there are many important additional terms in most offers, these are the only terms called the material terms because without them there can be no contract.

If Andy offered to paint Betty's house without specifying a price and she accepted, there would be no breach of contract if Andy did not perform as promised because there was no valid offer. If the offer does not contain a price term, it is indefinite and cannot be accepted to create a contract. Andy and Betty did not agree on a price for the painting services. Similarly, no valid offer would have existed if Andy had offered to do "some" painting for Betty for $700 because the quantity would be indefinite. Also, no offer would have existed if Andy had offered to "do some work" for Betty for four hours at the rate of $6 per hour because the description of the work would have been missing. Without all three material terms, there can be no offer or resulting contract.

[Time for performance is an important term, but it is not a material term because the courts will enforce the contract even in the absence of agreement on this detail by requiring that the parties perform within a reasonable time.] If the parties include the material terms in the offer, a failure to agree on the time for performance does not affect the enforceability of the contract.

If Carla offered to pay Dina $10 for washing her car and Dina accepted, the price, $10, the quantity, one car, and the description, Carla's car, were specified. There was, therefore, an enforceable contract when Dina accepted even though they never discussed when this washing should take place. Dina must wash the car within a reasonable time. Most courts would probably determine that the car should have been washed the day the contract was made.

Essential Vocabulary

1. offer
2. offeror
3. offeree
4. intent to make an offer
5. communicated
6. definite
7. material terms
8. price
9. quantity
10. description

IV. OFFER TERMINATION

An offer can be terminated by time, rejection or revocation.

[The offer creates a power of acceptance in the offeree that can be terminated by the passage of time.] How long does this power to form a contract last? Could an offer to sell an automobile made in October of 1945 be accepted in 1950? [When the offeror does not specify how long the offer should remain open, it will remain open for a reasonable time.] The length of a reasonable time is determined by the court after considering all the circumstances of a particular case. [At the end of that time, the offer terminates and ceases to exist. Upon "termination of the offer," it can no longer be accepted.]

If Frank offered to cut George's grass for $15, the offer would remain open for a reasonable time - probably the duration of the conversation. George could probably not call Frank and accept a week later. If the offeror specifies how long the offer will remain open, it will not remain open beyond the length of time specified. If Frank had told George that the offer to cut his grass would be open for two days, George could not accept it after the expiration of the two days.

[An offer can also be terminated by the rejection of the offeree.] [A rejection of an offer can be express or implied.] [An "express rejection" is made with words.] An "implied rejection" is made by actions.] Once the offeree rejects the offer, it can no longer be accepted even if the offeree changes his mind. An offer can be rejected by any action or words that indicate that the offeree is not interested in it.

If Frank had told George that the offer to cut his grass would be open for two days, George could not accept Frank's offer after telling him that he was not interested even if the two days had not yet elapsed. If, after rejecting Frank's offer, George had changed his mind he could have called Frank and told him so, but this would have amounted to George's making a new offer. If Frank indicated that he would still like to cut the grass, Frank would be accepting George's new offer because Frank's original offer had ceased to exist when George rejected it.

[An offer also ceases to exist when it is revoked by the offeror. An offer can be revoked by the offeror anytime before it is accepted.] After an offer has been accepted, revocation is no longer possible because the offer and acceptance become a contract.] An ["express revocation" is a revocation made by the offeror using words, and an "implied revocation" is a revocation made through actions.]

If Howard offered to sell John his house and keep the offer open for three days to give John time to think about the purchase, the offer would remain open for three days unless Howard revoked it within that time. Howard's selling his house to someone else would be an implied revocation of his offer. Howard could also have expressly revoked his offer by telling John that the offer was revoked. If Howard had revoked his offer, John could no longer accept even though the three days promised had not yet expired. A promise must be a contract to be enforceable. Since the promise to hold the offer open for three days was not supported by consideration, it was not a contract and would not be binding on Howard.

Essential Vocabulary

1. termination of the offer
2. express rejection
3. implied rejection
4. express revocation
5. implied revocation

V. OPTION CONTRACT

An option contract is a promise to hold an offer open for a certain length of time which is supported by consideration.

A promise to hold an offer open for a certain length of time is called an "option." Most options are not contracts and are not enforceable because they are not supported by consideration.[2] A promise to hold an offer open for a certain length of time that is supported by consideration is called an "option contract." Option contracts are enforceable.

Leonard offered to sell his television set to Mable for $200. Mable promised to pay him $5 if he would agree to hold the offer open for three days. Leonard agreed to hold the original offer open for three days. In this case, an option contract was created because Leonard's promise to hold the offer open was supported by consideration. If Leonard does not hold the offer open for the three days promised, he will be liable for breach of this option contract.

Essential Vocabulary

1. option
2. option contract

---

[2] See page 279 (16-IV) for an exception to the requirement of consideration for the formation of a merchant's firm offer for the sale of goods.

VI. ACCEPTANCE

An acceptance is an intentionally communicated and matching assent to the offer.

Once an offer has been made, the offeree has the power to accept it until it is terminated. An effective acceptance must reasonably appear to be made intentionally. As in the case of the offer, the court will judge whether the acceptance was intentionally made by considering appearances rather than the actual subjective intent of the offeree. "Intent to make an acceptance" is the reasonable appearance that an acceptance was intentionally made.

Paula offered to sell Julie her hat for $20, and Julie sarcastically answered, "Oh sure!" There would be no acceptance if a reasonable person present would not have taken Julie seriously even though Paula unreasonably believed that her offer had been accepted. However, Julie's response would have been an acceptance if she had appeared to be serious even if she subjectively did not intend to accept the offer at that time.

An acceptance is normally communicated when the offeree lets the offeror know that she intends to accept the offer. This can be done in any reasonable manner. Acceptances are normally effective when sent even if the offeree never receives the message. An offer is not normally accepted by silence unless the parties agree that silence will be an acceptance in advance. Therefore, an offeror cannot require the offeree to reject his offer or be bound by an assumed acceptance without some prior agreement of the parties.

Thomas received a letter from Alice in which she wrote, "Unless I hear from you by noon tomorrow, I will assume that you have accepted my offer to purchase your painting for $200." There would be no contract even if Thomas didn't contact Alice at all because the acceptance would not have been communicated. If, however, during negotiations, Thomas and Alice had agreed that Thomas would sell the painting to her for $200 unless he contacted her by noon the next day, Thomas' silence would have been an acceptance and a contract would have been formed if Alice did not hear from Thomas by noon.

Acceptances can be communicated in a variety of ways depending upon the offer. If the offer specifies that acceptance must be communicated by telegram, the acceptance must be communicated by that means or a substantially similar method.

Offers to create "bilateral contracts" or contracts in which both parties make promises can be accepted by the offeree promising to perform as required by the offer. Offers to create "unilateral contracts" or contracts in which only one party makes a promise must generally be accepted by the offeree's performance.

For example, an offer in which Sally promised to build Tina a fireplace in exchange for Tina's promise to pay $1200 could be accepted by Tina's promising to pay as required. A bilateral contract in which both parties would be making promises was proposed by the offer. However, if Sally had promised to build Tina a fireplace upon Tina's payment of $1200, the offer could only have been accepted by Tina's actual payment as required. In this case, the offer proposed a unilateral contract or a contract in which only one side or party would be making a promise.

[Acceptance requires a "matching assent" to the offer. A matching assent is consent to be bound to the exact terms of the offer with no alterations or additions.] This requirement is sometimes called the "mirror image rule."[3] The mirror image rule requires that the acceptance match the terms of the offer as exactly as a mirror's image matches the object reflected. Essentially, the offer must contain all of the terms of the proposed contract with the acceptance being merely an assent to the exact terms of that offer. If the acceptance purports to add to or change any of the terms of the offer, it is not an acceptance at all but, rather, a rejection of the original offer accompanied by a "counter offer." [A counter offer is a new offer made by the offeree after rejecting the offeror's original offer. This new offer can be accepted or rejected by the original offeror.]

Betty offered to build a fence for Dan for $450, and Dan accepted by saying, "I accept, but you will also need to paint it for that price." No contract was formed because the acceptance contained terms that differed from the offer. Dan's attempted acceptance actually made a counter offer that Betty could accept or reject. However, unless the counter offer was accepted by Betty, no contract would exist between the parties since the original offer was terminated rather than accepted by Dan's words.

Essential Vocabulary

1. acceptance
2. intent to make an acceptance
3. bilateral contract
4. unilateral contract
5. matching assent
6. mirror image rule
7. counter offer

VII. CONSIDERATION

Consideration is the new and bargained for promise, performance or forbearance given for a promise.

[In the absence of "consideration," a promise is merely an unenforceable promise to make a gift.] A party to a contract must receive something for her promise or be entitled

---

[3] See 277 (16-II) for an exception to the Mirror Image Rule in accepting offers for the sale of goods.

to receive something for her promise or she is generally not required to keep it under the law. Consideration may take one of three forms: a promise, a performance, or a forbearance.

Consideration may be in the form of a promise. If Audrey promises to pay $80 for a purse and Bill promises to deliver the purse, a contract has been formed even if the money and purse have not yet been delivered because the parties received each other's promises in exchange for their own promises.

Similarly, consideration may be in the form of a performance. A party may promise to pay or deliver consideration only after the object of the contract has been received. If Carl pays cash for a movie ticket, the consideration for his payment is the theater's promise to allow him to view the movie while the consideration for the theater's promise is Carl's performing the contract by paying for the ticket.

Consideration may also take the form of a "forbearance." A forbearance is the non-exercise of a legal right. If Debra offers to pay Ellen $200 if she will not travel to Florida next weekend, Debra will be required to pay if Ellen does not make the trip. The consideration for Debra's promise to pay Ellen is Ellen's temporarily giving up her right to travel to Florida. The consideration for Ellen's forbearance is Debra's promise to pay $200. It is important to remember that the right given up must be a legal right. If Debra promised to pay Ellen to stop vandalizing her home and Ellen agreed, there would be no forbearance and, therefore, no consideration for Debra's promise to pay because Ellen would have no legal right to vandalize Debra's property.

Normally, the value of the consideration is not important in determining whether or not a contract is enforceable. The courts simply require that the consideration be "new" and "bargained for." "New consideration" is something that the person making the promise does not already own. "Bargained for consideration" is the consideration obtained through a genuine sale and not through a gift disguised to look like a sale.

If Kelly promised to pay $300 for a used car that Pat was selling, the promise to pay would be supported by consideration as long as Kelly did not already own the car. However, if Pat had stolen Kelly's car and merely offered to sell it back to her for $300, Kelly's promise to pay would not have been supported by consideration since she already owned the car.

If Carl offered to paint Jake's house for $700, and Jake accepted the offer, any promise by Jake to pay more for the same job would be unenforceable because Jake "owned" the right to have his house painted when he accepted the offer. If Carl were to demand $800 for the job after contracting but before painting, and Jake agreed, the only consideration for Jake's promise to pay the additional $100 would be the painting of his house. This would not be "new" because Jake owned the right to have his house painted when he accepted the offer at the time of contracting.

The law also requires that the consideration must have been "bargained for" rather than included in the agreement as a mere formality. The courts take all circumstances into account in deciding whether consideration is merely a pretense in an effort to make a gift look like a sale or the subject of genuine bargaining.)

If Sandy offered to sell a farm worth $150,000 to her son for $85,000 without seeking any other buyers, she would only be making a promise to make a partial gift of the farm. The court would probably not enforce the contract if Sandy changed her mind because her promise was not supported by consideration. While the $85,000 was "new," it was not the subject of genuine bargaining since Sandy would not have sold the farm to anyone else for that price.[This type of inadequate consideration is called "nominal consideration." Nominal consideration is consideration in name only. It will not support a contract because it is not the actual object of the bargain.)

The fact that Sandy was selling to her son at a price that was dramatically lower than the market value of the property without seeking other buyers leads to the conclusion that the entire transaction was made merely to disguise a gift of $65,000 to her son. The price was actually nominal consideration for the sale with the actual motivation being Sandy's affection for her son. If, however, Sandy had contracted with a stranger after attempting to get the best price possible for the property, she would probably be required to go through with the sale or pay damages because the object of the transaction would have been the price.[Courts are usually more concerned with the presence or absence of bargaining than the actual value of the consideration being exchanged for promises.]

Essential Vocabulary

1. consideration
2. forbearance
3. new consideration
4. bargained for consideration
5. nominal consideration

VIII. MODIFICATION OF CONTRACT

Agreements modifying existing contracts must be supported by consideration to be enforceable.

[Consideration is required to make any "modification of a contract" enforceable.[4] A modification of a contract is any change in its terms.] [This rule is merely an explicit

---

[4] See page 278 {16-III} for an exception to the requirement of consideration to modify contracts for the sale of goods.

statement of the rule that consideration must be new. Once the offeree accepts an offer, it turns into a contract binding both parties as of the instant the offer was accepted. Each party owns the promises of the other. Any change must be made by agreement of both parties and be supported by new consideration.

In our previous example in which Carl had contracted to paint Jake's house for $700, a later promise by Jake to pay Carl more for the same job would not be enforceable because Jake would not be getting anything new for his promise to pay more. However, if Carl and Jake had agreed that the color specified in the original contract would be changed, this alteration is what Jake would be receiving would have satisfied the requirement of new consideration. This would have been true even if it had not cost Carl any more for the new color than the original color because the change would be something new and support the promise to pay the additional $100.

Essential Vocabulary

1. modification of a contract

IX. PROMISSORY ESTOPPEL

A promise is enforceable without consideration if the promisee justifiably and detrimentally relied upon it.

Under certain circumstances, a person will be stopped or "estopped" from refusing to honor a promise even in the absence of consideration. Since everyone is presumed to know the law, one may not ordinarily be justified in relying on a promise made by another without consideration. However, if the individual making the promise has made similar promises in the past without consideration and honored them, there may be legal grounds for relying on a similar promise made in the present. "Promissory estoppel" is a legal reason for stopping a person from avoiding legal liability for breaking a promise that is not supported by consideration.

If Jean promises Carl that she will pay his rent this month, Carl would not be justified in relying on the promise if it was not supported by consideration. However, if Jean had made similar promises in the past and kept them, Carl would be justified in relying on the current promise. Jean would still not be required to pay the rent, however, even though Carl's reliance was justifiable unless Carl suffered some detriment by virtue of her failure to pay the rent. If Carl lost a security deposit because of Jean's failure to pay the rent on time, the requirement of some detriment resulting from the broken promise would be met. Jean would be liable for damages — possibly the rent and the security deposit. However, if Carl had been able to straighten things out with his landlord without loss in spite of Jean's failure to keep her promise, she would not have been liable because there was no consideration for her promise and without detriment the court would not enforce her promise on the ground of promissory estoppel.

Essential Vocabulary

1. promissory estoppel

X. QUASI-CONTRACT

In the absence of a contract, people are liable for the reasonable value of property or services received if their acts or omissions were instrumental in getting the benefit.

[People who are active in obtaining a benefit must pay the supplier its reasonable value when no gift is intended.]The legal doctrine of "quasi-contract" has developed in the law to prevent a person from being unjustly enriched due to a failure to enter into an enforceable contract.[Quasi-contract is an obligation resembling a contract. It arises only when there is no contract between the parties and allows recovery for benefits given to another without the intent to make a gift.] In general, the courts have determined that it is unjust to allow a person who is active in getting a benefit to retain it without payment when no gift was intended. The benefit may be property or services.

In the case of medical services, the doctor and patient rarely negotiate a price prior to the rendering of the services. Often the agreement resembles an implied contract. However, no implied contract is formed because the price is not known by both parties prior to the services being rendered. If the patient does not pay for the services, the doctor may not resort to an action for breach of contract because neither an express nor an implied contract was formed due to the failure to specify the material term of price. It would be unjust, however, to allow the patient who actively sought the services to be enriched by receiving them without payment.

The theory of quasi-contract can be used by a doctor to recover the reasonable value of medical services. The reasonable value of the services may or may not be what the doctor attempted to charge the patient. If there had been a contract between the doctor and patient specifying a price for the services, the patient would be liable for the agreed price even though other doctors were charging much less. In this case, the agreement of the parties would be enforced because it would be a contract. Quasi-contract can be used as a theory of recovery only in the absence of an express or implied contract.

Essential Vocabulary

1. quasi-contract

CHECK YOUR UNDERSTANDING

DIRECTIONS: Read each of the following questions. Choose the best answer and study the discussion of the question.

1. Which of the lists below, according to the text, shows the elements of contract in the proper order?

    a. acceptance, offer, consideration, legality
    b. mutual assent, capacity, legality
    c. offer, acceptance, consideration
    d. offer, acceptance, performance
    e. investigation, consideration, mutual assent, performance

DISCUSSION

   (c)   The elements of an enforceable contract are offer, acceptance and consideration. These elements should be considered in the order listed because there is no need to consider acceptance if a valid offer creating a power of acceptance has not been communicated. Similarly, there is no need to engage in analysis of the consideration passing to each party if the offer has not been accepted. The legality of the subject matter and the capacity of the parties to enter into binding contracts are presumed and problems in these areas must be raised as affirmative defenses under the rules of civil procedure in force in most states. As defenses, they are not issues unless the elements of an enforceable contract can be proved. The term, "mutual assent," is another name for the elements of offer and acceptance and refers to the parties' agreement to be bound by the contract. Performance and investigation are not elements of a contract and are not important in determining whether a contract exists.

2. Amy built a house for Roy. When Roy refused to take possession or pay for the house, Amy sued for $125,000. During the trial, Amy proved that she had presented Roy with a contract bearing her signature regarding the construction of the

home. She also had expert witnesses testify that $98,000 was a reasonable price for the house. Amy did not introduce any other evidence. Amy will probably:

a. win the full $125,000 because she had performed as promised in the contract.
b. win $98,000 in quasi-contract.
c. lose because Roy never accepted her offer or took possession of the house.
d. lose because she had overcharged Roy.
e. obtain a new trial to introduce any further evidence the court deems necessary to her action.

DISCUSSION

(c)   To be victorious in an action for breach of contract, Amy would need to prove the existence of a contract. She would need to prove offer, acceptance and consideration. In her action against Roy, she proved only that she had presented Roy with a signed offer and built the house. She failed to prove that Roy accepted her offer. Under these circumstances, the value of the house which was the consideration was irrelevant because no acceptance had been proven. Amy would not be entitled to anything for breach of contract. If her failure to prove acceptance was merely an oversight, it was a costly mistake because the doctrine of res judicata would prevent her from bringing another action against Roy. The courts will not normally grant new trials merely to present additional evidence that could have been presented earlier. Quasi-contract will not afford Amy a remedy because Roy did not take possession of the house. He was not enriched since he had not received any benefit. Whether or not Amy had overcharged Roy would probably be irrelevant in most actions for breach of contract because the value of the consideration is not a factor in determining the adequacy of consideration.

3.   Arnold parked his car in a pay parking lot while no one was on duty and read a sign indicating that an hourly parking rate of $30 per hour would be charged. Arnold came back three hours later. Arnold is:

a. not liable to the parking lot owner because the contract was unconscionable.
b. not liable to the parking lot owner because he never agreed to pay the fee.
c. liable to the parking lot owner only for a reasonable fee based upon quasi-contract.
d. not liable to the parking lot owner because the parties were in pari delicto.
e. liable to the parking lot owner for $90 based upon an implied contract.

DISCUSSION

(e)   Arnold entered into an implied contract by parking his car in the lot while aware of the price he would be charged. His actions were an implied acceptance of the offer made by the sign. He would need to pay the full $90 for parking. The contract was not unconscionable even if the price was high because Arnold could have taken his business elsewhere. Quasi-contract would not be an action available in this case because of the existence of a valid, implied contract. The term "pari delicto" means equal wrong. Whether the parties to a contract are equally at fault is sometimes important when a contract is illegal. However, it is irrelevant in this case because the parking contract did not violate the law.

4.   Carl promised to buy Fred's house, and Fred agreed to sell. When the contract was drafted Fred wanted $98,000, but Carl wanted to pay only $75,000. They agreed on all other terms including the legal description of the property. Rather than let the written contract go to waste, they finally added a provision in which they agreed to decide on the price within six months. Both parties signed. About a week later, Fred sold the house to another person, and Carl sued for breach of contract. Carl will probably:

   a.   win because Fred did not agree to a price as promised.
   b.   win, but he'll have to pay $98,000 for the property.
   c.   win, but he'll have to pay the reasonable value of the property.
   d.   lose, because no contract was formed.
   e.   not be able to recover the property, but he will be entitled to damages for Fred's breach of contract.

DISCUSSION

(d)   No valid offer was made in this case because the material terms were not specified. The price of the property was left to be determined later. Since the offer was indefinite, it could not be accepted to form a contract. Since no contract was formed, Fred's sale of the property to the other person would not generate liability for breach of contract. Carl would not be entitled to any legal relief at all.

5.   Carol offered to wash Steven's fleet of trucks for $3,000. Steven told her that he would like to check around before accepting her offer and that he would give her $30 to hold the offer open for one week. Carol agreed to hold the offer open. Before the week was over, Steven called Carol to accept her offer. She told him that

she could no longer work for him because she had accepted other employment. When Steven sued Carol, he probably:

a. won because this was an enforceable option contract.

b. won because his promise to pay $30 created an implied contract for Carol to wash his trucks.

c. lost because he had not paid $30 before the offer was revoked.

d. lost because Carol's accepting other work was an implied revocation of her offer.

e. lost because option contracts are not enforceable.

DISCUSSION

(a) Carol and Steven entered into an enforceable option contract because Carol's promise to hold her offer open for one week was supported by consideration. This option contract was express rather than implied because the parties used words in its formation. The fact that Steven had not paid Carol at the time he called her would not have affected the enforceability of the option contract. His promise to pay the $30 was the consideration for Carol's promise to hold the offer open. Steve would need to pay Carol within a reasonable time. Carol could not revoke her offer during the week she promised to hold it open due to the option contract. Although a mere option is not enforceable because it lacks consideration, the option in this situation became an option contract because Steven promised to pay Carol $30 to hold her offer open.

6. Dromio offered to sell Antipholus his house and lot for $78,000. Antipholus asked if he could have his wife look at the place the following day. Dromio assured Antipholus that he would keep the offer open for two days and wrote the promise down, signed it, and delivered the letter to Antipholus. The next day, Dromio called Antipholus and told him that the deal was off because a better price had been negotiated with someone else. Antipholus can probably:

a. force Dromio to sell to him if he accepts the offer within the two day period.

b. not recover the property, but he can recover damages if he has been legally inconvenienced.

c. recover nothing from Dromio, but he may have an action against the buyer for interference with contract.

d. recover nothing because the offer was withdrawn prior to acceptance.

e. recover damages or the property because Dromio promised in writing to hold the offer open for two days.

DISCUSSION

(d)   An offer can be withdrawn anytime prior to acceptance. Promises to hold offers open are called options and are not enforceable in the absence of consideration. Dromio's promise to hold the offer open was not supported by consideration. Antipholus could not maintain a tort action for interference with contract because no contract existed. The fact that Dromio gave Antipholus a written option did not affect its enforceability due to the absence of consideration.

7.   Tom told David that he would pay him $435 if he would agree to build a hot tub in Tom's back yard within two months. To accept this offer David must:

   a. build the hot tub.
   b. write the agreement out, and require Tom to sign it.
   c. set a definite time for performance.
   d. apply for a building permit.
   e. make an express or implied promise to build the hot tub.

DISCUSSION

(e)   Tom proposed a bilateral contract to David in which both parties would be making promises. David's acceptance could be express or implied. An express acceptance would be an agreement or promise to perform. David could have implied his acceptance by starting to build the tub or taking any other action indicating that he intended to accept Tom's offer. It would not have been necessary for him to actually build the tub, reduce the agreement to writing, set a definite time for performance or apply for a building permit. Some of these actions would constitute an implied acceptance, but an express acceptance would work as well when the offer proposes a bilateral contract.

Unlike the offer in this case, offers proposing unilateral contracts require that the party accepting the offer accept by performance. If Tom had told David that he would pay him $435 to build a hot tub for him, the offer could only be accepted by the actual construction of the tub. In this case, Tom would not be asking David for a promise or to agree to anything. He would be requiring David to perform. Small changes in the wording of the offer can change an offer proposing a bilateral contract to an offer proposing a unilateral contract.

8.   Lucus offered to build a trailer for Andrew. The cost would be $2,000 for labor if Andrew supplied the materials. Andrew wrote, "I accept your offer. However, if

you are not finished within 30 days, you will pay me $20 per day for each day of delay." Andrew sent the materials to Lucus. Thirty days later Andrew discovered Lucus had not touched the materials or begun construction. Which of the following is probably true?

   a. Lucus will be liable for $20 per day until Andrew can get someone else to build the trailer.

   b. Lucus will be liable for breach of contract, but not for the late charge.

   c. Lucus will not be liable because Andrew did not accept his offer.

   d. Lucas will not liable because there was no consideration supporting Andrew's promise to pay $2,000 since he had to pay for the materials besides.

   e. Lucus will be liable for breach of contract and the late charge since his silence amounted to an acceptance of Andrew's counteroffer.

DISCUSSION

   (c)   Andrew did not accept Lucus' offer. An acceptance must be an intentional, communicated and matching assent to the offer. Andrew's acceptance did not match the offer. It violated the mirror image rule because he attempted to add the liquidated damage clause in his acceptance. Andrew's attempted acceptance merely rejected Lucus' offer and presented a counteroffer that Lucus was free to accept or reject. Lucus was under no duty to communicate his rejection of Andrew's counteroffer because silence is not an acceptance in the absence of some prior agreement.

9.   Lee borrowed $3,000 from MetaBank. The loan carried interest at the rate of 2% per month. The principal and interest were due on April 1st. On that date, Lee informed the bank that he would not be able to pay the full amount. Instead, he offered to pay the accrued interest if MetaBank would promise not to sue for six months. In addition, he promised to pay off the loan at the end of that time with six months additional interest. The bank agreed, and Lee paid the interest. One month later, Lee's financial situation was worse so the bank filed suit for breach of the loan contract. Lee defended on the ground that the bank had agreed not to sue for six months. The bank will probably:

   a. win because there was no consideration to support the extension.

   b. win if they could prove that Lee would probably breach the new agreement.

   c. win because Lee had breached the original loan contract.

   d. lose because Lee's reliance on the bank's promise was justifiable.

   e. lose because the bank's promise to extend the contract was supported by consideration.

DISCUSSION

(e)   The bank's promise to forbear from suing Lee for six months was supported by consideration and was, therefore, binding on the bank. The bank already "owned" the right to be paid in full by Lee. However, the additional six month's interest that Lee would pay after the due date was not owned by the bank until it accepted Lee's offer. Promissory estoppel, which is a substitute for consideration requires justifiable and detrimental reliance. There is no need to consider promissory estoppel because consideration was present. If the bank had agreed to allow the extension without the necessity of Lee's paying interest during the extension, the bank could have sued successfully because its forbearance would not have been supported by consideration. In that event, Lee would not have been able to successfully assert promissory estoppel to require the bank to wait for six months before filing suit. His reliance on the bank's promise would not have been justifiable because the bank's forbearance in this situation was without precedent. He also would have been unable to show that his reliance on the bank's promise was detrimental to him. He could have been sued even if the bank had never made the promise because he was unable to honor his obligation on time.

10.   Kelly and Igor entered into a contract in which Igor was obligated to repair the transmission in Kelly's car for $300. After he had completed the repairs, he demanded that Kelly pay him $400 for the work and refused to return her car unless she agreed to the change in fee. Kelly agreed and paid him $300 at that time with the promise to pay the remaining $100 when she got paid in approximately two weeks. Igor released the car to Kelly. When Kelly did not pay the additional $100 as promised, Igor sued her for breach of contract. Igor probably:

a. lost because he failed to get her promise in writing.
b. lost because the modification of the contract was not supported by consideration.
c. won because he had released the car to Kelly based upon her promise to pay the additional fee.
d. won if the transmission had actually turned out to be more work than the parties had anticipated.
e. won if Kelly had deliberately lied about the additional money.

DISCUSSION

(b)   Any modification of an existing contract must be supported by consideration to be enforceable. If consideration is not present, whether or not the promise was written is irrelevant. Igor's reliance on Kelly's promise was not justifiable. Generally, a person's reliance on a promise that is not supported by consideration is justifiable only when similar promises have been made and kept in the past or there are other exceptional circumstances. This was not the case here. Igor was bound by the agreed price regardless of how much work was involved. Igor did not have an action against Kelly for the tort of fraud in the inducement even if he could prove that Kelly lied because his reliance on her promise was not justifiable and he did not suffer damages. He had no right to demand the additional fee.

11. Which of the following statements about the use of promissory estoppel as a substitute for consideration is correct?

   a. Reliance on the promise must be justifiable.
   b. A preexisting contractual obligation to perform the promise is required.
   c. A moral obligation to perform the promise is required.
   d. An equitable injunction estopping the promisor from making a gift is required.
   e. Requiring the promisor to perform must not result in a burden or detriment to her.

DISCUSSION

   (a) Promissory estoppel is used in the absence of consideration to make a promise enforceable when the person asserting it has justifiably relied on the promise to her detriment. For reliance on a promise made without consideration to be justifiable, there must be some special reason for the reliance such as similar conduct in the past. If a preexisting contractual obligation existed, there would be no need to consider promissory estoppel as a means of requiring the promise to be honored. Moral obligations are not enforced by the courts. The courts are concerned with legal and equitable obligations. An injunction is a court order directing a person to do something or refrain from doing something in the future. No injunction would be granted unless a contractual obligation existed that could not be enforced with an award of damages. Promisors's obligations must be performed whether or not they are viewed as burdens.

12. John was cutting his front lawn one day when Dan, a stranger, drove by and asked John if he would like some help. When John said he would like some help, Dan cut the back lawn. When Dan finished, he presented John with a bill for $58. John would probably:

   a. be liable to Dan for the reasonable value of his work.
   b. not be liable to Dan for anything because he had volunteered to help.

c. be liable to Dan for $58 on an implied contract theory.

d. be liable to Dan for $58 on a promissory estoppel theory.

e. not be liable to Dan for anything because no accord had been reached or satisfied.

DISCUSSION

(a)   No contract came into existence between the parties because the consideration was not discussed prior to Dan's helping John. Similarly, no promises were made regarding payment that could be enforced by promissory estoppel. In the absence of a contract, a party must pay for services received if he was active in getting them. In this case, Dan could collect the reasonable value of his services in quasi-contract. This may not be as much as the $58 demanded. John was active in obtaining Dan's assistance because he told Dan he would like some help. Since Dan was a stranger, it was not reasonable for John to assume that Dan wanted to make a gift of his help. Accord and satisfaction is a type of discharge of contract that will be discussed in a later chapter. It does not arise in the absence of a dispute between the parties over what an existing contract requires. There was no contract in this case because the price was not known or established by the parties prior to Dan's performance.

Chapter 8
Contract Defenses

A defendant in an action for breach of contract needs no defense unless the plaintiff can prove that the contract existed. The plaintiff must prove offer, acceptance, consideration in an action for breach of contract. Once these elements of contract are proved, the plaintiff must prove the extent of the damages to be granted relief. The court will dismiss any action based upon a breach of contract if the plaintiff fails to prove each of the elements of a contract. When, however, the plaintiff successfully proves the elements of a contract, the defendant can avoid liability by pleading and proving one of the defenses to contracts discussed in this chapter. Illegality and lack of capacity are sometimes discussed as elements of a contract because no contract can come into existence if the subject matter of the contract is illegal or one of the parties lacks capacity. However, these objections to a contract are treated as defenses because they must be raised and proved by the defendant in the same manner as the other defenses discussed in this chapter. With the exception of illegality, parties successfully pleading and proving a defense to a contract are awarded the remedy of rescission and restitution which is discussed in more detail below under the section, "II. Incapacity."

I. ILLEGALITY

Contracts that are illegal or violate public policy will not be enforced.

Contracts to commit crimes and torts are illegal and will not be enforced by the courts. The courts will refuse to grant relief to either of the parties where illegal contracts are "executory." An executory contract is a contract that has not been performed. In cases where an illegal contract has been partially or fully performed or "executed," the courts will usually refuse relief to both parties unless the contract is illegal merely because one of the parties lacked a required state license to render the service. In these licensure cases, the courts have occasionally allowed relief in construction cases where the contractor provided services that were otherwise satisfactory. Some contracts are not illegal in the sense that entering into them is a crime or tort, but they will not be enforced because they violate good public policy by encouraging irresponsible behavior. An exculpatory clause waiving the right to sue for negligence is an example of a promise the courts will not enforce because it violates public policy by removing responsibility for carelessness.

Bob gave Anne $200 in exchange for her promise to beat Alfred with a steel pipe. Anne took the money but failed to beat Alfred as promised. If Bob sued to recover damages or get his money back, the court would refuse to award him damages because a contract to have another person beaten is an illegal contract to commit a crime. Similarly, if Bob had not paid in advance and Anne had beaten Alfred as agreed, she would not be able to recover the $200 if Bob refused to pay her. The courts will not enforce illegal contracts like this for either party since the parties are "in pari delicto." To be in pari delicto means to be equally at fault. When the parties to an illegal contract are not in pari delicto, the courts will sometimes award rescission and restitution to the party who is the lesser at fault. This rescission and restitution is a remedy that is discussed in a later chapter.

Statutes typically require that persons wishing to engage in certain professions and trades obtain a license from the state. Professions such as law, medicine, education, etc. and trades such as construction, barbering and the like require state licensure. Licensure statutes often make the act of entering into a contract to perform certain services without the required license a crime. Executory contracts to render services without the proper license are not enforceable.

Jake and George entered into a contract in which Jake promised to remove George's tonsils. Jake was not a doctor and did not have a license to practice medicine. State statutes made the unlicensed practice of medicine a crime. Since performing a tonsillectomy on George would constitute the practice of medicine, the contract would be illegal and unenforceable. If George had not known that Jake was unlicensed, George would not have been as much at fault as Jake. In this case, the parties would not have been in pari delicto so the courts may have allowed George to cancel the contract and get back any money he had paid. If George had known that Jake was unlicensed, it might have been more difficult for George to recover any payments he had made to Jake because the parties would have then been in pari delicto. If the contract had been for construction rather than medical services and Jake had performed as agreed, some courts would award Jake the reasonable value of his services while others would not.

Another type of contract that is frequently illegal is the gambling contract. Because of the use of contracts resembling gambling contracts in business contexts, it is important to be able to distinguish between "gambling contracts," "promotional schemes," "games of skill" and "insurance contracts."

A gambling contract is, in essence, a sale of a chance to win a prize. If any of the elements of selling, chance or prize is removed, the contract is not a gambling contract and will not be illegal although it may be unenforceable for other reasons.

Promotional schemes can be games used by businesses to attract customers. These schemes are illegal as gambling when the customer is required to purchase a product, service or admission to play the game. Such contracts have all the requirements of gambling contracts. The customer buys and the company sells a chance to win the prize. If, however, no purchase is necessary to play the game, the element of buying and selling is removed. Promotional games in which no purchase is necessary to play are legal even where gambling is prohibited.

The use of games in a business setting and charging money to allow people to play is legal as long as the game is a game of skill rather than chance, or there is no prize for winning. Charging $2 per attempt to make a basket with a basket ball and offering a stuffed toy if the player is successful is not gambling because a player with sufficient skill could win every time. Charging $1 for the opportunity to play a video game of roulette or poker would not be gambling if there were no prize for winning other than being named the winner. Of course, the use of such games in casinos is gambling since money prizes are paid to winners.

Insurance contracts require that the purchaser pay the insurance company for taking a specified risk. If the insured loss does not occur, the insurance company keeps the premium. However, if the loss does occur, the company will reimburse the policy holder for the loss. An insurance contract could be described as a contract in which the purchaser bets the premium that a given loss will occur and the insurance company bets that the loss will not occur. These contracts are legal provided that the purchaser has an "insurable interest" at the appropriate time. An insurable interest is the risk of loss arising from the occurrence that is insured against. The requirement of an insurable interest removes the element of prize from the contracts. The amount paid by the insurance company will only reimburse the policy holder for the loss sustained so, theoretically, there is no profit or prize.

The purchaser of a life insurance contract must have an insurable interest in the life of the insured at the time the policy is purchased. This means that the purchaser must be able to demonstrate that he is likely to suffer some loss if the insured dies. A person has an insurable interest in themselves, their children and their spouse. Partners and others in business relationships can also sometimes demonstrate sufficient possibility of losses arising from a death to be able to purchase life insurance on the lives of key people in their firms. If an insurable interest is present when the policy is purchased, the insurance company is obligated to pay the policy amount when the death occurs even if there is no insurable interest at that time. In the absence of an insurable interest at the time of purchase, the insurance company is only required to return the premium payments because the insurance policy resembles a gambling contract and violates public policy .

The purchaser of casualty insurance must have an insurable interest at the time the loss occurs. A person must be able to demonstrate some loss to recover on the policy. If the insured has no insurable interest nothing can be recovered from the insurance company. In the absence of a loss, any benefits paid would resemble the prize offered in a gambling contract.

Paula purchased life insurance on Quark, her husband, and casualty insurance on the couple's new car. About a year later, she and Quark got a divorce. Due to Paula's superior earning capacity, Quark was awarded the car and was relieved of any further duty to support her. Soon after the divorce became finalized, Quark was killed in an accident that demolished the car. Although both insurance policies were in force at the time of the loss, Paula could only recover on the life insurance policy. She had an insurable interest in Quark's life at the time the policy was purchased. However, in the case of the casualty insurance on the car, she did not have an insurable interest at the time of the loss so she would not be entitled to any proceeds from the policy.

"Exculpatory clauses" are contract promises that purport to release a party from liability. Such contract provisions are usually unenforceable to the extent that they are intended to limit liability for negligence. It is not illegal to include an exculpatory clause in a contract. However, the courts will not normally enforce these clauses because they violate good public policy by allowing people to eliminate their duty to exercise due care for the protection of others. The courts typically enforce the remainder of any contracts containing such a clauses as though the clauses were not part of the contracts.

Carla entered into a contract with a licensed contractor for the construction of a swimming pool. The contract would be enforceable even if it contained an exculpatory clause releasing the contractor from liability for negligence in performing the work. However, Carla could still successfully sue the contractor for negligence as well as breach of contract if he failed to exercise due care in building the pool. Only the exculpatory clause would be unenforceable. The remainder of the contract would be enforced as though the offending clause had not existed.

Essential Vocabulary

1. illegality
2. executory contract
3. executed contract
4. in pari delicto
5. gambling contracts
6. promotional schemes
7. games of skill
8. insurance contracts
9. insurable interest
10. exculpatory clause

II. INCAPACITY

Contracts made with minors, mentally incompetent or severely intoxicated persons are subject to rescission and restitution.

A voidable contract is an otherwise enforceable contract that can be "avoided" or "disaffirmed" by one of the parties due to special circumstances. This means that the contract is enforceable only at the pleasure of the party having the power to avoid the contract. A contract is avoided or disaffirmed when a party lacking capacity to enter into a contract expressly or by implication indicates that he will not be bound by it. A contract will not be enforced if it is avoided by a person lacking contractual capacity. "Minors," "children," and "infants" may avoid or disaffirm their contracts anytime until a reasonable time after they reach the "age of majority." Minors, children, and infants are people younger than 18 years of age. The age of majority is the age at which a person receives full capacity to enter into binding contracts. The law limits the legal capacity of minors to enter into contracts as a protection from adults who would take unfair advantage of their limited experience.

Amy sold Phil, a minor, an automobile. Phil could honor the contract and perform it as agreed, or he could avoid it anytime until a reasonable time after he turned 18 years of age, i.e. the age at which the minor's contractual incapacity ceases. If he chose to avoid the contract, he could expressly disaffirm it simply by telling Amy that he no longer wanted it, or he could disaffirm the contract by implication by returning the automobile to her. If he avoided the contract, he would be required to return the car, and Amy would be required to return his payments.

Parties avoiding contracts are required to make "restitution." A party makes restitution by returning the value of property and services received from the transaction. The duty to make restitution is more limited for a minor than an adult. An adult must return everything received by virtue of the transaction, but a minor needs to return only whatever he has left under his control. Consequently, in our example, Amy would need to return all of the money Phil had paid her even if Phil could only return the wreckage after the automobile had been destroyed. Similarly, Amy would be required to return any property Phil had given her in payment or its reasonable value if she could no longer return the property.

Adults can lack capacity to contract by virtue of their mental incapacity or severe intoxication. Mental incapacity can be permanent or temporary e.g. retardation, senility, brain damage, or a temporary psychosis or other disorder that impairs one's ability to bargain effectively. Mere lack of education, experience or judgment will not be sufficient to make a contract voidable. Severe intoxication is temporary and may be due to exposure to alcohol or other drugs or poisons. In the case of voluntary intoxication, the intoxication must be so severe that it removes the individual's capacity to form the intent to enter into a contract. Merely impairing a person's judgment is not enough. A person who is obnoxiously drunk can still have the capacity to enter into a binding contract if his offer or acceptance is intentionally made notwithstanding the fact that he would not have entered into the contract if he had been sober.

As in the case of a minor, an adult lacking capacity due to mental incapacity or severe intoxication can perform a contract or avoid it by express or implied disaffirmance anytime until a reasonable time after her disability ceases. In the event that the contract is disaffirmed, the parties must make full restitution. If all parties are adults, they must each return everything they received under the contract and pay the reasonable value of property or services that cannot be returned. In our example above in which Amy sold Phil an automobile, Phil would have been required to restore the automobile or pay for the damage when he disaffirmed the contract if he had been a mentally incompetent or severely intoxicated adult rather than a minor.

Once the disability ceases for minors, mentally incompetent or severely intoxicated people, they must exercise their power to avoid the contract within a reasonable time or forever lose it. Giving up the power to disaffirm a contract formed during a period of disability is called "ratification" of the contract. A ratification can be express or implied. An express ratification can be accomplished by notifying the other party that one intends to perform the contract. An implied ratification can be made by any action that indicates that the contract will be performed, e.g. making a payment, trying to sell the property, negligently damaging it, using it, or keeping it without disaffirming the contract after the lapse of a reasonable time. In determining the length of a reasonable time, the court will consider all of the circumstances of the case.

If the store where a minor had purchased something was closed on his eighteenth birthday, it might be reasonable for him to wait until the store opened to disaffirm the contract. However, waiting a few days because he was "busy" might constitute an implied ratification of the contract. If a person with a temporary mental disability does not recall the contract after he regains his mental faculties and does not find out about the contract for two months, it would probably be reasonable for him to disaffirm the contract promptly after he learned of it even though two months had elapsed since the disability ended. Once a contract is ratified, it remains binding even if the disability returns.

The contractual incapacity of minors and their limited duty to make restitution could render it impossible for them to care for themselves in the absence of their parents. For this reason minors are liable for the reasonable value of "necessaries" they purchase in quasi contract if they avoid the original contract. This allows them to care for themselves while according them protection from their lack of experience in bargaining. Necessaries are things and services needed to maintain oneself. They usually include reasonable food, clothing, shelter, medical treatment and education. The court will look at the facts of each case to determine whether or not a given contract was for necessaries.

Dirk, a minor, entered into a contract with George to purchase a meal for $45 that was reasonably worth only $7. Dirk can perform the contract and pay $45 for the food, or he can avoid the contract. If he avoids the contract, George can sue him for the reasonable value of the meal in quasi contract because food is normally a necessary. However, George will recover $7 rather than the full $45 promised because only the reasonable value of the meal can be recovered in quasi contract. In short, by allowing liability in quasi contract for necessaries the law allows minors to purchase items and services to meet their own needs while protecting them from being treated unfairly.

Essential Vocabulary

1. incapacity
2. avoid a contract
3. disaffirm a contract
4. minor
5. age of majority
6. restitution
7. ratification
8. necessaries

III. MUTUAL MISTAKE

Contracts based on mutual mistakes of material facts are subject to rescission and restitution.

A "mutual mistake" is a mistake made by both parties. Mutual mistakes are also referred to as "bilateral mistakes", or two-sided mistakes. To constitute a defense to a contract, a mistake must be mutual or bilateral. "Unilateral mistakes", or one-sided mistakes, will not excuse a contract.

Sid offered to sell Lisa a valuable gem that both believed to be merely an unusual piece of glass and Lisa accepted. If the error was later discovered, the contract would be subject to "rescission and restitution" because the mistake was mutual, material, and factual. Rescission is the cancellation of a contract. Restitution is the restoration of the parties to the same condition they were in prior to contracting. If Lisa had known that the object was a gem while Sid believed that it was only glass, Sid would not have been able to rescind the contract when he later discovered his error. Since the mistake was only made by Sid, it would have been only a unilateral mistake.

The law requires that the mistake be a mistake of "material fact." A material fact is an important fact subject to verification. To be important, the fact must have had an effect on the decision of at least one of the parties to enter into the contract in the first place. If the truth or falsity of the mistaken fact would not have influenced a reasonable person in entering into the contract, it would not be material and would not provide either of the parties with the defense of mutual mistake.

Andrea and Tanya entered into a contract in which Andrea promised to trim Tanya's trees for $100. Both of them mistakenly believed that one of the trees to be trimmed was an elm when it was in fact an oak tree. The contract would not have been subject to rescission if it was no more difficult to trim an oak than an elm tree. This contract would not have been subject to rescission even though the mistake was mutual because the type of tree involved was not important to the contract. If, however, oak trees required a significantly different treatment than elms, the mistake would have been material, and the defense of mutual mistake would have been available to the parties.

The courts will not usually allow this defense when the mistake is a "mistake of opinion" or a "mistake of law." Opinions are subjective judgments made by the parties or others. The courts will not allow rescission and restitution in cases where the parties are only mistaken in their opinions because they are not subject to independent verification. A mistake of law is a mistake regarding some rule the courts will enforce. Mistakes of law can include errors regarding the existence, meaning, or application of any legislative, judicial or administrative law. The courts will not normally allow rescission and restitution in cases in which there is a mutual mistake of law because of the ancient presumption that everyone knows the law, and those who do not should consult lawyers or proceed at their peril.

Even if both parties to a contract for the sale of a dog believed that the dog was the most attractive animal of its breed, the contract would not be subject to rescission if dog show judges unanimously agreed that the dog was not at all extraordinary. Although the mistake was mutual and material to the parties, whether or not a dog is attractive is a matter of opinion and not subject to independent verification.

Similarly, where the parties are mutually mistaken about how a tract of real estate is zoned, the contract is not subject to rescission because the mistake relates to zoning ordinances. Zoning ordinances are laws because they are rules enforced by the government regarding land use The parties are presumed to know the law so a mistake will not provide grounds for a defense.

Albert and Sylvia both mistakenly believed that Albert's farm land could be used by Sylvia to build a four story building. Based upon this belief, the parties entered into a contract in which Albert sold the property to Sylvia for development. When Sylvia contacted the city offices to obtain a building permit, she was informed that no permit could be issued because a four story building violated local zoning ordinances. This contract would be fully enforceable despite the fact that the mistake was mutual and material because zoning ordinances are laws.

Essential Vocabulary

1. unilateral mistake
2. bilateral mistake
3. mutual mistake
4. rescission
5. restitution
6. material fact
7. mistake of opinion
8. mistake of law

IV. MISREPRESENTATION

Contracts based upon intentional or innocent misrepresentations of material facts are subject to rescission and restitution.

An "intentional" or "innocent misrepresentation" of a material fact that is justifiably relied upon will make the contract subject to rescission and restitution. An intentional misrepresentation is a deliberate lie told with the intent to influence another to do something or refrain from doing something. Intentional misrepresentation is also referred to as "fraud" or "deceit" and is actionable as a tort. A "fraud in the inducement" is an intentional misrepresentation used to induce a person to knowingly enter into a contract. A "fraud in the factum" or a "fraud in the execution" is an intentional misrepresentation of the nature of a contract. In this type of fraud, a person misrepresents a contract to be some other type of document or contract so the victim is not aware that he is entering into the contract when he signs it. A contract is "executed" when a person signs it or performs it. In the context of fraud in the execution, the word, "execution," refers to the signing of the contract.

An innocent misrepresentation is a statement of a material fact that the speaker believes to be true, but which is actually false. An innocent misrepresentation is not normally actionable as the tort of intentional misrepresentation; however, it may be actionable as negligence. Whether the misrepresentation is intentional or innocent, a party to a contract successfully raising this defense will be awarded only rescission and restitution. This remedy only allows the victim to cancel the contract and recover any property he has given to the other party after returning everything he has received. A victim of an intentional or innocent misrepresentation must sue in tort to recover damages caused by the misrepresentation.

Where Donna told Betty that a painting she was selling was an original when in fact it was a less valuable copy, Betty could rescind the contract to purchase the painting if she had relied on the representation being correct when she entered into the sales contract. It would not matter whether the misrepresentation was a deliberate lie or merely an honest mistake. However, if the misrepresentation was intentional, it might also constitute the tort of "intentional misrepresentation." If the elements of the tort are present, Betty could sue for compensatory and punitive damages in addition to having the contract set aside.

Essential Vocabulary

1. intentional misrepresentation, fraud or deceit
2. fraud in the inducement
3. fraud in the factum or fraud in the execution
4. innocent misrepresentation

V. NONDISCLOSURE

Contracts based upon a failure to disclose a material fact by a party owing a fiduciary duty, actively concealing facts or knowing that the other party is mistaken in assumptions are subject to rescission and restitution.

Usually, there is no duty for a party to a contract to tell the other party important facts without being asked. The law requires people to be careful and protect themselves under the ancient doctrine of "caveat emptor." Caveat emptor is Latin for "let the buyer beware." However, exceptions are made to this rule when a party owes a "fiduciary duty" to the other party, actively conceals important facts or knows that someone is acting under false assumptions. A "fiduciary relationship" imposes a "fiduciary duty" upon one or both of the parties to the relationship. Fiduciary relationships are relationships in which one or both of the parties have the legal right to rely upon and trust the other. These relationships are relatively rare. Some common examples are husband-wife, investor-broker, doctor-patient, priest-penitent, and lawyer-client. A fiduciary duty is a legal obligation to act in the best interests of another.

Sam offered to sell Tom a car that Sam knew needed extensive work. Sam had no duty to disclose this information to Tom. However, if Sam had been Tom's lawyer, he would have needed to tell Tom about the necessary repairs because lawyers owe a fiduciary duty to their clients. Interestingly, if Tom were selling the car to Sam, Tom would have no duty to disclose the condition of the car to Sam because clients do not owe a fiduciary duty to their lawyers. This result follows from the fact that in the fiduciary relationship of lawyer and client, the client must trust the lawyer with money and confidential information while the lawyer does not need to entrust the client with anything. In fiduciary relationships, the party who must be trusted owes the fiduciary duty to his client. A fiduciary duty requires a person to act in the best interests of another by making a full disclosure of material facts in any contractual setting.

If Doris offered to sell Sally a tract of land, she normally would not have had a duty to disclose that there was quicksand on the property. However, Doris would have needed to tell Sally about this condition if she placed a swing set over it, and thereby concealed the true nature of the quicksand by making it look like a sand box. Similarly, Doris would be required to tell Sally that there was quicksand on the property if Sally had made a comment that let her know that Sally was assuming it was an unfinished play area. Remember that even if Doris was not required to tell Sally about the quicksand under contract law, Doris might still have been liable for negligence in not disclosing this important fact if someone was injured due to her failure to exercise reasonable care in warning Sally of the danger.

Essential Vocabulary

1. nondisclosure
2. caveat emptor
3. fiduciary relationship
4. fiduciary duty

VI. UNDUE INFLUENCE

Contracts made by parties deprived of their free will by a controlling relationship are subject to rescission and restitution.

"Undue influence" is excessive influence arising from a controlling relationship that allows the dominant person to unfairly take advantage of a position of trust. When a party to a contract does not really have the ability to say "no" to the offer because of his relationship with the other contracting party, the contract lacks genuine assent to the offer. The courts will not enforce such agreements. It is not enough that a relationship merely influenced a party to accept or make the offer. To successfully raise the defense of undue influence, the relationship must be of such a controlling nature that it resembles the traditional parent-child relationship. Young children do not have the freedom to refuse their parents in the same way that adults or strangers do. Their dependency makes them more susceptible to their parents' demands. If the father of an eight year old were to request that his child do something, the child would not feel the need to look after his own interests. In the same way, an elderly person may not have sufficient freedom of will in a transaction with a person upon whom he is dependent.

If an elderly man is under the 24 hour care of a resident nurse who decides what he eats, when he eats, which parties he can attend, and what time he goes to bed, the man's dependency upon may deprive him of his free will. This relationship is much like a parent-child relationship with the nurse being the parent figure and the elderly man being the child figure. Any contract the man might make with the nurse will be suspect due to this dependency. The nurse is in a position to take unfair advantage of the man's trust and exercise undue influence in contracting. Contracts that are the product of such undue influence are subject to rescission and restitution. If, however, the elderly man in this situation had retained his independence by making his own decisions during treatment, the contracts with the nurse would probably be enforceable. The mere fact that he may enter into a contract with his nurse because of his affection for her will not give rise to undue influence in the absence of a controlling relationship. The defense of undue influence requires a showing that a controlling relationship deprived a party of his free will.

Essential Vocabulary

1. undue influence
2. parent-child relationship

VII. DURESS

Contracts made by parties deprived of their free will by threats of illegal action are subject to rescission and restitution.

"Duress" is the use of threats of "illegal action" to deprive a person of her free will. Contracts formed under duress are subject to rescission and restitution. Illegal action is activity that violates the law or public policy. Threatening to take action that one has a legal right to take does not constitute duress even if it influences the threatened party to enter into a contract.

Dan threatened to blow up a building unless Sam agreed to sell him a cement mixer for a very low price. Sam entered into a contract to sell Dan the cement mixer as demanded. Sam could later rescind the contract on the ground of duress if he believed the threat. If Sam had not believed the threat, the contract would have been enforceable because the threat must deprive the victim of free will in the transaction. Generally, threats to commit crimes or torts will amount to duress if they are reasonably believed. If, however, Dan had threatened to squirt Sam with a squirt gun that Sam believed to be loaded with very cold water, the contract would have been enforceable because this would not ordinarily be sufficient to deprive a person of free will. This would be the case notwithstanding the fact that squirting someone constitutes a tortious battery and would therefore be illegal action. Similarly, the contract would have been enforceable if Dan had merely threatened to sue Sam because suing someone is not normally illegal or against public policy.

Essential Vocabulary

1. duress
2. illegal action

VIII. STATUTE OF FRAUDS

Executory contracts requiring payment of the debt of another, performance that cannot be completed in one year, conveyance of real property, or something in consideration of marriage must be evidenced by a written contract or memorandum.

A "Statute of Frauds" has been enacted in each for the purpose of preventing fraud by requiring that certain types of contracts be evidenced by written documentation. The written documentation may be either a written contract or a written memorandum of an oral contract. While most contracts may be written or oral, the Statute of Frauds requires that certain types of contracts be evidenced in writing.

If contracts within the Statute of Frauds are fully "executory," the courts will not enforce them in the absence of written evidence of their terms. Executory contracts are contracts that have not yet been performed. However, if such contracts have been partially or fully "executed" by one of the parties, the courts may enforce the contracts or order recession and restitution even in the absence of written documentation. Once a contract obligation has been performed it is referred as executed.

While other statutes require that additional types of contracts be evidenced by writings to be enforceable, the Statute of Frauds deals with four basic types of promises:

    (a)   promises to pay the *debt of another*;
    (b)   promises that by their terms cannot be performed in *one year* or less;
    (c)   promises to buy or sell *real property*; and
    (d)   promises made in consideration of *marriage*.[1]

---

[1] See 255 (17-I) for an addition to the number of promises that require a writing. Contracts for the sale of goods for $500 or more must also be evidenced by a written contract or memorandum.

A convenient acronym that some students find helpful in remembering the underlined words is "DORM."

Promises to pay the debt of another must be evidenced by a written contract or memorandum to be enforceable while promises to pay one's own debts are enforceable even if they are entirely verbal. Of course, a promise to pay the debt of another must be supported by consideration to be enforceable. Such contracts are often "third party beneficiary contracts." A third party beneficiary contract is a contract in which the consideration flows to a person who is not a party to the contract. The person receiving the benefit of the contract is called a "third party beneficiary." These contracts are valid and will be discussed in a later chapter.

John owed his dentist $200, and the dentist intended to sue to collect the debt. John's good friend, Dan, persuaded the dentist to give John a little longer to pay by promising to pay the debt if John did not pay within two months. The consideration for Dan's promise to pay John's debt was the dentist's promise not sue for two months i.e. a forbearance. The benefit of this contract went to John who was a third party beneficiary of the promise and not a party to the contract. Dan's promise would need to be evidenced by a written contract or a written memorandum of an oral agreement to be enforceable. Notice, however, that if Dan had met with the dentist before the services were rendered to John and told the dentist to take care of John and charge the services to his own account rather than John's, Dan would have been liable even though there was no writing because Dan would have offered to pay the bill as his own debt.

Promises that by their terms cannot be performed within one year or less must be evidenced by a writing to be enforceable. These contracts typically contain a provision specifying more than one year for performance by referring to a date that is more than a year in the future or by referring to a specific number of days, weeks, months or years that are longer than one year. Contracts which do not specify a length of time for performance or specify an indefinite time, e.g. "forever", "for the rest of one's life," etc., can be performed within one year since the contract would be terminated when a party died and that could take place within one year.

A contract in which Allen promised to restore 200 paintings for a museum would not need to be in writing even though Allen and other experts would agree that the job would take at least three years because the contract did not specify that Allen would work on the project for more than one year. Similarly, the contract would not need to be evidenced by a writing if Allen had promised to maintain the paintings for the remainder of his life. If Allen had promised, however, to work on the project for three years, the contract would have needed to be evidenced by a writing because the promised period of performance would have exceeded one year.

Promises to buy or sell real property must be evidenced by a writing to be enforceable. Nearly all interests in real property other than "leases" are covered by this provision. A lease is a contract under which real property is rented. Leases are not considered real property and do not need to be evidenced by writings unless they are required to continue for more than one year. Real property consists of land and things permanently attached to it. In addition, "easements" and "profits" are considered real property. An easement is a right to cross over or under someone's land and a profit is a right to take something from the land. Contracts in which easements or profits are bought or sold need to be evidenced by written contracts or memorandums.

If Sam wants to purchase a building for his business, a written contract or written memorandum of an oral contract will be required. The same is true if Sam wants only to purchase an easement, i.e. the right to cross someone's land. If Sam contracts with Ruth to pay $10,000 to her for an easement over her property to give his trucks easier access to his adjoining property, Ruth will not need to sell, and Sam will not need to pay, if the contract is not evidenced by a writing because the contract calls for the conveyance of an interest in real property, i.e. the easement. If Sam had only promised to lease the right to cross the property for ten months, an oral contract would have been enforceable because Ruth would have been leasing rather than conveying the easement. Notice, that if Sam had leased the easement for thirteen months, the contract would have required a writing because the lease, by its terms, could not have been performed within one year.

Promises made in consideration of marriage must be evidenced by a writing to be enforceable. Since marriage is the consideration for the promises made in these contracts, they must be made prior to the marriage and for this reason are called "antenuptial" or "prenuptial" agreements. Antenuptial or prenuptial agreements are agreements entered into prior to marriage in which the consideration is the impending marriage. These contracts are commonly used to define the claims of the engaged couple to each other's property after marriage.

Where Peggy, an elderly widow, and George, an elderly widower, want to get married but keep their property from being commingled after their marriage, they would need to enter into a prenuptial contract in which they each disclosed the extent of their respective property and renounced any claim to the property of the other by virtue of their marriage. This would ensure that their property would go to their own respective children upon their deaths. Agreements such as these are typically regulated by statute and must be evidenced by written contracts or memorandums to be enforceable.

In closing, it is necessary to discuss the differences between written contracts and written memorandums of verbal contracts. A written contract begins as a signed offer. When the second party signs the signed offer, he makes his acceptance. The second signature is an acceptance and no contract is formed if the second signature is withheld. A "memorandum," in contrast, is made after the parties enter into a verbal contract in which the offer, acceptance, or both were verbal. A signature on the memorandum is neither an offer nor an acceptance. It is an agreement to be bound by the terms of the memorandum. Consequently, a memorandum is binding on any party who signs it even if one or more of the other parties has not signed.

Pete signed an offer to sell his farm to Quincy for $1,000,000, and Quincy signed the contract indicating his acceptance of the offer. A valid contract for the sale of the farm was formed since the offer was accepted and the contract was evidenced by a written contract. If Quincy had refused to sign the contract, no contract would have come into existence because there would have been no acceptance. In such a situation, Pete could not force Quincy to buy the property, and Quincy could not force Pete to sell. If Pete and Quincy had merely made their offer and acceptance verbally, the contract would not have been enforceable because contracts for the sale of real property must be evidenced by a written contract or memorandum to be enforceable. However, if Pete and Quincy had verbally agreed on the sale of the farm and then reduced the agreement to writing, the written document would have been a memorandum of their verbal contract. Memorandums are enforceable against the parties who sign them whether or not all parties sign. A signature on a memorandum is an agreement to be bound by the terms of the memorandum. If Pete had signed the memorandum, but Quincy had not, Quincy could force Pete to go through with the sale because Pete had agreed to be bound by the terms of the memorandum. However, Pete could not have forced Quincy to go through with the purchase if he refused because Quincy had not signed.

Essential Vocabulary

1. Statute of Frauds
2. executory contracts
3. executed contracts
4. promises to pay the debt of another
5. third party beneficiary contracts
6. third party beneficiary
7. promises that cannot be performed in one year
8. promises to buy or sell real property
9. lease
10. easement
11. profit
12. promises made in consideration of marriage
13. antenuptial agreement or prenuptial agreement
14. memorandum

CHECK YOUR UNDERSTANDING

DIRECTIONS: Read each of the following questions. Choose the best answer and study the discussion of the question.

1. Andrew offered his customers the opportunity to put their business cards into a bin after they had made purchases. Purchases were required to participate in the drawing. Once each month, he drew out a card and awarded the winner $5,000. Bob did business with Andrew so that he could participate in the drawing. He placed his card in the bin and was the lucky winner. Unfortunately, Andrew was short of cash so he refused to make the award as promised. Gambling is illegal by statute. Bob sued Andrew for breach of contract. Bob probably:

   a. lost because the contract was illegal.
   b. lost because Andrew's promise to pay the winner was not supported by consideration.
   c. lost because he had no damages.
   d. won because he had detrimentally relied on Andrew's promise.
   e. won in quasi contract.

DISCUSSION

   (a)   A gambling contract is a sale of a chance to win a prize, and gambling is illegal in this case. Andrew's promise to pay the winner of the drawing would be an illegal gambling contract. The element of buying and selling is present because customers must make a purchase to play the game. The cost of the game is part of the price. The element of chance is present because a customer may or may not win. The element of prize is present because Andrew promised to pay the winner $5,000. Andrew's promises to pay the winner of the drawing were not enforceable because they constituted an illegal gambling contract. Andrew's promise to pay the winner was supported by consideration. The consideration required was a customer purchase. Bob suffered damages in the amount of the $5,000 he had won but not been paid. Detrimental reliance on a person's promise is required for asserting that a contract that is not supported by consideration should be enforced anyway on the ground of promissory estoppel. However, the doctrine of promissory estoppel cannot be used to make an illegal gambling contract enforceable. Quasi contract cannot be raised when there is a contract, and it can only be used to recover the reasonable value of property or services actually received by the plaintiff. Quasi contract cannot be used when the intended contract is illegal and the parties are in pari delicto.

2. Sam, who was sixteen years old, entered into a contract with Alan, an adult, for the purchase of an automobile which was not a necessary. Sam traded in his old car and paid $8,000 cash for the new car. The contract was executed. Alan sold the car Sam traded to an elderly man from Brazil. Sam negligently demolished the new car in an accident. If Sam disaffirmed the contract, he could:

a.   recover $8,000 from Alan and his old car from the man who bought it.

b.   recover only the $8,000 he paid for the car.

c.   recover $8,000 and the reasonable value of his old car from Alan.

d.   recover what he gave for the new car less its reasonable value.

e.   recover nothing because he could not return the new car.

DISCUSSION

(c)   Minors may disaffirm their contracts anytime until a reasonable time after they reach the age of majority. Sam was a minor since he is younger than 18 years of age. The contract was voidable by Sam because he lacked contractual capacity. He had the option of honoring or avoiding the contract on the ground of his incapacity. If Sam had chosen to honor the contract, he would have suffered the loss of the automobile. However, he also had the option of disaffirming the contract. If he disaffirmed the contract, he would be entitled to the return of everything he had given Alan. Since Alan could not return the Sam's old car, Alan would have needed to give Sam its reasonable value in addition to the the $8,000 he had received from Sam. Sam could not recover his old car from the man who bought it from Alan because the man was an innocent purchaser who was unaware of Sam's minority and his former ownership of the car prior to the purchase from Alan. Sam did not need to return anything other than the wreckage that he still had to Alan. Minors only need to return what they have left to the adult when they disaffirm a contract. If Sam had been an adult with some type of mental incapacity, he would have had to pay Alan the reasonable value of the car when he disaffirmed the contract. If he had not been overcharged for the car, Sam would not have recovered anything if he had been an adult.

3.   Simpson offered to sell Walter a glass jewel for $100. Walter accepted because he thought he was buying a diamond. Simpson made no representations regarding what type of jewel he was selling, and had no idea that Walter thought the jewel was a diamond. Walter probably:

a.   can avoid the contract on the ground of fraud.

b.   can avoid the contract on the ground of innocent misrepresentation of material fact.

c.   can avoid the contract on the ground of mistake.

d   cannot avoid the contract on the ground of mistake.

e.   has an action for breach of contract against Simpson.

DISCUSSION

(d)   Walter would be bound by the contract. He could not raise fraud or innocent misrepresentation as defenses because Simpson did not make any misrepresentations regarding the nature of the jewel. Walter could not raise mutual mistake of a material fact as a defense because only a unilateral mistake had been made. Only Walter had been mistaken regarding the nature of the jewel. Walter would not have had an action for breach of contract against Simpson unless Simpson failed to deliver the jewel as agreed.

4.   Yoda needed insulation to place inside some partitions in an apartment. Stanley, among other things, told Yoda the insulation was blue in color because he knew Yoda's favorite color was blue. Yoda was unable to inspect the insulation because of its packaging. Yoda bought the insulation because he thought Stanley gave him the best price in town. Later, Yoda found a dealer that would sell identical insulation cheaper. While inspecting the insulation, Yoda discovered that the insulation was yellow in color. Yoda probably:

a.   can avoid the contract on the ground of fraud if Stanley knew that the insulation was yellow.
b.   can avoid the contract on the ground of innocent misrepresentation if Stanley intended to deceive Yoda by lying about the color.
c.   cannot avoid the contract.
d.   can avoid the contract unless he was not deceived by Stanley's misrepresentation regarding the color.
e.   cannot avoid the contract unless he can prove that Stanley and he were in a fiduciary relationship.

DISCUSSION

(c)   An intentional misrepresentation is a deliberate lie told with the intent to influence another to do something or refrain from doing something. Stanley's misrepresentations, in this case, may have amounted to fraud in the inducement if Stanley intended to induce Yoda to enter into the contract. However, Yoda cannot avoid the contract because the fact misrepresented was not important. The color was not a material fact. Insulation is normally installed between partitions and does not show. The fact that Yoda wanted to rescind the contract because of the price is evidence that the color was not important. Avoiding a contract on the ground of misrepresentation requires that a party misrepresent an important fact. Whether or not Yoda was deceived and the presence or absence of a fiduciary relationship between the parties would not be relevant in the absence of a material misrepresentation.

5. Anderson sold his car to Rollo. Anderson knew that the brakes needed to be relined, the clutch was going out, and the car used about one quart of oil every thirty miles. Rollo discovered the problems after he had purchased the car and sued to have the contract rescinded. Anderson:

   a. would probably be liable to Rollo for fraud in the inducement.
   b. did not need to tell Rollo about the problems with the car so the contract would not be subject to rescission.
   c. was legally required to disclose the problems to Rollo.
   d. was legally required to disclose the problems only if Rollo did not take a test drive in the car.
   e. was legally required to disclose the problems unless he told Rollo that he was selling the car "as is."

DISCUSSION

   (b)   The rule of caveat emptor places the responsibility for examining an item to be purchased on the buyer. The seller does not usually need to anticipate the purchasers needs and concerns and disclose any facts at all. The law provides an exception to this doctrine when the seller owes a fiduciary duty to the buyer, when he has concealed something from the buyer and when he has reason to believe that the buyer is acting on false assumptions. When any of these circumstances exist, the seller has a duty to make a full disclosure of all material facts to the buyer. This would be the case whether or not the buyer took a test drive. Rollo probably should have taken a test drive in the car. The condition of the car may have been discovered if Rollo had taken reasonable steps to protect his own interests. However, Anderson had no duty to disclose important facts about the car because none of the special circumstances discussed above were present, and Rollo's failure to take the car for a test drive was largely irrelevant here. Likewise, selling something "as is" does not relieve a person of the duty to make a full disclosure if the special circumstances mentioned above exist.

6. Although she owned a home, June had lived with her daughter, Sandra, in a small apartment in the basement of Sandra's home. June was quite independent and handled her own business affairs. June decided to teach her other children "a lesson" because she was disappointed in them. After attempting to sell her home for some time without success, she decided to reduce the price and sell it to Sandra.

She died shortly after the sale to Sandra was completed. June's other children sued Sandra to have the contract rescinded so that June's home would become a part of the estate which they could inherit. They will probably:

a. be successful on the ground of duress.
b. be successful on the ground that there was a mutual mistake of fact regarding the value of the property.
c. be successful on the ground of caveat emptor.
d. be successful on the ground of undue influence.
e. be unsuccessful because June was not unduly influenced by Sandra.

DISCUSSION

(e)   June's children will probably not be successful in obtaining the rescission of the contract. There was no duress because Sandra had not threatened June with any illegal action. There are no facts to indicate that June and Sandra were both mistaken as to the value of the property. The rule of caveat emptor merely requires the buyer to exercise caution to protect her interests in a sales contract. There was no undue influence because June was not dependent upon Sandra, and there was no controlling relationship. Although she may have been influenced by her affection for Sandra, she was not deprived of her free will by her relationship with her daughter.

7.   Ben and Russ had a dispute over the precise nature of the performance Russ was required to render under the contract. Russ suggested a compromise that was not at all beneficial to Ben. He told Ben to accept the compromise, or he would contact his attorney and instruct him to seek declaratory relief in the courts. Ben agreed to the compromise because Russ' threatened action could ultimately cost Ben thousands of dollars in legal fees and losses due to delay. This agreement is probably:

a. invalid due to duress.
b. invalid due to unconscionability.
c. an illegal contract of adhesion.
d. valid because Russ' threats were not wrongful.
e. valid only if Russ' threats did not deprive Ben of his freedom of choice.

DISCUSSION

(d)   There was no duress in this case even though Russ threatened action in the courts. Russ had a right to bring a lawsuit to settle the dispute. Duress requires the threat of some type of illegal activity. To be unconscionable, a contract must take unfair advantage of one of the parties and be the result of grossly unequal bargaining power. The defense of unconscionability was codified by the Uniform Commercial Code and applies primarily to contracts for the sale of goods and might not apply to this situation in any event since no goods were being sold. A contract of adhesion is a contract formed between two parties when one of the parties has disproportionately less bargaining power than the other and is offered the contract on a take it or leave it basis. These contracts are enforceable unless the party with the disproportionately greater bargaining power takes unfair advantage of the other. When this occurs, the contract is said to be unconscionable and is not enforced by the courts. In this case, there are no facts to indicate that the parties had grossly disproportionate bargaining power or that Russ had unfairly taken advantage of Ben. The compromise is valid even if Ben felt he had no choice in light of Russ' threats to sue because Russ had the right to seek relief in the courts if a compromise could not be reached.

8. Ron couldn't pay his dental bill so the dentist threatened suit. Sally contacted the dentist and orally promised to pay Ron's bill if Ron failed to do so within the next six months. No documents were signed. The dentist agreed and promised not to sue Sally or Ron for six months. Ron never did pay so the dentist sued Sally. The dentist probably:

   a. lost because Sally's promise was not in writing.
   b. lost because there was no consideration for Sally's promise.
   c. won under the main purpose doctrine.
   d. won because Sally had intervened in the contractual relationship between Ron and the dentist.
   e. won because promises that can be performed within one year do not need to be in writing.

DISCUSSION

   (a) Sally entered into a third party beneficiary contract with Ron's dentist. Ron was the third party beneficiary of the consideration for Sally's promise to pay Ron's bill. The consideration was the dentist's forbearance in not suing Ron for six months. Unfortunately, contracts to pay the debt of another must be evidenced by a writing to be enforceable. Sally's promise was not made in a written contract or memorandum so she would not be liable.

   The main purpose doctrine is an exception to the rule that promises to pay the debt of another must be evidenced by a writing. Under this doctrine, promises to pay the debt of another do not need to be evidenced by a writing if the main purpose for making such a promise was to secure some benefit to the promisor. Since Sally would not be receiving any benefit from the dentist's giving Ron six months to pay his bill, the main purpose doctrine would not apply here. The main purpose doctrine was not discussed in this text because it is beyond the scope of the course. It was included as a wrong choice in this question to underscore the importance of exercising caution with unfamiliar legal terms.

Sally did not intervene in the contractual relationship between Ron and the dentist. She and the dentist formed their own separate and collateral contract in which the dentist's forbearance was the consideration for her promise to pay Ron's bill. This did not result in making Sally's promise merely a promise to pay her own debt that would not need to be in writing.

Although promises that can be performed within one year do not normally need to be evidenced by a writing, they may need to be in writing under other provisions of the Statute of Frauds. Promises to pay the debt of another, promises to buy or sell real property or promises given in consideration of marriage must all be evidenced by a written contract or memorandum of a verbal contract even if they can be performed within one year.

Chapter 9
Contract Discharges

A valid offer creates a power of acceptance in the offeree. Once the offeree has accepted the offer, it turns into a contract which is binding on the parties as of the instant the offer is accepted. In the absence of special circumstances, each party to a contract is bound to keep the promises made. This chapter deals with the "discharge" of the obligations produced by the contractual relationship. The discharge of an obligation is its termination. A discharged obligation no longer exists.

I. PERFORMANCE

Most contracts are discharged when both parties perform their promises as agreed.

Once a party has completely performed as promised in a contract, her promise is discharged and is no longer enforceable. The "performance" required to discharge a contract is accomplished by a party completely performing the contract as promised. A contractual promise or obligation is discharged when it ended under the law. Once a contractual obligation is discharged it cannot be revived and the contractual relationship of the parties is at an end. During the study of business law, it is easy to lose sight of the fact that most contracts are discharged by performance. Our economic system could not function if any more than a very few of the contracts formed in business were taken to the courts for enforcement

Donna entered into a valid contract in which she was required to do some accounting work for Bob's Shoe Store, and Bob, the owner, was required to pay her $3,500 for her work. Donna performed as agreed and was paid for her services. About one month later, Bob contacted her and asked her to assist him in accounting for some new transactions as part of the earlier job at no cost to him. If Donna refused, she would not be liable to Bob. Once she had completed the accounting work she promised, her contractual obligation to Bob was discharged by performance. She had no further liability on the contract. Similarly, she could not successfully sue Bob for a second payment of $3,500 because his obligation to pay her had been discharged by his performance.

Essential Vocabulary

1. performance
2. discharge

II. MUTUAL RESCISSION

A contract is discharged by an agreement of the parties to mutually rescind it.

Another way a contract can be discharged is by "mutual rescission." A rescission of a contract is a cancellation. A mutual rescission occurs when both parties agree to cancel a contract and release each other from their contractual obligations. A "unilateral rescission," or cancellation of the contract by only one of the parties, does not operate to discharge contractual obligations. In the absence of agreement, such an attempted cancellation would amount to a breach of contract. The consideration for one party's rescission of a contract is the other party's rescission.

Jack and Jill entered into a valid contract in which Jack promised to repair Jill's bicycle, and Jill promised to pay $80 to Jack. The contract could be discharged by mutual rescission if they both agreed to cancel the contract and release each other from liability on it. If, however, only Jack wanted to cancel the contract, he would be liable for breach of contract if he failed to perform. Rescission, to be effective in discharging a contract, must be mutual.

Essential Vocabulary

1. rescission
2. unilateral rescission
3. mutual rescission
4. consideration for mutual rescission

III. ACCORD AND SATISFACTION

A disputed contract is discharged by an accord and satisfaction.

When a contract is the subject of a genuine dispute as to what it requires, the parties may agree to settle their dispute with a compromise agreement. An agreement to settle a dispute is called an "accord." The settlement of the dispute is the consideration for the parties' promises in an accord. For this reason, there can be no accord and satisfaction in the absence of a "bona fide dispute." A bona fide dispute is a genuine, good faith dispute between the parties regarding what the contract requires. The mere fact that one party does not want to perform as agreed or made a mistake in making or accepting the offer does not constitute a dispute in the absence of a disagreement regarding what the contract requires.

The original contract is not discharged even if the parties have reached an accord until there is a "satisfaction." Satisfaction is the full performance of the accord as agreed. Once the accord has been performed, the disputed contract is discharged and cannot be revived even if it can later be proven that one of the parties was in error in the dispute.

Larry offered to install tile in Sam's bathroom for $800 payable by Sam in payments of $100 each month for eight months. Sam accepted the offer, and a valid contract was formed. Later, a dispute over how much Sam had paid developed. Sam claimed that he had paid $500, but Larry only had records of Sam's paying $300. Unfortunately, both Larry and Sam had lost some of their records. Larry and Sam decided to settle their dispute by Sam's paying $375 to Larry. Sam subsequently paid the $375 in satisfaction of the accord. The original contract was discharged by accord and satisfaction. If Larry later found his records and could prove that the correct balance owing at the time of the dispute was $500, he could not recover the $125 difference between what Sam had paid and what was owed. If, however, Sam had failed to satisfy the accord, Larry could have pursued his claim for $500 on the original contract since an "executory accord" would not discharge the original contract. An executory accord is an accord that has not been satisfied by performance.

Essential Vocabulary

1. accord and satisfaction
2. accord
3. satisfaction
4. executory accord
5. consideration for the accord
6. bona fide dispute

IV. IMPOSSIBILITY OF PERFORMANCE

A contract that becomes impossible to perform without the fault of either party is discharged subject to restitution.

When a contract becomes impossible to perform, it is discharged if neither party was at fault. A party is at fault if he negligently or intentionally renders the contract impossible to perform. If one of the parties is responsible for the conditions that made performance impossible, the contract is not discharged. Rather, the party at fault is liable for breach of contract. To be discharged, a contract must be impossible to perform and not merely difficult or unprofitable. The courts have consistently held that contracts requiring a party to purchase something are not discharged by impossibility of performance merely because the purchaser cannot obtain financing. For this reason, a purchaser should make contracts conditional upon obtaining financing at a specified rate of interest if money must be borrowed to pay for the purchase. Otherwise, the purchaser would be liable for breach of contract if she was unable to make payment due to her failure to qualify for a loan.

Carol and Georgia entered into a valid contract in which Georgia was obligated to shingle the roof on Carol's house and Carol was obligated to pay $3,000 for the labor and materials. The house burned down before Georgia could perform the contract. The contract was discharged by impossibility of performance. If, however, Carol had intentionally or negligently set fire to the house, the contract would not have been discharged; rather, Carol would have been liable for breach of contract. She would have been at fault for the impossibility of Georgia's performing as agreed. If someone stole Georgia's truck after she had entered into the contract but before she had performed, Georgia would still be required to perform even though neither Carol nor Georgia were at fault for the loss of the truck. The theft of the truck would not make Georgia's performance impossible because she could rent or purchase another one. This would be the case even if Georgia's renting of another vehicle would result in a financial loss to her because the action of the thief merely resulted in the contract being rendered unprofitable rather than impossible to perform.[1]

---

[1] See 287 (17-III) Causualty to Identified Goods and 288 (17-IV) Failure of Presupposed Conditions for the more lenient rules applied to contracts for the sale of goods that become unprofitable or "commercially impracticable" without the fault of either party.

Essential Vocabulary

   1. impossibility of performance

V. BREACH OF CONTRACT

   A party's duties under a contract are discharged by breach of contract.

   A "breach of contract" occurs when a party breaks his promise. Each party's duties under a contract are conditional upon the performance of the other party's duties. Therefore, if one party breaches the contract, the other party's obligations to perform are discharged, and he is left with the right to seek relief in the courts.

   If Henry and Norman enter into a contract in which Henry promises to convey a farm to Norman in consideration of Norman's payment of $60,000, Henry's duty to convey the property is conditional upon Norman's payment of the price. If Norman does not pay as agreed, Henry's duty to convey the property is discharged, and Norman will be liable to Henry for breach of contract.

Essential Vocabulary

   1. breach of contract

CHECK YOUR UNDERSTANDING

DIRECTIONS: Read each of the following questions. Choose the best answer and study the discussion of the question.

   1. Francis entered into a contract with Gina in which she was obligated to pay $120 to purchase curtains for her kitchen. Gina delivered the curtains and collected the $120 due. After Francis had paid the amount due, Gina misplaced the money on the way back to the shop. After failing to locate it, she demanded that Francis pay $120 again for the curtains. Francis refused so Gina sued her. Gina probably:

   a. lost because Francis' contract had been discharged by performance.
   b. lost because Francis had not guaranteed payment.
   c. won because Gina no longer had the payment for the curtains.
   d. won because Gina had not issued Francis a receipt.
   e. won if she sued in quasi contract because Francis had been unjustly enriched.

DISCUSSION

(a)   Francis had a contractual obligation to pay for the curtains. When she paid for them, her contractual obligation was discharged. Gina cannot revive the obligation merely because she lost the payment. Gina did not lose because Francis had not guaranteed payment. When Francis entered into the contract with Gina, she was bound to pay for the curtains so she did, in effect, personally guarantee payment. The obligation to pay for curtains was discharged when Francis gave the money to Gina. A receipt is only evidence of payment. A payment is effective to discharge the duty to pay even if a receipt is not issued. Francis had not been unjustly enriched because she had paid for the curtains she received.

2.   Harold, a jeweler, entered into a valid contract with Maud to repair her ring for $275. Harold got busy and asked Maud if he could cancel the contract. Maud agreed to the cancellation. Later, Harold changed his mind, but Maud refused to deliver the ring for repair. Harold sued Maud for breach of contract. Harold probably:

   a.   lost because there was an accord and satisfaction.
   b.   lost because there was a mutual rescission.
   c.   won because there was no consideration to modify the contract.
   d.   won because the contract was impossible to perform since Maud kept the ring and breached the contract.
   e.   won if the contract was in writing.

DISCUSSION

(b)   The valid contract between Harold and Maud was mutually rescinded by the agreement of the parties. The consideration for Harold's abandonment of the contract was Maud's abandonment. Once the contract had been discharged by mutual rescission, it could not be revived by Harold's changing his mind. There was no accord and satisfaction because there was no dispute for the parties to settle when the contract was in force. Impossibility of performance operates to discharge the parties' obligations under a contract only if the impossibility is not caused by the fault of either party. In this case, Maud would have been at fault for making the contract impossible to perform and would have been liable for breach if the contract had been in force at the time she refused to deliver the ring for service. This does not apply, however, because the contract had been mutually rescinded prior to her refusal to deliver the ring. This type of contract is not required to be evidenced by a writing. In any case, all contracts can be mutually rescinded whether or not they are in writing.

3. Alice and White entered into a valid contract in which White was to build Alice a swimming pool. During performance, Alice and White disagreed over construction methods. Eventually White agreed to use Alice's technique for an additional $500. Alice agreed to pay the additional fee to avoid the necessity of obtaining a court interpretation of the contract. However, when the pool was finished as agreed, Alice refused to pay the additional money. If White sued Alice, he would probably:

   a. lose because there was no consideration for Alice's promise to pay the additional fee.
   b. lose because modifications of service contracts are illegal.
   c. lose because Alice was forced to agree to avoid a law suit.
   d. win because $500 was a nominal amount in this case.
   e. win because the parties had entered into an accord and satisfaction.

DISCUSSION

(e) The original contract was discharged by accord and satisfaction. The parties had a dispute over what the contract required. They entered into an accord to settle the dispute. Satisfaction occurred when White performed the accord as promised. Alice will need to pay the additional $500 required by the accord. Modifications of service contracts are legal and enforceable if they are supported by consideration. No modification of the contract was involved in this case because the original contract was disputed by the parties. Rather than modify the contract, the parties entered into an accord and satisfaction that discharged it. No duress was involved in obtaining Alice's agreement to enter into the accord because White had the right to seek relief in the courts. Alice was not "forced" into entering into the accord in the sense that would render it unenforceable due to duress. The $500 Alice was required to pay under the accord was not "nominal." The word, nominal, means that it was consideration in name only and not real. If there had been no accord and satisfaction, White would not have been entitled to anything more than the original consideration for the job.

4. Gordon, a painter, entered into a contract with Hank to paint his garage for $250. Prior to painting as agreed, the garage burned to the ground. The cause of the fire was unknown. Gordon sued Hank for his expected profit on the job. Gordon probably:

   a. won because the fire prevented him from painting.
   b. won if Hank had the garage insured.

   c. lost because the contract was discharged by impossibility of performance.

   d. lost unless he was willing to paint the ashes.

   e. could require Hank to allow him to paint his next garage.

DISCUSSION

(c) The contract between Gordon and Hank was discharged by impossibility of performance. The contract was impossible to perform due to the fire which was not the result of any intentional or negligent act of either party. The presence or absence of insurance does not affect Gordon's rights because he would not be a party to the insurance contract. The law will not require the parties to enter into economically wasteful actions such as painting the ashes of the garage. Because the contract was discharged by impossibility of performance, it would not be binding upon Hank when he built another garage.

5. Pete and Quark entered into a valid, written contract in which Pete promised to build Quark a custom pool table for $10,000. Quark was required to pay $5,000 on June 1st and the remaining $5,000 on July 1st while Pete was required to deliver the pool table by August 1st. Quark made the first payment of $5,000 on June 1st as agreed, but he missed the second payment. Pete did not deliver the pool table on August 1st so Quark sued him for breach of contract. Quark probably:

   a. won because Pete had not delivered the pool table as agreed.

   b. won, but he will need to pay $5,000 for the pool table.

   c. lost because Pete was discharged from the contract by Quark's breach, but he may be able to recover some of his $5,000.

   d. lost unless he paid the remaining $5,000 prior to filing suit.

   e. lost unless he could prove that Pete had not started on the construction of the pool table.

DISCUSSION

(c) Pete's duty to perform on the contract was conditional upon Quark's making payments as agreed. When Quark missed his second payment, Pete's obligation to build the pool table was discharged. Pete would not be liable to Quark for breach of contract. Rather, Quark would be liable to Pete for breach. Pete would need to prove his damages, however. Pete would only be entitled to his profit in this case. If he could show that his profit on the contract would have been $3,000, Pete would need to return $2,000 of Quark's payment to him. If, on the other hand, Pete's expected profit had been $6,000, Quark would have needed to pay him an additional $1,000. Whether or not Pete had begun construction of the pool table would have been irrelevant because the contract merely required Pete to deliver a finished pool table on or before August 1st. How and when Pete constructed the pool table was left up to him.

Chapter 10
Assignment and Delegation

Contracts create enforceable rights and duties the instant they come into existence. Each party to a contract owns valuable rights and owes the burden of performing the specified duties the instant the offer is accepted. However, this state of affairs is subject to change by the parties. This chapter deals with the rules governing the transfer of these rights and duties to others who are not parties to the original contract. The rights acquired from the contractual relationship can be sold or given away to others, and the duties imposed by the contract can be delegated to others for performance.

If Li offers to paint Holly's house four months from today for $500 and Holly agrees, a contract is formed the instant Holly accepts Li's offer even though the painting and payment are to take place in the future. At the instant the contract is formed, each party owns a valuable property right. Li owns Holly's enforceable promise to pay him $500 when he paints her house, and Holly owns Li's obligation to paint her house. These rights are transferable by assignment. Rights are accompanied by corresponding duties. Li has the duty to paint, and Holly has the duty to pay. These duties can be delegated to other parties.

Li might need money now. Rather than wait until he can paint Holly's house, he could sell the contract right to be paid by Holly to Big City Finance. The finance company might be willing to pay $400 for the right to collect $500 in four months. This would provide a very good return on the company's money, and Li could have the money he needs right now. If Holly decided to install aluminum siding on her house, it may be a waste of her money to have it painted. However, if she simply refuses to allow Li to paint as agreed, she would be in breach of the contract and be liable to Li for whatever profit he would have made on the job. One solution to her problem would be to assign the right to have the painting done to an acquaintance who needed the painting. The acquaintance could pay Li for painting her house, and Holly would not need to waste her money painting a house that she intended to cover with siding. This section deals with the basic rules under which contract rights and duties are assigned and delegated.

I. ASSIGNMENT

Contract rights can be assigned if the corresponding duties are not materially altered, but the assignee is subject to the same discharges, defenses, and set-offs as the assignor.

One may "assign" a contract right without the consent of the other party if the corresponding duties imposed upon that party are not "materially altered." A party assigns a contract right when she gives, sells or trades it to another person who was not a party to the original contract. A duty is materially altered when it is changed in an important way. An "assignment" is an agreement to transfer contract rights. Assignments may transfer only the rights or both the rights and obligations arising under contracts.

In the introductory example, Holly could assign her right to have the house painted provided that Li's duties would not be materially altered. While she could assign the right to another homeowner who owned a similar house in the same area, she could not assign the contract to a person who owned a larger house or a house that was more difficult to paint or who lived substantially farther away from Li because the assignment must not materially alter Li's duty or burden.

The parties to an assignment are referred to as the "assignor" and the "assignee." The person assigning a contract right is called the assignor, and the person receiving the right is called the assignee. The assignee is not better able to enforce the contract than the assignor. If the assignor would not be able to enforce the contract due to the existence of some discharge, defense or "set-off," the assignee cannot enforce the contract either. In short, the assignee will be treated as though he were the assignor when he sues to enforce the contract. A set-off is a claim against the assignor that can be deducted from the amount owed on the contract.

If Li assigned his right to receive payment to Big City Finance, the finance company would be vulnerable to all the discharges, defenses, and set-offs to which Li himself would be vulnerable. If Li had failed to paint Holly's house as agreed, Big City Finance could not collect anything from Holly because her obligation to pay Li was discharged by his breach of contract. If Li had forced Holly to accept his offer to paint by threatening her with illegal harm, Holly could use the defense of duress to avoid the contract with Li even after it was signed. She could also assert the defense of duress against Big City Finance as well and would not be liable on the assigned contract. In addition, Holly could set-off any debt that Li owed her against the amount she was obligated to pay Big City Finance by virtue of the assignment. If Li had painted the house as agreed but put his ladder through Holly's picture window causing damage in the amount of $100, Holly could set that amount off against the $500 she had promised to pay for the painting services. She would need to pay Big City Finance only $400.

Essential Vocabulary

1. assign
2. materially altered
3. assignment
4. assignor
5. assignee
6. set-off

II. NOTICE OF ASSIGNMENT

Notice of assignment directs performance to the assignee and stops set-offs from accruing.

An assignment of a contract right is valid and binding upon the assignor and assignee even if no "notice of assignment" is given to the other party to the original contract. A notice of assignment is simply a verbal or written notification that performance should be directed to the assignee rather than the assignor. While notice of assignment is not required to make an assignment valid, it is highly desirable. Usually, a notice of assignment is merely a letter from one of the parties to a contract informing the other that the contract has been assigned and that the required payments or other performances required by the contract should be made to someone new. The new person entitled to receipt of the performance is the assignee.

Fresh Furniture Co. makes its money by selling furniture. Many of its customers do not pay the full price of the furniture at the time of purchase; rather, they sign contracts to pay for the furniture over time in installments. Eventually, Fresh Furniture Co. has no inventory remaining to sell so it assigns its accounts receivable, the installment contracts, to Quick Investment Co. If Tom's contract is one of the contracts assigned, neither of the companies needs to give Tom notice for the assignment to be valid and enforceable between them. However, if no one lets Tom know about the assignment, he will send his monthly payments to Fresh Furniture Co. as usual. He will be given credit for his payment as though he made it to Quick Investment Co. because he was not given notice of the assignment. Fresh Furniture Co. will be liable to Quick Investment Co. for the payments it receives after the assignment because the assignment is valid. After Tom has been given notice of the assignment, i.e. after he finds out about it, he will need to make his payments to Quick Investment Co. A notice of assignment directs the performance required by the contract to the proper party. If Tom forgets about the assignment and mails his payment to Fresh Furniture Co. after he has received notice of the assignment, he will be liable to Quick Investment Co. for the payment and will need to recover his payment from Fresh Furniture Co.

While notice of assignment will not protect an assignee from discharges and defenses to which the assignor would be subject, it will stop set-offs from accruing after the notice has been given. A party to a contract can deduct set-offs from the amount owed to the other party only if the debt arose prior to the receipt of a notice of assignment. Debts arising after the notice of assignment has been received must be collected directly from the original party and cannot be deducted from the amount owed on the contract.

Allan entered into a contract with Carla to build a dog house with an indoor swimming pool for $2,000 and assigned his fee to Hank. Hank can insure that Carla will pay him rather than Allan and protect his right to collect the $2,000 fee by giving notice to Carla of the assignment. The notice would let Carla know who to pay for the work. In addition, she would not be able to set claims against Allan off against her obligation to pay the $2,000 fee to Hank. Suppose that, after Carla had been notified of the assignment, Allan had borrowed $500 from her and failed to pay her back as agreed. Carla would still have been obligated to pay Hank the full $2,000 because the notice of assignment would stop this potential set-off from accruing. If Hank had not given her notice of the assignment, Carla could have deducted the $500 Allan had borrowed from the $2,000 she owed to him.

Essential Vocabulary

1. notice of assignment

III. DELEGATION

Contract duties can be delegated if they do not require special judgment or expertise, but both the delegator and delegatee are liable for performance in the absence of a novation.

A party to a contract delegates a duty when he gives an obligation he has under the contract to someone else to perform. A "personal duty" is a duty that cannot be delegated because its performance requires the special judgement of the person owing the duty. The courts have had difficulty in deciding what duties require so much judgement that allowing delegation of them would materially alter the corresponding benefits expected under the contract. In general, the courts have fairly consistently held that duties performed by tradesmen can be delegated because competent tradesmen can do equivalent work. However, they have held that duties to be performed by professionals cannot be delegated because it is the element of judgement that sets professions apart from trades. Hence, an automobile mechanic could delegate an engine repair to another qualified mechanic even over the objection of the other contracting party because trade services are being delegated. However, a doctor could not delegate the duty to perform surgery to another surgeon over the objection of the patient even if the surgeon was more qualified than the original doctor. Medicine is a profession, and the duties arising under contracts to perform medical services are personal duties that cannot be delegated.

In allowing the delegation of duties that are not personal, the courts impose liability for breach of contract on both the delegator and the delegatee. Making both liable for breach of contract protects the original party from delegations of duties that result in breach of contract and provides delegators with an incentive to make sure that delegatees are competent and financially responsible. From a purely legal standpoint, the original party entitled to receive the delegated performance is better off due to the delegation of duties imposed by the contract because he is able to sue two parties rather than one in the event of breach. This increases his chances of collecting a judgement in the event of a breach of the contract.

Ron and Chu entered into a valid contract in which Ron was required to repair Chu's truck, and Chu was required to pay $390 for this service. Ron could delegate the duty to repair the truck to a different shop even if Chu objected. Because truck repair is a trade, Ron's duty to repair would not be a personal duty. If Chu refused to allow the shop to which Ron delegated his duty to work on the truck, Chu would be liable for breach of contract. However, if Chu allowed the work to proceed and the new shop breached the contract by not performing as agreed, both Ron and the new shop would be liable to Chu for breach of contract.

As a general rule, making both the delegator and the delegatee liable for the performance of the delegated duty protects the interests of both parties. Sometimes however, it is necessary for a delegator to have a new party substituted for her on the contract and to be released from further liability. This can be accomplished by the original parties entering into a "novation." A novation is an agreement between the original parties to a contract to substitute a new party for one of the original parties and to release that party from further liability.

Pat borrowed money from a bank to purchase a home. The bank secured the loan with a mortgage that provided that the bank could take possession of the property and resell it if Pat defaulted on her payments. Subsequently, Pat decided that she wanted to sell the property to Julie. Julie wanted to buy out Pat and assume her mortgage. This would be an assignment of the mortgage contract in which Pat delegated her duty to make payments to Julie. If the assignment was made without a novation, Pat would be liable along with Julie if for any default in making payments to the bank. If the bank and Pat had entered into a novation in which Julie was substituted for Pat on the mortgage contract and Pat was released from further liability, Pat would not have been responsible if Julie was to default. A bank's consent to an assumption of a mortgage does not release the original obligor from liability on the loan in the absence of a novation.

Essential Vocabulary

1. delegation
2. personal duty
3. novation

IV. THIRD PARTY BENEFICIARY RIGHTS

A third party beneficiary can enforce the contract but is not liable for breach.

Many times a person will enter into a contract for the benefit of a "third party beneficiary." A third party beneficiary is a person who is not a party to the contract but, nevertheless, is entitled to receive some benefit from it. Such a beneficiary of a contract is called a "third party" because the first and second parties to the contract are offeror and offeree. People who are not parties to the contract at all but receive some benefit from them are called "third party beneficiaries" regardless of how many parties there are to the original contract. The question that often arises when a third party beneficiary is involved is which parties can enforce the contract and which parties are liable in the event of breach. While both the original parties and third party beneficiaries can enforce the contract, only the original parties are liable.

Gordon and Sarah, a caterer, entered into a contract in which Gordon agreed to pay Sarah $5,000 for planning and catering Bob's wedding. If Sarah performed as agreed, she could sue Gordon if she was not paid because he was a party to the contract. She could not successfully sue Bob, however, because he had never promised to pay for her services. Bob was merely a third party beneficiary of the contract between Gordon and Sarah. Both Gordon and Bob could successfully sue Sarah if she failed to cater the wedding as agreed. Gordon could sue because he was the original party to the contract, and Bob could sue because he was the intended recipient of the services. While both of them could sue Sarah, they could only collect damages once and would need to share the award according to their respective losses.

Essential Vocabulary

1. third party beneficiary

CHECK YOUR UNDERSTANDING

DIRECTIONS: Read each of the following questions. Choose the best answer and study the discussion of the question.

1. Frosty and Sunny entered into a valid contract whereby Frosty was obligated to shovel snow from the walks of Sunny's residence located in Nebraska. Sunny later assigned the benefit of the contract to Bill as a birthday present. Bill lived in a similar house located in Alaska. If Frosty objected, the assignment would probably be:

    a. invalid because it would materially increase Frosty's burden.
    b. Invalid because a written notice of assignment was not given.
    c. invalid because snow removal is a personal service.
    d. invalid because the contract did not prohibit assignment.
    e. invalid because Sunny did not delegate his duties as well.

DISCUSSION

    (a)   Benefits arising under a contract can be assigned without the permission of the parties obligated to provide them as long as their burdens in providing the benefits are not materially altered. The original contract required Frosty to shovel snow at a residence in a town in Nebraska. The assignee lived in Alaska. The increased distance to Bill's home and the increased amount of snow to be expected would materially increase the burden on Frosty so the assignment cannot be made without his agreement. Assignments are valid whether or not a notice of the assignment is given. When they are given, notices of assignment may be written or verbal. Snow removal is a trade rather than a profession so the duty to remove the snow could be delegated. However, the duty was not being delegated by Frosty in this case. A contract can prohibit assignment or be conditional upon no benefit being assigned. Benefits arising from contracts that prohibit assignment can be assigned anyway but the assignor will be liable for any damages resulting from the assignment. Benefits arising from contracts cannot be assigned if the parties agreed that the contract would be conditional upon there being no assignment. Where the contract is expressly conditional upon there being no assignment, an attempted assignment of the contract results in the contract being terminated and the parties being required to make restitution to each other.

2. Gaylord and Jentz entered into a valid written contract in which Gaylord promised to pay Jentz $3,000 for a sculpture he owned. Jentz delivered the sculpture to Gaylord, but he assigned the right to collect the $3,000 to his favorite charity. Neither the charity nor Jentz gave Gaylord notice of the assignment so Gaylord paid Jentz the money he owed. The charity sued Gaylord. The charity probably recovered nothing because:

   a. the assignment violated the Statute of Frauds.
   b. the assignment involved a personal duty.
   c. Gaylord was not given notice of the assignment.
   d. Gaylord did not consent to the assignment.
   e. charities cannot sue to enforce assignments of contract rights.

DISCUSSION

(c) The charity could not successfully sue Gaylord because Gaylord had not received notice of the assignment. His payment to Jentz discharged his obligation to pay on the contract because assignees are subject to the same discharges as the assignor. The charity could successfully sue Jentz to recover the $3,000 he received from Gaylord because the assignment was valid and binding on him even in the absence of notice to Gaylord. The assignment did not violate the Statute of Frauds since it was not a promise to pay the debt of another, a promise that could not be performed within one year, a promise to sell real property or a promise made in consideration of marriage. Jentz merely gave his right to receive the payment from Jentz to the charity. The duty to pay money does not require special judgement or discretion and is not, therefore, a personal duty. The assignment to the charity of the right to receive Gaylord's payment did not require Gaylord's consent to be binding on Jentz and the Charity. Charities are corporations that can sue to enforce contract rights in the same manner as any other corporation.

3. Remington borrowed money from Big Bank to buy a home. He later sold the home to Winchester and all parties agreed to the assumption of Remington's mortgage by Winchester. Winchester bought Remington out and began making payments to Big Bank. When he was laid off, Winchester defaulted on his payments to Big Bank. Which of the following is true?

   a. Remington is no longer a party to the Big Bank loan because Winchester assumed it.
   b. Winchester is not liable to Remington because he completely paid for Remington's equity.

c. Winchester is liable to both Big Bank and Remington, and Remington is liable to Big Bank.

d. Both Winchester and Remington are liable to Big Bank, but Winchester is not liable to Remington.

e. Only Remington is liable to Big Bank, and Winchester is liable to Remington.

DISCUSSION

(c) Remington assigned his contract with Big Bank to Winchester. Winchester was the assignee of Remington's contract with Big Bank. Along with the benefits of the contract, Remington delegated the duty to pay Big Bank to Winchester. In the absence of a novation entered into between Big Bank and Remington, Remington would continue to be liable on the contract after the assignment. If Winchester failed to pay Big Bank as agreed, Remington would be liable to the bank. Since the assignment of the contract required Winchester to pay the bank, Winchester would be liable to Remington for any damages arising because of his breach of contract. Under these circumstances, both Remington and Winchester would be liable to the bank, and Winchester would be liable to Remington for whatever the bank collected from him. The fact that Winchester completely paid for Remington's equity would not excuse him from liability arising out of Remington's being forced to pay the bank for damages caused by Winchester's failure to make payments as promised.

4. Rebecca took her adult daughter Sally to a dentist. Rebecca and the dentist entered into an oral contract whereby Rebecca promised to pay $325, and the dentist promised to cap one of Sally's teeth. Rebecca felt the dentist did a poor job so she refused to pay. The dentist disagreed and demanded payment. Which of the following best describes potential liabilities in this case?

a. Rebecca and Sally may be liable to the dentist, and the dentist may be liable to Rebecca and Sally.

b. Rebecca and Sally may be liable to the dentist, but the dentist could be liable only to Rebecca.

c. Rebecca and Sally may be liable to the dentist, but the dentist could be liable only to Sally.

d. Only Sally could be liable to the dentist, but the dentist may be liable to both Rebecca and Sally.

e. Only Rebecca could be liable to the dentist, but the dentist could be liable to both Rebecca and Sally.

DISCUSSION

(e)   Rebecca entered into a third party beneficiary contract with the dentist. Sally, her daughter, was the third party beneficiary. Rebecca would be liable to the dentist for any failure to pay the bill because she was a party to the contract. Sally, however, was not a party to the contract. She did not promise to pay anything to the dentist so she would not be liable. She would not be liable in quasi contract for the services she received if Rebecca did not pay the bill because quasi contract is available only in the absence of a contract. The dentist would be liable to both Rebecca and Sally if the services were poor or not given. Rebecca could sue for breach because she was a party to the contract. Sally could sue because she was the intended third party beneficiary of the contract. If the dentist was liable to both Rebecca and Sally, he would need to pay damages only once. Rebecca and Sally would need to divide the damages awarded between them.

Chapter 11
Remedies

A contract is a set of promises the courts will enforce. When contractual relations break down, the aggrieved party may seek relief. The various types of relief are used to provide the benefit of the bargain or at least return the parties to their original condition when this is not possible. These remedies are often not mutually exclusive and can be used in combination to achieve a just result. A party to a breached contract may decide to try to work out a compromise rather than seek relief through the courts. This often saves all of the parties money and time. However, when all else fails, the remedies listed below are important tools used by the courts to fashion appropriate relief for parties to contracts that are breached as well as contracts that should not be performed due to some impropriety.

I. RESCISSION AND RESTITUTION

When a contract is rescinded, adult parties must make full restitution while minors need to return only what they have left.

When a contract cannot be enforced due to circumstances that allow a party to raise a defense, the courts usually order the remedy of "rescission and restitution." The rescission of a contract is its cancellation. If the contract is "wholly executory" when it is rescinded, the parties simply end the contractual relationship and go their separate ways or sue for damages in tort. A wholly executory contract is a contract that has not yet been performed at all. When the contract has been "partially" or "fully executed", the parties must be restored to their original condition. A partially executed contract is a contract that has been partially performed, and a fully executed contract is a contract that has been completely performed by the parties. This is accomplished by the court's ordering "restitution." Restitution is each party's giving back whatever was received pursuant to the contract. Generally, adults are required to give back everything they received pursuant to the contract while minors are required only to return whatever they have left when the contract is rescinded.

Amy offered to sell a horse to Carla for $300. Carla asked her whether or not the horse was well trained and gentle for riding. Amy told her that the horse had been well trained and would be excellent for riding although she knew that the horse had not been trained at all. Amy was also aware that several expert riders had been injured attempting to ride the horse. Carla relied on Amy's representations regarding the horse and accepted the offer. If Carla had learned of Amy's deception prior to taking the horse or paying for it, she could rescind the contract. No restitution would be required since neither party had received anything under the contract. Carla could assert the defense of intentional misrepresentation of a material fact if Amy sued her on the contract. Amy would be entitled to nothing because she induced Carla to enter into the contract by intentionally misrepresenting the training and temperament of the horse.

Sometimes the situation is made more complicated by the partial execution or performance of the contract that is rescinded. Where this has occurred, the parties must make restitution. By ordering restitution, the courts require each party regardless of fault to restore to the other party whatever they received under the contract. In our example above, restitution would have been required if Carla had paid $100 down and taken possession of the horse and been injured by it. Carla could still have rescinded the contract for Amy's misrepresentation, but both Amy and Carla would have needed to make restitution. Carla would have been required to return the horse, and Amy would have been required to return Carla's $100 payment. Assuming that Carla was an adult, she would have had to pay Amy the remainder of the purchase price for the horse if she was unable to return it due to theft or other loss. If Carla had been injured by the horse and wanted damages for her injuries, she would have needed to sue Amy in tort for negligence or intentional misrepresentation.

In summary, adults must make "full restitution," while minors are only required to make "partial restitution" by restoring that portion of the consideration that remains in their possession when they avoid a contract. Full restitution is made by returning everything one has received pursuant to a contract while partial restitution is made by returning only that which the minor has left. In the example discussed above, Carla would have been able to get her money back even if she no longer had the horse if she had been a minor because a minor's duty to make restitution is limited to returning whatever remains in her possession when the contract is rescinded.

Essential Vocabulary

1. rescission
2. restitution
3. wholly executory contract
4. partially executed contract
5. fully executed contract
6. full restitution
7. partial restitution

II. ANTICIPATORY REPUDIATION

A party to a contract which has been breached prior to the time for performance may sue for breach immediately.

A special type of breach of contract is called an "anticipatory repudiation." An anticipatory repudiation of a contract is a breach of contract prior to the time for performance. When a contract requires a performance in the future, a party can sue for anticipatory repudiation of the contract anytime the other party breaks his promise even if the time for performance has not yet arrived. The repudiation can be express or implied. A party expressly repudiates the contract when he informs the other party that he will not be performing as promised prior to the time performance is due. A contract can be repudiated by implication if a party makes it impossible to perform prior to the time for performance. In both of these instances, the aggrieved party can seek relief for breach of contract immediately without waiting for the time of performance to arrive.

Bill and Sandy entered into a contract in which Bill promised to install Sandy's sprinkler system six months from the date of contracting. Bill called her about a month later and told her that he had changed his mind and would not perform as promised. This act of breaking a contractual promise five months before the performance was due constituted an anticipatory repudiation of the contract. Sandy could sue for breach of contract immediately and would not need to wait until the date of performance.

Essential Vocabulary

1. anticipatory repudiation

III. LIQUIDATED DAMAGES

A party to a contract breached by another is entitled to reasonable liquidated damages.

It is often difficult to prove damages for breach of contract. To alleviate this problem, the parties to a contract may agree to what the damages will be in the event of breach of contract. Damages that have been fixed by the parties in advance of a breach of contract are called "liquidated damages." Clauses in contracts that specify the amount of damages to be awarded for breach are called "liquidated damage clauses." The courts will enforce these agreements only if they are reasonable. If they are unreasonable or punitive, the parties will be required to prove their damages as though the clause was not part of the contract.

Gerald entered into a written contract to purchase a field from Helen for $50,000. The contract contained a written clause requiring Gerald to pay Helen $1,000 if for any reason he breached his contract to purchase the field. This liquidated damage clause would probably be reasonable because the price of the land was $50,000. If, however, the contract had required Gerald to pay Helen $20,000 in the event of a breach, the provision would probably have been unenforceable as a penalty because damages are very unlikely to approach 40% of the value of the property. In this case, the court would have ignored the liquidated damage clause and required Helen to prove her actual damages.

Essential Vocabulary

1. liquidated damages
2. liquidated damage clause

IV. FULL PERFORMANCE

A party who has completely performed the contract is entitled to the consideration promised.

When a party has fully performed her obligations under a contract, she is entitled to receive the consideration for her promises. The consideration for her promises would be whatever performance she was promised by the other party. We shall refer to this performance as the "price" for convenience whether or not the performance is a payment of money.

Peggy and Tom entered into a contract which required Peggy to sell Tom a vase for $150. Peggy delivered the vase to Tom, and he took possession of it. If Tom changed his mind and took the vase back to Peggy before he paid, she could refuse to accept the return of the vase and insist on the price. If Tom failed to pay as agreed, Peggy could successfully sue for breach of contract and collect the entire $150 promised. Peggy would be entitled to the price because she had completely performed at the time of Tom's breach of contract.

Essential Vocabulary

1. price

V. SUBSTANTIAL PERFORMANCE

A party who has substantially performed the contract is entitled to the consideration less damages.

A party who has "substantially performed" the contract but nevertheless breaches it is entitled to the price reduced by the damages caused by the breach. Substantial performance is the completion of a contract in all important respects. A good rule of thumb is that a contract has been substantially performed if it ninety percent or more of the required duties have been properly performed. Although substantial performance is something less than full performance it is still enough to entitle the party in breach of the contract to obtain something for coming close to performing as promised.

Dan and Fred entered into a valid contract requiring Dan to assemble a boat for Fred and paint it green. The contract required Fred to deliver a certain gold watch to Dan in payment. Dan built the boat but inadvertently painted it blue. Painting the boat was less than a tenth of the work required of Dan under the contract. Fred refused to deliver the watch to Dan because the boat had been painted the wrong color. Because he had substantially performed the contract, Dan would be entitled to the gold watch, but he would be required to pay for a new paint job first. If Fred would not deliver the watch, Dan would be entitled to the reasonable value of the watch less the cost of painting the boat green. In short, Dan would be entitled to the price less damages.

Essential Vocabulary

1. substantial performance

VI. BREACH

A party who has breached a contract is not entitled to anything under the contract but is liable for damages.

A party's duty to perform as promised on a contract is conditional upon the performance of the other party. Since a contract is a promise, a "breach of contract" is a broken promise. Breach of contract occurs when a party fails to keep the promises he made in a contract. If a party breaches a contract, he is not entitled to anything under the contract and cannot obtain partial payment in quasi contract.

Quinn and Robert entered into a contract in which Robert promised to remodel Quinn's kitchen and Quinn promised to pay $10,000 to Robert. Quinn completed half of the work valued at approximately $5,100 and quit. Since Robert's duty to pay Quinn is conditional upon Quinn's performing as promised, Robert is under no duty to pay Quinn for the work completed. Quinn will not be able to obtain compensation for the work completed in quasi contract either because a contract had been entered into by the parties. Robert may keep the work Quinn has performed without payment because Quinn breached the contract.

Diane and Gertrude entered into a valid contract requiring Diane to lay carpet in Gertrude's home. Gertrude was required to pay $700 for this service. If Diane did not lay the carpet, Gertrude would not be required to pay because her duty to pay under the contract is conditional upon Diane's carpet laying. In fact, if Diane had laid 60% of the carpet, Gertrude would still not be required to pay.

If Diane stopped short of substantially performing the contract, she could not recover anything under the contract. In addition, she would not be entitled to anything in quasi contract either since there had been a contract. Quasi contract is an equitable remedy available only in the absence of a contract. Diane would not be excused from performance even if she became too ill to perform or died because the contract duties to lay carpet could be delegated. Carpet laying is a trade that can be performed by any competent tradesman.

Essential Vocabulary

1.   breach of contract

VII. COMPENSATORY DAMAGES

A party who has breached a contract is liable for compensatory damages sufficient to provide the injured party with the benefit of the bargain.

If one party does not keep her promises, the other is not required to keep her promises either. However, the party that breached the contract is liable for damages caused by the breach. The damages awarded for breach of contract are "compensatory damages" designed to compensate for or make up for the losses suffered by the injured party. The courts will award enough compensatory damages to provide the aggrieved party with the "benefit of the bargain" and no more. The benefit of the bargain is the value of whatever she would have gained had the contract been performed. This is the profit or economic advantage the contract would have produced.

It is important to remember that the aggrieved party must prove her damages with particularity. If a party to a contract fails to prove the extent of her damages, the court may award only "nominal damages." Nominal damages are generally limited to $1 and whatever satisfaction one receives from "winning" the lawsuit. The courts normally do not award "punitive" or "exemplary damages" in actions for breach of contract. Punitive damages and exemplary damages are damages awarded to punish offenders and make examples of them to discourage similar misconduct in the future.

Harold and Cindy entered into a valid contract in which Harold was required to sell Cindy a car, and she was required to pay $300 for it. Harold breached the contract by refusing to deliver the car. If Cindy would need to pay $380 to purchase another car like the one Harold had promised, Harold would be liable for $80. This amount would be the benefit of the bargain because Cindy could add the $80 in damages from Harold to the $300 she was planning to spend and obtain a car just like the one she had been promised. Cindy would not be required to actually purchase another car. She would have the option of purchasing another car or just keeping the $80 in damages. However, Cindy would be awarded only nominal damages of $1 if she failed to prove the value of the car Harold had promised her. In any case, Cindy would have been entitled to the return of any payment she had made to Harold, and Harold would not have been entitled to anything since he breached the contract.

If, after Harold's breach, Cindy had found another car like the one Harold promised for $300 or less, she would not have been entitled to any damages other than the return of any payment she may have made to Harold. In this situation, she would have been able to purchase another car like the one promised without Harold's paying damages. The courts do not generally award punitive damages for breach of contract even when the breach is willful. If Cindy had found several cars like the one Harold had promised offered at different prices, her damages would have been based on the car that was the least expensive because the victims of a breach of contract have a duty to "mitigate" their damages. A party mitigates damages by keeping them to a minimum. A breaching party is not liable for any damages that the other party could have reasonably avoided.

If, in our example, Cindy had breached the contract rather than Harold by not accepting the car, Cindy would have been liable for the benefit of the bargain to Harold. If Harold could resell the car to another person for only $225, Cindy would be liable for $75. This is the benefit of Harold's bargain because the $225 he could realize from selling the car to another plus the $75 in damages he could collect from Cindy would total the $300 he was promised. Harold would not need to actually sell the car; rather, he would have the option of reselling the car or just keeping the damages. If Cindy had made a $100 payment to Harold, she would be entitled to the return of the $25 difference between her payment and the damages she owed Harold for breach. If Harold could resell the car to someone else for $300 or more, Cindy would not be liable to Harold for any damages at all, and she would be entitled to the return of any payments she had made. If Cindy had taken possession of the car and then failed to make payments as agreed, Harold's damages would be the payments due when he sued. Many contracts have "acceleration clauses" which are contractual provisions that allow a party to declare the entire unpaid balance due on breach. In such contracts the breaching party is liable for all future payments as well as all past due payments.

When a person contracts with a merchant, the merchant is entitled to her "profit" as the benefit of the bargain. Profit is typically figured by subtracting the price paid by the merchant from the price at which the item was sold to the customer. This is necessary because merchants typically sell their products at or near the market price due to competition. Theoretically, a purchaser could purchase a similar item for about the same price anywhere. This makes finding a difference between the sales price and the market price useless in computing damages for a merchant. A merchant earns her living by selling things. She has earned her profit when the customer enters into the sales contract.

Lisa entered into a valid contract to purchase a plane from All Makes Plane Company, a merchant, for $175,000. If Lisa took possession of the plane and then refused to pay for it, she would be liable to All Makes for the price of the plane because All Makes would have fully performed the contract by delivering the plane as promised. However, if Lisa had refused to take possession of the plane, she would have been liable to All Makes for the profit the company would have made on the sale. If All Makes had paid $100,000 for this plane when it purchased it from the wholesaler, Lisa would have been liable for the $75,000 profit All Makes would have realized from the sale.

Contracts for the sale of services are handled similarly. Where Alice and Bud entered into a valid contract in which Alice was required to pay Bud $200 for grooming her pet orangutan, Bud would be entitled to his profit if Alice breached the contract. If Bud's fee was entirely his labor, he would have been entitled to the entire $200 if he was unable to find another job to mitigate his damages. Bud would have been required to try to find another job when Alice breached her contract to keep his damages at the lowest level possible. An aggrieved party mitigates his damages when he takes reasonable steps to minimize them. If Bud had found another job grooming a chimpanzee for only $125, Alice would have been liable for only the $75 difference. In this case, Bud's damages would have been limited to $75 even if he had refused to take the other job because Alice would be liable only for the damages he could not avoid.

Essential Vocabulary

1. compensatory damages
2. benefit of the bargain
3. nominal damages
4. punitive damages or exemplary damages
5. duty to mitigate damages
6. acceleration clauses
7. profit

VIII. CONSEQUENTIAL DAMAGES

Consequential damages may be awarded when both parties are aware of the special consequences of a breach prior to entering into the contract.

Most of the time, damages result directly from a breach of contract and are foreseeable by the parties. Sometimes, however, problems caused indirectly by a breach of contract result in damages that would be unforeseeable by a party that had not been forewarned. Damages caused indirectly are called "consequential damages." Consequential damages usually result when a party's breach forces the innocent party to breach a contract with someone else.

Phyllis offered to pay Bill $5000 to appear in her movie as an "extra," and Bill accepted. The contract required Bill to walk down a street wearing a hat that needed to be specially made and purchased by Bill. Bill ordered the hat for $35 from a hat maker and told him that he needed it by 2:00 p.m. on the following Monday. This was about one hour before the scene was to be filmed. The hat maker forgot about Bill's order, and the hat was not ready when Bill went to get it. When Bill appeared for the filming of the scene, he was fired because he did not have the required hat. If Bill could get another hat maker to make a similar hat for $50, Bill's damages would be $15 – the difference between the cost of the hat as promised and the amount he had to pay to replace it. Unfortunately, this measure of damages does not come close to Bill's loss. The hat maker would not be liable for $5000 in consequential damages resulting indirectly from the breach because he was not aware of the special consequences of breach prior to entering into the contract. Had he been aware, he could have taken special precautions, purchased insurance, and adjusted the price of the hat accordingly. Consequential damages are awarded only when both parties are aware of the special consequences of breach prior to entering into the contract. If Bill had discussed his special circumstances with the hat maker prior to entering into the contract, the hat maker could have been liable for $5015 in compensatory damages for breach of the contract — $15 damages for the benefit of the bargain and $5000 for consequential damages. The damages arising out of the loss of the movie would have been available only if Bill was unable to mitigate his damages by getting another hat in time.

Essential Vocabulary

1. consequential damages

IX. SPECIFIC PERFORMANCE

A party to a contract for the sale of property is entitled to specific performance if the property is unique.

Money damages are usually adequate to provide the benefit of the bargain in an action for breach of contract. With the damage award, the aggrieved party can purchase whatever the contract promised from another source. However, if the contract is for the purchase of a "unique" item, the aggrieved party cannot purchase a similar item for any amount of money and damages will not provide the benefit of the bargain. Property is unique when it is the only one of its kind or the only one for sale. Land and art works are usually held to be unique no matter how similar other tracts of land or art objects are to the subject of the contract. In other cases, the circumstances determine whether or not property is unique.

When the contract is for the sale of unique property, a party to a contract breached by another can elect specific performance as a remedy. Specific performance requires the breaching party to specifically perform the contract for sale and deliver the property as agreed when the purchaser has paid as promised. Specific performance cannot be used as a remedy to obtain unique services from a breaching party because of the constitutional prohibitions against slavery. This remedy is also not available if the property has been sold to another party who was unaware of the prior contract. In these cases, the aggrieved parties must settle for monetary damages.

Tony and Harold entered into a contract in which Tony was required to sell, and Harold was required to buy, a pen. If Tony refused to deliver the pen as agreed, Harold would need to sue for damages because pens are not ordinarily unique. If the pen had once been owned and used by a president of the United States, and its prior ownership was material to the contract, the pen would be unique if no other pens used by the same president were for sale. Harold would be entitled to elect damages or specific performance. If Harold sued for specific performance, the court would require Tony to deliver the pen, and Harold would need to pay for it. If Harold sued for damages he could use appraisers to estimate the value of that particular pen. He would then be entitled to the difference in price between the value of the pen and what he had promised to pay for it. If the appraisers could not estimate the value of the item, Harold would only be entitled to nominal damages.

Essential Vocabulary

1. unique

X. QUASI CONTRACT

In the absence of a contract, people are liable for the reasonable value of property or services received if their acts or omissions were instrumental in obtaining them.

Quasi contract is included in this list of remedies for the sake of completeness. Quasi contract is not actually a remedy for breach of contract at all. It is an equitable cause of action provided to prevent unjust enrichment in the absence of an enforceable contract. When there is no contract, there can be no remedies for breach. However, in the absence of a contract, an action in quasi contract is available to prevent the unjust enrichment of a party. Parties who have breached a contract are not normally entitled to recover anything for their partial performances because actions in quasi contract are available only in the absence of a contract. A more complete discussion of this topic is included in the chapter on contract formation.[1]

CHECK YOUR UNDERSTANDING

DIRECTIONS: Read each of the following questions. Choose the best answer and study the discussion of the question.

1. Molly, a mentally incompetent adult, entered into a contract to purchase an expensive desk and took possession of the desk after making a down payment. The price charged for the desk was reasonable. Upon the advice of a trusted friend, she sued to disaffirm the contract because she had no need for the desk. She probably:

    a. lost unless the contract was unconscionable.
    b. lost unless the other party was aware of her incompetence.
    c. lost if she made the offer, and the other party accepted it.
    d. won, but she would need to make only partial restitution by returning whatever she had left.
    e. won, but she would need to make full restitution by returning the desk or paying for it.

---

[1] See 100 (7-X) for a more complete discussion of actions in quasi contract.

DISCUSSION

(e)   Molly could avoid the contract due to her lack of capacity whether or not it was the product of gross overreaching and grossly unequal bargaining power and therefore unconscionable. Molly could disaffirm this contract even if the seller was unaware of her mental disability. However, she would need to make full restitution for any benefits she received under the contract because she was an adult. Only minors are allowed to make partial restitution when they avoid contracts. Molly would need to return the desk or pay for it. If the desk had been damaged, Molly would have needed to return the desk and pay the costs of depreciation and repair.

2.   Peter entered into a valid, written contract to sell Jones his famous checker-playing cow for $15,000. Payment and delivery were to have taken place eight months after the contract was signed. Two months after the contract was signed, Peter caught the cow cheating so he had a barbecue with the cow being the featured attraction (the main course). Jones could probably:

a.   recover for breach of contract immediately after the barbecue.
b.   recover for breach of contract only after the agreed date of delivery and payment.
c.   recover for breach of contract only if he could prove the cow was not cheating.
d.   not recover anything because he had not yet paid for the cow.
e.   not recover anything because the contract was excused by impossibility of performance.

DISCUSSION

(a)   Peter breached the contract prior to the time for delivery by barbecuing the cow. This act made performance as promised impossible. The contract would not be discharged by impossibility of performance because it was Peter's fault. Jones had the right to sue him immediately for breach by anticipatory repudiation of the contract. Jones would be entitled to damages even though he had not yet paid for the cow. He owned the right to future delivery of the cow at the moment the contract was formed. His damages would have been the difference in price between the market value of the cow and what he had promised to pay for it.

3. Stuart entered into a valid written contract to build an office complex for Warren. Because Warren would need to begin renting the building prior to completion and any delay would result in legal problems with the renters, the contract contained a clause in which Stuart agreed to pay Warren $10,000 per day for every day the project took to complete after the due date. This was a reasonable estimate of the costs Warren would incur in the event of delays. Stuart was 30 days late so Warren sued him for $300,000 on the liquidated damages clause. Warren probably:

   a. lost because liquidated damages violate public policy.
   b. lost if Stuart's health made it impossible for him to complete the project.
   c. won a judgement for $300,000.
   d. won only the damages he could prove.
   e. won only if he could prove that Stuart was negligent in failing to complete the project on time.

DISCUSSION

   (c)   The contract between Stuart and Warren contained a liquidated damages clause. This clause would be enforceable as long as it was reasonable and did not constitute a penalty or forfeiture. Stuart's health would be irrelevant because his duties under the contract could be delegated to any competent tradesman. If the court determined that the liquidated damages were reasonable, Warren would not have been required to prove the extent of his actual damages. Stuart would have been liable for damages for finishing the project late even if the delay had not been caused by his negligence or other fault.

4. Nicole offered to sell Andrea a painting for $10,000, and Andrea accepted the offer. The painting was delivered to Andrea, and she took possession prior to payment. Andrea later tried to return the painting and refused to pay for it when she found that the "artist" was an earthworm that had been repeatedly dipped in paint and allowed to crawl over the canvas. Nicole probably:

   a. can recover the $10,000 on a quasi contractual theory.
   b. cannot recover more than the reasonable value of the painting.
   c. cannot recover anything if a reasonable person would find that the painting is worthless.
   d. cannot recover anything because Andrea's promise to pay was not supported by adequate consideration.
   e. can refuse to accept the return of the painting and recover the $10,000 price.

DISCUSSION

(e)   Nicole had completely performed her duty to deliver the painting under the contract so she was entitled to the $10,000 contract price. She could not recover anything in quasi contract because this remedy is available only in the absence of a contract. The reasonable value of something is important only when one seeks relief in quasi contract. When the remedy is for breach of contract, the price or benefit of the bargain is the measure of damages. The actual value of the painting would not be important as long as the painting met the requirements of consideration. The painting would have been sufficient consideration to support Andrea's promise to pay $10,000 because the painting was "new" to her and she had "bargained for" it. Since Andrea did not own it at the time the contract was formed, and she had not been disguising a gift to Nicole to look like a purchase, the painting was sufficient consideration to support the contract. No misrepresentation had taken place, and Nicole had no duty to disclose the method she had used for producing the painting.

5.   Harvey entered into a contract to build a swimming pool with an oak deck for Alice. The total cost of the project was $250,000. Harvey did a good job, but he built the deck using pine. The cost of replacing the pine deck with oak was $10,000. Alice refused to pay Harvey anything. When Harvey sued her, he probably:

   a.   lost because he had breached the contract.
   b.   lost, but he could take his materials back.
   c.   won $240,000 because he had substantially performed.
   d.   won $250,000 if pine would wear as well as oak.
   e.   lost unless he was willing to personally rebuild the deck.

DISCUSSION

(c)   Harvey breached the contract by using pine instead of oak to build the deck. However, since he had almost completely performed the contract, he met the requirements of substantial performance. This defect in performance impaired the value of the project by only 4% of the total contract price, the contract was completed in most important respects. Harvey would, therefore, be entitled to the contract price less damages for breach or about $240,000. He would not have to rebuild the deck because Alice could hire someone else to take care of the problem for the $10,000 she could deduct from the contract price. She would have the option of learning to appreciate the beauty of pine and keeping the $10,000 or using it to correct the problem.

6. In October, the Lazy Lizards, a dance band, contracted with Don's Dive, a private club, to play for customers on December 3rd. On November 20th, the band leader informed Don that the Lizards would not be able to play as agreed because they were tired of playing club dates. In the past, Don had made from $10,000 to $12,000 on liquor sales when the band had been featured. Don probably:

   a. could have obtained specific performance.
   b. could have recovered $10,000 from the Lizards.
   c. should have tried to hire another band to mitigate his damages.
   d. could have closed his club and obtained his lost profits.
   e. could have recovered only nominal damages from the Lizards.

   DISCUSSION

   (c)   The Lazy Lizards breached their contract with Don by anticipatory repudiation. Don could sue for damages immediately without waiting for the date of the performance. Don could not have obtained specific performance because forcing the Lizards to perform would have violated the constitutional prohibitions against slavery. Don would have been required to mitigate his damages by attempting to hire another band. He would have been entitled to the amount he had to pay for another equivalent band over the amount he had promised to pay the Lizards. In addition, he would have been entitled to his lost profits if he could have proved that his losses resulted from the Lizards' breach of contract. Don would have been limited to recovering $1 as nominal damages only if he was unable to prove the extent of his actual damages.

7. Pam entered into a valid, written contract with Betty in which she agreed to supply steel for Betty's project and to pay $1,000 per day for every day that expired after the due date until the steel was delivered. Pam then contracted with a steel mill to purchase the steel she needed to deliver to Betty without mentioning her contract with Betty. Due to problems at the mill, Pam received the steel 5 days later than promised. She was, therefore, 5 days late delivering the steel to Betty. Betty demanded that Pam pay her $5,000 in late fees as required by the liquidated damage clause in the contract. Pam paid as required and sued the steel mill for this amount. Pam probably:

   a. lost because the mill had specifically performed its contract.

b. lost because the mill's representatives had not known about the late fee before contracting with Pam.

c. won because the mill did not deliver the steel by the due date.

d. won if the $1,000 per day constituted a lawful penalty.

e. won if the $1,000 per day was reasonable.

DISCUSSION

(b)   Pam could probably not recover $5,000 in damages from the mill. The damages Pam suffered due to the mill's delayed delivery of the steel were consequential damages resulting indirectly from the mill's breach of its contract with Pam. Consequential damages can be recovered only when the breaching party was aware of the special circumstances that would produce the consequential damages prior to entering into the contract. If Pam had informed the mill about the liquidated damage clause contained in her contract with Betty, the mill may have been liable to reimburse Pam for the late fee. Even so, the late fee would have needed to be reasonable because penalties are not allowed as damages for breach of contract. Whether or not the liquidated damages were reasonable was irrelevant because the mill had not been informed of Pam's contract with Betty prior to entering into its contract with Pam.

8. George contracted to sell Thomas a meteorite which was one of only ten known to be in existence on earth. Although the contract was valid, George repudiated it and refused to sell. If none of the other nine owners want to sell, Thomas can probably:

a. recover only money damages for breach.

b. force George to deliver the meteorite if Tom performs his obligations.

c. exercise eminent domain.

d. recover both compensatory and punitive damages.

e. recover exemplary damages.

DISCUSSION

(b)   Thomas would probably be entitled to the remedy of specific performance because the meteorite was unique. It was unique because it was the only one for sale. Thomas could elect to recover money damages by having an appraiser testify as an expert witness to establish the value of the meteorite. However, he would not have been required to accept monetary damages if George still had possession of the meteorite. If Thomas had elected specific performance, he would have been required to pay for the meteorite upon delivery as promised. Thomas could not exercise eminent domain which is a police power of the government that allows it to take private property for a public use after compensating the owner. If Thomas decided to seek damages, he would only be entitled to compensatory damages sufficient to give him the benefit of his bargain. Punitive damages are not normally awarded in actions for breach of contract even when the breach was willful. Exemplary damages are punitive damages.

9. George went to the doctor for an injection. Neither the doctor nor George discussed the price of this service. The doctor later sent George a bill for $150, and George refused to pay. The doctor sued him. The doctor probably:

   a. lost because the price was not specified.
   b. lost because George would have been justified in assuming that the services were free.
   c. won in an action for specific performance.
   d. won based on an implied contract if the charge was reasonable.
   e. won the reasonable value of his services in quasi contract.

DISCUSSION

   (e)   No contract was formed between George and the doctor because the price of the doctor's services was not part of the offer. No offer can be made without the material terms of price, quantity and description. Since there was no offer, there could be no contract. However, George was enriched by receiving the doctor's services, and he was active in obtaining the services because he went to the doctor seeking an injection and consented to the procedure. George would be liable in quasi contract for the reasonable value of the injection. The doctor would have needed to seek relief in quasi contract rather than on an implied contract theory because the price was not specified. When a person sues on a quasi contractual theory, the remedy awarded is the reasonable value of the property or services delivered.

Chapter 12
Contract Critique

The previous chapters presenting contract law deal with the formation and enforcement of contracts more than with the desirability of specific contract provisions. When managers are asked what they think about a contract, the enforceability of the contract is only part of the information sought. How well the contract expresses the agreement of the parties and how well it gives the parties notice of what is expected are extremely important. A "good" contract is a contract that prevents disagreements from arising due to unexpected circumstances. Both parties to a contract hope that it will be performed according to its terms with mutually beneficial and fair results. Good contracts help maintain customers and attract new business.

This section deals with a method for evaluating the merits of a particular written contract or memorandum of a contract. Managers should not draft contract provisions because this constitutes the unlicensed practice of law. However, a working knowledge of how a contract can be evaluated will allow more efficient use of professional legal services.

I. INVESTIGATE

Examine the contract and develop a descriptive word list.

The process of preparing to critique a contract is the same as the investigation described in the chapter on research. It is critical that managers become very familiar with the contract, the parties to the contract, and their expectations. It is also often helpful to become familiar with similar transactions completed in the past. This information is required to develop the descriptive word list that will be used in research.

II. RESEARCH

Find similar contracts in form books by searching indexes, texts, pocket parts and interim supplements.

Once the descriptive word list has been prepared, the researcher is ready to search a contract form book for similar contacts. An excellent source for such a search is American Jurisprudence Legal Forms 2nd. This set contains numerous helpful checklists and contract forms dealing with every aspect of business. It is updated frequently in pocket parts and other supplements. Once a similar contract is located, it should be copied and the volume replaced for others to use.

III. MEMORANDUM

Compare the contract to be critiqued to the forms copied and note common provisions omitted and uncommon provisions included.

The first step in the process of critiquing a contract involves the identification of "common provisions" which are not included in the contract to be critiqued. Common provisions are provisions that are included in the sample contracts and checklists in the form books. The company attorney should be consulted about any common provisions that are missing to determine if they are needed. The missing common provisions should be described or listed in a memorandum for easy reference when consulting the company's attorney. Such provisions should never be added without legal counsel because local variances in law or practice may make them inappropriate in some circumstances. If no common provisions are missing, it should be noted in the memorandum to indicate that the contract was examined for these potential defects.

The next step is to examine the contract for "uncommon provisions" that are included in the contract to be critiqued. Uncommon provisions are provisions that are not included in the checklists and forms in the form books. These provisions should be examined by the company attorney to make certain that they fit the contemplated transaction and that the parties understand their intended use and probable effects. These provisions should never be removed without legal counsel because they may be required by changes in the law or the special circumstances of the transaction. These uncommon provisions should be listed or referenced in the memorandum so that they are readily accessible. If there are no unusual provisions, it should be noted so that it is apparent that the contract has been examined for these potential points of disagreement.

Essential Vocabulary

1. common provisions
2. uncommon provisions

CONTRACT CRITIQUE EXERCISE

The following exercise will provide you with an opportunity to critique a contract. The contract presented to be critiqued would be a binding contract if it were properly signed with the required attachments. The elements of a contract are offer, acceptance and consideration. The brief contract to be critiqued contains all of the material terms of an offer in that it specifies price, quantity and description. Still, it is a very inadequate and, therefore, dangerous instrument to be used in the sale of a multi-million dollar business. The law studied in connection with contracts does not deal with how desirable a valid contract may be for use in a given situation. The method of contract critique presented in the text will enable a manager to effectively interact with professional legal counsel and to recognize when legal help is necessary.

The contract to be critiqued is entitled "CONTRACT FOR THE SALE OF COR-PORATE ASSETS." This contract omits many very important standard provisions and contains one unusual provision. You should be able to identify the common provisions omitted and the unusual provision included by comparing it with the sample contract form provided. The legal form entitled "SAMPLE CONTRACT FORM" supplied for this exercise is not an actual form from a form book. It would be a more effective exercise if an actual form could be used. However, the advantage of the form supplied is that it is relatively brief and easily understood. This form should not be used for any purpose other than this exercise.

The memorandum embodies and preserves the contract critique. The memorandum deals with the usual provisions omitted and the unusual provisions included in the contract. When there are no usual provisions omitted or unusual provisions included, the memorandum should state these findings. The memorandum should include enough information about each provision listed to enable the writer to find the actual provision in the contract being critiqued and to explain the purpose of the provision. Determining if a specific provision is desirable is the job of professional legal counsel. However, identifying provisions that are questionable is a valuable skill for which a well trained manager will find many uses. A typical memorandum might be organized somewhat like the following:

Contract Critique Memorandum

Date:

To:

From:

Re:

   I.   The CONTRACT FOR SALE OF CORPORATE ASSETS has been reviewed. This
        contract omits provisions which are commonly included in contracts of this type.
        The provisions omitted involve the following:
        A.
        B.
        C.
        D. etc.

  II.   This contract includes provisions not commonly included in contracts of this type.
        The unusual provisions involve the following:
        A.
        B. etc.

 III.   Recommendations:

Instructions for the Exercise

Compare the "Contract for the Sale of Corporate Assets" with the "Sample Contract
Form" provided. Take note of the common provisions contained in the sample but omitted from the contract. Be sure to make a note of any unusual provisions included in the
contract that are not included in the "Sample Contract Form." Compile your findings in a
memorandum. You can compare your memorandum with the model provided at the end
of this exercise.

Contract for the Sale of Corporate Assets[1]

(CONTRACT TO BE CRITIQUED)

I

We, the Board of Directors of Short Swing, Inc., a private corporation incorporated in the State of _____ having its principal office at _____ hereby bargain and sell all of the assets of the aforesaid corporation to Hungry Giant, Inc. for the sum of $13,500,000.

II

A description of the assets is attached hereto and incorporated herein.

III

The closing for this transaction shall be held at Big Bank at its main office at 2:00 p.m. on April 15, _____.

IV

If for any reason other than the lack of cooperation of Short Swing Inc. the closing is not held on the agreed date, Hungry Giant shall be liable to Short Swing, Inc. for liquidated damages in the amount of $1,000 per day for every day of delay after the agreed closing date. At the time of the closing, the seller shall execute all documents necessary to transfer title to the buyer, and deliver them to Big Bank. At the same time, the buyer shall deliver a certified check in the amount of $13,500,000 to Big Bank for collection. At such time as the funds have been collected and deposited to the account of Short Swing Inc., Big Bank will release all documents to Hungry Giant, Inc. Short Swing, Inc. will deliver its assets to Hungry Giant, Inc. within ten days.

Short Swing, Inc.

_____   _____
Agent for Short Swing, Inc.   Date

Hungry Giant, Inc.

_____   _____
Agent for Hungry Giant, Inc.   Date

---

[1] This contract should not be used in an actual transaction. It is presented here merely for illustrative purposes.

Sample Contract Form[2]

(A SUBSTITUTE FOR A CONTRACT FROM A FORM BOOK FOR THIS EXERCISE)

This agreement is made this _____ day of _____, __, between _____, a corporation incorporated in the state of _____, herein referred to as "seller" and _____, a corporation incorporated in the state of _____, herein referred to as "buyer." In consideration of the mutual covenants presented herein seller and buyer agree to the following:

I
SALE OF ASSETS

The seller hereby bargains, sells and assigns to the buyer, and the buyer hereby accepts and purchases, on the closing date, all the assets and properties owned by the seller of every description including but not limited to all property tangible or intangible, real or personal, the good will of the seller and the right to use the names of the seller. The seller further sells and assigns to the buyer and the buyer hereby purchases a parcel of real estate consisting of approximately _____ acres and located at _____ along with all improvements built upon it.

II
PAYMENT AND ASSUMPTION OF LIABILITIES

In consideration of this sale of assets by the seller to the buyer, the buyer promises to pay to the seller the sum of _____ on the closing date and shall assume and pay all of seller's liabilities as reflected on its balance sheet dated _____, __. Seller warrants that the said balance sheet was prepared according to generally accepted accounting principles and that the information included thereon is accurate and complete. A copy of the balance sheet is attached to this contract and made a part of it by this reference. The buyer's assumption of the seller's liabilities shall not include the following:

(a)   Any liabilities not reflected by the balance sheet.
(b)   Any liabilities incurred after the date of the balance sheet.
(c)   Any tax liabilities in favor of the state or federal government.
(d)   Any liabilities connected with or resulting from the negotiation or consummation of this contract.

---

[2] This form is not an actual form from a form book. It is presented here merely for illustrative purposes and should not be used in an actual transaction.

III
REQUIRED INSTRUMENTS AND DOCUMENTS

The transfer of assets to the buyer by the seller shall be accomplished by deeds, bills of sale, commercial paper, title certificates and other instruments and documents as required or reasonably requested by the buyer. The seller shall prepare all necessary instruments and documents in appropriate form and submit them to the buyer for inspection at least _____ days prior to the closing date. The seller will also submit to the buyer any additional instruments and documents requested by the buyer and reasonably necessary to accomplish the transfers of title contemplated by this contract.

IV
ASSIGNMENT OF CONTRACT RIGHTS

The seller will use its best effort to obtain the consent of all other parties to contracts assigned to the buyer pursuant to this agreement if such contracts cannot be assigned without their consent. If any contract right cannot be assigned without the consent of the other party and consent cannot be obtained, the seller shall reduce the amount owing under this contract by the market value of the contract right that cannot be assigned. The seller shall provide a list of the names and addresses of all parties to contracts assigned to the buyer at least _____ days prior to the closing date.

V
ACCOUNTS RECEIVABLE

The buyer shall have the authority to collect all accounts and debts owing to buyer as of the date of the balance sheet. The seller shall transfer all commercial paper to seller without recourse and without warranties. Any accounts receivable collected by seller after the date of closing shall be transferred to the buyer.

VI
COMPLIANCE WITH THE BULK TRANSFERS LAW

The seller shall deliver to the buyer a list of the names, addresses, with amounts of debts owed or claimed by all of its creditors including but not limited to all persons, companies, corporations, and taxing authorities asserting any claim against the seller whatsoever and whether uncontested or contested by the seller. This list shall be delivered by the seller to the buyer at least _____ days before the closing date and shall contain a statement that it is complete and accurate and be signed by an authorized agent of the seller and notarized. It shall be the buyer's responsibility to give the notices to creditors required by the bulk sales provisions of the Uniform Commercial Code as enacted and in force in the state of _____.

VII
CLOSING

The closing shall be held on the _____ day of _____, __ at the hour of _____ at the offices of _____ located at _____ or at such other time and place as the parties shall agree.

VIII
COVENANT AGAINST COMPETITION

The seller hereby agrees that it will not engage in any business involving or related to its current business and shall not assist any other person, partnership, corporation or other business organization to engage in the same or a similar business for a period of _____ years in the geographic area of _____. The seller also agrees not to advise or provide customer lists, inventions, patents, data or other information to anyone involved in a similar business.

IX
EXPENSES

Each party shall pay its own expenses including but not limited to legal fees, transfer fees, taxes and the like incurred in the consummation of this contract. The sellers shall pay all costs incurred in the preparation of the documents and instruments used to transfer ownership of its assets to the buyer. The buyer shall pay all filing costs, recording fees and costs associated with sending any required notices of bulk transfer in compliance with the Uniform Commercial Code.

X
MERGER CLAUSE

This contract constitutes the entire agreement between the parties. Any other agreements, representations, or understandings between the parties relating to the subject of this contract are merged into this written expression of the agreement. Any modifications or additional agreements between the parties shall be void and of no legal effect unless reduced to writing and signed by authorized representatives of both parties.

The parties to this contract, by their authorized agents, hereby execute the same this _____ day of _____, __.

_____
(signature)

_____
(signature)

Example Memorandum[3]

I. The CONTRACT FOR SALE OF CORPORATE ASSETS has been reviewed. This contract omits provisions which are commonly included in contracts of this type. The provisions omitted involve the following:

    A. the buyer's assumption and payment of liabilities reflected on the seller's balance sheet;

    B. the seller's preparation of instruments and documents necessary to transfer the assets to the buyer;

    C. the assignment of contract rights and adjustments in the price paid by the buyer if the seller cannot obtain any required consent to assignment;

    D. the buyer's right to collect the seller's accounts receivable;

    E. the seller's transfer of commercial paper to the buyer without warranties;

    F. the seller's collection of account's receivable after the closing date;

    G. the seller's and buyer's duties relating to compliance with the Uniform Commercial Code bulk transfers law;

    H. the seller's promise not to compete with the buyer;

    I. the payment of expenses resulting from performance of this contract by the parties;

    j. a merger clause indicating that this contract contains the entire agreement of the parties.

II. This contract includes a provision not commonly included in contracts of this type. The unusual provision is located in Section IV and involves the imposition of liquidated damages upon the seller in the event the closing is not held on the agreed date.

I suggest that we contact our attorney to review the advisability and possible impact of the common provisions omitted and the unusual provision included in this contract.

---

[3] This memorandum is merely provided for illustrative purposes and should not be used otherwise.

SECTION IV
BUSINESS ORGANIZATIONS

Principal and Agent
Partnerships
Corporations

Chapter 13
Principal and Agent

When an individual has a small sole proprietorship, she can handle most transactions by herself. Larger businesses cannot be run by only one person. Fortunately, the law allows a person to enter into a contract through an agent. The person actually entering into a contractual relationship is called the "principal." The person contracting on the principal's behalf is called the "agent." In partnerships, each partner is an agent for the other partners and the partnership. Corporations must do all of their business through agents because the corporation itself is considered a person in the eyes of the law. The officers and employees of a corporation who enter into contracts for it are the agents of the corporation. The law of agency is much broader than presented here. For the sake of brevity, the discussion will be limited to the topics and applications that deal most directly with business law.

Essential Vocabulary

1. principal
2. agent

I. AGENT AND PRINCIPAL

An agent has authority to act in the place of the principal in making an offer, an acceptance, or receiving a performance.

Although agents can act for their principals in many other ways, this generalization is limited to agents entering into contracts on behalf of their principals. Agents must have "authority" to legally bind their principals in some way. Authority, in the context of this discussion, is the power to enter into a contract. The agent must obtain his authority directly or indirectly from the principal. The principal may be a person, a partnership, or a corporation. Not all employees, officers, independent contractors and the like are agents. In business law, the most important way an agent obligates a principal is through entering into contracts on his behalf. The tasks that result in a principal's being contractually bound are: making an offer, making an acceptance, or receiving a performance.

Louis owned a dairy with three employees working for him. Andrew contacted potential customers and made offers on behalf of the dairy to provide milk to them at their homes. Barney delivered the milk and monthly statements to the customers. Carol cared for the cows. Louis did everything else. Louis was the principal and Andrew was his only agent because he was the only employee authorized to make offers on Louis' behalf. If Barney had been authorized to collect from the customers in addition to delivering the statements, he would have been an agent because he would have had authority to receive the payment or performance from them.

In the eyes of the law, the agent acts in the place of the principal. When an agent has actual authority to act for the principal, the agent is not a party to the contract. The actions, capacity and knowledge of the agent are those of the principal. In short, the courts apply a legal fiction and analyze cases as though the principal and not the agent was present for the transaction. This legal fiction can produce some surprising results.

Mila, an adult, told Betty to purchase a case of whiskey for her club and have it delivered directly to her by the distillery. Betty was a minor, and it was illegal to sell liquor to a minor. Betty entered into the contract on Mila's behalf. Before the liquor was delivered, Mila changed her mind and refused to take delivery. When the distillery sued her for breach of contract, Mila defended on the ground that the contract was illegal.

The contract was legal, and Mila was liable for breach of contract. When Mila told Betty to purchase the liquor for her, Betty received actual authority to enter into the purchase contract on Mila's behalf. Since this required Betty to make an offer to purchase the liquor for Mila, Betty became Mila's agent. An agent acts in the place of the principal so, in the eyes of the law, Mila entered into the contract rather than Betty. The contract was lawful and binding on Mila. It is the capacity of the principal and not that of the agent that governs the transaction because the agent acts "in the place of the principal." An easy way to remember this is to imagine that the principal is present when the agent is exercising her authority to make an offer, an acceptance, or receive a performance for the principal.

Another interesting result of this fiction is that the principal is held to have knowledge of all material facts known by the agent. Jim read an advertisement in the newspaper that described a tract of land as a beautiful and quiet location for a home. The tract was represented as being covered with trees and far from noisy streets. Jim decided to purchase the tract based on the description in the advertisement. He instructed Ken to examine the tract and purchase it for him. Ken contacted the owner and visited the tract. When he got there, he observed that there were only two trees on the lot and that is was positioned between a mink farm and a busy freeway. The lot was covered with debris and over half of it was under water due to the fact that it was part of a swamp. Ken accepted the owners offer on behalf of Jim anyway. When Jim saw the land, he did not want it, and he attempted to rescind the contract on the ground that the seller had made intentional misrepresentations in the advertisement.

Jim was not successful because Ken was his agent. Jim was held to know everything Ken knew about the land at the time of contracting. Since Ken learned the true state of the land prior to contracting, he did not rely on the owners representations made in the advertisement.

For the purposes of this transaction, Ken was Jim in the eyes of the law. In keeping with the legal fiction, it was Jim who inspected the property and entered into the contract despite the actual condition of the land. In this case, Ken would have been liable to Jim for breach of fiduciary duty. We will discuss the fiduciary duty of an agent under later in this chapter.

Essential Vocabulary

1. authority

II. DISCLOSURE

An agent will be liable with the principal unless both the agency and the principal's identity are disclosed.

An agent is required to fully disclose to the other contracting party that the principal and not the agent is entering into the contractual relationship. If the agent fails to do this, she will be liable on the contract along with the principal. To make a "full disclosure," the agent must advise the other contracting party of the identity of the principal and of her status as agent. While this may be done in writing or orally, it is often preferable to make the disclosure in writing to make it easier to prove in the future. One way to make a full disclosure in writing is to sign documents as follows:

Kelly Smith, Principal
by *John Jones*, Agent.

The italicized name represents the signature in this example. This form of signature makes it quite clear that Kelly Smith is the principal and that John Jones is merely signing on her behalf. Other forms of signature may be acceptable, but one must be cautious because the agent will be liable along with the principal if the signature is ambiguous.

An agent will be liable on a contract if only a "partial disclosure" of the agency is made. A partial disclosure is the disclosure of the identity of the principal without disclosing that the person signing is merely an agent, e.g. Thomas, an agent for Ben, signs a contract on behalf of Ben by simply signing Ben's name and his own name without indicating that he is signing merely as an agent. Another type of partial disclosure is the disclosure of the fact that one is an agent without disclosing the identity of the principal, e.g. Thomas, Ben's agent, signs a contract for Ben by merely signing his own name followed by the word "agent" without indicating the identity of his principal.

Similarly, an agent will be liable on a contract if "no disclosure" of the agency is made. This takes place when the agent enters into a contract in her own name without mentioning that she is an agent acting for a principal e.g., Sue, an agent for Fred, signs a contract on behalf of Fred by merely signing her own name without mentioning the agency at all.

Terry instructed Paul to sign a contract for landscaping services for him. Paul signed his own name to the contract without mentioning that he was an agent or that Terry was the principal. Terry failed to pay for the services that were rendered by the landscaper. When the landscaper sued Paul, he disclosed that he was merely an agent for Terry. The landscaper amended its complaint to sue Terry along with Paul. Both Terry and Paul would be liable. Terry would be liable because he was the principal and, therefore, a party to the contract. Paul would be liable because he had failed to make a full disclosure of the agency.

A full disclosure could have been made by Paul's indication that Terry was the principal and that Paul was signing only as agent, e.g. by signing "Terry, principal, by *Paul*, agent." Paul would not have been liable on the contract if he had made this full disclosure. A partial disclosure could have been made by Paul in any of the following ways: Paul's signing the contract in Terry's name without indicating that he was acting only as an agent, e.g. by merely signing the principal's name, "*Terry*;" Paul's signing the contract in his own name and indicating that he was an agent but failing to indicate the identity of the principal, e.g. "*Paul*, agent;" Paul's signing the contract in both his own name and Terry's name but failing to indicate that he was signing merely as an agent, e.g. "*Terry* and *Paul*."

Paul may have failed to mention capacity as an agent and the identity of the principal by merely signing his own name, e.g. by signing "*Paul*." This would have been no disclosure at all. Anything less than full disclosure can result in the agent's being liable on the contract. When a partial disclosure is made, the courts will sometimes require the other contracting party to make an election to take a judgment against either the principal or the agent, but not both. When no disclosure is made, the courts typically allow a judgment to be taken against both the agent and the principal.

Essential Vocabulary

1. full disclosure
2. partial disclosure
3. no disclosure

III.   EQUAL DIGNITY RULE

If a written contract or memorandum is required by law, the agent must have a power of attorney.

The actual authority given by the principal to the agent can be given orally or in writing. If it is given in writing, the document is called a "power of attorney." Notice that the power of attorney is not a "power" at all but rather a document that purports to give the agent authority to make offers or acceptances or receive performances for the principal. Powers of attorney are required only when the agent is authorized to enter into contracts which are within the Statute of Frauds or otherwise required by law to be in writing. When the law requires that a contract be dignified by written evidence, the "Equal Dignity Rule" requires that the agent's authority to be given equal dignity by being evidenced by a power of attorney. If the parties merely decide to use a written contract when the law does not require it, no power of attorney is required even though the agent will be signing a contract for the principal. When the law does not require that the contract be dignified by a writing, the agent's authority may be given orally by the principal. It should be noted, however, that good business practice usually dictates that powers of attorney be used to evidence agents' authority even when the law does not specifically require them.

Dana verbally authorized Miko to purchase an apartment complex for her. Miko fully disclosed the agency by placing Dana's name on the contract as principal and indicating that Miko's signature was made only in the capacity of agent for Dana. While the original owner still had the property in her own name and before Dana had taken possession of the complex, Dana changed her mind and denied giving Mike authority to make the purchase. The owner could not successfully sue Dana for breach of contract because Miko did not have a power of attorney. A power of attorney was required because contracts for the purchase of real property must be evidenced by written contracts or memorandums. The Equal Dignity Rule required that Miko's authority be dignified by being evidenced by a power of attorney.

Essential Vocabulary

1. power of attorney
2. Equal Dignity Rule

IV. ACTUAL AUTHORITY

If an agent has actual or both actual and apparent authority, only the principal has liability on the contract.

One type of authority is "actual authority." Actual authority is the term for the authority directly, and intentionally given by a principal to an agent to make an offer, an acceptance, or receive a performance. This actual authority may be given verbally or in writing. An agent with actual authority is not a party to the contract he enters into for his principal if he fully discloses the agency. The law applies a legal fiction in analyzing transactions entered into by an agent for his principal. Cases are analyzed as though the principal is actually present at all important times in the transaction. The agent with actual authority who has made a full disclosure of the agency is not liable on the contract to the principal or to the other contracting party. If the principal breaches the contract, the other party to the contract may sue only the principal. If the other party to the contract defaults, the principal's only remedy would be to sue the other party to the contract.

Sam gave Ward actual authority through a power of attorney to purchase a truck for him from Trucks Unlimited. The contract required Sam to make payments to Trucks Unlimited for five years. Ward fully disclosed the agency and properly signed the contract. Since Sam had given Ward actual authority to enter into the contract and full disclosure was made, Ward would not be liable on the contract. If Trucks Unlimited breached their warranties under the contract, Sam could sue the company but not Ward. If Sam failed to make payments, Sam, and not Ward, would be liable to Trucks Unlimited.

Essential Vocabulary

1.   actual authority

V. APPARENT AUTHORITY

If an agent has only apparent authority, both the principal and the agent have liability.

Another type of authority is "apparent authority." Apparent authority is the term for the authority given to an agent when the principal creates the appearance that the person is her agent. A person with apparent authority may or may not also have actual authority. If the agent has both apparent and actual authority, she would not liable on any transactions entered into on behalf of the principal. If the agent has only apparent authority and the principal did not actually give the agent authority to contractually bind her, the agent is liable on the transaction and may be liable to both the principal and the other party to the contract. In addition, the principal is liable because she created the appearance upon which the other party to the contract relied. This is the case if a person tells others that a given individual is her agent when, in fact, that individual is not actually authorized to act as her agent.

Connie hired Paula to be the purchasing agent for her pet store. Company stationary, the switchboard operator, and correspondence with vendors identified Paula as the company's purchasing agent. When Paula was hired for the position, Connie gave her actual authority to be the company's agent for purchasing inventory. By authorizing the stationary, switchboard procedures and correspondence, Connie created the appearance that Paula was her agent and gave her apparent authority in addition to her actual authority. This resulted in Paula's having both actual and apparent authority to enter into contracts for the pet store. Paula would not have liability on any contract she entered into for the company because she had actual authority.

Connie later told Paula not to enter into any contracts to purchase animals for a month because inventory was excessive. This terminated Paula's actual authority to purchase additional animals. However, Paula still appeared to the vendors to have the authority to purchase inventory because no one let them know of the limitation on Paula's actual authority. If contrary to instructions, Paula entered into contracts to purchase additional inventory, Connie would be bound by the contracts because Paula still had apparent authority. Since Paula would not also have actual authority to enter into the contracts, she would be liable on the contracts made during the month along with Connie. Connie would be liable to the vendors because she created the appearance that Paula had authority to make the purchases. Paula would be liable on the contracts and liable to Connie because Connie had not actually authorized the contracts.

Essential Vocabulary

1. apparent authority

VI. NO AUTHORITY

If an "agent" has no authority, only the "agent" has liability.

Authority must be given to the agent by the principal directly or indirectly. No one can act as agent for someone else without some type of authority. If someone claiming to be an agent has no actual or apparent authority, he is not an agent at all. Such a person is liable on any contract he makes without authority. The principal is not liable because he has neither given the "agent" actual authority nor created the appearance of authority.

Dan had stationary made with letterhead that listed him as the personnel manager for Edward's Fashions. Dan did not work for Edward's Fashions, and no one from the company knew that he had purchased the misleading stationary. Dan used the stationary to play a "joke" on Fred, one of his enemies, who was without a job at the time. He wrote to Fred and offered him a job with Edward's Fashions for $1200 per month. Fred wrote back to him and accepted the offer. Fred discovered the ruse when he reported for work at the appointed time and was not amused. If Fred sued Edward's Fashions for breach of employment contract, Edward's Fashions would not be liable to Fred because Dan had neither actual nor apparent authority to enter into employment contracts on its behalf.

The stationary did not confer apparent authority because it was not authorized by Edward's Fashions. Although the stationary made Dan appear to be the personnel manager for the company, it did not give him apparent authority to enter into contracts for Edward's

Fashions. The appearance of authority must be created by the principal to confer apparent authority. The stationary was made by the "agent" and not the purported principal. Fred would have an action against Dan for breach of the employment contract because the offer reasonably appeared to have been intentionally made.

VII. TERMINATION OF ACTUAL AUTHORITY

Actual authority is terminated by informing the agent of revocation.

A person ceases to be an agent for another with the "termination of authority." The termination of authority is the removal of an agent's power to bind the principal. The "termination of actual authority" takes place when the agent learns that his authority has been terminated by the principal or by the law. The principal may terminate the authority simply by telling the agent that he no longer has authority to enter into contracts for the principal. Actual authority terminates by law when the principal dies, becomes incompetent or files for bankruptcy.

Gary gave Han authority to purchase some tools for him. Before Han purchased the tools, Gary informed him that the tools were no longer needed. Han purchased the tools anyway. Han, and not Gary, would be bound by the purchase contract because Han had no actual authority to purchase the tools after Gary told him that the tools were no longer needed. Gary would not be liable on the contract because Han had neither actual nor apparent authority. If Gary had told Han he no longer wanted the tools after he had made the purchase, Gary, and not Han, would have been liable on the contract because Han would have had actual authority to enter into the contract at the time the tools were purchased.

If Gary had given Han a power of attorney, Gary would have been liable on the contract because the power of attorney would have given Han apparent authority in addition to actual authority by creating the appearance that he was Gary's agent. Han would have had both actual and apparent authority in the beginning. When Gary told him the tools were no longer needed, the actual authority would have been terminated. However, the appearance that Han was Gary's agent would have remained as long as Han retained the power of attorney. Apparent authority could be terminated by Gary's recovery of the power of attorney or his informing the tool vendor that the power of attorney was no longer valid.

Essential Vocabulary

1. termination of authority
2. termination of actual authority

VIII. TERMINATION OF APPARENT AUTHORITY

Apparent authority is terminated by informing everyone with whom the agent has done business of revocation.

Since apparent authority is created by the principal's creating the appearance that someone is her agent, the "termination of apparent authority" takes place when the appearance that the person is an agent is terminated. Informing the agent that her authority has been terminated merely terminates actual authority leaving any apparent authority intact. Apparent authority is unaffected until those who have done business with the agent receive "actual notice" of the termination of authority, and those who were aware of the agents authority without having done business through her receive "constructive notice." Actual notice is written or verbal notice mailed or actually given to the parties that have done business with the principal through the agent. People who were aware of the agent's authority but had never actually done business through her should be notified by "constructive notice." Constructive notice is notice printed in a newspaper or magazine of general circulation in the area where the agent entered into contracts on behalf of the principal.

Julie gave Kelly a power of attorney authorizing her to enter into a contract to lease a warehouse for two years. Kelly had both actual and apparent authority to enter into the contract at that time. However, before Kelly entered into the contract, she had a disagreement with Julie. Julie told her that she was fired and demanded that Kelly return the power of attorney. Kelly refused. Firing Kelly terminated her actual authority but left the apparent authority created by the power of attorney intact. Kelly later entered into a contract to teach Julie a lesson. Both Julie and Kelly would be bound by the contract. Julie would be bound because Kelly had apparent authority by virtue of the power of attorney in her possession. Kelly would be bound because she did not have actual authority to enter into any contract on Julie's behalf. To terminate Kelly's apparent authority, Julie would have needed to destroy the power of attorney or inform the people who might be misled by it that Kelly was not authorized to enter into any contract. In cases where a number of people have dealt with an agent with apparent authority, it would be necessary to give everyone who had done business with the agent in the past actual notice.

Essential Vocabulary

1. termination of apparent authority
2. actual notice
3. constructive notice

IX. DOCTRINE OF RESPONDEAT SUPERIOR

Employers are liable with their employees and partners for torts committed within the scope of employment.

"Respondeat superior" literally means let the master answer. The "Doctrine of Respondeat Superior" makes employers liable with their employees for torts committed within the scope of employment. People working for an employer may be employees or independent contractors. The Doctrine of Respondeat Superior applies only to employees so it is important to be able to distinguish between the two. Employers are not liable for the torts of the independent contractors working for them. Lists of factors to be considered in making this determination range from five or six items to twenty or more depending on the source of the lists. Using three criteria will generally allow the prediction of whether or not an individual is an employee or an independent contractor with some accuracy. If someone meets at least two of the three following tests for being either an independent contractor or an employee, he would probably be found to be in the same category using the longer, more accurate tests.

The tests are as follows:

1. *Separate Business Test* — Independent contractors generally offer their services to the general public, i.e. they maintain a separate business. Employees generally offer their services only to a particular employer or small set of employers.

2. *Supervision and Control Test* — Independent contractors generally are not supervised in their work by their employer. They are employed merely to produce a desired product or result. Employees, on the other hand, are employed to participate in a process or job which their employer may supervise and control.

3. *Supply of Tools and Workplace Test* — Independent contractors generally supply their own tools and maintain their own workplace and shops while employees receive these things from their employers.

Larry, a lawyer, was involved in an automobile accident while on his way to court to represent Mandy. Larry was negligent and the other driver claimed that Mandy had "vicarious liability" under the Doctrine of Respondeat Superior for the damages he suffered . A person has vicarious liability for a tort when the law imposes liability for harm caused by another. To determine whether the Doctrine of Respondeat Superior will impose vicarious liability upon Mandy for Larry's negligence, it must first be determined if Larry was an employee or an independent contractor. If Larry was an employee, Mandy would be liable for his negligence. If Larry was an independent contractor, Mandy would not have vicarious liability.

Larry handled all of Mandy's legal matters, and she was his only client. He was free to handle Mandy's cases without supervision. Mandy provided Larry with an office, library, office furniture and secretarial support in her office building. In this case, Larry did not have a separate business, or supply his own tools or workplace. He was probably an employee under both the Separate Business Test and the Supply of Tools and Workplace Test. Under the Doctrine of Respondeat Superior, Mandy would probably have vicarious liability for the damages caused by Larry in the scope of his employment to handle Mandy's legal matters. If Larry had other clients, the result may have been otherwise because he would have appeared to be an employee under only the Supply of Tools and Workplace Test. An employee will generally appear to be an employee under at least two of the three tests for employees given above.

The employer is not liable for all torts committed by his employees. Vicarious liability extends only to those intentional and negligent torts committed within the "scope of employment." An employee is within the scope of his employment when he is doing something in connection with the job for which he was hired. The liability attaches for torts committed by an employee doing his job whether or not he was doing his job properly.

Olivia was Nancy's employee hired to deliver auto parts to Nancy's customers. While Olivia was trying to make a delivery downtown, she found a vacant parallel parking space and pulled over while signaling to use it to make a delivery. Pete slipped into the space with a small car before Olivia could back into it. She got out of the truck and asked Pete to move his car because she had gotten there first. Pete refused. Olivia then struck Pete in the face with her fist and repeated her demand. Pete again refused and was struck again. The process continued until Pete finally recognized the pattern and moved his car after having been severely beaten about the head and shoulders. Pete sued both Olivia and Nancy. Olivia was liable for battery. Nancy was vicariously liable for the battery because Olivia was acting within the scope of her employment to make deliveries. Although Nancy did not authorize this rough treatment of other motorists with poor manners, she was liable because getting a parking place was part of Olivia's job in making deliveries.

Essential Vocabulary

1. respondeat superior
2. Doctrine of Respondeat Superior
3. Separate Business Test
4. Supervision and Control Test
5. Supply of Tools and Workplace Test
6. vicarious liability
7. scope of employment

X. FIDUCIARY DUTY

An agent owes a fiduciary duty to the principal to:

   (1) *account,*

   (2) *avoid competition* **with the principal,**

   (3) *obey,*

   (4) **use** *reasonable* **care, and**

   (5) **make full** *disclose.*

Since a principal must place trust and confidence in the agent, the relationship of principal and agent is a "fiduciary relationship." A fiduciary relationship is a relationship in which one or both of the parties has the legal right to rely upon and trust the other. The fiduciary relationship between the principal and the agent imposes a "fiduciary duty" upon the agent. A fiduciary duty is a legal obligation to act in the best interests of another. Because the principal must trust and depend upon the agent to act in his best interest, the agent owes the principal a fiduciary duty. The agent, however, is not as vulnerable to the principal so the fiduciary duty is owed by the agent to the principal but not by the principal to the agent. The fiduciary relationship of principal and agent imposes at least five duties upon the agent: the duty to account, avoid competition, obey, use reasonable care, and make full disclosure. Some students find the acronym "AACORD" a useful way to remember these duties.

The fiduciary duty to account requires the agent to keep accurate records for the principal of any business he handles. In any dispute between the principal and the agent over matters for which the agent was required to keep records, the agent has the burden of proving that he behaved properly. If the principal sues the agent in a dispute over the agent's actions, the agent will lose to the principal if he cannot produce the required records.

An agent may not represent the principal's competitors at the same time as he represents the principal without the principal's consent. In addition, the agent may not compete with the principal himself by taking any of the principal's business opportunities or accepting secret profits such as "kick-backs."

The agent's fiduciary duty to the principal requires him to obey the instructions of the principal. The agent will be liable for any failure to follow the principals instructions. When the instructions are ambiguous, the agent is required to obtain more specific instructions.

The fiduciary relationship imposes a duty to exercise reasonable care to protect the interests of the principal. Agents are liable for any damage or harm they negligently cause the principal to suffer. They also have a duty to rescue the principal as discussed in the chapter on negligence.

The duty to disclose all material facts to the principal requires the agent to disclose facts important to the principal in any contracts between the agent and the principal. In addition, the agent is required to notify the principal of any important information he acquires during the handling of the principal's business. This is required because the law charges the principal with the agent's knowledge as discussed under the first generalization in this section.

Essential Vocabulary

1. fiduciary relationship
4. fiduciary duty
5. AACORD

CHECK YOUR UNDERSTANDING

DIRECTIONS: Read each of the following questions. Choose the best answer and study the discussion of the question.

1. Gary advertised a race horse for sale as being in top condition for $250,000. Andy sent his agent, Bill, to look at the horse and purchase it for him. When Bill looked at the horse, he saw that it was lame, sway backed, approximately 300 pounds overweight, and blind in one eye. Nevertheless, he purchased it for Andy. Andy can:

   a. avoid the purchase, and Bill is liable to Andy for negligence.
   b. not avoid the purchase, but Bill is liable to Andy for breach of fiduciary duty.
   c. avoid the contract, but Bill is liable to Gary on the contract.
   d. not avoid the contract, but Bill is liable to Gary for negligence.
   e. avoid the purchase because Gary induced the sale by fraud.

DISCUSSION

(b) Andy is bound by the contract. He cannot avoid the contract based upon Gary's misrepresentation because Bill bought the horse without relying on Gary's misrepresentations. Since the agent acts in the place of the principal, the courts apply the fiction that the principal knew what the agent knew. Andy will be charged with Bill's knowledge of the true facts. Therefore, Andy knew the true state of affairs and purchased the horse anyway. He was not misled by Gary's misrepresentations. Bill's action in binding Andy to the contract was negligent. Bill's fiduciary duty to Andy required him to exercise reasonable care to protect Andy's interests in the transaction. The reasonable person would not have purchased the horse under the circumstances of this case. Bill would be liable to Andy for breach of fiduciary duty by being negligent in purchasing the horse and by failing to disclose the condition of the horse to Andy prior to entering into the contract.

2. Mark, the bookkeeper for Big Realty, was authorized to sign all contracts on behalf of the company. When the company borrowed $23,000 from the bank for six months, Mark was sent to sign the papers and pick up the check. Mark signed his name to the loan papers on the blank line at the bottom. The papers clearly indicated that the money was to go to Big Realty, and the check was made out to the company. When Big Realty defaulted on the loan, the bank sued Mark along with the owners. Mark was probably:

    a. liable because his authority was not in writing.
    b. liable because he picked up the check.
    c. liable because he failed to fully disclose his agency status.
    d. not liable because no power of attorney had been delivered to the bank to evidence his liability as an agent.
    e. not liable because he had actual authority, and he did not keep the money.

DISCUSSION

   (c)   Mark had actual authority to sign all contracts on behalf of the company. He would, therefore, not be a party to the loan contract with the bank if he fully disclosed the identity of the principal which was Big Realty in this case and the fact that he was acting only as agent for the company. Unfortunately, Mark did not disclose the fact that he was signing merely as agent when he signed his name at the bottom of the contract. Since the contract was made between Big Realty and the bank, the disclosure of the principal may have been made by the circumstances. However, this was only a partial disclosure of the agency because his status of agent was not disclosed. Mark's authority would not need to be in writing under the equal dignity rule unless the contract required Big Realty to make payments for more than a year. If a power of attorney was required, it would not affect Mark's liability or the liability of Big Realty in this case because Mark accepted the loaned money for the company. Contracts required to be evidenced by a writing under the Statute of Frauds will sometimes be enforced in the absence of a writing when one party has completely performed and the other party has accepted the performance.

3. Jan wanted to give Pete authority to enter into a contract on her behalf with the owner of a large office complex. It was agreed that the contract would be in writing because Jan was to be obligated to maintain the building and grounds for a period of five years at a cost of $40,000 to the owner. Pete's authority:

a. should have been in writing but oral authority would be sufficient.

b. had to be in writing because more than $500 was involved.

c. had to be in writing because the contract could not be performed within one year.

d. had to be in writing because the contract involved realty.

e. would have been sufficient if oral, and Pete could have delegated it to another person if he could have proved that his subagent had more expertise than he did.

DISCUSSION

(c) The Statute of Frauds would require that the contract between Jan and the owner of the office complex be evidenced by a written contract or memorandum because the contract could not be performed within one year. The Equal Dignity Rule requires that Pete's authority also be evidenced by a writing. The written embodiment of an agent's authority is called a power of attorney. Therefore, a power of attorney would be required. The contract was not a contract for the sale or purchase of real property. Jan was merely going to maintain the property by rendering a service. Pete could have delegated his authority to enter into the contract to a subagent only if his duty as Jan's agent merely involved the signing of the contract. The duty could not have been delegated if Pete was required to negotiate or exercise any judgement in entering into the contract.

4. Sam was hired by Tom to sign a contract to sell his home while he was out of town. Tom gave Sam a power of attorney. What type of authority did Sam have to sign Tom's name to the deed?

a. fiduciary authority

b. general authority to manage all of Tom's business affairs

c. implied authority

d. actual and apparent authority

e. no authority

DISCUSSION

(d) Sam was given actual and apparent authority to act for Tom. The term, fiduciary authority, is bogus. General authority is actual authority that is not limited to specific transactions while special authority is actual authority that is limited to a specific transaction or set of transactions. Sam would have had special authority in this case to handle only the sale of Tom's home. Sam had apparent authority because Tom gave him a power of attorney to create the appearance that Sam was his agent. Since this transaction involved the selling of real property, Tom was required to give

Sam a power of attorney. Once he had given Sam the document, Sam had apparent authority in addition to actual authority. Implied authority is authority given by implication when a person is authorized to do a particular job. When a person is given authority to collect money, he is given the authority to issue a receipt by implication because this is required to carry out the job of collecting money.

5. Paul was the owner of a store. One day while working he realized that he had forgotten to turn the oven off at home. He asked Kim to watch the store while he went home to take care of the problem, and Kim consented. Paul asked Kim to wear a distinctive apron worn by store employees, but he told her to make no sales at all until he returned. If Kim made a sale to a customer who thought she was an employee, Kim would have:

   a. no authority.
   b. authority by necessity.
   c. fraudulent authority.
   d. actual authority.
   e. apparent authority.

DISCUSSION

(e)   Kim would have apparent authority because Paul gave her the apron and created the appearance that she was a sales person authorized to make sales on behalf of the store. She did not have actual authority because Paul had instructed her to refrain from making any sales until he returned. Both Paul and Kim would be bound by any sales contracts made by Kim in his absence. Paul would be bound because he created the appearance that Kim was an agent, and Kim would be liable because she lacked actual authority to do so. The terms, authority by necessity and fraudulent authority, are bogus.

6. Anne walked into a used car dealership and purchased a used car for Bonnie, her girlfriend, as a birthday surprise. She signed the contract, "Bonnie, principal, by Anne, agent." The contract required the purchaser to pay $450 for the car. Bonnie knew nothing of Anne's purchase of the car and had not instructed her to sign any contract on her behalf. Bonnie refused to accept the car when Anne presented it to her so Anne left it on the side of the street where it was vandalized. Bonnie is probably:

   a. not liable on the contract because Anne had no authority to sign the contract for her.

b. not liable on the contract because she did not like the car.

c. liable on the contract because Anne had apparent authority to sign for her.

d. liable on the contract because she ratified the purchase.

e. liable on the contract because she was negligent in failing to return the car to the dealership.

DISCUSSION

(a) Anne had no authority to enter into a contract on behalf of Bonnie. Bonnie would not, therefore, be liable. Only Anne would be a party to the contract. The fact that she signed the contract as agent for Bonnie would have no effect on her liability because she did not have actual authority from Bonnie to enter any contract at all. Principals are liable on contracts entered into by their agents with actual authority whether or not they like the fruits of the contract. Bonnie would not be liable for the car even if she liked it because she did not enter into a contract to purchase it, and she never took possession of it. Anne had no power of attorney and Bonnie had not represented that she was her agent so Anne did not have apparent authority. Bonnie would have been liable for the car if she had ratified the contract. She could have ratified the contract expressly by indicating that she would pay for it or by implication by taking possession of the car. In this case, she did neither of these things. Bonnie had no duty to return the car because she had nothing to do with Anne's purchase of it.

7. Henry and Jan entered into a written contract whereby Henry agreed to pay Jan $500 per month for one year in exchange for Jan's acting as Henry's sales agent in Denver. Henry gave Jan a power of attorney so that she could sign contracts for him. After two months, Henry told Jan that the deal was off, and she was fired. Which of the following is probably true?

a. Jan's apparent authority is terminated.

b. Jan's actual authority is terminated.

c. Both Jan's actual and apparent authority are terminated.

d. Jan's authority cannot be terminated until Henry pays her the remainder of her salary.

e. a court will enforce Jan's right to be Henry's agent.

DISCUSSION

(b) Actual authority is terminated when the agent is informed that the authority has been withdrawn or when the agent learns of facts that would result in the authority being terminated by law. Henry's informing Jan that she was fired terminated her actual authority. Jan's apparent authority could be terminated only by destroying the appearance that she was his agent. This could be accomplished by giving people who had contracted through her actual notice of the termination of authority and by destroying the power of attorney given to her. If a person's role as agent for the principal is widely known, constructive notice, in addition to actual notice, is sometimes required to terminate the apparent authority. Jan's authority can be terminated even if Henry is in breach of his contract with her. Jan's remedy would be to sue Henry for her salary in an action for breach of contract. Jan could not continue to act as Henry's agent once her actual authority was terminated. She may have had a right to be paid for her services, but this would not have included the right to continue to act as Henry's agent.

8. Donna had been Page's agent for twenty years. On the twenty-first year of her employment, Page fired her. After being fired, Donna entered into a typical contract with Warwick on Page's behalf without Page's consent. Warwick had done business with Page through Donna in the past but was particularly pleased with this deal because the terms gave him the usual amount of goods at an unusually good price. Page was probably:

    a. liable on the contract unless Warwick knew Donna had been fired.
    b. liable on the contract only if it was profitable for her.
    c. not liable on the contract because Donna had no actual authority.
    d. not liable on the contract because Donna had no apparent authority.
    e. liable on an undisclosed agency theory.

DISCUSSION

    (a)   When Warwick had done business with Page through Donna in the past, Donna acquired apparent authority to act as Page's agent in addition to her actual authority. Page's firing of Donna terminated her actual authority but not her apparent authority. Page would be bound by Donna's contract with Warwick unless Warwick had been given actual notice of the termination of Donna's authority, i.e. unless Warwick knew Donna had been fired. Whether the contract was profitable or not would be irrelevant unless Warwick was collaborating with Donna in defrauding Page. The term, undisclosed agency theory, is bogus.

9. Emma was Scott's employee. While driving the company truck to make a delivery, she decided to take a 25 mile detour to visit her girlfriend. Just before she reached her friend's house, she negligently ran down Ted. Ted sued Emma and Scott. Which of the following is probably true?

a. Neither will be liable if Ted has insurance.
b. Only Emma will be liable.
c. Only Scott will be liable if Emma had no property, money, or insurance.
d. Both Emma and Scott will be liable.
e. Only the insured party will be liable.

DISCUSSION

(b)   Only Emma will be liable to Ted whether or not Scott has insurance. If Ted has insurance, he could collect twice - once from the insurance company and once from Emma. However, most insurance policies contain a subrogation clause that requires the victim to reimburse the insurance company for any benefits received if money is collected from a tortfeasor. Scott would not be liable to Ted under the Doctrine of Respondeat Superior even though Emma was his employee because she was not within the scope of her employment when she took the detour to visit her friend. Since Scott would not be liable, his insurance would not pay for Ted's injuries.

10. Ken hired Eric to examine real property in Florida and, if the property was a good investment, to sign a promissory note in Ken's name and purchase the property for him. Eric liked the property and purchased it in his own name for himself using his own money. Ken probably:

a. can't sue Eric if his fees weren't paid prior to the purchase.
b. can recover damages or the property from Eric for breach of fiduciary duty.
c. has no remedy if the seller knew of Eric's agency and put the property in Eric's name anyway.
d. is liable to the seller if Eric's check bounces.
e. has breached his fiduciary duty to Eric.

DISCUSSION

(b)   Ken could successfully sue Eric for breach of fiduciary duty because Eric's action of purchasing the property for himself amounted to competition with the principal. The seller's knowledge of the agent's authority has no effect on the agent's liability for breach of fiduciary duty. Since Eric purchased the property for himself rather than for Ken, Ken would not be liable for payment for the property. Ken would owe no fiduciary duty to Eric because the fiduciary duty generated by the principal and agent relationship is owed only by the agent to the principal and not by the principal to the agent. The fiduciary duty of an agent comes into existence when a person consents to be the agent for another whether or not he has been paid.

Chapter 14
Partnerships

At common law, a business owned by a single individual, or proprietor, is called a sole proprietorship. If a business has more than one owner, it is a partnership. Corporations, limited partnerships and other limited liability business organizations were not generally available at common law. After the Revolutionary War, the colonies were faced with the choice of retaining the English Common Law or writing totally new systems of laws. It was decided that writing totally new laws would not be in the best interest of the states because it would take the courts many years to interpret their meaning during which the economy would suffer unnecessarily.

Instead, each state with English origins continued to embrace the English Common Law until such time as the state legislature changed it. Therefore, the common law became the law of most of the states of the United States after the Revolutionary War. The important consequence of this is that, in many respects, the courts treat organizations that are not clearly corporations or other entities entitled to limited liability as partnerships. Joint ventures, syndicates, improperly formed charities, improperly formed corporations, etc. are treated in much the same manner as partnerships because they have not been formed in compliance with statutes that alter the common law treatment of business organizations. Business organizations with more than one owner are still treated as partnerships in the absence of compliance with a statute making another type of organization possible. This chapter deals with the basic principles governing partnerships and the limited liability versions of these organizations authorized by statutes enacted since the Revolutionary War — limited partnerships.

I. PARTNERSHIP

A partnership is a group of co-owners carrying on a business for profit.

A "partnership" is a group of co-owners carrying on a business for profit. Partners must be co-owners of a business intended to earn a profit. They must contribute to the capital of the partnership to be co-owners. Their contribution can be money, property or services. Merely sharing in the profits of a business does not normally make one a partner in the absence of some contribution to the capital of the business. The partnership must also be organized for the purpose of making a profit. A charity or a nonprofit cooperative cannot be organized as a partnership because these organizations are not formed for the purpose of making a profit for the co-owners.

A partnership must also be organized for the purpose of carrying on a business. "Joint ventures" are not partnerships. A joint venture is an organization formed for the purpose of a single transaction or limited set of transactions rather than for carrying on a business. Joint ventures are treated in much the same manner as partnerships. However, it is important to remember the term, joint venture, for future research because there are a few differences between partnerships and joint ventures due to the fact that only a limited number of transactions is intended.

Terry and Lisa agreed that Lisa would purchase a $60,000 truck equipped for cleaning septic tanks. Terry would use the truck to answer calls for assistance, and the fees collected would be split between them with Terry receiving 30% and Lisa receiving 70%. They also agreed that Lisa would be solely responsible for all expenses. When they began business, Terry and Lisa were not partners because they were not co-owners. Lisa was the sole proprietor of the business, and Terry was merely an employee working for a commission because he had not contributed to the capital.

Paula and Carol decided to open a dry cleaning business together. Paula contributed the land and building while Carol contributed all of the necessary equipment. They shared profits after the expenses were paid each month. They were partners because they were co-owners carrying on a business for profit. They would have been partners even if the business consistently realized losses because the business must only be intended to earn a profit. If they had purchased a sail boat for recreational use instead of the dry cleaning business, they would not have been partners because the boat would not have been used in a business for the purpose of earning a profit.

Essential Vocabulary

1. partnership
2. joint venture

II. PARTNERSHIP AGREEMENT

A partnership is formed by express or implied agreement to last for a term or at will.

All partnerships are formed by "express" or "implied" partnership agreements. Since partnership agreements are comprised of promises that the courts will enforce, they are contracts. An express partnership agreement is a partnership contract made with words that can be verbal or written. A written partnership agreement is called "articles of partnership." An implied partnership agreement is an agreement that is imposed upon the parties by the law because they have behaved like partners. An implied partnership is formed when two or more parties carry on a business as co-owners for profit without an express partnership agreement or with only an incomplete express partnership agreement.

In express partnership agreements, partners agree to whatever terms they desire. In implied partnership agreements, the terms are provided by state partnership acts published in state codes. The terms of partnership in the state partnership acts are generally binding upon the parties only in the absence of an express agreement to the contrary. If the parties to express partnership agreements fail to deal with some aspect of their relationships, state partnership acts are used to settle their rights and responsibilities. The partnership acts in force in most states are quite similar.

When partnerships are created, they are either intended to last for a definite or indefinite duration. Partnerships organized for a definite length of time are called "partnerships for a term." Those partnerships in which the duration is not specified or cannot be determined are called "partnerships at will." A partner can withdraw from a partnership any time. However, withdrawal from a partnership for a term before the term has ended is called a "wrongful withdrawal." A partner is liable for wrongful withdrawal from the partnership as a breach of the partnership contract. A withdrawal from a partnership for a term after the term has ended is not a breach of the partnership agreement and is not actionable. Such a withdrawal is often called a "rightful withdrawal." Withdrawals from a partnership at will are rightful at any time since the parties only agree to remain partners as long as they desire or "will" to do so.

The withdrawal of a partner results in the dissolution of the partnership. This may or may not actually mean the end of the business itself. In some cases, the existing partners and others may buy the withdrawing partner's interest and continue to operate the business under the same name. Sometimes after dissolution, the partners will wind up the business by selling the partnership assets and using the proceeds of the sale to pay the creditors. After the creditors have been paid, any money remaining is distributed to the partners.

When a partnership is created for a term longer than one year, articles of partnership are required by the Statute of Frauds. Partnerships in which the duration is not specified are partnerships at will that can terminate within a year so no writing is required. Notice that articles of partnership are normally not required under the Statute of Frauds for partnerships that are at will or organized for a term shorter than one year. The partnership interest that one purchases when she becomes a partner is a contractual right to share in management, profits, losses and the other incidents of partnership rather than specific partnership property. A partnership interest is intangible personal property rather than real property regardless of what type of property the partnership owns. If, however, the partnership agreement itself is intended to function as a power of attorney authorizing the partners to enter into contracts for the purchase or sale of real property, articles of partnership would be required since a power of attorney is a written document.

Alice and Boris entered into a partnership agreement in which they agreed to invest $800,000 each and purchase an apartment complex to manage for profit. They would not be required to have articles of partnership because their partnership was organized without stating a duration. It is, therefore, a partnership at will that can be completed within one year. The Statute of Frauds does not require articles of partnership even though the partnership will be purchasing real property. The contract between Alice and Boris is for the purchase of partnership interests which are contractual rights regardless of what assets the partnership will own or acquire. The contract between the partnership and the owner of the apartment complex in which the partnership purchases the complex will need to be evidenced by a written contract or memorandum because that contract, rather than the partnership agreement, will be for the purchase of real property.

Essential Vocabulary

1. express partnership agreement
2. articles of partnership
3. implied partnership agreement
4. partnerships for a term
5. partnerships at will
6. wrongful withdrawal
7. rightful withdrawal

III. AUTHORITY

General partners have both actual and apparent authority in the regular course of business; otherwise, they have no authority.

Partners are not merely "special agents" of the partnership. They are the "general agents" of the partnership for the purpose of entering into contracts on behalf of the partnership. A "special agent" is an agent that is authorized to conduct only a single transaction or a limited number of transactions. General agents are agents that have authority to enter into all contracts connected with a particular business. Unless the partners have limited the actual authority of a partner, a partner, as the general agent of the partnership, has actual authority to make offers, acceptances and receive performances on behalf of the partnership in the regular course of business. Also, partners may have apparent authority to enter into such contracts with parties who know that they are partners by virtue of the other partners' creation of the appearance of partnership.

In this way, the rules governing the actual and apparent authority of agents are applied to partners. This authority extends only to transactions in "the regular course of business." The regular course of business is the usual manner in which the partnership does business. A retail hardware store usually sells its inventory to its customers a few items at a time. Such sales would be in the regular course of business. If the store were to sell its entire inventory to a single purchaser, the transaction would not be in the regular course of business. A partner in the hardware business described above would have actual and apparent authority to enter into the usual contracts for the sale of the inventory to customers. However, he would have no authority to enter into the bulk sale of the store's inventory. All partners in the hardware business would need to enter into such a contract together to bind the partnership.

As agents of the partnership, partners owe each other the same fiduciary duties that all agents owe their principals. Partners have a fiduciary duty to: account, avoid competition, obey, use reasonable care, and disclose. Some students find the acronym "AACORD" a useful way to remember the fiduciary duties. Any violation of this duty is actionable by the partners through suing for breach of fiduciary duty. The partnership can, however, be bound by a partner's acts in violation of his fiduciary duty by virtue of his actual and apparent authority to enter into contracts on behalf of the partnership in the regular course of business.

Carl, Doris and Elvis entered into a partnership to operate a small restaurant. The three introduced themselves to the sales manager of a restaurant supply house as partners in the restaurant business and opened an account. After purchasing supplies in a number of transactions over the year, the three decided in a meeting that Doris and Elvis would not have authority to enter into contracts for the purchase of supplies in the future. Instead, Carl would be the sole purchasing agent for the partnership. Prior to this meeting, all of the partners had actual authority to enter into contracts for the purchase of supplies because they were partners. They also had apparent authority to contract for the partnership because they had created the appearance of being partners by virtue of their representations to the sales manager of the restaurant supply house. The meeting terminated the actual, but not the apparent, authority of Doris and Elvis to purchase supplies. The partnership would be bound by Carl's contracts with the supply house because he had both actual and apparent authority. However, the partnership would also be bound by the contracts of Doris and Elvis with the supply house because they would retain their apparent authority until the sales manager was notified of the new arrangement. If, however, Doris or Elvis had entered into contracts with the supply house without actual authority, they would have been liable to Carl and the partnership for breach of fiduciary duty in failing to obey their instructions.

Essential Vocabulary

1. special agent
2. general agent
3. the regular course of business
4. fiduciary duty of partners

IV. MAJORITY AND UNANIMOUS APPROVAL

Partnership action requires majority approval in the regular course of business; otherwise, unanimous approval is required.

When partners vote on usual business matters, only a "majority" approval of the proposed action is required. Majority approval is approval by more than half of the partners. If the matter is not within the regular course of business, a "unanimous" approval is required or no action can be taken. A unanimous approval is approval by every partner. If a partner undertakes some action on behalf of the partnership without the necessary approval, he may be liable to the partnership. The fiduciary duty requiring partners to obey instructions require partners to obey the will of the majority on matters within the regular course of business and to obtain unanimous approval for actions that are not within the regular course of business. Unusual actions or matters that are not within the regular course of business include, but are not limited to, admitting a new partner, filing for bankruptcy, selling the business, and changing the partnership agreement.

Frank, Gary and Harold entered into a dry cleaning partnership. Frank decided that it would be a good idea for the partnership to purchase a new steam iron. When the partners voted, Frank and Gary were in favor of the purchase, but Harold was not. Purchasing equipment necessary to conduct the partnership business was within the regular course of business so only a majority vote was required. The new steam iron could be purchased. If, instead, Frank had wanted to purchase and operate a car wash, a unanimous vote would have been required because this is not in the regular course of this partnership's business. No car wash could be purchased because Harold disagreed.

Essential Vocabulary

1. majority approval
2. unanimous approval

V. PARTNERSHIP BY ESTOPPEL

People creating the appearance of partnership will be liable as though they are partners.

People who represent themselves as partners give each other apparent authority to contract on behalf of the partnership. This is an application of the agency rules governing apparent authority since partners are general agents for the partnership. If the parties representing to others that they are partners are actually partners they have both actual and apparent authority to contract for the partnership in the regular course of business. If people present themselves as partners to others when they are not in fact partners, they create the appearance of a partnership and give each other apparent authority to enter into contracts for the spurious partnership. In this case, the parties are said to be "partners by estoppel." Partners by estoppel are parties that are liable to third parties as partners even though they are not actually partners. The word, "estop," is an archaic form of the modern word, "stop." A person becomes a partner by estoppel when the law estops or stops him from denying that he is a partner due to his representations regarding the existence of a partnership. The law will stop parties who misrepresent themselves to be partners from denying their liability to creditors who relied on their representations. This doctrine affects only the liability of the parties making the fraudulent representations and does not result in any of the other incidents of partnership listed as rules in this chapter.

Julie and Candace were partners who operated a garden shop called "The Nursery." The partnership was able to purchase gardening supplies wholesale from Wholesale Gardens Co. because of the volume of their business. In an effort to help Leslie, a close friend, landscape a new home, Candace introduced Leslie as a partner to the salespeople at Wholesale Gardens so that she could purchase her supplies at the same price as the partnership. Candace did not inform Julie of this, and she told Leslie to pay cash and refrain from charging any of her supplies to the partnership account. Leslie did not follow these instructions. She charged supplies costing $2000 to the partnership account. Later, the partnership had financial difficulties and gradually became an additional $10,000 in arrears on its account with Wholesale Gardens.

Wholesale Gardens sued Julie, Candace and Leslie. Julie would be liable only for the $10,000 charged by the partnership. She would not be liable on the $2,000 charged by Leslie because Leslie was not a partner and had no authority to contract for her or the partnership. Since Julie was not a party to creating the appearance that Leslie was a partner, she would not be liable under the doctrine of partnership by estoppel. Candace would be liable for $12,000. She would be liable for the partnership debt of $10,000 because she was Julie's partner in The Nursery. She would also be liable for the $2,000 charged by Leslie under the doctrine of partnership by estoppel because her representations to the salespeople at Wholesale Gardens created the appearance that Leslie was a partner. Leslie would also be liable for $12,000. She would be liable for $2,000 because she charged the material without actual authority. She would also be liable for $10,000 charged by The Nursery after her introduction to the salespeople at Wholesale Gardens under the doctrine of partnership by estoppel. She created the appearance that she was a partner by going along with the ruse. The law will estop her from denying liability now that Wholesale Gardens, a creditor, has relied upon her being a partner by extending credit to The Nursery.

Essential Vocabulary

1. partners by estoppel
2. estop

VI. PROFITS, LOSSES AND VOTES

Absent contrary agreement, profits, losses and votes are shared equally regardless of investment.

When the partners expressly agree as to how profits, losses, and voting rights will be divided among themselves, the express partnership agreement will be enforced as a contract according to its terms. In the absence of an express agreement, the partners have an implied agreement with the terms supplied by the state partnership act. These statutes indicate that in the absence of agreement, profits, losses, and voting rights will be allocated equally among the partners regardless of investment.

Mark, Paul and Nemo entered into a partnership. Mark invested $30,000 in cash. Paul contributed a building valued at $200,000. Nemo contributed $50,000 in cash and $20,000 labor for the partnership. The partnership was developed so rapidly that the only detail they had agreed upon was that Mark and Nemo were entitled to 1/4 of the profits each and that Paul was entitled to 1/2 of the profits. During the first year of operation, the business made a profit of $20,000. During the second year, Mark and Nemo wanted to hire an additional clerk, but Paul disagreed. At the end of the second year, the partnership had not made a profit and $9,000 was needed to be paid to various taxing authorities.

The agreement regarding the division of profits was binding on the partners. Mark's and Nemo's shares of the profits would each be $5,000, and Paul's share would be $10,000. Since the agreement was silent as to voting rights and losses, each of the partners would be entitled to one vote each on partnership business regardless of their investment. Hiring the clerk would have been within the regular course of business so only majority approval would have been required. The clerk could be hired over Paul's objection. In the absence of agreement, losses must be allocated equally among the partners so, at the end of the second year, each partner would have needed to contribute $3,000 to cover one-third of the tax debt. If a partner could not contribute his share of the losses, the other partners would be liable for it and would need to pay it for him. The partner that could not pay his share of the losses would then be liable to the partners who had paid the obligation for him.

VII. LIABILITY

Partners have unlimited, joint liability for partnership debts and unlimited, joint and several liability for partnership torts.

Of course, the partnership is liable for all partnership debts. If, however, partnership assets are insufficient to cover partnership liabilities, the partners' personal assets are subject to the claims of partnership creditors. Since the creditors can seize partners' personal assets and are not limited to using partnership assets to satisfy their claims, partners' liability for partnership debts is called "unlimited liability." Unlimited liability is liability that extends to all of the assets of a debtor. This is understandable since at common law everyone has unlimited liability for their debts. Partners also have "joint liability" for partnership debts arising from the partnership business. Because partners carry on a business together, or jointly, claims against the partnership must be resolved against all of the partners together. Partners must be sued together in one action when claims against the partnership are taken to court. Combining these two terms, it can be said that partners have unlimited, joint liability for partnership debts other than debts arising from tort liability.

Partners are responsible for the torts of their employees and each other that are committed within the scope of partnership business under the Doctrine of Respondeat Superior. Since a tort is a wrongful action, it is specifically the responsibility of the partner or partnership employee committing it. For this reason, the individual committing the tort has "several liability" for the tort. A person has several liability when his liability can be severed from the liability of others so he can be sued alone and without other parties being joined in the lawsuit.

The Doctrine of Respondeat Superior subjects partnerships to vicarious liability for torts committed in the course of partnership business. Partners have "joint and several liability" for torts committed by employees and other partners within the scope of partnership business as well. Partners have joint and several liability for torts because they can be sued jointly with the other partners in an action or severally by themselves in separate actions. The victims of torts are not limited to partnership assets to satisfy their claims so the liability for tort claims is unlimited. Hence, the liability for tort claims against the partnership is "unlimited, joint and several Liability."

Rita and Sandy were partners in a retail shoe store. They had one employee, Tina. One day, Tina was instructed by Rita to purchase a special rotating shoe display from a supplier and charge it to the partnership. Tina obtained the display as she was instructed. While she was assembling it, her hair became entangled in the gears. When a customer laughed, Tina grabbed him and tied him to a shelf with an electrical cord so that when the shelves rotated, the customer was rotated as though he had been attached to a giant rotisserie. The customer finally extricated himself and sued for battery and false imprisonment. Rita then refused to pay for the display and the supplier sued for breach of contract.

Tina was liable for the torts because she had committed them, and Rita and Sandy were vicariously liable by the Doctrine of Respondeat Superior since Tina had committed the torts while engaged in her work for the partnership. Because the partnership has unlimited, joint and several liability for torts committed within the scope of the partnership business, the customer can sue Tina and the partners jointly in one action, or he can sue Tina in one action and the others separately. If partnership assets are inadequate to satisfy the customer's claims, the customer can pursue the personal assets of Rita, Sandy, and Tina because their liability for tort claims against the partnership is unlimited.

The partnership is liable to the supplier for the display since Tina was its agent in entering into the purchase contract. Rita and Sandy had given Tina actual authority to purchase it so Tina would not be liable for payment. The supplier would need to sue all of the partners jointly in a single action against the partnership since the liability for partnership debts is joint. If partnership assets are inadequate to satisfy the claim of the supplier for the price of the display, the partners' personal assets are subject to the claim since partners have unlimited liability for partnership debts arising from breach of contract.

Essential Vocabulary

1. unlimited liability
2. joint liability
3. unlimited, joint liability
4. several liability
5. joint and several liability
6. Doctrine of Respondeat Superior
7. unlimited, joint and several liability

VIII. LIABILITY OF NEW GENERAL PARTNERS

New general partners have limited liability for antecedent debts and unlimited liability for subsequent debts.

A basic principal of law is that liability follows control. The more control an individual has of something, the more responsible she will be for the consequences of exercising that control. When a new partner is admitted to the partnership by unanimous vote of the existing partners, she comes into an existing business with existing liabilities that were incurred by the partnership prior to her becoming a partner. Since she had no control over incurring these "antecedent debts," she will have only limited liability for them. Antecedent debts are debts incurred by a partnership prior to the admission of the new partner to the partnership. New partners have only "limited liability" for antecedent partnership debts. Limited liability is liability that is limited to the assets invested by the new partner. Creditors are limited to the new partner's investment for satisfying antecedent claims against the partnership. If the partnership assets are not sufficient to satisfy the creditors' claims, they will not be able to reach the new partner's personal assets.

Once the new partner has been admitted to the partnership and has acquired the right to vote on partnership business, she has control over partnership affairs. Therefore, the liability for "subsequent debts" is "unlimited liability." Subsequent debts are debts that are incurred by the partnership after the new partner has been admitted to the partnership. Unlimited liability is liability that is not limited to the partnership assets. Creditors are allowed to satisfy their claims against the partnership for subsequent debts from both the assets invested in the partnership by the new partner and her personal assets if partnership assets are inadequate. A partner's personal assets include all assets not invested in the partnership e.g. television sets, skis, pool tables, etc. Partnership creditors could also seize a partner's wages, bank account deposits, and accounts receivable which are unrelated to the partnership to obtain payment of partnership debts.

Unis and Vern were partners in a chicken hatchery, and they both unanimously agreed to allow Warren to purchase a one-third interest in the partnership and become a partner for $1,000. At the time Warren joined the partnership, it had assets worth $2,000 and owed creditors $24,000. After Warren joined, the firm incurred an additional $10,000 in debt, and all but $1,000 of the assets were used to cover operating expenses. When the creditors took the remaining $1,000 to satisfy partnership debts, the partnership would be left owing $33,000.

Ultimately, Unis and Vern would each have had unlimited liability for the full $33,000 remaining debt, but Warren would have had unlimited liability for only $10,000 of the partnership debts. Warren would not have had unlimited liability on the $24,000 debt incurred prior to his joining the firm. Warren's liability for these antecedent debts is limited to the $1,000 he invested.

Although Unis and Vern, and to the limited extent of $10,000, Warren, would face ultimate responsibility for all of the remaining debts of the partnership, each partner should contribute to the payment of the remaining partnership debts. If each partner had sufficient personal assets to pay his share, Vern and Unis would each pay one-half of the $24,000 owing on antecedent debts and one-third of the subsequent debts or $15,000 each. Warren would pay nothing on the antecedent debts, but he would be responsible for one-third of the subsequent debts, or $3000.

If Unis and Warren did not have sufficient assets to pay their share, the creditors could collect the entire $33,000 debt from Vern leaving him with an action for contribution against Unis for $15,000 and Warren for $3,000. Hopefully, he could have pursued his actions for contribution at a later date when financial conditions improved. A similar result would have followed if Vern and Warren did not have sufficient assets to pay their share. In this case,

Unis would have been required to pay the entire debt and pursue Vern and Warren for contribution.

If Unis and Vern were unable to pay their share, Warren would have been liable for a maximum of $10,000 since this is the total of the debts incurred subsequent to his joining the firm. Creditors would not have been able to recover any of the $24,000 antecedent debts from Warren's personal assets. If Warren paid the entire $10,000 for which he was ultimately liable, he could have pursued Unis and Vern for their contribution to payment of the partnership debts. If the creditors were unable to collect portions of the debt from the partners due to their lack of partnership and personal assets, they would have needed to accept their losses without relief. It is, therefore, very important for creditors to carefully examine assets, debts, payment histories, and other factors prior to advancing credit. When debtors have no assets, creditors often go unpaid.

Essential Vocabulary

1. antecedent debts
2. subsequent debts
3. limited liability
4. unlimited liability

IX. LIMITED PARTNERSHIPS

A limited partnership is a group of general and limited partners carrying on a business for profit after filing a limited partnership certificate with the state.

A limited partnership is one type of "limited liability business organization." A limited liability business organization is a form of business that affords all or some of its owners limited liability. Unlike general partners, some of the owners of such organizations risk only their investment in the company. Creditors are limited to the company's assets for satisfaction of their claims whether their claims arise from contracts or torts. Limited liability business organizations were not available under the English Common Law and were not incorporated into the common law adopted by each state after the War for Independence. Consequently, all states have enacted statutes altering the common law by allowing the formation of limited liability business organizations. These statutes require investors seeking limited liability to take specific steps in the formation of their businesses and to file some form of documentation with the state for recognition. Failure to file as required by statute may result in the business being treated like a partnership. In fact, businesses that don't fall into any of the statutorily defined categories of limited liability business organizations are generally treated as partnerships.

A limited partnership affords protection for some partners by limiting their liability for partnership debts to their investment. "General partners" have all the powers and responsibilities of partners as discussed above. General partners are the partners who control the partnership and, therefore, have unlimited liability for the partnership debts. "Limited partners" merely join the limited partnership as investors. Limited partners are the partners who invest in the partnership in expectation of a return without the power to control partnership business. Limited partnerships must be authorized by state statute because this type of business organization was unknown at common law. To qualify for special treatment as a limited partnership, the organizers must comply with the statute authorizing this form of business organization. The limited partnership acts published in the state codes require that a "certificate of limited partnership" be filed with a governmental office. These certificates operate as notice to the public that the partnership provides some of the partners with limited liability. Failure to file the certificate as required can result in unlimited liability for both general partners and partners intended to have limited liability.

Essential Vocabulary

1. limited liability business organization
2. general partners
3. limited partners
4. certificate of limited partnership

X. LIABILITY OF LIMITED PARTNERS

Limited partners lose their limited liability by improper certificate, name, management or payment for interest.

If the partners do not comply with the state statute that makes the formation of a limited partnership possible, they will incur unlimited liability as general partners. This means that partnership creditors will have unlimited access to the assets owned by the limited partners and can reach their personal assets as well as their investment in the business.

Failure to file the required certificate of limited partnership or filing improper or fraudulent certificates can result in the limited partnership being treated as an ordinary partnership with unlimited liability for general and limited partners alike. The filing is required to give creditors and others notice of the limited liability of some of the partners. If improper filing results in someone being misled, all of the partners are responsible.

While it is permissible for the name of the limited partnership to contain the "given name" or "Christian name" of a limited partner, it must not contain a limited partner's "surname." A person's given name, sometimes called his Christian name, is his first name. These terms come from the custom in Christian faiths of giving children their first names as infants when they are christened. A person's surname is his family name or last name. A limited partner's surname may not be used in the partnership name because this could mislead creditors into believing that the limited partner is a general partner with unlimited liability. If the surname of a limited partner is included in the name of the limited partnership, the limited partner whose name was used loses his limited liability and incurs unlimited liability for partnership debts.

Since liability follows control, limited partners cannot enjoy limited liability while exercising control over the business. The general partners have unlimited liability because they have control over the operation of the business by virtue of their power to vote on partnership affairs. If a limited partner votes on partnership business or otherwise participates in management, he will have unlimited liability for the partnership debts.

Some limited partnership statutes require that the limited partners invest only property or money. Investments of services will not be allowed. Partnership interests for which the partnership has not received proper payment are called "watered interests." This metaphor comes from the illicit practice of diluting liquor with water and selling it as full strength when it is not. A limited partner is liable for the amount of "water" on his share. Water is the amount owing on his interest in the partnership. His liability for the water is unlimited in that the partners can reach his personal assets to satisfy his unpaid obligation. He does not, however, have unlimited liability for other partnership obligations by virtue of owning a watered interest. The liability for the water on a limited partnership interest is discharged once the limited partner fully pays for his interest.

Essential Vocabulary

1. surname
2. given name or Christian name
3. watered interest

XI. DISSOLUTION

A partnership dissolves when a partner withdraws, and the actual authority of remaining partners is limited to winding up while their apparent authority is unaffected until terminated by notice.

Once a partner leaves the partnership, the "dissolution of the partnership" instantly results. A partnership is dissolved when the partnership can no longer continue to conduct new partnership business. Dissolution of a partnership results in the actual authority of the partners to conduct partnership business being limited to "winding up the partnership." Winding up the partnership is the process by which the former partners gather the partnership assets, pay the partnership creditors, and distribute any remaining assets to the partners or their "personal representatives." When a partner dies, her business affairs are concluded by her personal representative. A personal representative winds up the business affairs of a decedent.

Dissolution of the partnership terminates the actual authority of the partners to conduct new business on behalf of the partnership that is not necessary to wind up the business. The apparent authority of partners, however, is unaffected by dissolution of the partnership until parties who have done business with the partnership receive "actual notice" of the dissolution and those who were aware of the partnership without having done business with the partners receive "constructive notice" of the dissolution of the partnership. Actual notice is written or verbal notice given to the parties that have done business with the partnership. People who were aware of the partnership but had never actually done business with it should be notified by "constructive notice." Constructive notice is notice printed in a newspaper or magazine of general circulation in the area where the partnership did its business.

Winding up the partnership business can mean that the assets are actually gathered and liquidated with creditors being paid in full while the remaining funds are distributed to the partners according to their investments and the partnership agreement. The final payment of creditors and distribution to partners results in the "termination of the partnership." The termination of a partnership is its end in the eyes of the law. Sometimes, however, some partners may wish to form a new partnership to continue the business. When this occurs, the winding up process is merely carried out on paper so that the withdrawing partner can be paid for her interest. Once the distribution to the withdrawing partner has been made, the partnership is terminated, and all subsequent transactions are completed by a new partnership. The new partnership could use the name of the terminated partnership so customers may never know of the change. In both cases, the dissolution is the point in time marking the beginning of the process of winding up, and the termination of the former partnership is the point marking the end of this process.

Sally and Arnold entered into a partnership without specifying its duration. Arnold died leaving his interest in the partnership to his wife, Alice, by will. After attending the funeral, but before creditors had been notified, Sally borrowed money for the business from a lender that did not know of Arnold's death. The loan was made to the partnership with Sally signing on behalf of the partnership for the purpose of remodeling her office. A few months later, the lender, who had not been paid according to the contract sued the partnership for breach of contract. All partnership assets would be subject to the lender's claims because no notice of dissolution had been given. Although Sally's actual authority was limited to winding up the affairs of the partnership when she learned of Arnold's death, her apparent authority could only be terminated by giving actual notice to those who had done business with the partnership in the past and constructive notice to those who were familiar with the partnership but had not actually done business with it. Since Sally would have had only apparent authority to enter into the loan contract, she would have been liable to Arnold's estate and the lender. If any of the money owed to the lender had to be paid out of Arnold's share of the partnership assets, his personal representative would have an action for breach of fiduciary duty against Sally.

Essential Vocabulary

1. dissolution of the partnership
2. winding up the partnership
3. personal representative
4. actual notice
5. constructive notice
6. termination of the partnership

XII. PRIORITIES ON DISSOLUTION

On dissolution claims will be satisfied in the following order:

(1) creditors,

(2) loans from partners,

(3) investment,

(4) profit.

The dissolution of a partnership is followed by the process of winding up or liquidation. The assets of the partnership are gathered and the creditors are paid. If the assets do not generate enough money to pay the creditors and return the partners' investments to them, the question of who will be paid first arises. This is really a question of the priority of claims against the partnership assets. When bankruptcy is not filed, the parties' claims against the partnership are satisfied as follows:

(1) Claims of *creditors* who were not partners in the partnership must be fully paid before any of the investors can be paid.

(2) *Loans* made to the partnership by partners are satisfied after all other creditors have been paid because the partners had control of the business while the other creditors did not.

(3) The *investments* of partners are returned after the creditors have been fully paid.

(4) Any *profits* remaining in the partnership are distributed after all claims against the partnership have been satisfied.

Some students find that the list of priorities above can be conveniently remembered by memorizing the acronym, "CLIP." The key words in the list used to form the acronym are italicized. The theory behind the list is simply that creditors will be paid before partners and liability or responsibility for losses follows control.

Larry and Margaret were partners in a tire recapping business. Margaret informed Larry that she was withdrawing from the partnership. At the time of her withdrawal, the company owed rubber suppliers $30,000. It also owed Larry $10,000 for a loan he had personally made to the partnership. Larry and Margaret had each invested $20,000 to get the business going. These claims against the partnership from both creditors and Larry and Margaret totaled $80,000. If the assets at the time of the dissolution were worth $35,000, the rubber suppliers would receive $30,000, and Larry would receive only $5,000 of the $10,000 owed by virtue of his loan.

This would leave a loss of $45,000 that would need to be shared equally in the absence of an agreement to the contrary. Margaret and Larry would each need to contribute $22,500 to cover this loss. After this was contributed, Larry would be entitled to receive the $5,000 due on his loan to the partnership and his $20,000 investment. Margaret would be entitled to the return of her $20,000 investment. Notice that the net effect of this transaction requires Margaret to pay Larry $2,500 to equalize their losses so that each party loses $22,500.

Further practice may be useful to be certain that the application of this rule is clearly understood. Using the example above, assume that at the time of Margaret's withdrawal, the company owed rubber suppliers $30,000. Assume it also owed Larry $10,000 for a loan he had personally made to the partnership. And assume that Larry had invested $30,000 and Margaret had invested $10,000 to get the business going. These claims against the partnership would have totaled $80,000. If the assets at the time of the dissolution were worth $35,000, the net loss to the partnership would be $45,000. The rubber suppliers would receive $30,000 from the partnership assets, and Larry would receive only $5,000 of the $10,000 owed by virtue of his loan.

This would leave the loss of $45,000 to be shared equally in the absence of an agreement to the contrary. Margaret and Larry would each need to contribute $22,500 to cover this loss. After contribution, Larry would be entitled to receive the $5,000 due on his loan to the partnership and his $30,000 investment. Margaret would be entitled to the return of her $10,000 investment. Notice that the net effect of this transaction would require Margaret to pay Larry $12,500 to equalize their losses so that both Margaret and Larry would wind up losing $22,500.

Essential Vocabulary

1. CLIP

CHECK YOUR UNDERSTANDING

DIRECTIONS: Read each of the following questions. Choose the best answer and study
                   the discussion of the question.

1. Frank and Derrick entered into business together. Frank contributed all of the assets
    and managed the business. Derrick contributed his expertise as a salesperson and
    handled all sales for the company. It was agreed that Derrick would receive 20% of
    the gross amount of sales, and Frank would take 80%, pay the bills, and keep
    whatever was left. Which of the following is probably true?

    a. Frank and Derrick will be jointly and severally liable for business debts.
    b. Frank and Derrick will be jointly liable for business debts.
    c. Creditors will only be able to reach business assets to satisfy business debts.
    d. Frank will be liable for 80% of business debts, and Derrick will be liable for
        20%.
    e. Frank will be liable for 100% of business debts, and Derrick will not be liable
        for them at all because he was not a partner.

DISCUSSION

    (e)   Frank's business was a sole proprietorship because it did not meet the
definition of a partnership. A partnership is a group of co-owners carrying on a
business for profit. Derrick was not a co-owner because he had not invested in the
business. Merely sharing in the gross receipts of a business is not sufficient to make
one a co-owner in the absence of an investment. Since Derrick was not a partner, he
would not be liable for company debts. The creditors would be able to reach Frank's
personal assets if company assets were inadequate to satisfy the business debts.
Frank's liability for these debts would be unlimited.

2. Adrian and Slim entered into a partnership. The articles of partnership provided that
    the partnership would have a duration of five years. Slim withdrew from the
    partnership over Adrian's objection after only two years because he was bored by the
    business. Adrian sued Slim for damages. Slim would probably:

    a. be liable for tortious withdrawal.
    b. be liable for wrongful liquidation.

c. be liable for wrongful withdrawal.

d. not be liable if he could show that he could make more money in a different business.

e. not be liable if he could show that Adrian's conservative attitude had severely limited the partnership's business opportunities.

DISCUSSION

(c) Adrian and Slim entered into a partnership for a term of five years that was evidenced by written articles of partnership. Slim's withdrawal was wrongful because the term had not yet expired. This constituted a breach of the partnership agreement. Wrongful withdrawal is a breach of contract rather than a tort. The liquidation of a partnership is the winding up of its affairs by gathering the assets, selling them, and distributing the proceeds to creditors and partners. This is not involved here. Wrongful withdrawal constitutes a breach of contract regardless of the fact that the withdrawing partner could make more money in a different venture. Legitimate disagreements over company policy do not justify withdrawal of a partner before the end of the term of the partnership.

3. George, Lyndon, Washington, Bains, and Johnson entered into a partnership agreement wherein they agreed to open and operate a truck tire distributorship. George contributed 80% of the capital invested and each of the others contributed 5%. At a partnership meeting, George suggested buying the land next door to rent to people as part of the business. All of the partners voted in favor of the purchase of the rental property except Bains. In a vote on whether to increase the company's selection of tires, Washington, Bains, and Johnson voted in favor while George and Lyndon voted against the proposal. Which of the following is probably correct?

a. The land cannot be purchased, and the inventory cannot be increased.

b. The land can be purchased, but the inventory cannot be increased.

c. The land cannot be purchased, but the inventory can be increased.

d. The land can be purchased, and the inventory can be increased.

e. The voting was invalid due to lack of meeting of the minds.

DISCUSSION

(c) Partnership action requires majority approval in the regular course of business; otherwise, unanimous approval is required. The partnership was organized to distribute truck tires. Renting land was not part of the business contemplated by the parties. Increasing inventory, on the other hand, would be a normal part of operating a tire distributorship. The land could not be purchased to produce rental income without unanimous approval of the partners. The selection of inventory could be increased because the majority of the partners approved of the action. George's vote would have no more weight than any other partner's vote in the absence of a provision in the partnership agreement linking voting power to the amount of capital invested in the partnership.

4.   When partners disagree about whether or not to fire one of their employees, which of the following is probably true?

   a.   A majority vote will decide the issue.
   b.   A 2/3 majority vote is necessary to decide the issue.
   c.   A unanimous vote is required to terminate an employee.
   d.   Partners cannot fire employees in this case.
   e.   Legal action would be necessary to authorize termination.

DISCUSSION

   (a)   Firing an employee is within the regular course of business of any partnership. Partnership action within the regular course of business can be taken upon the approval of a majority of the partners. No legal action is required to fire an employee. However, if the employee's termination is wrongful or without cause, it may involve the partnership in litigation or an increase in the company's unemployment insurance contributions.

5.   Abe, Bill, and Carl are partners in a business known as "American Pencil Company." Carl introduced his cousin, Paul, to the manager of Office Supply, Inc. as a partner so that he could get the American Pencil Company discount on office supplies. Paul was not a partner. Paul later charged supplies worth $3000 to American Pencil Company without authorization and used them in his own business. Who is liable to Office Supply Inc.?

   a.   Paul only
   b.   Paul and Carl
   c.   Paul, Carl, Abe, and Bill
   d.   Paul, Carl, Abe, Bill, and American Pencil Company
   e.   Paul, Carl, and American Pencil Company

DISCUSSION

   (b)   When Carl introduced Paul as a partner and Paul participated in the misrepresentation, they became partners by estoppel. Each had apparent authority to enter into transactions with Office Supply on behalf of the other. Paul was not actually a partner so he had no actual or apparent authority to charge the supplies to American Pencil Company. The partners of American Pencil Company other than Carl would not be liable for the supplies charged because they did not participate in creating the false appearance that Paul was a partner. Carl would be liable for the $3,000 debt as a partner by estoppel. Paul would be liable for charging the supplies without actual authority. If Carl ultimately paid the bill, he would have an action against Paul because Paul received the supplies.

6. West and Knoll entered into a partnership. Although the Partnership Act in their state provided for equal division of profits and losses, they agreed to divide the profits as follows: 70% for West and 30% for Knoll. If Knoll provided 80% of the assets and all of the labor for the business, he will get:

   a. 80% of the profits.
   b. 50% of the profits.
   c. 30% of the profits.
   d. nothing because the partnership is illegal.
   e. equitable relief because the agreement is unconscionable.

DISCUSSION

   (c)   The provisions of the state partnership statute would provide for the equal division of profits in the absence of a partnership agreement to the contrary. However, agreements dividing profits unequally are not illegal and will be enforced. The court would honor the agreement to give Knoll 30% of the profits. The agreement would not be unconscionable in the absence of gross misconduct on the part of West.

7. Rumpole and Hilda operated a trucking company. Their partnership agreement provided that only Hilda would drive company trucks. Rumpole decided to move a company truck that was blocking access to a company storage facility. Unfortunately, he negligently backed into Brown's Mercedes. Which of the following is probably correct?

   a. Rumpole and Hilda are jointly liable to Brown.
   b. Rumpole and Hilda are jointly liable to Brown, and Rumpole is liable to Hilda.
   c. Rumpole and Hilda are jointly and severally liable to Brown.
   d. Rumpole and Hilda are jointly and severally liable to Brown, and Rumpole is liable to Hilda.

e.   Only Rumpole is liable to Brown.

DISCUSSION

(d)   Rumpole and Hilda are jointly and severally liable to Brown for Rumpole's negligence. Negligence is a tort, and partners are jointly and severally liable for damages arising from torts committed in the scope of partnership business. Moving the truck to obtain access to a company storage facility was part of operating the business. Rumpole is liable for his own negligence and the partnership is liable under the Doctrine of Respondeat Superior. Rumpole and Hilda can be sued together or separately, i.e. jointly or severally. Rumpole will be liable to Hilda for violating the partnership agreement and his fiduciary duties to obey instructions and exercise reasonable care.

8.   Andy and Ben were partners who operated a janitorial business. After incurring liabilities in the amount of $100,000, they allowed John to purchase an interest in the partnership for $10,000. In two weeks, the three decided to dissolve the partnership. The only asset was the $10,000 contributed by John and the liabilities had not changed. Which of the following is probably correct?

a.   John is not entitled to the return of his $10,000, but he is not personally liable for the debts of the partnership.
b.   John is entitled to the return of his $10,000, and he is not liable for the debts.
c.   John is entitled to the return of his $10,000, but he will be liable for the debts.
d.   John is not entitled to the return of his $10,000, and he will be liable for the debts.
e.   John will not be liable to creditors, but he will be liable to Andy and Ben for 1/3 of the partnership debts remaining after the $10,000 has been paid to creditors.

DISCUSSION

(a)   The liabilities incurred prior to John's admission to the partnership as a new partner were antecedent debts. John's liability for antecedent debts was limited to his investment because he had no control over the company's activities when they were incurred. John will lose his investment due to his limited liability for the debts, but he will not be liable for any antecedent debts. Andy and Ben would have unlimited liability for all debts of the partnership. The creditors could reach their personal assets to satisfy claims.

9. Clark and Lois formed a limited partnership in which Clark was the general partner, and Lois was a limited partner. Each invested $30,000. When they decided to dissolve the partnership, only assets worth $30,000 remained, and the company owed $100,000 in debts. Lois will probably:

    a. lose her investment, but she will not be liable for the debts.
    b. lose her investment and be liable for $35,000.
    c. recover her investment but she must pay half of the debts.
    d. be liable for $70,000.
    e. be entitled to $15,000, but she will not be liable on the debts.

    DISCUSSION

    (a)   Limited partners have limited liability. Their risk is limited only to the assets invested in the limited partnership. Lois would not recover her investment, but she would not be liable for any portion of the remaining $70,000 in debts. Clark would have unlimited liability for the remainder of the debts because he had control of the company as a general partner.

10. Linn and Carol wanted to purchase limited partner interests in a limited partnership. The interests were worth $1000 each. In payment, Linn negotiated certain promissory notes she had received from a corporation to the firm without recourse, and Carol worked for the firm for one month as a nurse for her contribution. The promissory notes were not honored by the corporation and could not be collected. The creditors sued both Linn and Carol. Which of the following is probably true?

    a. Neither Linn nor Carol will be liable because they were limited partners.
    b. Linn will be liable because his contribution was ultimately worthless.
    c. Carol will be liable because her contribution was not money or property.
    d. Both Linn and Carol will be liable for their contributions.
    e. Both Linn and Carol will be personally liable for all of the debts of the limited partnership that cannot be satisfied out of partnership property.

    DISCUSSION

    (c)   Carol will be liable because her contribution was not money or property. Limited partners must contribute property or money for their limited partnership interests. Linn contributed the promissory notes which constituted property even though his indorsement without recourse would result in his release from liability if the notes were not honored. Carol's contribution violated the requirement that limited partnership interests must be purchased with money or property rather than services. Carol would be liable for the price of her share because her payment was not valid.

Her liability for the price of her interest would be unlimited and the partnership, partners, and creditors could reach her personal assets to satisfy this debt. She would not, however, have unlimited liability for any of the partnership debts. Her unlimited liability would be limited to the price of her interest. Some states have modified the requirement that limited partnership interests be purchased with money or property. The more restrictive rule is used in this text for ease of learning. As with all legal questions, one must actually research the laws of the state when a question arises to obtain a definitive answer. Memorization of the more restrictive rules will protect a manager until research can be completed.

11. Dissolution of a partnership:

   a. is caused by any partner withdrawing from the partnership.
   b. terminates the partnership immediately.
   c. always results in the end of the business.
   d. is the process of liquidation of assets, payment of creditors, and distribution of the residue to the partners.
   e. does not occur at the death of a partner if living partners wish to continue operating the business.

DISCUSSION

   (a) Dissolution of a partnership results anytime a partner withdraws. It does not terminate the existence of the partnership. The partnership must continue to exist during the process of winding up. Sometimes, some of the partners wish to continue the business after a partner withdraws. When this occurs, the winding up is primarily done on paper with the partners who wish to continue the business purchasing the withdrawing partner's interest. When a partner dies, he withdraws from the partnership so the partnership dissolves.

12. When a partnership was dissolved, all but two of the creditors had been paid. The partnership owed Rand Co. $50,000 for supplies purchased on account, and it owed Boggs, a partner, $50,000 for money he loaned the partnership to cover operating expenses. The only remaining asset was a bank account containing $50,000. Which of the following is probably true?

   a. The $50,000 will escheat to the state government.
   b. Investors must be paid before creditors.
   c. Rand Co. and Boggs are each entitled to $25,000.
   d. Rand Co. is entitled to the full $50,000.
   e. Boggs is entitled to the full $50,000.

DISCUSSION

(d) On dissolution, the order of payment of claims from the partnership assets can be recalled from the acronym, CLIP. The creditors must be fully paid before partners can be paid for loans made to the partnership. Boggs would not receive any of the partnership assets under the circumstances because they would be exhausted by paying Rand Co. This result is justified because Boggs had control of the partnership by reason of his power to vote as a partner while Rand Co. had no control. Boggs may still recover something from the partnership when the partners make their required contributions to cover partnership losses.

Chapter 15
Corporations

The "corporation" is an amazingly flexible business organization. The term, corporation, literally means body. Although a corporation is actually a group of investors operating a business, it is treated like an artificial person with legal rights and responsibilities. A corporation can sue and be sued in its own name, enter into contracts, commit torts and crimes, etc. in much the same way as a natural person can.

The primary advantages of the corporation over the common law organizations of sole proprietorship and partnership are its capacity to accommodate a large number of investors, limited liability, and perpetual existence. It allows numerous investors to pool their money to create gigantic businesses that would be virtually nonexistent if the sole proprietorship and partnership were the only business organizations allowed by law. Investors in a corporation are called "stockholders."

As partnerships grow larger, they encounter difficulties resulting from the partners' rights to participate in the management of the business. Allowing all owners a voice in the day to day management of a business makes sense for small businesses but soon becomes unmanageable when the number of owners of a business becomes large. A corporation, on the other hand, is flexible enough to accommodate any number of owners. It would be virtually impossible for a partnership to conduct management meetings if it had 70,000 owners each of whom had the right to vote on every management decision. Corporations can easily accommodate any number of investors because they are managed by a board of directors rather than the individual owners.

The investors in a corporation are accorded limited liability while sole proprietors and general partners have unlimited liability. Corporate creditors are limited to looking to the assets owned by the corporation to satisfy their claims. If corporate assets are insufficient to pay creditors, the stockholders are not personally liable for corporate debts. The creditors of sole proprietorships and partnerships, on the other hand, can take the personal assets of the owners when the assets owned by the company are insufficient to pay their claims. This is justified by the relatively limited control that stockholders have over corporate business. Unlike partners who can vote on every issue of partnership management, corporate stockholders may vote only on the directors who handle the corporate business and on a few other extraordinary matters.

Partnerships terminate each time a partner withdraws or dies. This can be disruptive to the business and limit the existence of a given partnership to the lifetime of its owners. This is not the case with a corporation which can be organized to exist forever. As the owners of a corporation withdraw or die, the corporation can continue in business without disruption.

Corporations are not without their disadvantages, however. Corporations are often subject to "double taxation" while partnerships are not. Corporations must pay a corporate income tax on the profits they earn. After the corporate income tax is paid, the remainder of the profits are distributed to the stockholders as "dividends." Dividends are payments made by corporations to their stockholders. When stockholders receive dividends from corporations, they must pay personal income tax on them. This results in taxes being paid twice on the same profits — once by the corporations and once by the stockholders. Small corporations and other small limited liability organizations are sometimes accorded tax treatment analogous to that of partnerships. Partnerships do not pay income tax on their profits. Rather, the profits are distributed to the partners who then pay personal income tax on them. Partnership profits are therefore taxed only once.

While corporations sometimes find it easier to acquire large amounts of capital from many investors, small corporations sometimes find it more difficult to borrow money since only the corporate assets are available to creditors. Partnerships can often borrow money more easily because the partners' personal assets are available to creditors along with the partnership assets. If the partners of a small partnership have substantial personal assets, lenders may be more willing to advance credit than they would for a similarly sized corporation.

Essential Vocabulary

1. corporation
2. stockholders
3. double taxation
4. dividends

I. INCORPORATION

A corporation is created by incorporators filing articles of incorporation and receiving a certificate of incorporation.

Corporations were not known at common law so each state needed to enact a corporation statute that recognized this type of limited liability business organization. The statutes require "incorporators" to file a statement called "articles of incorporation." Articles of incorporation give notice of the type of business, the number of shares of stock that can be sold to finance the venture, and the name and address of the agent authorized to receive legal papers on behalf of the corporation. The incorporators are the individuals who sign the articles of incorporation. Once the articles are filed with the appropriate state office, most states issue a "certificate of incorporation." Certificates of incorporation are documents that indicate that the state recognizes the existence of the new corporations.

A corporation is called a "de jure corporation" if the incorporators have strictly complied with the incorporation statutes. The stockholders of a de jure corporation have limited liability. A corporation is called a "de facto corporation" if the incorporators have substantially complied with the incorporation statutes. Substantial compliance is compliance without serious deviations. The stockholders of a de facto corporation have limited liability also. When the incorporators have not substantially complied with the incorporation statutes, the organization is called an "unincorporated association." An unincorporated association is usually treated like a partnership resulting in stockholders having unlimited liability for the debts of the business. In most states, a corporation is a de jure corporation once the certificate of incorporation is issued no matter how defective the articles of incorporation may be.

Louise, Mary, and Paula decided to incorporate a grocery store business which they owned. They filled out articles of incorporation but neglected to file them. If creditors later sued them, they would probably have unlimited liability for the debts of their business. Without receiving a certificate of incorporation, the owners would merely be an unincorporated association. Unincorporated associations are treated like partnerships in most cases and the creditors of the business can reach the personal assets of the owners.[1] If the owners had filed articles of incorporation and the state had issued a certificate of incorporation, they would have had only limited liability for the corporate debts and creditors would not have been able to reach their personal assets. The corporation would have been a de jure corporation even if the articles of incorporation were in some way defective or the certificate of incorporation was negligently issued.

Essential Vocabulary

1. incorporators
2. articles of incorporation
3. certificate of incorporation
4. de jure corporation
5. de facto corporation
6. unincorporated association

---

[1] In doing research on this type of business organization, it is important to look under the term, unincorporated association, rather than the term, partnership, because there are sometimes subtle differences in how the parties will be treated if they intended to operate a corporation.

II. STOCK

Investors receive par or no-par stock, and their investments are accounted as capital stock (stated capital) or capital surplus (paid in capital).

The corporation must sell "shares" of the business to raise "capital." Capital is the total of assets invested and used to conduct the corporate business and a share is a portion of the capital owned by an investor. At any given time, shares of the corporation are usually sold at a uniform price so, for example, two shares require twice the investment of one share. Corporate shares are often referred to as "stock." "Stock certificates" are issued as evidence of ownership of shares in the business. "Par stock" refers to shares of the corporation with a minimum price fixed by the articles of incorporation. Par stock is useful to ensure that later investors will not be able to purchase stock below the price earlier investors were required to pay and thereby dilute the relative size of their investment.

It is important to understand how accountants record investments in corporations. State statutes typically limit the use of capital received for the issuance of stock. For example, it is often illegal to pay dividends from the stated capital and capital surplus accounts. Since the restrictions on the uses of each of these accounts varies, it is necessary to have an understanding of what they represent. When par stock is sold, the par value of the shares issued is recorded in the "capital stock account" which is sometimes called the "stated capital account." Any amount above par that is received by the corporation is recorded in the "capital surplus account" which is sometimes called the "paid in capital account." If the stock is sold below par, the stock is "watered" and the stockholder is liable to the corporation for the difference between what she paid and par. Watered stock is stock for which the investor has not fully paid.

Neil, Orin, and Peter purchased stock from a corporation that was authorized to issue 10,000 shares of $50 par stock. Each of them purchased interests at different times at different prices. Neil paid $50,000 for 1,000 shares; Orin paid $60,000 for 1,000 shares; and Peter paid $20,000 for 1,000 shares. Neil's investment would be recorded by placing $50,000 in the capital stock account since he paid par value for his shares. Orin's investment would be recorded by placing $50,000 in the capital stock account and $10,000 in the capital surplus account because he paid $10 per share more than par value for his shares.

Since Peter paid less than par for his stock, his shares were watered. He would be liable to the corporation for the $30,000 difference between par and what he had paid. Allowing Peter to pay less than par for his stock injured the corporation by diluting the investments of Neil and Orin. After Neil and Orin had purchased their stock from the corporation, there were 2,000 shares outstanding, and the corporation owned the $110,000 they had invested. If the corporation had dissolved at that point, Neil and Orin would have received $110,000 ÷ 2000 or $55 per share in liquidation dividends. This would have been $5 more per share than Neil had invested and $5 per share less than Orin had invested. However, in each case, it would have been more than the $50 par value per share required by the articles of incorporation.

After Peter's investment of $20,000, there were 3,000 shares issued, and the corporation would have owned the $130,000 invested. If the corporation had dissolved at that point, Neil, Orin, and Peter would have received $130,000 ÷ 3000 or $43.33 per share in liquidation dividends. This would have been about $23.33 more per share than Peter had invested, about $6.67 per share less than Neil had invested and about $16.67 per share less than Orin had invested. In addition to diluting the investment of Neil and Orin, Peter's watered shares would dilute their voting power by giving Peter an equal number of votes despite his smaller investment. The corporation would need to rectify this problem by suing Peter on the watered stock he owned and requiring him to pay the remaining $30 per share for a total of $30,000.

While some investors prefer par stock as a way to protect their investment from dilution by later sales of stock at a lower price than they paid, others prefer the flexibility of "no-par stock." No-par stock has no minimum price. The board of directors determines at what price the stock will be issued and how to allocate the money received as capital stock or capital surplus.

In our example above, if the stockholders amended the articles of incorporation to allow the company to issue 1,000 shares of no-par stock. The board of directors could decide to issue the new class of stock for $40 per share. The board could also decide that they would allocate $30 per share to capital stock and $10 per share to capital surplus on each share sold. If the stock could not be sold for $40 per share, the board of directors could lower the price and allocate the proceeds to the accounts the board deemed appropriate.

Essential Vocabulary

1. shares
2. capital
3. stock
4. par stock
5. stated capital account or capital stock account
6. capital surplus account or paid in capital account
7. watered stock
8. no-par stock

III. STOCKHOLDERS

A quorum of stockholders vote on directors, new articles, mergers, consolidations, and liquidations.

Stockholders must make their will known by voting in meetings. The final decision must represent the will of a "quorum of stockholders." Since stockholders get one vote for each share of the corporation they own, their importance is based upon the extent of their investment. A corporation raises capital for its business by "issuing stock." Stock is issued when the corporation sells it for the first time to raise capital. A quorum of stockholders, therefore, is enough owners to represent a majority of the shares issued by the corporation rather than merely a majority of the people and companies that own the stock. Owners of a corporation sell their shares by "trading stock." Stock that is sold by investors after it has been issued by the corporation is referred to as traded stock. Stockholders can vote their stock in person by attending stockholders' meetings. When it is inconvenient for stockholders to attend these meetings, they can vote their shares by sending an agent to the meetings. The agent is called a "proxy." In addition, the instrument giving the agent or proxy the authority to vote the principal's stock is sometimes referred to as a proxy.

Big Inc. was a corporation that had issued 1000 shares of stock which were owned by Amy, Ben, Carl, Don, and Emily. Their ownership in the company was as follows: Amy 300 shares; Ben 300 shares; Carl 200 shares; Don 100 shares; and Emily 100 shares. A regular meeting of the stockholders was attended by Carl, Don and Emily, but the other stockholders did not attend. No business could be undertaken because a quorum of stockholders was not present. Although a majority of stockholders was present, a majority of the shares was not represented by them since they collectively owned only 400 shares. If the meeting had been attended by only Amy and Ben, they could have transacted business because together they formed a quorum of the stockholders. They owned 600 shares between them which was more than a majority of the 1000 shares issued by the corporation.

Stockholders are granted limited liability because they have correspondingly limited control of the corporation. The management of the corporation is handled by the board of directors elected by the stockholders. The stockholders' right to vote is generally limited to voting on directors, changes in the articles of incorporation, mergers, consolidations, and liquidations of the corporate assets.

The election of the directors by the stockholders is accomplished by "ordinary voting" or "cumulative voting" as prescribed by the articles of incorporation. When ordinary voting is used, the stockholders can cast one vote for each share of stock they own to elect a director for each position that is available. When cumulative voting is used, the stockholders can cast a number of votes equal to the number of shares they own multiplied by the number of directors' positions that need to be filled. Since all of these votes can be cast for one director, this allows for more protection of minority stockholders than does ordinary voting. Majority stockholders still have more votes than minority stockholders because they own more stock. However, to control the entire board, the majority stockholders are forced to spread their votes among several director's positions while the minority stockholders can focus their votes on a single position. When the voting is over, the majority stockholders will have more of their representatives on the board than the minority stockholders, but the minority stockholders are often able to elect at least a single representative.

Little Mine, Inc. was a corporation that had issued 100 shares of stock which were owned by Fred, Gary, Hank, Irene, and Jenny. Their ownership in the company was as follows: Fred 30 shares; Gary 30 shares; Hank 10 shares; Irene 20 shares; and Jenny 10 shares. When the time came to elect the three directors, Fred, Gary and Hank presented three friends as their nominees. Irene and Jenny wanted to elect their own candidates to protect their interests. If ordinary voting was prescribed by the articles of incorporation, Irene and Jenny would not be able to elect any directors if Fred, Gary, and Hank voted as a block because they could cast only one vote for each share they owned on each director being elected. This would mean that on any one director, Irene and Jenny could together cast only 30 votes while Fred, Gary and Hank could cast 70 votes and consistently elect their nominees as directors.

If cumulative voting for directors was allowed by the articles, each stockholder would be entitled to cast a number of votes equal to the number of shares owned multiplied by the number of directors' positions that needed to be filled, and all directors would stand for election at the same time. This would result in Fred, Gary, and Hank being entitled to 210 votes which is the number of director's positions times the number of shares they owned or 3 x 70 while Irene and Jenny would be entitled to 3 x 30 or 90 votes. Since all directors stand for election at the same time, Fred, Gary, and Hank would need to divide their 210 votes between their candidates and could only cast up to 70 votes for each of their three candidates. Irene and Jenny could cast their entire 90 votes for one candidate and be assured of electing at least one director to protect their interests in the corporation.

Stockholder voting on "amendments to the articles of incorporation," "mergers," "consolidations" and "liquidations" of substantially all of the assets of a corporation is accomplished by ordinary voting. An amendment to the articles of incorporation is a change to the articles originally filed with the state to obtain corporate recognition through the issuance of a certificate of incorporation. A merger is a corporate reorganization in which two corporations combine their assets and one of them is terminated. The surviving corporation becomes liable for the debts and other obligations of the corporation that went out of existence. For example, in a merger of Apples, Inc. and Big Fruit, Inc., the assets of Apples, Inc. could be transferred to Big Fruit, Inc. This would result in the termination of Apples, Inc. and Big Fruit, Inc. being liable for Apples' debts and other legal obligations. A consolidation is a reorganization in which two corporations combine their assets in a new corporation and are both terminated. The new corporation becomes liable for the debts and other obligations of the corporations that were terminated. For example, Apples, Inc. and Big Fruit, Inc. could be consolidated into a new corporation called California Fruits, Inc. This would result in the assets of Apples, Inc. and Big Fruit, Inc. being transferred to California Fruits, Inc. Both Apples, Inc. and Big Fruit, Inc. would be terminated leaving California Fruits, Inc. with liability for their debts and other legal obligations.

A liquidation of substantially all of the assets of a corporation is accomplished by the corporations' selling all of its assets. This converts the assets of the corporation into money, commercial paper, or other payments. Unlike a mere sale of inventory or other assets in the regular course of business, a liquidation of substantially all of the corporation's assets deprives the corporation of the means to carry on the business that it was organized to conduct. In addition, stockholders and creditors are placed at risk because money is more easily misappropriated and hidden than other forms of property. Stockholders must, therefore, approve this fundamental change.

Essential Vocabulary

1. quorum of stockholders
2. issuing stock
3. trading stock
4. proxy
5. ordinary voting
6. cumulative voting
7. amendments of the articles of incorporation
8. mergers
9. consolidations
10. liquidations

IV. STOCKHOLDER APPRAISAL RIGHTS

The corporation must appraise and purchase the shares of dissenting stockholders in mergers, consolidations and liquidations.

The very nature of a corporate investment can be changed by a merger, consolidation, or sale of substantially all of the corporate assets. In a merger or consolidation, a stockholder's influence on corporate affairs through voting rights will be reduced because the stockholders of another corporation will also be owners of the surviving or new corporation. When substantially all of the assets of a corporation including its plant and equipment are sold, it can no longer carry on the business for which it was originally organized. For these reasons, the state corporation statutes allow stockholders to vote on corporate activities that fundamentally change the nature of the corporation. "Dissenting stockholders" are also accorded the additional protection of being able to force the corporation to purchase their stock at its fair value just prior to the change in the event that the action is approved by the required number of votes. Dissenting stockholders are stockholders who disagree with a fundamental change approved by the majority shareholders. The dissenting stockholders' right to force the corporation to purchase their stock is called their "stockholder's right of appraisal."

The statutes require that the dissenting stockholders file a "stockholder's notice of dissent" to any proposed merger, consolidation, or sale of substantially all of the corporate assets prior to the stockholders' voting on the issue. A stockholder's notice of dissent is a written notice that indicates that the stockholder opposes the proposed fundamental change in the corporation. This gives other stockholders notice of how much the proposed action may cost the corporation if it is required to purchase the dissenters' stock. The dissenting stockholders must then vote against the action at the stockholders' meeting. If the action is approved by the majority of stockholders, the dissenting stockholders must then file a "stockholder's demand for payment" with the corporation. A stockholder's demand for payment is a written demand that the corporation purchase their shares at "fair value." Fair value is the value of the shares at the time the fundamental change was approved without the effects on the price of speculation resulting from the announced change. The statutes that give appraisal rights to dissenting stockholders require that the procedure prescribed by the statute be strictly followed or the right to require the corporation to purchase the dissenters' stock will be lost.

The board of directors of Anne's Grill, Inc., a corporation that manufactured gas grills, wanted to sell the corporation's manufacturing plant, inventory, and raw materials to World Wide Barbecue, Inc. They voted in favor of a resolution to present the proposal to the stockholders for approval. Lisa, a stockholder, disapproved of the action because she believed that the manufacture of gas grills would continue to be profitable for Anne's Grill, Inc. She contacted her attorney who carefully followed the procedure for dissenting stockholders to exercise their appraisal rights. Prior to the meeting at which the votes for and against the proposal would be cast, her attorney filed a notice of dissent with the corporation. At the meeting, Lisa voted against the proposed sale. If the sale to World Wide Barbecue was approved, Lisa's attorney would need to file a demand for payment within the time limit prescribed by statute to exercise Lisa's right to require the corporation to purchase her stock. The corporation would then be required to pay fair value for the stock. The fair value of the stock would be the price of the stock before it was affected by notice of the proposed liquidation. Any deviation or delay in exercising

Lisa's appraisal rights would result in the corporation's being released from its duty to purchase her stock.

Essential Vocabulary

1. dissenting stockholders
2. stockholder's right of appraisal
3. stockholder's notice of dissent
4. stockholder's demand for payment
5. fair value

V. DERIVATIVE ACTIONS

Stockholders may sue on behalf of the corporation when the corporation has a cause of action but does not pursue it.

Stockholders can sue the corporation on their own behalf if it injures them by failing to pay declared dividends or acknowledging their voting rights or rights of appraisal, etc. However, stockholders can sue a third party on behalf of the corporation through a "stockholders' derivative action" when the corporation has suffered some injury and the board of directors refuses to sue. A stockholders' derivative action is a law suit filed by a stockholder against a third party on behalf of the corporation. The corporation is a necessary party to a derivative action, and the judgement is awarded to the corporation if the suit is successful. Sometimes, stockholders who bring successful derivative actions can require the corporation to reimburse them for their costs. Derivative actions allow stockholders to protect the corporation's interests when the board of directors refuses to pursue a corporate claim against a third party.

Tom traded some land worth $75,000 to Slinky, Inc. for some stock in Slinky carried on its books at $100,000. This masterpiece of accounting was accomplished by simply overvaluing Tom's land as worth $100,000. When it was discovered that Tom's shares were watered, the board of directors refused to pursue legal action against Tom to recover the unpaid purchase price of the stock because Tom was a powerful stockholder. A small minority of stockholders objected to this dilution of their interests and filed suit against Tom in a stockholders' derivative action on behalf of the corporation. The parties to the suit were the stockholders filing the action, Slinky, Inc. and Tom. The judgement would have been awarded to Slinky, Inc. rather than to the stockholders who filed the action. Tom would probably have been required to pay $25,000 to Slinky, Inc. because his stock was watered. The damages would need to be paid to the corporation since the corporation was technically the victim and the plaintiff in the derivative action brought by the minority stockholders.

Essential Vocabulary

1. stockholders' derivative action

VI. PIERCING THE CORPORATE VEIL

The stockholder will be liable for watered shares, fraud, inadequate capitalization, and failure to observe corporate formalities.

The term, "corporate veil," has been used to refer to the protection accorded stockholders from liability for corporate debts. Stockholders within the corporate veil enjoy limited liability which restricts their financial risk to their investment. Although they can lose their investment, their personal assets are not normally subject to the claims of corporate creditors. Stockholders can lose this protection by abuse of the corporate entity. "Piercing the corporate veil" is a term coined for the imposition of unlimited liability upon stockholders. Four abuses that may result in the courts' piercing the corporate veil and imposing unlimited liability on stockholders are the following: the ownership of "watered stock," the use of the corporation to perpetrate a "fraud," the "inadequate capitalization" of the corporation, and the "failure to observe corporate formalities" resulting in the corporation's becoming the mere "alter ego" of its owners.

"Watered stock" is a term used for stock for which a purchaser has not fully paid. Stock is watered if the purchaser paid less than the par value of the stock when it was issued or, in the case of no-par stock, less than the price set by the corporation's board of directors. When stock is sold by shareholders following the initial sale of the stock by the corporation, it can be traded for any price the market will bear. Restrictions regarding the minimum price of stock apply only to sales of stock by the corporation when it is issued. Purchasing watered shares does not make the investor liable for the debts of the corporation. However, the purchaser would have unlimited liability to the corporation for the difference between what was paid and the par value in the case of par stock or the amount paid and the issue price set by the board of directors in the case of no-par stock. Allowing investors to purchase stock from the corporation at less than the par or the issue price set by the board results in the dilution of the interests of other investors.

Amy, Bill, Carla, and Don each owned 25 shares of Bronco Inc.'s $100 par value stock. These were the only shares issued by the corporation at that time, and the total corporate assets were $10,000. If the corporation later issued an additional 25 shares of the stock to Edward at $40 per share, the stock would be watered to the extent of $60 per share or $1,500. Edward would be liable to the corporation for that amount. Allowing Edward to buy the stock at less than par would have diluted the investments of the other stockholders.

After the transaction, Edward would have owned 25 shares of a total 125 issued shares or one-fifth of the total stock. This would be as much as each of the other stockholders owned. If the corporation were terminated at that moment and there were no liabilities or other assets, each investor would receive one-fifth of $11,000, the total assets. This would mean that each investor, including Edward, would receive $2,200. This would be $300 less than Amy, Bill, Carla and Don paid for their interests and $1,200 more than Edward had paid for his interest. Allowing investors to purchase stock at less than par increases the value of the stock held by the investor with the watered stock at the expense of the other investors. The corporation must correct this by collecting the $1,500 deficiency in investment on the watered shares from Edward. The corporation could reach Edwards personal assets for this deficiency since his liability for watered shares is unlimited.

Sally, Todd, and Unis were the sole stockholders of Big Band Booking, Inc. (BBB). BBB booked popular bands at fairs around the country and mounted a huge advertising campaign to attract customers. Fair organizers were required to pay in advance for the bands that BBB booked for them. In an effort to increase profits and bring down overhead, BBB did not actually book any bands. Sally, Todd, and Unis took the money paid by fair owners for themselves as salaries and bonuses. If angry fair owners sued the corporation and found the assets inadequate to answer their claims, Sally, Todd, and Unis would have unlimited liability for the damages owed by the corporation to victims of this "fraud." A fraud is committed by intentionally misrepresenting material facts upon which others justifiably rely. Sally, Todd, and Unis collected money by intentionally misrepresenting to fair owners that BBB would book bands for them.

Alice, Ben, Carl, and Donna were the sole stockholders in City Cement, Inc. State statutes required that at least $1,000 be invested in each new corporation. Each of the stockholders, therefore, invested $250 to make up the required $1,000. They borrowed money and loaned the other assets to the corporation to minimize the assets that were at risk in the company. Alice loaned the corporation a lot with a building to house their offices. Ben loaned his fleet of 25 cement trucks to the company. Carl loaned all of the office furnishings and equipment to the corporation. Donna loaned the corporation its rock crushers and cement mixing equipment. The company operated using assets worth $20 million. However, only $1,000 of these assets belonged to the corporation. The remainder had been loaned by the stockholders or borrowed from other lenders.

The courts would pierce the corporate veil in this situation to impose unlimited liability upon the stockholders due to the corporation's "inadequate capitalization." Corporations must have sufficient "equity" in their business to provide creditors with significant access to the assets used to operate the business. The equity of a corporation is the net amount invested in the corporation. Corporations are inadequately capitalized when they lack the capital to pay ordinary business expenses. This can occur when corporations borrow too many assets from the owners as in the case above or when they borrow too much money resulting in a ratio of debt to equity that is too high.

An "alter ego" is a second self. A corporation becomes the alter ego of its stockholders when the stockholders use the corporation merely to conduct their personal business. When a corporation becomes nothing more than the alter ego of its owners, the owners become liable for the corporate debts. Unlimited liability follows their exercise of control of the corporation beyond the limitations set by corporate formalities. Stockholders can fail to observe corporate formalities by failing to hold meetings or commingling corporate assets with private assets.

When a "parent corporation" fails to keep the business of a "subsidiary corporation" separate by observing corporate formalities, holding proper meetings, and keeping assets separate, the alter ego theory can also be used to impose liability on the parent corporation for the debts of the subsidiary. A parent corporation is a corporation that owns at least a majority of another corporation's stock. The corporation who has issued the stock owned by a parent corporation is referred to as the subsidiary corporation. A parent corporation has control over its subsidiary due to its majority interest.

Three brothers incorporated their family's automobile shop. No meetings of the board of directors were held. Money received as fees was divided among the brothers informally throughout each month. Each of the brothers had used the corporate checking account to purchase groceries and pay personal bills as well as shop debts. When the corporation became short on cash and parts were needed, the brothers would sometimes deposit their wives' checks into the account to cover expenses. The three brothers in this situation would be liable to creditors for the corporate debts because the absence of corporate formalities suggests that the corporation was not a separate entity. It was merely the brothers' alter ego.

Essential Vocabulary

1. corporate veil
2. piercing the corporate veil
3. watered stock
4. fraud
5. inadequate capitalization
6. equity
7. alter ego
8. parent corporation
9. subsidiary corporation

VII. DIRECTORS

A quorum of directors has actual authority to run the business through agents, officers, and employees.

A "quorum of directors" is a majority of the directors qualified to vote on an issue. A quorum has actual authority to bind the corporation to contracts. The board gives this authority to officers and employees so that they can contract on behalf of the corporation. It is important to remember that it is the board itself that has the authority and not individual board members. Officers, employees, and independent contractors that work for the corporation have no authority other than that given to them by the board. It is not safe to assume that an officer or employee has authority to enter into a contract that is not within the regular course of business for the corporation. It is customary in such situations to require the board to issue a power of attorney to its agent signed by each board member and notarized to evidence that the signatures are genuine. Some lenders require corporate officers signing for loans to present a written, signed, and notarized copy of the board resolution authorizing the transaction and appointing a specific officer as its agent for signing the contract.

Jack, Kim, Lucy, Mary, and Nina were the directors for Fabulous Farm Products, Inc. which did business under the name "FFP." Jack and Kim instructed the president of the corporation, to sell the processing plant in Denver and gave him a power of attorney to present to World Wide Vegetables, Inc. The president subsequently signed a contract on behalf of the corporation to sell the plant to World Wide Vegetables, Inc. When the board of directors for FFP met on the issue, only Jack and Kim were in favor of the sale so FFP refused to honor the contract. World Wide Vegetables sued FFP for breach.

FFP would not be liable for breach of contract because the president had no authority to sign the contract selling the plant. Jack and Kim could not delegate the authority to bind the corporation to the president because the resolution was not approved by a quorum of directors. At the time Jack and Kim had instructed Tom to sell the plant, the board had not even met on the issue. Jack and Kim would ultimately have been liable to World Wide Vegetables, Inc. as principals in the contract signed by the president. The president, on the other hand, would probably avoid liability unless he was negligent in following the instructions of Jack and Kim without further inquiry into whether or not the board had authorized the transaction.

At least three of the five board members would have needed to vote in favor of the sale if all members attended the meeting. It would be possible for fewer than all members of the board to take action if a quorum of directors attended the meeting. When there are five directors, three directors are required to form a quorum. If the meeting mentioned in the fact pattern above had been attended by only Jack, Kim, and Lucy, the sale could have been approved over Lucy's objection, and the corporation would have been bound.

If a quorum of directors is present, a majority of those voting can approve a resolution. Jack and Kim erred by taking action before the board had met.

Board members are required to attend board meetings. If they are absent or abstain from voting on an issue, they are liable as though they voted with the majority. Sometimes absent directors can avoid liability with the majority if they file a "notice of director's dissent" with the secretary of the meeting upon discovering the board's action. A notice of director's dissent is a written notification that a director disagrees with the action taken by the board along with an explanation of why. This does not always result in avoidance of liability so the best practice is for directors to attend all meetings. In the case above in which Mary and Nina were absent from the meeting in which the sale of the plant was voted upon by Jack, Kim, and Lucy, Mary and Nina would have been liable for negligence if the sale had amounted to mismanagement unless they filed directors' dissents immediately upon learning of the board's action. Lucy would not have been liable because she attended the meeting and voted against the sale.

Essential Vocabulary

1. quorum of directors
2. notice of director's dissent

VIII. DIRECTORS' MEETINGS

The board of directors follows its bylaws, makes its will known through resolutions, and records its meetings in minutes.

The rules which boards of directors adopt for themselves are called "bylaws." The bylaws are generally procedural and govern such things as how notice of special meetings should be given, how much notice is necessary, how and when agendas should be distributed, etc. The bylaws are made and changed at the will of the board of directors through majority approval. This makes them much easier to modify than the articles of incorporation. The agenda items considered by the board are called "resolutions." Resolutions are noted in the minutes of the meetings in which they are made and are sometimes additionally memorialized as separate documents. The "minutes" of each meeting record the issues and actions of the board along with how each board member voted on each resolution considered.

Essential Vocabulary

1. bylaws
2. resolutions
3. minutes

IX. DIVIDENDS

Dividends must be paid from earned surplus (retained earnings).

Corporations distribute their profits to their stockholders as dividends. Dividends must, therefore, be paid from the "earned surplus account" which is also sometimes called the "retained earnings account." Corporate profits made by conducting the business of the corporation are recorded in the earned surplus or retained earnings account. Dividends paid from the capital stock (stated capital) and the capital surplus (paid in capital) accounts are "liquidation dividends" that can be paid only after creditors have been satisfied. Dividends paid from these accounts prior to payment of creditors are generally illegal. Liquidation dividends are used to return the investments of stockholders when a corporation is terminated. Board members who vote in favor of declaring illegal dividends are liable to the corporation for them. Stockholders receiving illegal dividends are generally liable for their return only if they knew that the dividends were illegal or had knowledge of facts that would indicate that they were illegal.

The board of directors of Tough Luck, Inc. voted unanimously to pay a dividend to stockholders. Unfortunately, the corporation had suffered numerous losses and there was not enough revenue in the retained earnings account to cover the dividend. They decided to remedy this situation by paying the dividend from the capital stock account. Tough Luck, Inc. owed a little more than fifteen million dollars to its creditors. This dividend was illegal so the board members voting in favor of it would have been jointly and severally liable to the corporation for the dividends paid. Stockholders who accepted the dividend knowing that it was illegal would have been liable for the amount they received.

Essential Vocabulary

1. earned surplus account or retained earnings account
2. liquidation dividends

X.   CORPORATE DISSOLUTION

When a corporation dissolves, it must liquidate its assets and distribute the money to creditors and stockholders.

Corporate dissolution may be accomplished voluntarily by a vote of the stockholders or involuntarily by the action of creditors or the state. Once the process begins, the corporation can still sue and be sued until all corporate affairs are settled or "barred" by the "statute of limitations." A claim is barred when a party can no longer seek relief through the courts due to some legal prohibition against bringing the action. The Statute of Limitations is a statute enacted in every state that limits the time within which an action may be filed in court. After a prescribed length of time, an injured party can no longer bring an action for a tort, breach of contract, breach of fiduciary duty, or other injury.

Once dissolution begins, the authority of the board of directors to enter into contracts is limited to entering into those contracts necessary to wind up corporate affairs. When dissolution becomes necessary, the board of directors liquidates the corporation by selling its assets and paying corporate debts. If dissolution is involuntary or for any other reason it is undesirable for the board of directors to handle the liquidation, a "receiver" can be appointed by a court to handle the process. A receiver is a third party appointed by the court to take control of the liquidation process and account to the court and stockholders. Once the liquidation is complete, the creditors are paid. After the creditors have been paid, the corporation dissolves by distributing any remaining cash in a liquidation dividend. When the corporation is dissolved, it ceases to exist under state law.

The directors of Sherlock's Detective Agency, Inc. presented the stockholders with a resolution calling for the liquidation of the agency following the disappearance of its chief detective. A majority of a quorum of the stockholders voted in favor of the dissolution. The directors were charged with the task of "liquidation." Liquidation is the process of winding up the corporate affairs by selling the assets and paying the creditors of the corporation. During the liquidation process, the board decided to have the corporation enter into one last contract requiring the investigation of some chicken thefts that had just occurred. If, after the board's approval, but prior to the corporation's entering into the contract with the chicken farmer, a stockholder had sued the corporation to stop it from entering into the contract, the stockholder would have won because the board had no authority to enter into the contract once the stockholders had voted in favor of dissolution. The board's actual authority to bind the corporation to contracts was limited by the vote in favor of dissolution to contracts required to accomplish the liquidation.

If the corporation had entered into the contract with the chicken farmer before the stockholder had learned about it, the corporation would have been bound because the board members still had apparent authority to enter into contracts for the corporation. However, the board members would have been liable to the corporation and the chicken farmer because they lacked actual authority. If the board refused to bring an action against themselves in such a case, the aggrieved stockholder could have sued them on behalf of the corporation in a stockholders' derivative action.

Essential Vocabulary

1. barred
2. Statute of Limitations
3. receiver
4. liquidation

CHECK YOUR UNDERSTANDING

DIRECTIONS: Read each of the following questions. Choose the best answer and study the discussion of the question.

1. Sixty-one people decided to incorporate a business. The attorney they hired to accomplish this assured the owners that he would take care of the legal requirements for incorporation. Unfortunately, the entire project slipped his mind. Thinking the business had been incorporated, the owners elected a board of directors, issued stock, and commenced business. Their business organization was probably:

   a. a joint stock company.
   b. an investment group.
   c. a cooperative.
   d. a partnership.
   e. an unincorporated association.

DISCUSSION

   (e)   Failure to file articles of incorporation and obtain a certificate of incorporation from the state will result in the organization being classified as an unincorporated association. Unincorporated associations are generally treated like partnerships with the controlling stockholders incurring unlimited liability for corporate debts. A joint stock company is a partnership in which stock is issued to evidence the ownership of the partners. An investment group could use any type of business organization to accomplish their venture. A cooperative is a nonprofit corporation that must be properly incorporated to exist. A partnership is a group of co-owners carrying on a business for profit. However, since unincorporated associations are sometimes treated differently than partnerships, the term unincorporated association should be used in conducting research.

2. When a corporation issues no-par stock, the amount of the price to be allocated to the capital stock and capital surplus accounts is probably determined by:

    a. the United States Code Ann.
    b. the State Code.
    c. "Generally Accepted Accounting Principles."
    d. the stockholders.
    e. the board of directors.

DISCUSSION

(e)   When no-par stock is issued by a corporation, the board of directors determines how much of the price to allocate to each of the capital stock and the capital surplus accounts. This is important because there are restrictions in the use of funds placed in various accounts. The United States Code contains the legislative law enacted by Congress. The state codes contain the legislative laws enacted by the state legislatures. Generally accepted accounting principles (GAAP) provide accountants with general standards necessary to uniformly and accurately account for all business transactions and financial information. The stockholders are allowed to vote only on the members of the board of directors and extraordinary matters such as mergers, consolidations, and liquidations of all corporate assets.

3. Big Deal Inc. had ten stockholders who held 1,000 shares of stock. No other stock had been issued. At an annual meeting, seven of the stockholders were present. Those present owned 450 shares of stock. The stockholders elected Tom to the board of directors. During the meeting 300 votes were cast for Tom, and 150 votes were cast for another candidate. The election was probably:

    a. binding if the notice of the meeting was properly given.
    b. binding because Tom received a majority of the votes.
    c. binding because a majority of the stockholders participated.
    d. not binding because a quorum of stockholders was not present.
    e. not binding because fewer than 501 votes were cast for Tom.

DISCUSSION

(d)   A quorum of stockholders must be present to conduct any business such as the election of members of the board of directors. A quorum of stockholders would be enough stockholders to represent the majority of the stock issued by the corporation. In this case, a minimum of 501 shares would be required for a quorum. The fact that seven of the stockholders participated would be irrelevant because the number of shares represented rather than the number of owners present determines whether or not a quorum is present. If a quorum of stockholders is present, the majority of the stock that is voted in the meeting will determine the issue. If fewer than all shares of stock were represented at the meeting, Tom could have been elected by fewer than 501 votes. For example, if 600 shares were represented, a quorum of stockholders would have been present, and Tom could have been elected by as few as 301 votes.

4. Western Farms, Inc. was a corporation engaged in dry farming approximately 1,250 acres of land which the corporation owned along with sufficient water rights and an eight year old tractor. The board of directors approved a resolution calling for the sale of this land to Mega Farms, Inc. Saul owned approximately 3% of the Western Farms stock and was opposed to the sale. Saul could probably:

a. enjoin the sale.
b. obtain the impeachment of the directors.
c. exercise his right of appraisal.
d. require Western Farms, Inc. to dissolve.
e. require Mega Farms, Inc. to make a formal tender offer.

DISCUSSION

(c)   The resolution of the Western Farms board of directors called for a sale of substantially all of the corporate assets. This fundamental change in the nature of the business would need to be approved by a quorum of stockholders. Saul could exercise his right of appraisal by filing a stockholder's notice of dissent with the board of directors prior to the stockholder meeting held to allow stockholders to vote on the issue. This would give the other stockholders notice of how much the proposed action could cost the corporation if it was required to purchase Saul's stock. Saul would then need to vote against the action at the stockholders meeting. If the action was approved by the majority of stockholders, Saul would need to have his attorney file a stockholder's demand for payment with the corporation requiring the corporation to purchase his shares at fair value.

5. Ninety percent of a corporation's stock was owned by members of the same family. One of the corporation's bookkeepers, who also was a member of the family, took $72,000 from the company. When this came to the attention of the board of directors, it was decided to transfer the offending employee to a job that did not involve the handling of money. However, the board voted six to one against suing the employee for reimbursement. Travis heard about this, and, although he owned less than one percent of the stock, he wanted the corporation to attempt to recover the $72,000. Travis probably:

    a. could sue the employee directly for $72,000, but he'll need to give the money he recovers to the corporation.
    b. could sue the employee only on behalf of the corporation in a stockholder's derivative action.
    c. could sue the directors to force them to sue the employee.
    d. couldn't sue the employee unless the majority of the other stockholders agreed to the action.
    e. couldn't sue the employee because the directors had decided that it was not in the corporation's interest to take such action.

DISCUSSION

   (b) Travis could sue the employee on behalf of the corporation in a stockholders derivative action. The fact that he owns very little stock is not important. Any judgement against the employee would be rendered in favor of the corporation rather than Travis. Travis might have been able to sue the directors for mismanagement for breach of their fiduciary duty to the corporation in addition to suing the employee in the derivative suit. He could not, however, get an injunction requiring the directors to maintain an action against the employee. No approval from other stockholders would be necessary to bring a derivative action against the employee. If Travis was successful in his derivative action, he might be able to get the corporation to reimburse him for his court costs and attorney's fees.

6. Sam, Phil, and Arnold organized a corporation and contributed $1,000 for stock. Sam loaned his building to the corporation. Phil loaned the business a fleet of 35 cement trucks, and Arnold loaned the corporation all of its office equipment and furnishings. The gross income of the business was approximately 2.5 million dollars per year. When creditors attempted to collect debts, they found only the $1,000 contributed for stock because Sam, Phil, and Arnold only loaned the other assets to the corporation. Which of the following is probably true?

a. Only $1,000 is subject to creditors' claims.
b. Sam, Phil and Arnold will have unlimited liability for the corporate debts.
c. The creditors can reach the $1,000 and assets loaned to the business but Sam, Phil, and Arnold have limited liability.
d. Sam, Phil and Arnold will be liable under the corporation by estoppel doctrine for fraud.
e. The creditors are liable for contributory negligence.

DISCUSSION

(b)   The corporation was inadequately capitalized because it did not own enough assets to conduct its business. The corporate organization was merely being used to defraud creditors. The court would pierce the corporate veil and impose unlimited liability on the stockholders. The creditors of the corporation would be able to reach all of the stockholders' personal assets to satisfy the corporate debts and would not be limited to the assets loaned to the corporation. The Doctrine of Corporation by Estoppel prevents parties who deal with unincorporated associations from denying their contracts with them on the ground that no corporation existed so the unincorporated association was not a party to the contract. This has no application here. Since the corporation's negligence is not an issue, the creditors' contributory negligence would not be a defense.

7. Phil was a director on the board of directors for Longtree Inc. While he was out of town, the other members of the board voted to declare an illegal dividend to stockholders. In an action against board members for mismanagement, Phil would probably:

a. not be liable because he didn't vote.
b. not be liable unless his vote would have made a difference.
c. be liable only if he approved of the dividend.
d. be liable as though he voted with the majority unless he had filed a director's dissent.
e. be liable only if he was in a position to gain from the dividend.

DISCUSSION

(d)   Directors must attend board meetings and vote or be liable for whatever action the board takes with the majority. When a director misses a meeting, he can sometimes avoid liability through filing a director's dissent immediately upon learning of it. The members of the board who voted in favor of the illegal dividend would be liable to the corporation even if they were not in a position to benefit from it.

8. Sam, a member of the board of directors of a corporation, wanted at least 90 days written notice prior to special meetings of the board. The best way to accomplish this change of policy would be to:

   a. reincorporate.
   b. amend the bylaws.
   c. take a resolution to the stockholders.
   d. lobby for changes in the corporation statutes.
   e. have his wishes noted in the corporate minutes.

DISCUSSION

(b) The procedural rules followed by the board of directors are contained in the bylaws and can be conveniently changed at the will of a majority of the directors. Reincorporating would be expensive and not deal with the notice issue. Taking the resolution to the stockholders would be inappropriate because notice requirements do not fundamentally alter the business of the corporation and the process is expensive. Changes in the corporation laws of the state would not be necessary to deal with the notice issue. Merely noting a director's wishes in the minutes would have no effect at all on the rules imposed on the board.

9. Fish Inc.'s board of directors declared a dividend to be paid out of the capital stock account. This was necessary because the corporation's by-laws required a dividend amounting to a total of $100,000 to be paid at least once each year. There was nothing in the retained earnings account due to a prolonged slump in the economy. The stockholders were aware of the state of affairs and that the dividend was illegal at the time it was declared and paid. Which of the following is probably correct?

   a. Both stockholders and directors will be liable to the corporation.
   b. Only the directors will be liable to the corporation and its creditors.
   c. Only the stockholders will be liable because the directors were merely obeying the corporation's bylaws.
   d. The dividend is legal if capital stock is sufficient.
   e. Stockholders and directors will be liable only to creditors.

DISCUSSION

(a)   Dividends must be declared and paid from the earned surplus or retained earnings account. A dividend declared from the capital stock account would be a liquidation dividend. The claims of creditors have priority over the claims of stockholders for the return of their investment when dissolution takes place. The directors approving the dividend would be jointly and severally liable to the corporation for the amount of the dividend. Stockholders would be liable for the amount of the dividend they received because they had knowledge of the facts that made the dividend illegal.

10.   Beta Corporation's directors and stockholders decided that it was time to terminate the corporation's business. All of the stock in the company was owned by three stockholders: Alice owned 60% of the stock; Betty owned 30% of the stock; and Collins owned 10% of the stock. The corporation owned two fine automobiles and a pickup truck along with about two hundred acres of good farm land. Alice, Betty, and Collins agreed to sell the farm land and divide the money according to their holdings. However, they were in disagreement over who should get the pickup truck because both Betty and Collins wanted it. Betty will probably:

a.   get the truck if it is worth 30% of the total value of all of the vehicles.
b.   get the truck because she owns more stock than Collins.
c.   get the truck if she gave the corporation notice of her claim before Collins did.
d.   get a 30% interest in the truck.
e.   get 30% of whatever is left after the corporation sells all of the assets and pays its creditors.

DISCUSSION

(e)   When a corporation is dissolved, creditor's claims must be completely satisfied before stockholders are entitle to the return of their investments. None of the stockholders would be entitled to any specific piece of property. If the specific corporate property the parties attempted to divide still remained after all creditors had been satisfied, the stockholders could agree to distribute property instead of selling it and distributing cash. If the parties could not agree on the distribution of specific corporate assets, they would be required to sell the assets and distribute the proceeds of the sale. Of course, the property could be purchased by a stockholder at fair market value if this were done.

SECTION V
UNIFORM COMMERCIAL CODE

SALES CONTRACTS
SALES CONTRACT DEFENSES AND DISCHARGES
TITLE, RISK OF LOSS AND PERFORMANCE
SALES WARRANTIES
SECURED TRANSACTIONS
COMMERCIAL PAPER

Chapter 16
Sales Contract

Article II of the Uniform Commercial Code (UCC) is in force in every state and deals with sales of goods. Since this is a legislative law, the text of this statute is located in the state code. The sale of goods is so important to the economy that the common law of contract has been modified by state statute to facilitate commercial transactions. The generalizations that follow in this section represent exceptions to the law of contracts that apply only to sales of goods. Throughout the chapters dealing with sales of goods, the citations to the Uniform Commercial Code have been provided for convenient reference to the actual statute. Since most states have similar numbering systems for the UCC, the citations can actually be used to reference state statutes once a researcher determines the title numbers used in a given state. The generalizations presented are based upon these statutes. Because of this, the statutes should be consulted when actually researching a question relating to sales contracts. When learning these generalizations, it is important to remember that they generally apply only to "sales of goods" and do not apply to contracts for services, sales of real property, and sales of contract rights.

A "sale" is the passage of title to goods from a seller to a buyer for a price. Understanding the concept of "goods" requires a brief review of the general classifications of property. Property can be divided into two great classes: "real property" and "personal property." Real property consists of land and things permanently attached to it. Things that are permanently attached to land are called "fixtures." Buildings, trees, sod, and cement work are fixtures. "Personal property" is all property other than real property. Goods fall into the category of personal property.

Personal property can be classified as "tangible" or "intangible." "Tangible personal property" consists of things that are tangible or can be touched. Boots, cars, boats, and pencils are tangible personal property. Contract rights, causes of action, and other rights are classified as "intangible personal property." "Goods" are generally tangible personal property. The Uniform Commercial Code extends the definition of goods to fixtures that a sales contract requires to be severed from the land, i.e. fixtures that will be turned into tangible personal property when the contract is performed.

The generalizations that follow apply only to sales of goods and should be thought of as statutory exceptions to the contract rules that were presented in earlier chapters. The rules governing contracts apply to contracts for sales of goods unless the generalizations that follow establish an exception. Most of the generalizations presented in this and following chapters dealing with sales apply to all sales of goods whether or not they are made by merchants. A few of them apply only to merchants and are clearly labeled by including some form of the word, "merchant," in the name of the generalization. A merchant is a company or person who is in the business of selling goods of the type involved in the sales contract in question. This would include both retailers and manufacturers. A person or company that does not normally sell the goods involved in a transaction is merely a casual seller and would not be affected by the generalizations applying solely to merchant sellers. A used car dealership would be a merchant when selling cars but would be a casual seller when selling the lawn mower used for maintaining the grass surrounding the car lot.

Essential Vocabulary

1. sale
2. goods
3. real property
4. fixtures
5. personal property
6. tangible personal property
7. intangible personal property
8. merchant

I. OFFER UCC 2-305(1)

If the contract for sale of goods contains the quantity and description, the court may fix a reasonable price.

When parties enter into a contract other than for the sale of goods, the offer must contain the material terms of price, quantity, and description. If one of these terms is omitted in the offer, it is defective by reason of being indefinite and cannot be accepted to create a contract. To facilitate the formation of contracts for the sale of goods in situations where prices may fluctuate, the Uniform Commercial Code has made an exception to the rule requiring the offer to include the price. When the offer is for the sale or purchase of goods, the price does not need to be specified. If the parties intend to enter into a contract although the price is not settled, the price is a "reasonable price" at the time of delivery. A reasonable price is the market price prevailing at the time and place of delivery. Therefore, there are only two material terms that must be included in a valid offer for the sale of goods: description and quantity. The courts will enforce an otherwise binding contract and fix a reasonable price when the parties cannot agree.

Andy sold wheelbarrows at his hardware store. One day, he asked Ben if he wanted to purchase one of the wheelbarrows he had in inventory. Ben accepted his offer. Although they discussed the wheelbarrow, they never mentioned the price. Both of them intended to enter into a binding contract. When Ben went to pick up the wheelbarrow, he asked Andy how much he owed. Andy then told Ben that the price was $80. Ben felt that the wheelbarrow was worth only $40. If Andy and Ben could not agree on the price and Ben refused to accept and pay for the wheelbarrow, Andy could sue for breach of contract and recover his profit based on the reasonable price of the wheelbarrow. Ben would have been liable for the reasonable price of the wheelbarrow if he had accepted it without agreeing on the final price. If the parties had been contracting for the sale of a home instead of a wheelbarrow, no contract would have been formed because the offer did not specify the price. Since the contract was for the sale of goods, the contract was binding.

Essential Vocabulary

1. reasonable price

II. ACCEPTANCE UCC 2-207(1)(2)

An acceptance that does not match the offer for sale of goods creates a contract, but material changes in terms are not binding.

An acceptance is normally not effective to create a contract if it violates the mirror image rule by conflicting with the terms of the offer or attempting to add new terms to the contract. An acceptance that does not match the offer usually constitutes a counter offer and does not operate as an acceptance at all. The Uniform Commercial Code has modified the mirror image rule when the offer is for the sale or purchase of goods. When an offeree accepts an offer leading to a sales contract, she is bound by the contract even if her acceptance does not match the offer. The new or different terms are treated merely as proposals for addition to the contract. If the offeror objects to them, they do not become part of the contract, and the offeree is bound by the terms set forth in the offer.

Carla sent a letter offering to sell her car to Diane for $350. Diane mailed a letter of acceptance that read in part, "I accept your offer to sell your car for $350. Diane also wrote back that she expected Carla to rebuild the engine as soon as possible as part of the contract. Carla received the letter of acceptance and delivered the car to Diane. Carla objected to rebuilding the engine because the work would cost $500. When Carla refused to pay for rebuilding the engine, Diane sued her for breach of contract. Carla would probably prevail in this case because the contract was for the sale of goods. Diane's acceptance was effective to create a sales contract because she intended to enter into a binding contract. However, the new term she attempted to add in her acceptance regarding the rebuilding of the engine would not be binding on Carla because it was not part of the offer. If Carla had been selling the service of painting the car rather than the car itself, Diane's acceptance would not have been effective to create a contract at all because it violated the mirror image rule. It would have been a counteroffer.

III. MODIFICATION UCC 2-209(1)

An agreement modifying a contract for the sale of goods is binding without consideration.

Normally, agreements for the modification of an existing contract must be supported by consideration to be binding upon the parties. The Uniform Commercial Code has modified this rule in the case of sales contracts. An agreement for the modification of a sales contract is binding without consideration and can be made anytime after the sales contract is formed. It is important to remember that the parties to a sales contract must agree to the modification. If only one of the parties wants to modify the contract, the original contract will continue to bind the parties.

Edna contracted to sell paint to Fred for $200. Edna delivered the paint, and Fred paid her. About two weeks later, Edna contacted Fred and told him that the paint had been priced incorrectly - correct price was $350. Fred agreed to pay the $150 difference. Fred later changed his mind and refused to pay so Edna sued him. Edna won because Fred would be bound by the agreement to modify the contract price. This agreement was binding without consideration because the contract was for the sale of goods. If Edna and Fred had entered into a contract in which Edna was required to paint Fred's home, the agreement to change the price would not have been binding because it would not have been supported by consideration.

IV. MERCHANT'S FIRM OFFER UCC 2-205

A promise to hold an offer open is not binding unless it is an option contract or a merchant's firm offer.

Generally, options are not binding unless they are supported by consideration. When promises to hold offers open are supported by consideration they are binding and become "option contracts." In addition to creating an option contract, a merchant can make a binding promise to hold an offer open for the sale of goods without the necessity of consideration. Such an offer is called a "merchant's firm offer." A merchant's firm offer is a signed, written offer made by a merchant that specifies the material terms of the offer and the length of time it will remain open. Under the UCC, the time the offer is to be held open must not exceed three months.

Gary went to Herb's Used Cars to find a car for his son. He found a car he thought his son would like for $330 and asked Herb, a merchant, to hold it for him so that he could bring his son back to see it prior to purchase. Herb agreed to hold the car for two days. Gary returned with his son and was told that the car had been sold to someone else. Gary tried to find a similar car, but the least expensive car he could find was $430. Gary sued Herb for breach of his merchant's firm offer. Gary lost because Herb's promise to hold the offer open was not an option contract since it was not supported by consideration. It was not a merchant's firm offer, either, because it was not embodied in a signed, written document. Gary would have won $100 if he had either given Herb something for holding the offer open or had obtained from Herb a written, signed promise to hold the offer open for the two day period.

Essential Vocabulary

1. option contract
2. merchant's firm offer

CHECK YOUR UNDERSTANDING

DIRECTIONS: Read each of the following questions. Choose the best answer and study the discussion of the question.

1. Amy and Sue entered into a written contract in which Amy was required to deliver 123 gross of a certain type of ball to Sue for resale. Although they were quite specific regarding the type of balls, the price portion of the contract was left blank to be agreed upon later. After the balls had been delivered, Amy sent Sue an invoice for $1,230. Sue refused to pay that much for them, and she sent the balls back to Amy. Amy will probably:

   a. need to take the goods back because the offer lacked a material term dealing with price.
   b. need to take the goods back because contracts for the sale of inventory are voidable by a merchant.
   c. be entitled to a reasonable price if she refuses to allow Sue to return the balls.

    d. be entitled to $1,230 because Sue agreed to whatever price Amy demanded for the balls by accepting them when the contract was left partially blank.

    e. be liable for failing to disclose a material term during negotiations.

DISCUSSION

    (c)   Amy actually has three options in this case: (1) she can agree to a mutual rescission of the contract and accept the return of the balls; (2) she can accept the return of the balls and sue for breach of contract to recover the profit she would have realized from the sale if the goods were reasonably priced; or, (3) she can refuse to accept the return of the balls and sue for a reasonable price. Although the offer did not specify the price, it is a valid offer since the parties intended to be bound and the contract was for the sale of goods. If the contract had been for the sale of real property, intangible personal property or services, the failure to specify the price in the offer would have precluded the formation of a contract. Contracts for the sale of goods are not voidable by merchants in the absence of a valid defense or discharge. Amy will be able to recover $1,230 only if that was a reasonable price for the balls. Sue did not agree to whatever price Amy decided to charge. If she had agreed to allow Amy to fix a price, Amy would have been required to fix a reasonable price in good faith. There is no contractual or tort liability for failing to include a material term in an offer. If a material term is omitted from an offer, the offer is simply indefinite and cannot be accepted to form a contract.

2. Phil wrote Tom a letter in which he offered to sell him a used lawn mower for $300. Tom wrote back, "I accept your offer to sell the lawn mower for $300." He also added that Phil would pay for engine tune-ups and blade sharpening for five years. Phil delivered the lawn mower to Tom, and Tom paid for it. After about a year of use, the lawn mower needed to be tuned up and the blade needed to be sharpened. When Tom contacted Phil, he refused to pay for the work on the lawn mower. If Tom sued Phil for breach of contract, Tom would probably be entitled to:

    a. nothing because the acceptance did not create a contract.

    b. nothing because the contract was never written embodied in a single document.

    c. nothing because he accepted Phil's offer, and the offer did not contain the provision dealing with tune-ups or sharpening.

    d. damages because Phil accepted Tom's counteroffer when he delivered the mower to him.

e. rescind the contract because he was mistaken in thinking that Phil would have the lawn mower tuned up and sharpened.

DISCUSSION

(c) An acceptance that does not match the offer is effective to create a contract when the contract is for the sale of goods. The additional or different terms provided in the acceptance are treated as proposed changes in the contract. Phil did not agree to the additional terms so he had no duty to tune or sharpen the lawn mower. If Tom had made his acceptance conditional upon Phil's tuning and sharpening the lawn mower, no contract would have been formed if Phil did not agree. Tom could have done this by writing, "I accept your offer to sell the lawn mower for $300 on condition that you agree to tune-up and sharpen the lawn mower for five years." The Uniform Commercial Code imposes upon merchants the duty to object to proposed changes in the terms of the offer if the changes are not material. Neither Phil nor Tom were merchants so this rule does not apply here. If they had been merchants, Phil would probably not have been required to object to tuning and sharpening the mower in any case because the imposition of a $65 burden upon Phil would have been a material change in the terms of the offer. Even merchants have no need to object to changes in the terms of their offers if the changes are material. The contract between Phil and Tom was in writing even though the writing consisted of several documents. Tom could not rescind the contract based upon mutual mistake of material fact because he was the only party mistaken. Phil knew that he would not sharpen or tune the lawn mower.

3. Warren and Bill entered into a contract in which Warren sold Bill five parrots, and Bill paid $390 for them. About two months later, Warren called Bill and told him a mistake had been made in pricing the birds and demanded an additional $100. Bill agreed to pay the additional amount because the birds were exceptionally good at "talking." Bill later changed his mind so Warren sued him. Warren probably:

a. won because Bill's promise was an enforceable promise to make a gift.
b. won because Bill had agreed to modify the contract.
c. won on the ground of promissory estoppel.
d. lost because there was no consideration for Bill's promise to pay more.
e. lost because the contract had been completely performed prior to Bill's promise.

DISCUSSION

(b)   When Bill agreed to the change in price demanded by Warren, the parties had agreed to a modification of the contract. Since parrots are goods, the contract was a sales contract and could be modified without consideration at any time. Bill's promise was not a promise to make a gift. It was a promise to modify the consideration required under the previously executed sales contract in which he purchased the parrots. If Bill had refused to modify the contract, Warren would not have been entitled to the additional $100. No promissory estoppel was involved in this case because the consideration for Bill's promise to pay the $100 was the parrots. Promissory estoppel is a substitute for consideration when a party justifiably and detrimentally relies upon a promise that is not supported by consideration. Sales contracts can be modified without consideration at any time whether or not the contract has been performed.

4.   Allen was interested in purchasing a metal lathe from Industrial Tools, a tool merchant. The sales manager told Allen that the price quoted by Industrial Tools would be firm for five days. After three days, Allen went back to Industrial to purchase the lathe. When he met the sales manager, he was told that the price had gone up by $3,000. Allen was furious and sued Industrial to force the company to sell the lathe at the promised price. Allen will probably:

   a. lose unless he can prove that the sales manager quoted him the lower price.
   b. lose because the "accord" with Industrial Tools was not "satisfied."
   c. lose because Industrial's promise to hold its offer open was not binding.
   d. win on the ground of promissory estoppel.
   e. win because merchants' firm offers do not need to be supported by consideration.

DISCUSSION

(c)   Industrial Tools could withdraw its offer to sell the lathe at any time before it was accepted. No option contract was created because Industrial Tools did not receive any consideration for its promise to hold the offer open for Allen. Although Industrial Tools was a merchant, no firm offer was made by the sales manager because the offer was not written and signed. Accord and satisfaction was not an issue because there was no agreement to settle a dispute over an existing contract. Promissory estoppel would not operate to force Industrial Tools to keep its offer open as promised unless Allen could prove that his reliance on the sales manager's promise was justifiable and that he had suffered a detriment. In this case, he had suffered a detriment by relying on the sales manager's promise to hold the offer open. However, his reliance was not justified because he could not show that the manager had made similar promises in the past without consideration and kept them. While it is true that merchants' firm offers do not need to be supported by consideration to be enforceable, they are required to be written and signed. The promise to hold the offer open in this case was merely verbal.

Chapter 17

Sales Contract Defenses and Discharges

The Uniform Commercial Code adds additional defenses and discharges to those presented in previous chapters on contracts. These defenses and discharges generally apply only to contracts for the sale of goods.

I. WRITTEN SALES CONTRACTS UCC 2-201(1)(2)

Contracts for the sale of goods for $500 or more must be evidenced by a written contract, memorandum, or merchant's confirmation.

As you will recall, the Statute of Frauds requires written evidence of contracts for the payment of the debts of another, contracts that cannot be performed within one year, contracts made in consideration of marriage, and contracts for the sale of real property. In addition to the contracts required to be evidenced by writing under the Statute of Frauds, the Uniform Commercial Code requires contracts for the sale of goods for $500 or more to be evidenced by a written contract, memorandum, or "merchant's confirmation." When a written contract is used to evidence a sales contract, the offeree's signature constitutes acceptance. When the parties to a sales contract enter into a verbal contract for the sale of goods for more than $500, they can write a memorandum of their agreement. The memorandum will be binding upon the party signing it even if both parties do not sign. Signing a memorandum is an agreement to be bound by the terms of the memorandum. If both parties to a memorandum are merchants, the memorandum is called a "merchant's confirmation" and is handled differently than an ordinary memorandum. A merchant's confirmation is a memorandum sent by one merchant to another merchant. Unlike an ordinary memorandum, a merchant is required to object to a merchant's confirmation within 10 days of receiving it or be bound by its terms.

Debbie offered to sell a patio table to Eva for $625, and Eva accepted. Later, Eva denied that she had accepted the offer. If Debbie sued for breach of contract, she would probably not prevail because there would be no written evidence of the contract. If Debbie had sent Eva a memorandum of the contract, Eva would have been bound only if she had signed it. However, if they had been merchants, and Debbie had sent Eva a merchant's confirmation, Eva would have been bound on the contact if she failed to object in writing within 10 days even though she did not sign the memorandum.

Essential Vocabulary

1. merchant's confirmation

II. UNCONSCIONABILITY UCC 2-302(1)

Grossly unfair contracts resulting from grossly unequal bargaining power are unenforceable.

Contracts for the sale of goods that are grossly unfair due to the grossly unequal bargaining power of the parties are "unconscionable contracts." Unconscionable contracts are promises that shock the conscience of the court and will not be enforced. Contracts that are very unfavorable to one of the parties are enforceable even though they are bad bargains in the absence of grossly unequal bargaining power. The ability to take one's business elsewhere is a good indicator of the presence of bargaining power. When circumstances prevent a party from being able to take his business elsewhere, the bargaining power of the parties is not balanced. Contracts that are offered in the absence of competition on a "take it or leave it" basis are called "adhesion contracts." Adhesion contracts are enforceable as long as the gross difference in the bargaining power of the parties is not abused, i.e. they are fair. When grossly unfair bargaining power results in a grossly unfair bargain, the court may refuse to enforce the parts of the contract that it deems unconscionable. If the unconscionable portion of the contract cannot be severed from the contract as a whole, the entire contract is subject to rescission and restitution.

Frank needed a clothes dryer so he went to Gary's Used Appliances to purchase a dryer Gary had rebuilt. When he chose the one he wanted, Gary refused to sell it without a provision in the contract disclaiming all warranties and releasing Gary from all liability for any damages resulting from the product. All used appliance merchants within 100 miles had similar clauses in their contracts. Frank was forced to agree to Gary's terms to purchase the dryer. Frank signed the release of liability. The second time he tried to use it, the dryer malfunctioned burning Frank's house to the ground and injuring Frank. When Frank sued Gary, Gary raised the release as a defense. Gary lost because the release of liability allowed him to avoid all responsibility for the dryer's malfunction. This result was harsh, and Gary was able to obtain the release because Frank was unable to take his business elsewhere. All other nearby merchants required similar clauses to be in their contracts. The release was a contract of adhesion. The difference in bargaining power of the parties resulted in a grossly unfair bargain. Since the release could be separated from the sales contract as a whole, the court could refuse to enforce the release of liability on the ground that it was unconscionable and allow Frank to sue Gary.

Essential Vocabulary

1. unconscionable contracts
2. adhesion contracts

III. CASUALTY TO IDENTIFIED GOODS UCC 2-613

Casualty to identified goods without the fault of either party will excuse a sales contract and leave the buyer with the choice of avoiding the contract or purchasing the salvage at a discount.

"Casualty to identified goods" is damage to the goods selected to be the subject of a sales contract. The "casualty" or damage must occur without the fault of either party. If the casualty occurs due to a parties negligence or other misconduct, the party at fault is liable for breach of contract. Goods are "identified" when they are selected by the seller to fill the sales contract. When the goods are in inventory, they are unidentified because any of them could be used to fill a customer's order. However, once the seller has selected specific items to satisfy a sales contract and separated them in some way from the remainder of the inventory, they have been identified. Selection is typically informal and can be accomplished in any way the seller wishes such as by putting the goods in a separate pile, marking them, or putting them on a truck.

If the goods suffer casualty after they have been identified but before the seller has made the required delivery, the seller has risk of loss and the buyer has the option of canceling the contract or purchasing the salvage. The seller is not under an obligation to supply the buyer with undamaged goods under the contract. Since this rule could result in losses to the buyer, the Uniform Commercial Code gives the buyer an "insurable interest" in goods the moment they are identified to a sales contract. An insurable interest is required to purchase insurance. The presence of an insurable interest allows the buyer to purchase insurance on goods even though the risk of loss and title have not yet passed from the seller to the buyer. If the casualty occurs after the required delivery has been made, this generalization does not apply. Risk of loss has passed to the buyer, and the buyer must pay for the goods and rely on his insurance or the carrier responsible for delivery to reimburse him.

Helen entered into a contract in which she agreed to sell a stunt alligator named Rufus to Igor. Rufus was capable of diving off platforms and retrieving small objects from a river without harming them. After contracting, but prior to delivery, Rufus, the alligator, died of natural causes. Since alligators are goods, Helen and Igor had entered into a sales contract. The alligator was identified to the contract when the parties agreed that Helen would sell the specific alligator named Rufus. The alligator's death was a casualty to identified goods. Igor could avoid the contract or purchase the carcass at a reduced price. Helen would not be required to train and deliver another alligator under the contract. If Helen had been responsible for the death of Rufus, she would have been liable for breach of contract.

Essential Vocabulary

1. casualty to identified goods
2. casualty
3. identified goods
4. insurable interest

IV. FAILURE OF PRESUPPOSED CONDITIONS UCC 2-615

Failure of presupposed conditions will excuse a contract for the sale of goods.

In any contract for the sale of goods, the parties assume that usual conditions will continue to prevail throughout the transaction. The courts will allow the discharge of a sales contract when there is a "failure of presupposed conditions." A failure of presupposed conditions occurs when the parties are genuinely surprised by sudden changes in business conditions that make the contract "commercially impracticable." A sudden change in presupposed business conditions can be roughly defined as a a change in circumstances that the parties could not anticipate. A contract obligation is commercially impracticable when it is no longer commercially reasonable to perform it. When a sales contract is discharged by reason of failure of presupposed conditions, the contract is subject to rescission and restitution.

Tires, Inc. entered into a contract to sell a large quantity of special order tires to Beth's Retail Tires. After they entered into the contract, but before Tires, Inc. could procure the rubber necessary for the contract, the government imposed a trade embargo on rubber producing countries, and Tires, Inc. was unable to acquire rubber without paying three times the usual cost. This would result in a huge loss on the contract with Beth's Retail Tires. The contract would be excused because the embargo was not anticipated by either party, and it made the contract commercially impracticable.

Essential Vocabulary

1. failure of presupposed conditions
2. commercially impracticable

V. BULK TRANSFERS 6-104,105,106

A bulk transfer is ineffective against a merchant's creditors unless the buyer obtains a sworn list of creditors, gives notice of sale, and applies the price to the seller's debts.

A "bulk transfer" or "bulk sale" is a sale of a major part of the materials, supplies, merchandise, or other inventory of a business. Bulk sales are not made in the "regular course of business." The regular course of business is the usual way the seller conducts its business. For example, the usual way for a retail hardware store to sell inventory is to sell to customers who come into the store and pay for their purchases at a cash register. It would not be in the regular course of business for the store to sell its entire paint inventory by contract to another merchant. When a manufacturer or merchant sells a major part of its goods, creditors may be left without recourse to the seller's assets. To alleviate this problem, the UCC requires the buyer to give the seller's creditors notice of the impending sale so that they can make claims against the purchase price before it is given to the seller. If this is not done, the seller's creditors can recover the seller's goods even after the buyer has paid for them. If the assets are no longer in the possession of a buyer who has failed to comply with the notice requirements, the seller's creditors can recover the reasonable value of the goods from the buyer.

Kim's Auto Parts and Car Parts, Inc. entered into a contact in which Kim's Auto purchased all of Car Parts' inventory for $40,000. After Kim had paid and received Car Parts' inventory, the state tax commission contacted Kim and demanded payment for Car Parts' back taxes in the amount of $30,000, and Sports Cars Unlimited, one of Car Parts' suppliers, demanded $25,000 for parts supplied to Car Parts, Inc. Kim's Auto Parts will need to deliver the inventory to the creditors or pay $40,000. The limit of the liability for failure to comply with the notice requirements of the law is $40,000 in this case, because it was the reasonable value of the inventory purchased by Kim. Kim's Auto is not liable for all of Car Parts' debts, but Kim will lose her purchased goods or their reasonable value and be left with an unsecured claim against Car Parts, Inc. that she may or may not be able to collect. If Kim had required Car Parts, Inc. to provide a sworn list of creditors and sent notices to the creditors on the list, she would have been protected from the claims of Car Parts' creditors even if the list turned out to be incomplete. Car Parts' creditors would have been limited to seeking compensation from Car Parts, Inc. if the notice requirements of the UCC had been met whether or not they had actually received notice.

Essential Vocabulary

1. bulk transfer or bulk sale
2. regular course of business

CHECK YOUR UNDERSTANDING

DIRECTIONS: Read each of the following questions. Choose the best answer and study the discussion of the question.

1. Sally and Tim entered into an oral contract in which Tim promised to sell her a certain valuable book for $1,000. Tim later got an offer of $1,500 for the same book so he called her and demanded $1,500. When she refused to pay the additional money, Tim sold the book to another party. Sally sued Tim for breach of contract. If Tim denies that he entered into the contract to sell the book to Sally, she will probably:

    a. lose because the contract was not in writing.
    b. lose because valid sales contracts are revocable.
    c. win because Tim breached his contract to sell the book to Sally.
    d. win because estimates must be within 10% of the final price, and the $1,500 asked was well over the $1,100 demanded.
    e. win because there would be no consideration for Sally's promise to pay the additional $500 Tim demanded.

DISCUSSION

(a)   Books are goods. The Uniform Commercial Code requires that contracts for the sale of goods for $500 or more be evidenced by written contracts, memorandums, or merchant's confirmations. Since this contract was merely oral, it would be unenforceable unless Tim admitted the existence of the contract. When a party denies the existence of an oral sales contract for more than $500, the UCC allows enforcement if one of the parties has already performed. Sally could have enforced the contract even without written evidence if Tim had delivered the book and she had accepted it or if she had paid $1,000 for the book and Tim had accepted her payment. Valid sales contracts are not revocable by either party. No estimates were involved in this case because the price was fixed at

$1,000 by the parties. If Sally had promised to pay the additional $500 demanded by Tim, she would have needed to pay the new amount because sales contracts can be modified by agreement of the parties at any time without consideration.

2. Sam was unable to read and he didn't own a car. He needed a chair to furnish his apartment so he went to Quick Sell Furniture which was the only furniture store within five miles of his home. The sales representative at Quick Sell knew of Sam's situation so he offered to sell Sam a recliner for $300. Similar chairs were being sold at other stores for $125. Sam signed a contract to purchase the chair that indicated the chair was damaged and released Quick Sell from all responsibility for the damages. The contract was not read or explained to Sam. Sam refused to pay for the chair when he learned it was broken and returned it to the store. Quick Sell sued Sam. Quick Sell probably:

    a. lost because the contract was unconscionable.
    b. lost because the sales person misrepresented the condition of the chair.
    c. lost because contracts signed by people who cannot read are not binding.
    d. won because Sam signed the contract.
    e. won because Sam had already accepted delivery of the chair.

DISCUSSION

   (a)   Sam's contract was not enforceable because it was unconscionable. Grossly unfair contracts resulting from grossly unequal bargaining power are unenforceable. Grossly unequal bargaining power resulted from Sam's inability to take his business elsewhere and his lack of education. Quick Sell used its advantage to charge Sam more than twice what the chair was worth. There was no misrepresentation regarding the condition of the chair since the condition was disclosed in the contract and the sales person made no other representations. Contracts signed by people who cannot read are binding upon them unless someone uses that disadvantage to impose a grossly unfair bargain. The defense of unconscionability can be raised in cases involving both verbal as well as written contracts. The fact that Sam had accepted delivery of the chair does not preclude his raising the defense of unconscionability. However, if the court finds the contract unconscionable, Sam would be required to make restitution to Quick Sell.

3. Ron contracted in writing to deliver a certain trained racing chicken to Ling in consideration of which Ling promised to pay Ron $1,000. Delivery was to take place within three days. The next day, Ron's racing chicken was mistaken for a stewing chicken by an itinerant hobo and was eaten. Assuming that Ron was in no way negligent in the untimely demise of the chicken, which of the following is probably true?

a. Ron is liable to Ling for the reasonable value of the chicken.
b. Ron must train another chicken for Ling.
c. The contract is discharged.
d. Ling is entitled to specific performance.
e. Ling is liable to Ron for $1000 because Ron had the risk of loss.

DISCUSSION

(c) Since chickens are goods, the contract would be discharged by the casualty to identified goods which occurred without the fault of either party. Ling would have the option of purchasing any salvage at a reduced price or canceling the contract. Since the only salvage would have been bones and feathers, the only real option open to Ling would be cancellation. Ling could not require Ron to train another chicken for him under the original contract. Ling could not obtain specific performance because the chicken was no longer in Ron's possession. Ron did have risk of loss because he had not yet made delivery to Ling. However, Ron would not be liable to Ling for the loss because he did not cause it.

4. Ellie entered into a valid contract to manufacture gasoline for Warren. Due to coordinated terrorist attacks around the world there was an unforeseen shortage of oil. Ellie could obtain oil only at prices seven times as high as the highest price demanded prior to the crisis. The contract contemplated deliveries over several years' time. Ellie will probably need to:

a. deliver the gasoline as agreed and accept the loss.
b. deliver the gasoline as agreed but raise her contract price to a reasonable level.
c. deliver the gasoline as agreed and split the loss with Warren.
d. notify Warren of the unforeseen circumstances and inform him that she cannot perform in order to be excused by failure of presupposed conditions.
e. organize a counter terrorist group and finance them by selling arms to relatively benign terrorists.

DISCUSSION

(d) Ellie's obligation to deliver the gasoline under her contract with Warren would be discharged by a failure of presupposed conditions. The unforeseen attacks of terrorists changed the supply of oil that both parties assumed while negotiating their contract. The huge increase in the price of the oil made the transaction commercially impracticable or unreasonable. Ellie cannot raise the price of the gasoline without the agreement of Warren. If they agreed to a change in price, it would be binding because sales contracts can be modified without consideration at any time. There is no justification in the law for splitting the loss in the absence of an agreement to do so by the parties. Ellie would have an obligation to notify Warren of the circumstances to exercise good faith.

5. World Fruits, Inc. entered into a binding contract to purchase the assets of Ma's Produce, Inc. for 1.5 million dollars. No notice was sent to the creditors of Ma's Produce. The contract was executed, and all of Ma's assets were delivered to World Fruits. The price was distributed to Ma's shareholders. Ma's Produce owed Gary, a farmer, two million dollars. Gary could probably:

   a. recover $1.5 million of Ma's debt from World Fruits.
   b. recover all of Ma's debt from World Fruits.
   c. collect his debt from Ma's shareholders.
   d. not recover anything because the transaction had already been completed.
   e. not recover anything from World Fruits because he failed to comply with the Bulk Transfers Act.

DISCUSSION

(a) World Fruits would be liable to Gary because it failed to notify the creditors of Ma's Produce of the bulk sale in accordance with the bulk transfer provisions of the Uniform Commercial Code. World Fruits would have the option of delivering the assets it purchased to Gary or pay him their reasonable value. Gary had no obligation to comply with the Bulk Transfers Act of the Uniform Commercial Code. The UCC places the burden of compliance and the risk of noncompliance on the purchaser in a bulk sale. The contract for sale would not prevent Ma's creditors from recovering the goods or their value from World Fruits. If World Fruits had required a sworn list of creditors from Ma's Produce and sent notices of the sale as required, it would have been protected even if the list was incomplete. World Fruits' failure to comply with the statute did not make it liable for all of Ma's debts. It's maximum liability would be the value of the goods it received from Ma's or 1.5 million dollars. Ma's shareholders would not be liable in the absence of cause for piercing the corporate veil, i.e. fraud, watered shares, inadequate capitalization, or failure to observe corporate formalities. The fact that the transaction had already been completed would have no effect.

Chapter 18

Title, Risk of Loss and Performance

In sales contracts, the goods are often held by the seller temporarily after the contract has been formed awaiting delivery to the buyer. For this reason, it has been necessary to develop rules governing the passage of title and risk of loss from the seller to the buyer. Whether the buyer or the seller has title is especially important to creditors, taxing authorities, and insurance companies.

Creditors can take property to satisfy a debt only if the debtor has title to it. If the seller has title to goods which are the subject of a sales contract, the seller's creditors can take them to satisfy their claims. However, if title has passed to the buyer, it is only the buyer's creditors that can reach the goods. This is the case even if the seller or someone else still has possession of the goods in question.

When the government imposes property taxes on personal property, it is the person who holds title to the property who must pay the tax. The seller must pay tax on inventory if she holds title to it even if it is the subject of a sales contract.

The party with risk of loss should insure property so that if it is damaged or destroyed she can be reimbursed for the loss by her insurance company. If both the seller and buyer have insurance on goods that are the subject of a sales contract, the insurance company of the party with risk of loss will need to cover any loss to the goods.

I. TITLE AND RISK OF LOSS UCC 2-308, 2-319, 2-401, 2-509

Title and risk of loss pass from the seller to the buyer when the seller has performed the delivery required by the sales contract.

When a sales contract is not executed at the instant it comes into existence, it is important to be able to determine whether the buyer or the seller has title and risk of loss. "Title" may roughly be defined as ownership. A person who owns personal property has title to it. It is not a written document such as a title certificate for an automobile or a deed to real property. These things, by themselves, are merely evidence of title. Creditors can take property to satisfy debts only when debtors have title. In other words, a creditor can take only property owned by the debtor to satisfy its claims. Similarly, taxing authorities impose personal property taxes on the parties who have title to personal property, i.e. the parties who own it. In a sales contract, title to the goods sold passes from the seller to the buyer when the seller has completely performed the delivery required by the sales contract. Until this performance is complete, title remains with the seller.

Similarly, "risk of loss" is important to the parties to a sales contract. The risk of loss is the burden of replacing the goods or suffering the financial hardship resulting from any casualty or loss. If the goods are destroyed before the buyer takes possession, it is necessary to determine whether the buyer or the seller must stand the loss. As in the case of title, risk of loss generally shifts from the seller to the buyer when the seller has completed the delivery requirements of the sales contract. If the goods are insured, the issue is important to the insurance companies covering the risk for the buyer and the seller. The insurance company insuring the party with the risk of loss be required to compensate its insured for the loss sustained.

Since title and risk of loss generally shift from the seller to the buyer when the seller has performed the delivery required by the sales contract, it is necessary to be able to determine just what sort of delivery is required of the seller. The delivery requirements differ in four basic ways in sales contracts. Sales contracts may require:

(1) **delivery of the goods;**

(2) **shipment of the goods;**

(3) **delivery of a document of title without moving the goods;**

(4) **no delivery or shipment.**

Sales contracts that require the seller to deliver the goods to the buyer at a location other than the seller's place of business are often called "delivery contracts" or "destination contracts." In contracts that expressly require a seller to make delivery of goods to a buyer's place of business or other location set by the buyer, risk of loss and title pass from the seller to the buyer when the seller presents the goods at the address for delivery. A seller tenders the goods when he offers them to the buyer at the appropriate location. Whether the seller transports the goods to the destination himself or ships them with a "carrier", the seller retains both title and risk of loss until the goods arrive at the buyer's address whether or not the buyer has already paid for them. A carrier is a company that transports goods or people for hire, for example trucking companies, railroads, airlines, and bus companies, etc.

Connie, the buyer, entered into a contract with Debbie, the seller, to purchase goods valued at $20,000. The written contract required Debbie to deliver the goods to Connie's place of business in another city. Connie paid for the goods as agreed. Before the goods had been delivered, one of Debbie's creditors obtained a judgement and attempted to seize the goods in Debbie's possession. Title remained with Debbie because the delivery required by the contract had not yet been made. Debbie's creditors could, therefore, seize the goods, leaving Connie with an action against Debbie for breach of contract. Unfortunately, Debbie may not have been in any position to repay Connie since she had apparently been unable to pay the creditor who seized the goods. If, however, the goods had been delivered before the creditors could seize them, the creditors could not have taken them since title would have shifted from Debbie to Connie when delivery was made at Connie's place of business.

Contracts that merely require a seller to ship goods are called "shipment contracts." These contracts merely require the seller to deliver the goods to a carrier without the responsibility of actually getting the goods to the buyer at their final destination. In shipment contracts, title and risk of loss pass from the seller to the buyer when the seller safely delivers possession of the goods to the carrier for shipment. Once this has been done, title and risk of loss pass from the seller to the buyer whether or not the buyer has paid for the goods. The carrier has responsibility to care for the goods and may even arrange to insure the goods during transport. However, it is the buyer who has the risk of loss and would need to collect from the carrier or insurance company in the event of casualty to the goods.

George, the seller, entered into a contract for sale of goods to Harry, the buyer. The contract required George to ship the goods to Harry in a different city. Harry was required to pay for the goods within thirty days of their shipment. After George left the goods with the carrier for shipment, they disappeared. Harry refused to pay for the goods because he had not received them. This contract only required George, the seller, to ship the goods. It did not require him to actually deliver the goods. George would prevail in a suit against Harry for the price of the goods. The risk of loss passed to Harry when George had completed the delivery requirements of the contract by taking the goods to the carrier for shipment. Harry would need to pay for the goods and pursue the carrier and his insurance company for reimbursement if the carrier does not voluntarily settle under the shipping contract.

It is readily apparent that classifying a sales contract as a shipment contract or a delivery contract can have important consequences for the parties and that the difference can depend upon whether the word, "ship" or "deliver," is used. Being able to easily identify the difference can be critical. Section 2-319 of the Uniform Commercial Code has provided a convenient method for specifying the delivery requirements of sales contracts by use of the term, "F.O.B." F.O.B. is an abbreviation for "free on board." Free on Board is a delivery term that indicates that title and risk of loss will pass from the seller to the buyer when the goods are placed at the specified location free of the seller's ropes, tackle, and control. "F.O.B. destination" requires the seller to transport goods to a stated destination and tender delivery of the goods to the buyer at that location. "F.O.B. point of shipment" requires the seller to place the goods in the possession of the carrier for shipment to the buyer. Title and risk of loss pass from the seller to the buyer when the goods are safely placed in possession of the specified carrier.

In our example above, Connie, the buyer, entered into a contract with Debbie, the seller, requiring Debbie to deliver the goods to Connie's place of business in another city. The delivery term of the contract could have been written by specifying that Debbie would deliver the goods to Connie's place of business "F.O.B. 314 East 1st Street, Salt Lake City, Utah." This would have clearly indicated that the parties intended a destination contract. If the contract discussed above involving George and Harry had required George to ship the goods via Big City Trucking based in Reno, Nevada, the delivery term could have been clearly written by specifying that George would ship the goods to Harry, "F.O.B. Big City Trucking, Reno, Nevada."

Sometimes, it is advantageous to conclude a sales contract without physically delivering the goods. In cases such as these, the parties may elect to use "documents of title." A document of title is a "warehouse receipt" or a "bill of lading" that entitles the holder of the document to possession of the goods described. A warehouse receipt is a receipt issued by a company that stores goods for hire. Warehouse receipts are issued so that warehousers will know to whom to return the goods. A bill of lading is a receipt issued by a carrier for goods submitted for shipment. Carriers issue bills of lading so that they will know to whom to deliver the goods at the shipping destination. When a receipt authorizes a warehouser or carrier to deliver goods to whomever is in possession of the receipt rather than a specific person or company, the delivery of the document transfers the right to take possession of the goods from the seller to the buyer. When this is the only delivery required by the contract, title and risk of loss pass from the seller to the buyer when the document is delivered.

Unis had purchased 60,000 bushels of wheat from various farmers for resale to her customers. While she was negotiating contracts for its resale, she stored the grain in a grain elevator. The company that owned the elevator gave her receipts for the wheat that entitled the persons or companies that presented the receipts to take possession of the amount of wheat noted on the receipts. She entered into a contract with Vern to sell him 20,000 bushels. Vern did not have an immediate use for the wheat and needed to store it until he was ready for it. He also had not decided where he would use it at the time Unis contracted him.

Unis and Vern entered into a sales contract that required Unis to deliver a receipt allowing Vern to take delivery of 20,000 bushels of wheat when she received Vern's payment. A few days after they had entered into the contract but before Unis had delivered the receipt, the grain elevator exploded strewing puffed wheat for miles. Since the receipt had not been delivered at the time of the explosion, Unis still had title and risk of loss. The delivery requirements of their contract would not have been performed until the warehouse receipt issued by the grain elevator company had been delivered by Unis to Vern.

When a sales contract does not specify delivery or shipment and no documents of title are used, the buyer must pick up the goods at the seller's place of business or, if he has no place of business, at his residence. When the place of delivery is not specified, the risk of loss and title pass from the seller to the buyer at the time of contracting because the only delivery required is making the goods available to the buyer. The Uniform Commercial Code has made an exception to the passage of risk of loss in cases where the seller is a merchant because merchants typically have insurance that covers the goods in their possession. When the seller is a merchant and no delivery is required by the contract, title passes from the merchant to the buyer at the time of contracting but the risk of loss remains with the seller until the buyer actually takes possession of the goods. This allows the parties to take advantage of the seller's insurance when the buyer does not take the goods at the time of contracting. To facilitate memorization, the generalization presented for this section of the text does not include this distinction.

Essential Vocabulary

1. title
2. risk of loss
3. delivery contracts (destination contracts)
4. carrier
5. shipment contracts
6. F.O.B.
7. Free on Board
8. document of title
9. warehouse receipt
10. bill of lading

II. SALE ON APPROVAL UCC 2-326,2-327

In a sale on approval, the buyer may return the goods during the approval period, and title and risk of loss pass from the seller to the buyer when the buyer approves the sale.

III. SALE OR RETURN UCC 2-326,2-327

In a sale or return, risk of loss and title pass to the buyer when the seller has performed the delivery required by the sales contract, and the buyer can return the goods, title and risk of loss during the return period.

At times, a seller may allow a buyer to try goods prior to purchasing them. This may be accomplished through a "sale on approval" or a "sale or return." When the contract is silent as to whether it is a sale on approval or a sale or return, it will be interpreted as a sale on approval if the goods are being purchased for use by the buyer and a sale or return if they are being purchased for resale.

In a sale on approval, the title and risk of loss remain with the seller until the goods are accepted by the buyer. The purchaser may use the goods as agreed in the contract during the "approval period" and can return the goods to the seller at any time. The approval period is the time during which the buyer can cancel the contract by returning the goods to the seller. If the buyer uses the goods in a way that was not intended by the parties or keeps the goods past the end of the approval period, he will be deemed to have approved the sale. When the buyer approves the sale, title and risk of loss pass from the seller to the buyer.

In a sale or return, the title and risk of loss pass from the seller to the buyer when the seller has performed the delivery required by the contract. The purchaser can return the goods to the seller at any time during the "return period" provided that the goods have not been damaged. The return period is the time during which the buyer can cancel the sales contract by returning the undamaged goods to the seller. If the buyer exercises this option, title and risk of loss will pass from the buyer back to the seller when the buyer returns the goods unharmed.

Gloria sold Pat an electric car in a contract which they agreed was a sale on approval. The approval period was one week. During that week, an intoxicated man drove a bus into the car pushing it into a river. The electronics were completely destroyed in the mishap. Pat had the car towed back to Gloria on the last day of the approval period. Gloria had title and risk of loss because the approval period had not expired. Since the loss was not due to intentional or negligent misconduct on the part of Pat, Gloria would have to suffer the loss. Pat would have no liability if she exercised her right under the contract to return the damaged car during the approval period.

Jane entered into a contract with Paul in which she agreed to sell him an antique lamp in a sale or return. The contract allowed Paul to return the lamp if he was not satisfied within three weeks. During the return period, a burglar broke into Paul's home and cut the lamp into four-inch strips with Paul's skill saw after it shocked him during the burglary. He left a note explaining this to Paul. Paul gathered the pieces into a box and took them to Jane indicating that he no longer wanted the lamp because it was defective. Jane and

Paul had agreed that this contract would be a sale or return even though the lamp was being purchased for use by the buyer. Because the contract was a sale or return, Paul had title and risk of loss during the return period. Paul was unable to return the lamp to Jane because it had been damaged by the burglar. Paul would have to suffer the loss.

Essential Vocabulary

1. sale on approval
2. approval period
3. sale or return
4. return period

IV. PERFECT TENDER RULE UCC 2-601

If the seller makes a perfect tender of performance, the buyer must accept the goods and pay the price; otherwise, the buyer may accept all the goods at a discount, accept and pay for conforming goods and reject the rest, or reject all of the goods and pay nothing.

A "tender of performance" is an offer to perform a contract. A "perfect tender of performance" is an offer to perform a contract exactly as agreed. In a sales contract, the buyer is obligated to accept the goods when the seller makes a perfect tender of performance, i.e. when he offers to deliver the goods exactly as required by the sales contract. The buyer breaches the contract if it refuses to accept delivery. However, if the seller delivers the wrong goods or otherwise fails to perform exactly as promised, the buyer has three options prior to suing for breach of contract. The buyer may inform the seller of the problem and agree to accept the entire order with an adjusted price to which both parties agree. If they cannot agree on an adjusted price, the buyer has two other options: accept and pay for the conforming goods and reject the nonconforming goods without paying for them; or reject the entire order without paying for it. It is the seller's responsibility, when this happens, to give the buyer instructions regarding what to do with the goods.

Owen and Stella entered into a written contract in which Owen was required to deliver to Stella eight identical wooden chests with animals carved on them for $800. When the chests arrived, three of them were carved with animals, but the rest were plain. Stella called Owen and complained about the chests that had not been carved. If Owen and Stella agreed, Stella could accept all of the chests at an adjusted price. For example, Stella may have been willing to accept the entire order for $600.

If either party did not want the make such an agreement, Stella could accept and pay for the carved chests and reject the others. To do this, she would have needed to pay $300 for the three chests that conformed to the contract. She would then have been required to follow any instructions given to her by Owen regarding how the other chests should be returned. Stella would also have had the option of rejecting all of the chests and paying nothing for them. If she chose this option, she would have informed Owen and followed his instructions for the return of the chests.

If Stella had chosen either of the options in which she rejected some or all of the chests, Owen would have been entitled to a reasonable time to cure the defects by delivering the appropriate number of carved chests to Stella. When the chests arrived, she would have been obligated to accept and pay for them. If Owen had not cured the defects in tender within a reasonable time or if he had indicated that he did not intend to send the appropriate chests, Stella could have sued Owen for breach of contract.

Essential Vocabulary

1. tender of performance
2. perfect tender of performance

V. NOTIFICATION OF BREACH UCC 2-508,2-605

The buyer must notify the seller of any defect in tender so that he can cure it within a reasonable time after the due date or the buyer cannot use the defect in action or defense.

When there is any "defect in tender of performance," the buyer is required to inform the seller so that he can cure the defect within a reasonable time. A defect in tender of performance is any deviation from the requirements of the sales contract. A failure to inform the seller would prevent the seller from curing the defect so the buyer would lose the right to raise the problem in an action for breach of contract or in a defense to the seller's action for breach of contract.

Carl and Ellen entered into a contract in which Carl was required to deliver 12 Ford carburetors to Ellen's auto shop on July 1st. On June 30th, Carl delivered 12 Chevrolet carburetors by mistake. Ellen refused to accept the delivery. When Carl asked Ellen why she would not accept the goods, she told him he was an "incompetent fool." She offered no other reason, and Carl was unaware of his error. Ellen could not successfully sue Carl for breach of contact because she had not informed him of the reason she rejected the goods. Furthermore, Carl would probably have been successful in an action for breach of contract against Ellen because she would be unable to use his error as a defense.

Essential Vocabulary

   1. defect in tender of performance

CHECK YOUR UNDERSTANDING

DIRECTIONS: Read each of the following questions. Choose the best answer and study the discussion of the question.

1. George, who was located in Wasatch City, and Karen, who was located in Chicago, entered into a contract in which George sold Karen five tons of beef. The contract required George to ship the beef, "F.O.B. Speedy Trucking, Wasatch City," to Karen in Chicago. While the beef was on its way to Chicago with Speedy Trucking, an uninsured motorist negligently collided with the truck, and the entire load was consumed by fire. Karen sued George for breach of contract because the beef was never delivered. Karen probably:

    a. won because this was a "destination contract."
    b. won because the F.O.B. term required George to deliver beef.
    c. won because title had passed to Karen in Wasatch City.
    d. lost because the contract did not specify that the beef would be delivered raw.
    e. lost because she had the risk of loss.

DISCUSSION

    (e)   The F.O.B. term in this contract indicated that the contract was a shipment contract. Therefore, title and risk of loss passed from George to Karen when George delivered the beef to Speedy Trucking in Wasatch City. Karen would need to seek reimbursement from Speedy Trucking or her insurance company to the extent the loss was not covered by Speedy Trucking. If the delivery term had been "F.O.B. destination," the contract would have required actual delivery and George would have retained title and risk of loss until the goods had been delivered to Karen in Chicago. If no delivery or shipment had been specified by the contract, Karen would have been required to pick the goods up at George's place of business in Wasatch City. Risk of loss would have remained with George until Karen took possession of the goods if George was a merchant and Karen was a consumer.

2. Mutt sold a vacuum cleaner to Jeff on approval. The price was $405, and the approval period was ten days. Eight days after Jeff had taken possession of the vacuum, it was stolen. He reported the theft to the police and Mutt on the ninth day. Which of the following is probably true?

   a. Title to the vacuum passed to Jeff.
   b. Jeff is liable for $405 to Mutt.
   c. Jeff is liable for the reasonable value of the vacuum.
   d. Jeff is not liable to Mutt for the vacuum.
   e. Title to the vacuum passed from Jeff to Mutt when it was stolen.

DISCUSSION

   (d)   Since the vacuum was sold in a sale on approval, title and risk of loss would remain with Mutt, the seller, until Jeff approved the sale or the approval period expired. When the vacuum was stolen, Mutt had the risk of loss so Jeff was not liable to Mutt unless he was negligent in the storage of the vacuum.

3. In a "sale or return," title and risk of loss:

   a. pass to the buyer immediately and pass back to the seller if the goods are properly returned.
   b. remain with the seller until the buyer approves the sale.
   c. are divided with title remaining with the seller until approval and risk of loss passing to the buyer immediately.
   d. are divided with risk of loss remaining with the seller until approval and title passing to the buyer immediately.
   e. are of little practical importance if the goods are properly insured.

DISCUSSION

   (a)   In a sale or return, title and risk of loss pass to the buyer immediately and pass back to the seller only when the goods are properly returned to the seller by the buyer. In question 2, Jeff would have been responsible for the price of the vacuum if he had purchased the vacuum in a sale or return because he would have had the risk of loss when the vacuum was stolen. In a sale or return, the buyer must return the goods to the seller unharmed within the return period to cancel the contract.

4. Albert bought three refrigerators from Hall for $400 each. Albert was required to make monthly payments of $100 per month until the $1,200 balance was paid.

Hall was required to deliver the three refrigerators in one delivery within ten days of contracting. When the refrigerators arrived two were badly damaged due to Hall's poor packing technique, and one was in fine condition. When Albert called Hall to complain, Hall was uncooperative and told him to "take them or leave them." Which of the following statements is probably true:

a. Hall can avoid the contract.
b. Albert must accept the refrigerators, but he can recover damages.
c. Albert must accept or reject all of the refrigerators and then sue for damages.
d. Albert may accept the good refrigerator and reject the others, but he will have to pay the reasonable value of the accepted unit.
e. Albert may accept the good refrigerator and reject the others, but he will need to pay Hall the price of the accepted unit.

DISCUSSION

(e)   Hall did not make a perfect tender of delivery because the refrigerators were damaged due to his improper packing technique. In the absence of perfect tender, Albert had three options. (1) He could accept the refrigerators and pay a discounted price that he and Hall agreed upon. Unfortunately in this case, Hall would not agree to any reduced price. He was being uncooperative so this option was not available. (2) Albert could have paid the price for the conforming refrigerator and rejected the damaged refrigerators. If he had chosen this option, Hall would have had a reasonable time to deliver undamaged refrigerators to replace the damaged ones. If he did replace the refrigerators, Albert would have been required to pay the agreed price for them. If Hall persisted in being uncooperative, Albert could have also sued him for any damages resulting from his breach of contract. (3) Albert could have rejected all of the refrigerators after informing Hall of the problems. If he had chosen this option, he would not have paid. Hall would have had a reasonable time to cure the defect and make delivery as agreed. If he had cured the defect and delivered the refrigerators to Albert within a reasonable time, Albert would have been required to accept the conforming delivery and pay for the refrigerators.

It is important to notice that Albert would be required to pay the price rather than the reasonable value for the undamaged refrigerators he accepted. Parties to sales contracts pay the reasonable value for goods they receive only when the contract does not specify a price. If the refrigerators had been damaged after risk of loss and title had passed from Hall to Albert and the damage had not been Hall's fault, Hall would have made a perfect tender and Albert would have been required to pay the agreed price for the goods. It would have then been Albert's responsibility to collect from the carrier or his insurance company.

5. Vern and Wilde entered into a contract in which Vern was required to build and deliver twenty chests-of-drawers to Wilde. The chests required had seven drawers each. However, the chests tendered by Vern's truck driver had only five drawers. Wilde refused to accept them and refused to disclose the problem to Vern. Vern sued Wilde for breach of contract. Vern will probably:

   a. recover damages from Wilde for breach.
   b. be liable to Wilde for breach.
   c. recover nothing on the contract although he may have a quasi contractual remedy.
   d. be liable to Wilde in quasi contract, but not for breach of contract.
   e. recover the costs of delivery although he would be liable to Wilde for any damages Wilde sustained by reason of Vern's breach.

DISCUSSION

(a)   Vern will probably recover damages from Wilde for breach of contract because Wilde failed to disclose the defect in tender. When Wilde failed to disclose the problem, he deprived Vern of his opportunity to cure the defect in tender within a reasonable time. This failure to give notice of the defect in tender resulted in Wilde's losing the ability to sue Vern for breach arising from the undisclosed defect and to use the defect as a defense when Vern sued him for breach. The Uniform Commercial Code is designed to encourage the parties to settle their differences out of court by requiring reasonable behavior.

Chapter 19

Sales Warranties

Buyers are interested in sellers' promises regarding the quality, description, future performance, and ownership of the goods they purchase. You have probably heard someone purchasing something ask the seller how long the item was "guaranteed." The purchaser was asking how long the seller would be responsible for the performance of the item. If the seller answered that the item would be guaranteed for one year, the purchaser would be able to take the item back to the seller for repair, replacement, or credit if it failed to perform properly during the one year period. The purchaser might purchase the item in question from the seller making the promise rather than from a competing seller who would not promise to stand behind the item. The Uniform Commercial Code governs the formation and enforcement of promises made in connection with sales contracts. These promises are properly called "warranties."

In common parlance, a warranty is a guarantee that goods will have certain characteristics, last a certain length of time, or perform in a certain way. The terms "guarantee" and "warranty" come from the same root word. Many legal terms come from the Norman French language. The "g" of the Norman French is equivalent to the English "w." These terms are often used interchangeably in commercial transactions, and most students are more familiar with the term, guarantee. Technically, a warranty differs from a guarantee in that a warranty is a promise made by one of the parties to a contract that goods will have certain characteristics while a guarantee is a promise made in a separate contract. In most cases, people mean "warranty" when they use the word "guarantee." For example, where a seller promises that a knife will remain sharp for one year, it is common to say that the knife is guaranteed to remain sharp for a year. However, if the seller of the knife made the promise as part of the sales contract the knife would be "warranted" for one year. If the promise was made by the seller in a separate contract or by someone other than the seller, the knife would be "guaranteed" for a year.

Essential Vocabulary

1. guarantee
2. warranty

I. EXPRESS WARRANTIES UCC 2-313

Unless otherwise agreed, a seller is liable for breach of express warranties created by promise, description, or sample.

An "express warranty" is a warranty made with words regarding the goods that are being sold. Express warranties are created by the seller's promises relating to the goods. For example, a seller would make an express warranty when she promised that an automobile tire would last for 30,000 miles. This promise would be enforceable by the purchaser because the consideration for it would be the purchaser's promise to pay for the goods. A seller warrants that her description or sample of the goods accurately represents the goods themselves. A seller's making a statement of fact creates a warranty that the facts represented about the goods are accurate.

If the goods do not perform as warranted or conform to their description, the seller may be liable for breach of express warranty. This liability is conditional upon the buyer's informing the seller of any nonconformity within a reasonable time to allow the seller to cure the defect. When the buyer informs the seller of the failure of the goods to conform to the promises made in the warranty, the seller may cure the defect by replacing the goods or repairing them. If the seller refuses to cure the defect, the seller is liable for damages in the amount of the difference between the value of the goods as warranted and their actual value as well as for foreseeable "consequential damages." Consequential damages are damages that are caused indirectly by the breach of warranty.

If the tires mentioned above were warranted for 30,000 miles but were actually only fit for use for 15,000 miles, the difference in value between the tires as warranted and the actual tires sold would be half their value. If the tires were sold for $100 each, the damages for breach of warranty would be $50. However, the breach may have indirectly caused down time for the vehicle or damage to property being transported in the vehicle when the tire failure occurred. These losses are consequential damages. If it was foreseeable that the tire failure would cause loss of use of the vehicle or damage to the property being transported, the consequential damages for these losses could be collected in an action for breach of warranty.

The liability for breach of express warranty can be limited by the agreement of the parties. Consequently, most express warranties are "limited warranties." A limited warranty is a warranty that limits the seller's responsibility to the buyer in the event the goods do not conform to the promises relating to them. The limitations usually limit the seller's liability to replacement of the goods or to making a pro rata adjustment allowing the buyer credit for whatever part of the warranty period the goods failed to last. In the example given above regarding the defective tires, the seller could have limited her liability to the replacement of the tires by making a limited warranty. If the seller had done this, she would not have been liable for the resulting consequential damages arising from loss of use of the vehicle or damage to the property being transported.

Ron bought a battery from Auto Mart for $60. The battery came with a written, limited warranty which indicated that the battery would last for three years and limited the duty of the manufacturer to making a pro rata adjustment in the event of a failure. After two years, the battery failed, and $100 worth of food in the freezer in Ron's motor home was spoiled due to the failure. Ron took the battery back and demanded a new battery and $100 for the spoiled food. Ron was probably entitled only to a pro rata adjustment. The battery had lasted for 2/3 of its warranted life so 2/3 of its value had been used by Ron. Ron would have been entitled to an adjustment for the portion of the battery life that he didn't receive or $20. The limitation of liability for breach of warranty would protect Auto Mart from liability for the spoiled food. In the absence of this limitation of liability, Auto Mart might have been liable for the reasonable value of the spoiled food if the court had decided that the use of the battery to operate a refrigerator was foreseeable as well as that the battery's failure could result in the loss of food.

Essential Vocabulary

1. express warranty
2. consequential damages
3. limited warranty

II. IMPLIED WARRANTY OF TITLE UCC 2-312

Unless otherwise agreed, a seller is liable for breach of warranty of title if the buyer doesn't receive good title free of liens.

The Uniform Commercial Code states that sellers make a "warranty of title" to purchasers when they sell goods. The warranty of title is the promise that the seller owns the goods being sold and that there are no liens against them. A "lien" is a creditor's right to take possession of the property of the debtor and sell them to raise money to pay the debt. Most buyers assume that sellers own the goods that they offer for sale. Sellers make this warranty by implication when they sell goods to buyers whether or not words are used. In other words, the warranty of title is made even if the seller is silent as to the ownership of the goods and the absence of liens. A seller has breached the warranty of title if a third party is legally able to take the goods from the buyer either because the third party owns them or because the third party has a lien against them. The warranty of title is made anytime a seller sells goods unless the seller expressly limits liability for good title by indicating that the seller does not own the goods or that they are subject to a lien. While the warranty of title is made by a seller whether or not words are used, limitations of this warranty must usually be verbally or in writing.

Larry entered into a contract with Carla in which he sold her a television set. The television set was collateral for repayment of money he had borrowed from Big Bank. Although Carla had paid Larry for the television, Big Bank took the set away from her when Larry missed his payments. Larry is liable to Carla for breach of warranty of title even though Big Bank's lien was not discussed. Larry made the warranty of title when he sold the television set to Carla. He could have limited his liability by telling Carla about the lien prior to entering into the sales contract. The parties could then have agreed to adjust the price appropriately so that Carla could have paid Big Bank and kept the television set, or she could have waited to purchase the set until Larry had paid Big Bank and the lien had been terminated.

Essential Vocabulary

1. warranty of title
2. lien

III. IMPLIED WARRANTY OF MERCHANTABILITY UCC 2-314

Unless otherwise agreed, a merchant is liable for breach of the implied warranty of merchantability if the goods are not suitable for ordinary use.

Merchants make the "implied warranty of merchantability" when they sell their inventory. The implied warranty of merchantability is an implied promise made by merchants that goods sold are fit for their ordinary uses. The word, "merchantable," means fit for ordinary use and, therefore, fit for sale. One should be able to sit on a chair, mix eggs with an egg beater, etc. If the goods do not conform and cannot be used for their ordinary uses, the merchant seller has breached this warranty. The warranty can be expressly disclaimed or limited prior to the sale. Merchants can do this by communicating verbally or in writing to buyers that they are not making the warranty of merchantability, or that they are not making warranties of any kind, or that the goods are being sold "as is," or "with all faults." To limit this liability, it must be brought home to the buyer that the merchant seller is not warranting that the goods will work or be fit for their ordinary uses.

Fred purchased a pair of shoes from Men's Shoe Co. When he got home and tried them on again, the heel of one shoe fell off onto the floor. He took them back to the store. Since Men's Shoe Co. is a merchant, it made the implied warranty of merchantability when it sold the shoes to Fred even though the shoe salesperson did not tell Fred that the shoes would be fit to wear. The warranty was breached when the heel fell off so soon. Men's Shoe will be required to repair the shoes, replace them, or refund Fred's money because the company breached the implied warranty of merchantability. Men's Shoe could have avoided liability if Fred had been informed prior to purchase that the company did not warrant that the shoes would be merchantable. It would not have been enough to indicate that no refunds or exchanges would be made without a sales slip. Fred would have been entitled to relief for breach of warranty of merchantability even if he lost his sales slip because the mere indication that there would be no refunds or exchanges without sales slips would not communicate that the company would not be responsible if the goods were not fit for their ordinary uses.

Essential Vocabulary

1. implied warranty of merchantability
2. merchantable

IV. IMPLIED WARRANTY OF FITNESS UCC 2-315

Unless otherwise agreed, a seller is liable for breach of the implied warranty of fitness if the buyer relies on the seller's judgement to select goods for a special purpose and the goods are not suitable.

A seller makes the "implied warranty of fitness for a particular purpose" when a buyer relies on the seller's expertise to assist him in selecting goods fit for the buyer's special needs. The implied warranty of fitness is an implied promise that the goods will be fit for the use the buyer has in mind. No language is required to make this warranty, and the seller does not need to be a merchant. This warranty is implied when a seller helps a buyer select goods for the buyer's particular needs. This warranty can be limited or disclaimed only by a conspicuous, written disclaimer indicating that no warranty of fitness for a particular purpose is being made or that there are no warranties that extend beyond the description of the goods. Words indicating that the goods are sold "as is" or "with all faults" are sufficient to exclude the implied warranty of fitness.

Gary purchased a raft and two paddles from Big's Sporting Goods for use in salt water. He asked the salesperson where the paddles were located and was told to look on aisle 14. After looking at the paddles for a few moments, he selected two that he thought would work well in salt water. While he was looking at the rafts, he consulted a salesperson to find out which of the rafts the company sold could be used in salt water. He finally purchased the company's "Rad Raft" for $100 after the salesperson assured him that the product would be ideal for use in salt water . Unfortunately, the salesperson was mistaken because the raft was made for use only in fresh water. Although neither the paddles nor the raft were defective, the salt water dissolved the glue when Gary took the equipment out to sea. Gary lost the raft, paddles, and $900 worth of fishing gear so he sued Big's Sporting Goods. Big's Sporting Goods would have been liable for breach of implied warranty of fitness for a particular purpose with regard to the raft because the salesperson helped Gary select it. However, Big's would not have been liable for the loss of the paddles because Gary selected them without relying on the expertise of the salesperson.

Big's Sporting Goods would have been liable for the difference in cost between the raft as it was and as it was represented as well as for consequential damages. The raft was totally lost along with the fishing gear so the company would have been liable for $1,000. There would have been no liability for breach of the implied warranty of merchantability even though the seller was a merchant because the raft and paddles were not defective. The equipment failed only because it was used in salt water which was Gary's particular use for them. Big's Sporting Goods would have had no liability if Gary had selected the raft himself without relying on the salesperson to help him choose a raft fit for use in salt water.

Essential Vocabulary

1. implied warranty of fitness for a particular purpose

V. LIABILITY

A seller is liable for breach of warranty to any foreseeable victim for any foreseeable harm and liability for personal injury cannot be limited.

While it is generally possible to limit liability for breach of warranties resulting in "economic losses," limitations of liability are not generally enforceable for "personal injuries." Economic losses are damages to property or monetary losses while personal injuries are injuries to the bodies of people. Historically, the courts have struggled with whether or not third parties who were not in "privity of contract" but were nevertheless injured, could sue for breach of warranties made in sales contracts. Privity of contract is the relationship between the parties to a contract. In other words, parties who are injured by a breach of warranty but are not in privity of contract are third parties who are not parties to the contract and were not the intended recipients of the promises made in the contract. In modern times, the historical requirements of privity of contract have been dropped as more inclusive liability rules have been adopted by the various states. In most states, any foreseeable victim who suffers a foreseeable harm resulting from a breach of warranty can sue for any foreseeable injury. This is the same requirement discussed in connection with "proximate cause" in the section dealing with the tort of negligence.

Ben manufactured and sold fuel tanks for trucks. He sold one of the tanks to Carlos. The sales contract warranted Ben's workmanship but limited Ben's liability for defective tanks to replacing or repairing the tank. The tank exploded when it broke due to metal fatigue. Carlos' truck was damaged and both Carlos and his wife were injured. It was undisputed that the accident occurred due to a defect in the material rather than Ben's workmanship. Ben would probably be liable to Carlos for the physical injuries he and his wife suffered but not for damage to the truck. The disclaimer would have been effective to protect Ben from the economic losses resulting from damage to the truck. However, it would not have eliminated liability for the personal injuries that Carlos and his wife suffered. If other people had been injured when the tank exploded, they too could have sued for breach of warranty of merchantability if they were foreseeable victims suffering foreseeable harm.

Dan purchased a cake from Bakery, Inc. for his daughter's birthday. After dinner, Dan took his family to the movies intending to eat the cake when they returned. While they were gone, Elsie burglarized Dan's home and ate a piece of the cake. Unfortunately, due to the negligence of an employee of Bakery, Inc., the cake contained ground glass. Elsie was seriously injured and sued Bakery, Inc. for damages for breach of warranty of merchantability since the cake was not fit for its ordinary use, i.e. eating. Elsie lost because she was not a foreseeable victim. Only Dan, his family, and his guests would have been foreseeable victims. Elsie would not have been able to recover damages if she sued Bakery, Inc. for negligence either because she would not have been a foreseeable victim required for proximate cause.

Essential Vocabulary

1. economic loss
2. personal injury

CHECK YOUR UNDERSTANDING

DIRECTIONS: Read each of the following questions. Choose the best answer and study the discussion of the question.

1. Lisa sold Marlin her stereo system. Although the stereo had worked when she used it last, it did not work when Marlin took it home. Marlin sued Lisa. Marlin will probably:

   a. lose because he failed to take a security interest in the goods.

b. lose because Lisa made no express or implied warranties other than the warranty of title, and title was good.

c. win because Lisa breached the implied warranty of merchantability.

d. win because Lisa breached the implied warranty of fitness for a particular purpose.

e. win because Lisa failed to disclose the fact that it didn't work.

DISCUSSION

(b)   Lisa did not make any express warranties regarding the stereo. Since she was not a merchant, she did not make the implied warranty of merchantability when she sold the stereo to Marlin. She also did not make the implied warranty of fitness for a particular purpose because Marlin did not rely on her assistance to select a stereo for some special purpose he had in mind. The only warranty made by Lisa was the warranty of title. By selling the stereo to Marlin, Lisa warranted that she owned the stereo and that there were no liens against it. This warranty was not breached. A security interest is a type of lien that would have allowed Lisa to repossess the stereo if Marlin had failed to pay her. This will be discussed in the chapter dealing with secured transactions and is not relevant here. Lisa did not know that the stereo would not work. Buyers are governed by the rule of Caveat Emptor, or buyer beware, in the absence of facts allowing for the rescission of a contract based upon nondisclosure as discussed in the chapter on contract defenses.

2. Nevil sold Orvil a refrigerator. The refrigerator was later repossessed by one of Nevil's creditors who held a lien against it. Orvil sued Nevil. Orvil will probably:

a. win because Nevil breached the implied warranty of merchantability.

b. win because Nevil breached the implied warranty of fitness for a particular purpose.

c. win because Nevil breached the warranty of good title made by all sellers of goods.

d. lose because he failed to check for liens that had been filed with the state Commercial Code Department.

e. lose because Nevil made no representations about the absence of liens, and Orvil never asked.

DISCUSSION

(c)   Whether or not Nevil was a merchant, he made the warranty of title when he sold the refrigerator to Orvil. No words were necessary. Nevil's act of selling the refrigerator implied that he owned it and that there were no liens against it. When Nevil's creditor repossessed the refrigerator pursuant to its lien, the warranty was breached, and Nevil became liable to Orvil for breach of the implied warranty of title. No implied warranty of merchantability was made by Nevil because he was not a merchant. Even if he had been a merchant, there would have been no breach of implied warranty of merchantability if the refrigerator worked. Nevil did not make the implied warranty of fitness for a particular purpose because he did not help Orvil select a refrigerator appropriate for Orvil's particular needs. The warranty of title is made whether or not public notice of a lien has been given through filing with the state Commercial Code Department. In addition, the warranty of title is made even in the absence of express representations about the ownership of and liens against goods being sold. The buyer may assume that the seller owns goods being sold and that there are no liens against them. Furthermore, a buyer will not lose in an action for breach of the warranty of title merely because he failed to check for filed liens against the goods.

3. Richard, a merchant, sold a new toaster to Sylvia. The toaster did not work so Sylvia attempted to exchange it. Richard refused to allow the exchange because she had lost her sales receipt. He had posted a large sign that indicated that no refunds or exchanges would be made without a sales slip. If Sylvia sued Richard, he would probably:

    a. not be liable to Sylvia because she lost the sales receipt.
    b. be liable to Sylvia for breach of sales contract.
    c. be liable to Sylvia for breach of the implied warranty of fitness.
    d. be liable to Sylvia for breach of the implied warranty of merchantability.
    e. not be liable to Sylvia because there was no express warranty.

DISCUSSION

(d) Richard made the implied warranty of merchantability by selling the toaster to Sylvia because Richard was a merchant. The toaster was not merchantable because it did not work. The sign posted by Richard would not limit the implied warranty of merchantability because it did not mention that there would be no implied warranty of merchantability in the absence of a sales slip or that the goods were being sold "as is" unless the customer could produce a sales slip. Therefore, Richard would be liable to Sylvia for the toaster if the court believed that she had purchased the toaster from him. There was no breach of sales contract because Richard delivered the toaster to Sylvia as required. No warranty of fitness for a particular purpose was made because Sylvia did not rely on Richard's expertise to help her select an appropriate toaster. A merchant makes the implied warranty of merchantability merely by selling his inventory. No express warranty is required to make a merchant liable for goods that are not fit for their ordinary uses.

4. Theodore went into Uriah's Paint Shop and asked Tom, a salesperson, to show him some waterproof interior paint that would stand up to frequent washings. Although it was Tom's first day on the job, he listened carefully and helped Theodore select some paint. The paint Tom recommended washed off of Theodore's walls the first time they got wet. Under these circumstances, the paint Theodore received was of the same value as the waterproof paint. The paint was worth $600, and the labor to have it put on was $400. Theodore sued Uriah's Paint Shop. He will probably recover:

    a. nothing.
    b. $400.
    c. $600.
    d. $1,000.
    e. $1,000 plus damages for fraud in the inducement.

DISCUSSION

    (d)   Uriah's Paint Shop made an implied warranty of fitness for a particular purpose because Theodore relied upon the expertise of Tom, one of Uriah's salespeople, to help him select paint appropriate for his particular use. No express warranty was required. The warranty of fitness for a particular purpose was made when Tom helped Theodore select paint that would stand up to frequent washings. When the paint washed off the walls, the warranty was breached. Uriah's Paint Shop would be liable for the difference between the value of the goods as warranted and their actual value as well as any foreseeable consequential damages. The difference in value between the paint as warranted and the actual paint was zero in this case because the waterproof paint and the paint Theodore bought sold for the same price. However, the loss of the paint and labor were foreseeable consequential damages that could be recovered. Theodore's damages would have been $1,000. There would have been no liability for the tort of fraud in the inducement because there was no evidence that Tom intentionally misrepresented the characteristics of the paint to induce Theodore to purchase it.

5. Damages for breach of warranty are:

    a. the price of the goods or a full refund.

b. the difference between the market value of the goods and the contract price.

c. the price of the goods and, in the proper case, punitive damages.

d. the difference between the actual value of the goods and the contract price.

e. the difference between the actual value of the goods and their warranted value plus any consequential damages.

DISCUSSION

(e)   Damages for breach of warranty are the difference between the actual value of the goods and their warranted value plus consequential damages. Liability can be limited or disclaimed by an express disclaimer properly made prior to the sale of the goods. The damages are not the price of the goods or a full refund because the goods may have some salvage value even though they are defective. The difference between the market value or actual value of the goods and the contract price are not good measures for damages for breach of warranty because they fail to include the element of consequential damages. Punitive damages are damages only properly awarded in cases of intentional torts or recklessness. They are not normally awarded in cases of breach of contract or sales warranty.

Chapter 20
Secured Transactions

The parties to contracts generally perform as promised. In the event a promise is broken, the injured party can sue for breach of contract and obtain remedies designed to provide the benefit of his bargain. Most contracts are of this type and are called "unsecured transactions." An unsecured transaction is a contract that is enforceable only by obtaining a judgement in court against the party that breached the contract. Collecting judgements can be difficult or impossible if the breaching party has no property or income.

Article 9 of the Uniform Commercial Code allows parties to contracts to secure the performance of other parties through "secured transactions." A secured transaction is a contract that is enforceable by taking possession of the breaching party's property, selling it, and applying the proceeds to the debt prior to obtaining a judgement for any amount that is still owing after the sale of the property. This type of contract is advantageous because it greatly increases the probability that an injured party will obtain satisfaction for a breach of contract.

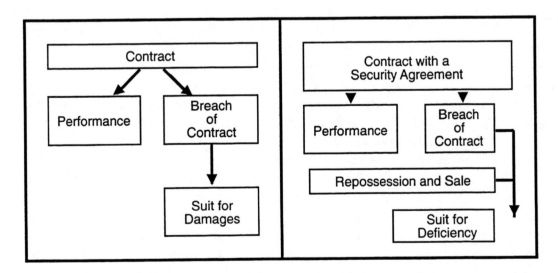

Figure 20-1 — Unsecured Transaction vs. Secured Transaction

Most automobile sales contracts are secured transactions so that the financing company can repossess the car in the event the purchaser does not make payments as promised. If the contracts were not handled as secured transactions, finance companies could only sue for amounts owed when a purchaser quit making payments. No repossession would be possible. The differences between unsecured transactions and secured transactions are summarized at a glance in Figure 20-1.

Essential Vocabulary

1.   unsecured transactions
2.   secured transactions

I. SECURITY INTERESTS UCC 9-203

A security interest is created when a secured party takes possession of collateral subject to a security agreement or the debtor takes possession of collateral subject to a written security agreement.

A secured transactions is a transaction in which a "security interest" is created in a debtor's property. A security interest is one of many types of liens created by statute or common law. A "lien" is the right to take possession of a debtor's property and sell it to raise money to satisfy a debt. A security interest is created when the parties to a contract enter into a "security agreement." A security agreement is an agreement between the parties that in the event of a default on a contract, the "secured party" can take possession of specific personal property belonging to the defaulting party and sell it to raise money to cover the debt. The secured party is the party that has the right to take possession of and sell property in the event of a default. The property that will be taken is called the "collateral" and must be described with specificity. It is the security agreement that creates a security interest. In the absence of a security agreement, a debtor's property cannot be taken by a creditor prior to judgement.

Allan sold his car to Bill pursuant to a contract that required Bill to make payments to Allan for eight months. When Bill missed a payment, Allan repossessed the car. If Bill sued Allan for conversion, he would be successful because the contract did not contain a security agreement. A creditor has no right to repossess collateral in the absence of a security agreement or some other lien. Allan and Bill would have needed to agree to the repossession in writing because Allan allowed Bill to take possession of the car. Security agreements do not need to be in writing when secured parties retain possession of the collateral.

Doris, a dentist, entered into a verbal contract with Charles in which she sold him dentures. The contract provided that she would keep the dentures until Charles paid for them as agreed. Charles failed to pay so Doris refused to give him the dentures. Charles sued Doris for conversion. Doris was probably not liable because this transaction created a valid pledge. A "pledge" is a secured transaction in which the secured party retains possession of the collateral until the debtor has performed. Although pledges are not generally required to be evidenced by written contracts or memorandums, it is good practice to require and maintain written documentation. Common pledges are "lay away contracts" and "pawns." A lay away is a secured transaction in which a retailer retains possession of the property purchased until the customer fully pays for it. If the customer fails to pay as promised, the retailer may retain the payments made and resell the merchandise. A "pawn" is a secured transaction in which a person borrows money from a pawn broker and leaves the collateral with the lender pursuant to a security agreement that allows the lender to sell the collateral and keep the proceeds if the loan is not repaid as agreed.

Essential Vocabulary

1. security interest
2. lien
3. security agreement
4. secured party
5. collateral
6. pledge
7. lay away contract
8. pawn

II. UNPERFECTED SECURITY INTERESTS UCC 9-301, 9-307

An unperfected security interest is enforceable against the debtor and subsequent purchasers of the collateral unless they were unaware of the security interest or purchased from a merchant.

One of the basic principals of due process is the idea that people are entitled to notice before action is taken against them. A debtor is given notice by the security agreement that the secured creditor will take possession of the collateral in the event of a default on the contract. Security interests can be enforced against everyone with notice of them. Since only the secured creditor and the debtor are parties to the security agreement, they are usually the only people with actual notice of the security interest.

In practical terms, this means that the secured creditor can enforce a security interest only so long as the debtor has possession of the collateral. If the debtor sells the collateral to another who is not aware of the security interest, the secured creditor cannot recover it from the innocent purchaser. Such a security interest is called an "unperfected security interest" due to this weakness. Unperfected security interests are good only against the original debtor and purchasers who are aware of the security interest before they purchase the collateral. Also, no security interest can be enforced against anyone who purchases goods in the regular course of business from a merchant. This exception to the enforceability of security interests has been placed in the law to encourage commerce. Purchasers from merchants get good title free of security interests whether or not they are aware of security interests in the goods.

Paula purchased a dining set from Wonder Furniture. The written sales contract required her to make payments for fifteen months and contained a valid security agreement in which the furniture was the collateral. Wonder failed to perfect its security interest. If Paula failed to make payments as agreed, Wonder Furniture could repossess the furniture if Paula still had it. If she had sold it, Wonder Furniture could not repossess the furniture from the new owner because it had not perfected its security interest. Its only recourse would be to sue Paula for damages. If Paula was not making payments because she had lost her job or suffered some other financial disaster, Wonder Furniture would be unable to collect from her. Interestingly, if Paula had made her payments she would have been safe from Wonder Furniture's secured creditors even if she was aware that the dining set was collateral for one of Wonder Furniture's loans. Wonder Furniture was a merchant so its customers in the regular course of business would take good title to all of its inventory.

Essential Vocabulary

1.   unperfected security interest

III. PERFECTION UCC 9-302,9-305

A secured party may perfect a security interest by taking possession of the goods or filing a financing statement.

IV. PERFECTED SECURITY INTERESTS UCC 9-307

A perfected security interest is enforceable against the debtor and subsequent purchasers who did not purchase from a merchant.

A "perfected security interest" is a security interest that is enforceable against subsequent purchasers as well as the original debtor. There are two ways to perfect a security interest — (1) the secured creditor can retain possession of the collateral; or (2) the secured creditor can file a financing statement with the appropriate governmental office. A "financing statement" is an announcement that the creditor claims a security interest in certain items of the debtor's property. The theory behind perfecting a security interest is that when the secured creditor retains possession of the collateral or files a financing statement, the entire world is given constructive notice that the secured creditor claims a security interest. It should be noted, however, that purchasers who buy goods subject to security interests can sue for breach of warranty of title even if the seller's creditors have perfected their liens by filing financing statements.

Secured transactions in which the secured party retains possession of the collateral are called pledges as mentioned above. A pledge effectively gives the world notice of the security interest because potential purchasers would need to go to the secured creditor to examine the goods prior to purchase. The filing of a financing statement gives the world notice because potential purchasers have an opportunity and obligation to check for the existence of security interests prior to entering into sales contracts. If they fail to protect themselves, they may suffer the consequence of having the goods they purchased from a nonmerchant seller repossessed by one of the seller's secured creditors.

Orville purchased five used typewriters from Paul, an attorney. He paid Paul for the typewriters and took them to his firm. A short time later, City Office Machines, Inc. took the typewriters from him because it held a perfected security interest for the purchase price. After Orville had purchased the typewriters, Paul had ceased to make payments on them. Orville would have an action against Paul for breach of warranty of title. However, if Paul did not have sufficient assets to cover his liability, Orville might be unable to collect any judgement he was awarded. Orville could have protected himself by checking with the state office in charge of commercial code filings. He should have gone to the appropriate state office and asked to check financing statements filed on Paul's property. To do so, he would have needed Paul's social security number or taxpayer identification number to aid in his search because there would probably have been many debtors with the same name as Paul.

Ellen worked for Mega Hardware. She purchased a table saw from her company in the regular course of business although she knew that it was part of the collateral for Hardware Wholesale's security interest in Mega's inventory. Mega defaulted on its obligation to Hardware Wholesale so Hardware Wholesale sued Ellen for return of the table saw. Hardware Wholesale lost because Mega Hardware was a merchant. Hardware Wholesale's security interest would not have been enforceable against Ellen even if it had perfected its security interest and even if Ellen had actual knowledge of the security interest because she purchased the saw from Mega Hardware in the regular course of business. The exception to the enforceability of security interests when the collateral is purchased from merchants is necessary because the state offices responsible for filings cannot accommodate the enormous numbers of people who purchase goods from merchants.

Essential Vocabulary

1.   perfected security interest
2.   financing statement

V. TERMINATION STATEMENTS UCC 9-404

A termination statement must be filed when a secured obligation perfected by filing a financing statement has been satisfied.

Once the contract has been performed, the secured party should terminate any filings that were made to perfect the security interest. This is done by filing a "termination statement" with the appropriate governmental offices. A termination statement ends the security interest and instructs the state office in charge of commercial code filings to remove the financing statement from the public records. A failure to promptly file a termination statement can generate liability for damages and penalties under state statutes and court decisions. Security interests that were perfected by taking possession of the collateral rather than filing are terminated by giving possession of the collateral to the debtor. Unperfected security interests are terminated without further action on the part of the secured party when the debtor has performed as agreed.

In our example above involving Orville's purchase of typewriters from Paul, if Orville had checked with the appropriate office and discovered City Office Machines, Inc.'s financing statement, he could have refused to purchase the typewriters until the security interest was terminated. If Paul had arranged with City Office Machines for the termination of its security interest prior to the sale of the typewriters, City Office Machines would have filed a termination statement. This would have made it possible for Orville to obtain title to the typewriters free of City's security interest.

Essential Vocabulary

1.   termination statement

CHECK YOUR UNDERSTANDING

DIRECTIONS: Read each of the following questions. Choose the best answer and study the discussion of the question.

1. Phil and Quincy entered into a valid written contract in which Quincy bought Phil's television set and was required to pay for it in 15 monthly installments of $20 each. After making five payments, Quincy defaulted on the contract. Phil probably can:

    a. only repossess the television set.
    b. repossess the television set and recover damages.
    c. repossess the television set, resell it, and recover any deficiency.
    d. force Quincy into bankruptcy by an involuntary petition.
    e. only sue for damages.

    DISCUSSION

    (e)   The contract between Phil and Quincy was valid but the transaction was unsecured because it did not contain a security agreement. Without a security agreement, Phil would have no security interest. A security interest is the right to take possession of the collateral and sell it on default. Phil could only sue for damages. No repossession is allowed in the absence of a security interest. Individuals who are debtors cannot be forced into involuntary bankruptcy.

2. Rudy and Stanley entered into a valid written contract in which Rudy sold Stanley a hair dryer, and Stanley was obligated to pay $800 for it in ten monthly installments. The contract contained a security agreement, but Rudy neglected to perfect it. If Stanley quit making payments, Rudy could:

    a. repossess the hair dryer and recover the unpaid purchase price.
    b. recover the full purchase price only.
    c. repossess the hair dryer and recover the unpaid purchase price plus damages.
    d. repossess the hair dryer, resell it, and recover any deficiency in a suit for damages.
    e. recover only the unpaid purchase price in a suit for damages because he failed to perfect his security interest.

DISCUSSION

(d)   Rudy had a security interest because he and Stanley had entered into a security agreement. The security agreement consisted of words that indicated that in the event of a default by Stanley, Rudy would have the right to repossess and resell the hair dryer. If the proceeds were insufficient to cover Stanley's debt to him, Rudy could have sued for the deficiency. Rudy's failure to perfect his security interest would not affect its enforceability because Stanley was aware of it. However, if Stanley had sold the hair dryer to a purchaser who was unaware of Rudy's security interest, Rudy would not have been able to repossess the hair dryer from the innocent purchaser due to his failure to perfect. Rudy could not both repossess the hair dryer and recover the unpaid purchase price because he would collect too much if Stanley had equity in the hair dryer. If Rudy had elected to sue for damages rather than pursue his security interest, he would have recovered the unpaid purchase price rather than the full purchase price.

3.   A financing statement:

   a.   may be written or oral.
   b.   is filed to give the world notice of the creditor's security interest in the debtor's property.
   c.   is usually a copy of the security agreement which is filed with a governmental office.
   d.   cannot be used to perfect a security interest in inventory.
   e.   may not attach to exempt property as defined by state and federal law.

DISCUSSION

(b)   A financing statement is filed with a state governmental office to give the world notice of a creditor's security interest in the property of the debtor. It is not the financing statement that creates the security interest. Rather, the security interest is created by a security agreement which is typically included in the contract between the parties. Inventory is routinely used as collateral in secured transactions, but the security interest is not enforceable against customers in the regular course of business. Property exempted from execution by state statutes can be taken by secured creditors and sold when it is listed as collateral in secured transactions despite the fact that ordinary creditors could not have taken the property even after judgement.

4. Brad, an appliance merchant, borrowed money from Big Finance Co. and secured the loan with his inventory. Big Finance Co. perfected its security interest. Brad sold a washer and dryer to Thompson, who knew about the security interest. If Brad quit making payments, Big finance Co. could:

   a. repossess the washer and dryer from Thompson.
   b. recover the reasonable value of the washer and dryer from Thompson.
   c. not repossess the washer and dryer from Thompson.
   d. recover damages from Brad for fraud on a creditor for selling the collateral.
   e. force Brad to recover the appliances from Thompson.

   DISCUSSION

   (c)   Brad was a merchant, and Thompson purchased the washer and dryer in the regular course of business. Thompson took good title to the property even though Big Finance Co. had perfected its security interest and even though Thompson was aware of it. Purchasers from merchants in the regular course of business take good title to the inventory they purchase. This is necessary to allow the state Commercial Code offices to function. They could not handle the volume of inquiries that would result if ordinary retail transactions with merchants had to be checked. Brad did not commit fraud by selling a portion of his inventory to Thompson. When secured parties take security interests in inventory, they understand that it will be sold to purchasers in the regular course of business. Their liens on the inventory are called "floating liens" because the actual property covered changes as inventory is sold and new inventory is acquired.

5. When a secured obligation that has been perfected by filing a financing statement has been completely performed, the secured party must:

   a. file a security agreement.
   b. file a termination statement.
   c. file a financing statement.
   d. destroy the security agreement.
   e. file a bill of sale.

   DISCUSSION

   (b)   When a security interest has been perfected by filing, it must be removed by the filing of a termination statement when the contract has been performed. The destruction of the security agreement would not terminate the filing with the state office. The security agreement creates the security interest and the filing of the financing statement perfects it. Bills of sale are merely evidence that purchasers have purchased property rather than stolen it. They have no applicability to secured transactions.

Chapter 21
Commercial Paper

It is often convenient to substitute written contracts for cash in business transactions. These written contracts are referred to as commercial paper. Commercial paper has some of the flexibility of cash without all of its risks. The ease of transferring cash and the difficulty of tracing it make it a less desirable medium of exchange than commercial paper. Although there are many variations, commercial paper can be divided into two broad categories: (1) promissory notes; and, (2) drafts. If you have purchased goods on an installment plan, you have probably signed a promissory note. Checks, which are a form of draft, are a common medium of payment. Nearly everyone has had some experience with commercial paper in connection with their personal business. This chapter will introduce the basic concepts underlying this important medium of exchange.

I. NOTES AND DRAFTS UCC 3-104

Commercial paper consists of promissory notes (promises to pay) and drafts (orders to pay).

Commercial paper takes two forms: "promissory notes", and "drafts." A promissory note is a written promise to pay money at a definite time or on demand. The person making the promise to pay money is the "maker" of the note. The person to whom the promise to pay money is first made is the "payee." Anyone who signs the note on the back is an "endorser." An "I.O.U." is not a promissory note. It is merely an evidence of indebtedness because no promise to pay is mentioned. A draft is an order to pay money. The "drawer" signs the draft and orders the "drawee" to pay money to a "payee." As in the case of a promissory note, anyone who signs the back of a draft is an "endorser." A check is a special type of draft, and a bond is a special type of note. There are many others, but the principals introduced in this chapter form the foundation of all commercial paper law.

Al gave Gary a signed letter containing the following words: "Dear Ben, please pay Gary $300. I'm short of cash. Thanks, Al." This letter was a draft in which Al was the drawer, Ben was the drawee, and Gary was the payee. If Al had given Gary a signed letter in which he had said, "Dear Gary, I promise to pay you $300," the letter would have been a promissory note in which Al would have been the maker and Gary the payee. In either case, anyone who signed the paper on the back would have been an endorser.

Notes and drafts are sometimes given more descriptive names, e.g. "certificate of deposit" or "check." The use of a name other than "note" or "draft" to classify commercial paper usually means that special rules apply to the particular promissory note or draft bearing the special name. A certificate of deposit is a promissory note issued by a bank to depositors, and a check is a negotiable draft drawn on a bank. They are given their more descriptive names because they are specially regulated in the banking industry. The "checks" issued by some credit unions are called "drafts" because the credit unions are not banks and some of the special rules governing checks do not all apply to the draft accounts provided by the credit union.

Essential Vocabulary

1. promissory note
2. Maker of a note
3. payee of a note
4. draft
5. drawer
6. drawee
7. payee of a draft
8. endorser
9. I.O.U.
10. certificate of deposit
11. check

January 3, 1951

Dear Ben,

Please pay Gary Doe $300.00. I'm short of cash.

Thanks,

Al

This paper is a draft because it orders Ben to pay Gary. Al is the drawer, Ben is the drawee, and Gary is the payee. Drafts used in business may contain additional terms. The date, "January 3, 1951," the presence of the words "please" and "thanks" and the explanation, "I'm short of cash." are not required parts of the draft and their omission would not change the character of the paper. This document is an order draft since the payee is named. In actual commercial paper, full names are used and additional terms would be included.

January 3, 1951

Dear Gary,

I promise to pay you $300.

Sincerely,

Al

This paper is a note by virtue of its promise to pay Gary. Al is the maker and Gary is the payee. Promissory notes used in business usually contain additional terms. The date, "January 3, 1951," and the presence of the word "sincerely" are not required parts of the note and their omission would not change the character of the paper. This document is an order note since the payee is named.

II. BEARER AND ORDER PAPER UCC 3-110, 3-111, 3-202

A note or draft in which the payee is not named is bearer paper, and paper in which the payee is named is order paper.

The payee may be named or unnamed on commercial paper. If the payee is not named, the note or draft is called "bearer paper" because the maker of the note or the drawee of the draft is authorized to pay the person who presents the paper for payment. Such a person is called the "bearer" because he "bears" or carries the paper to the person required to pay. Ownership of bearer paper can be transferred by merely delivering the paper to the new owner. Sometimes, the transferee of bearer paper will require the bearer to indorse the back in addition to making delivery as an additional precaution not required by law.

Alice owed Betty $25 for cleaning her windows. She wrote a check for the required amount and signed it. She neglected to write Betty's name on the line provided because she was not sure of the spelling. The check was bearer paper. If Alice had written the word "cash" or "bearer" on the line, the check would have remained bearer paper because the payee would not have been named. As long as no name was written on the payee line, the check could have been transferred merely by Betty's delivering it to someone else. If Betty had lost the check while it was "bearer paper," a stranger could have cashed the check. If this occurred, Betty could not have demanded repayment from Alice. Her only remedy would have been to find the stranger that cashed the check and sue for conversion.

When commercial paper names the payee, it is called "order paper." Notes and drafts in which the payee is named cannot be paid unless the payee orders them to be paid. This is accomplished by placing an "endorsement" on the back of the paper and delivering it to the new owner. Endorsements are signatures and words placed on the back of commercial paper relating to the transfer of ownership. There are several types of endorsements used on commercial paper, but the simplest is merely a signature on the back of the instrument. Endorsements will be discussed more fully in following sections. Mere delivery of order paper without the proper endorsement is not enough to transfer ownership.

Sylvia signed a promissory note that was payable to Tom. She gave the note to Tom as payment for gardening work he had done for her. Tom signed the back of the note and delivered it to Unis in exchange for sod. This promissory note was order paper because Tom was named as the payee. Unis received ownership of the note when it was delivered to her with Tom's endorsement. Sylvia will need to pay Unis when she presents the note for payment. If Tom had lost the note before endorsing it, he could have gotten another from Sylvia. If the lost note had been found by a stranger and presented for payment, Sylvia could not make payment because Tom would not have endorsed the note. If she had made payment on the note to the stranger in error, she would have suffered the loss

Alice
9999 Canal Street
Anytown, USA

545

February 14,   1973

PAY TO THE
ORDER OF _____

$ *25 and no/100*

Twenty-five and no/100 ——————————— DOLLARS

BIG CITY BANK
South Office
111 South 2222 East
Anytown, USA

cleaning windows   *Alice*

kljkjklsffffs   545aaafffddss

This paper is a draft by virtue of its ordering Big City Bank to pay the bearer. This check is bearer paper because the payee is not named.

March 3, 1973

I, Sylvia, promise to pay Tom $300.

Sylvia

This paper is a promissory note because Sylvia is promising to pay Tom $300. It is order paper because the payee is named — "Tom." Two alternative endorsements for this note are presented below. The endorsement on the left is a blank endorsement by Tom and the one on the right is a special endorsement by Tom to Unis. The special endorsement would require Unis to sign the note to transfer ownership to anyone else. This will be discussed more fully in the next section.

Tom

Tom
Pay Unis

rather than Tom. Her only remedy would have been to pay Tom and sue the stranger for conversion or intentional misrepresentation.

Essential Vocabulary

1. bearer paper
2. bearer
3. order paper
4. endorsement

III. BLANK AND SPECIAL ENDORSEMENTS UCC 3-204

A blank endorsement makes commercial paper bearer paper, and a special endorsement makes it order paper.

The simplest endorsement is the "blank endorsement." A blank endorsement is made by simply signing the back of a note or draft. As mentioned above, some sort of endorsement by the payee is required to transfer ownership to order paper. A blank endorsement changes order paper to bearer paper and allows bearer paper to remain bearer paper after it is endorsed. The maker of a note or the drawee of a draft can properly pay whoever presents the note or draft for payment once it has been endorsed with a blank endorsement.

Orville received a promissory note as payment for a shed he sold to Rita. The note was signed by Rita and read as follows: "I, Rita, promise to pay to the order of Orville or his assigns $700 on demand after June 1, 1993." Orville wanted to trade the note to Sylvia for some bricks. He signed his name on the back of the note and drove to Sylvia's brick factory. However, before he could deliver the note as intended, he lost it. Larry found it and presented it to Rita for payment before Orville could inform her that he had lost the note. When Orville found out that Rita had paid Larry, Orville demanded that Rita pay him because the note had been lost. Rita refused because she had already paid Larry.

When Orville sued her, Rita was not liable because she had paid Larry. The note was order paper when Rita gave it to Orville in payment for the shed because it named Orville as payee. If Orville had not endorsed the note before he lost it, he would have been able to collect from Rita even if Larry had forged Orville's endorsement. Orville converted the note into bearer paper by signing it on the back. Since Orville's signature was a blank endorsement, his only recourse would have been to sue Larry for conversion if he could be located.

Orville could have protected himself by waiting to endorse the note until he presented it to Sylvia as payment for the bricks. He also could have protected himself by using a special endorsement. A "special endorsement" could have been made by writing the words, "pay to the order of Sylvia," or "pay Sylvia," above his signature. Special endorsements convert bearer paper to order paper and allow order paper to remain order paper after it is endorsed. Order paper must be endorsed by the proper party to transfer ownership. In the example above, Rita would not have been allowed to pay Larry if the note had been endorsed with the words, "pay to Sylvia," written above Orville's signature. She could have paid only after Sylvia had ordered the note paid by endorsing it.

April 1, 1992

I, Rita, promise to pay to the order of Orville or his assigns $700 on demand after June 1, 1993.

Rita

This document is a promissory note because it contains a promise to pay Orville, the payee, made by Rita, the maker. It is order paper because the payee, Orville, is named.

Essential Vocabulary

1. blank endorsement
2. special endorsement

IV. RESTRICTIVE AND CONDITIONAL ENDORSEMENTS 3-205

Payors can be given instructions regarding payment through conditional and restrictive endorsements.

An endorser can give a payor instructions by making a "conditional endorsement" or a "restrictive endorsement." A conditional endorsement instructs the maker of a promissory note or the drawee of a draft to pay only if a condition is met. A restrictive endorsement is an endorsement that restricts further transfer of the instrument and instructs the party receiving the instrument to collect the proceeds for the endorser. Typically, these endorsements instruct a bank to collect the proceeds of the commercial paper for the owner who makes the restrictive endorsement. They are usually made with words such as "for deposit only," "for collection only," or "pay any bank." These endorsements lock the paper into the bank collection process by requiring the banks to collect the money and deposit it into the endorser's account.

Sam received a promissory note from Todd in which Todd promised to pay Sam $200. Sam needed cement so he entered into a contract with Unis for the delivery of twenty sacks of cement in exchange for Todd's note. When Sam delivered the note to Unis as agreed in the contract, he wrote the following words on the back in addition to his signature: "Pay Unis only if she delivers twenty sacks of cement by August 24, 1997." Sam's endorsement was a conditional endorsement that allowed Todd to pay Unis the $200 only if she delivered the cement as required by her contract with Sam. Neither Unis nor any later owner of the note could collect on the note until she had delivered the cement.

Allen owned and operated a service station. At the end of the day, he would gather all of the checks received and stamp the following words on the back: "For deposit only to the account of Allen # 8485." He would then prepare a deposit slip and give the deposit to a trusted employee to take to the bank. One night after work, the employee took one of the checks out of the deposit and asked the bank teller for cash in exchange for the instrument. The teller had the employee sign on the back of the check under the restrictive endorsement and gave him the cash. The employee left town and was never seen again. Allen learned of this when he received his bank statement and found that the deposit was not as large as his records indicated. The bank would be liable to Allen for conversion because it failed to credit his account by giving the employee the cash. Once the restrictive endorsement was in place, the bank was required to follow the instructions given and deposit the proceeds only into Allen's account pending the collection process.

PROMISSORY NOTE

August 1, 1994

I, Todd, promise to pay Sam $200 on August 31, 1994.

Todd

Sam
Pay Unis only if she delivers twenty sacks of cement by August 24, 1994.

Sam's endorsement is a conditional endorsement that allows Todd to pay Unis the $200 only if Unis delivers the cement as required by her contract with Sam. Neither Unis nor any later owner of the note can collect from Todd unless she delivers the cement.

The following endorsement is a commonly used restrictive endorsement that requires the collection and deposit of funds into Allen's account.

For deposit only to
the account of
Allen
#8485

Essential Vocabulary

1. conditional endorsement
2. restrictive endorsement

V. IMPLIED TRANSFERORS' WARRANTIES UCC 3-417

Transferors of commercial paper make the implied warranties of no defenses, no alterations, genuine signatures, and good title.

A person transfers commercial paper when he transfers "title" to the note or draft to another person. "Title" is ownership. Anytime a person sells or otherwise transfers ownership of commercial paper, whether by endorsement and delivery or just delivery, he makes four "transferors' warranties":

(1) **warranty against defenses**, i.e. those responsible to pay on the paper do not have any defenses to payment,

(2) **warranty against alterations**, i.e. the instrument has not been altered,

(3) **warranty of genuine signatures**, i.e. none of the signatures have been forged, and

(4)   **warranty of good title,** i.e. he can transfer title to the instrument to the buyer.

Allan was an antique merchant. He took a new desk and distressed it by chipping it and subjecting it to chemicals so that it appeared to be 150 years old. He then represented the desk as an antique and sold it to Bill for $5,000. Bill gave Allan a nonnegotiable promissory note for $5,000 to be paid in one payment five months after the date of sale. Allan endorsed the note and transferred it to Oak Furniture Specialists as payment for some oak paneling. When Oak Furniture attempted to collect the note, Bill would not pay because he had discovered Allan's misrepresentation. Bill was successful in an action to rescind the sale and the note in an action for fraud. Oak Furniture Specialists then sued Allan for $5,000 for breach of warranty against defenses to the note. Allan would be liable to Oak Furniture Specialists for breach of his warranty against defenses to payment. Although he did not discuss the issue of defenses, Allan warranted that Bill would not be able to assert any defense to payment by transferring ownership of the note to Oak Furniture Specialists. No words were necessary to make the implied warranty.

Sally issued a check to Tom for $70. Tom changed the amount from $70 to $700, and delivered it to Paula after endorsing it in exchange for a car. Paula endorsed it and delivered it to Ron in exchange for a stereo. Only $70 was paid when Ron presented the check for payment so he sued Sally and Paula. Tom could not be found. Sally would be liable only for the original amount of the check. Since that amount was paid, Sally would have no further liability. Paula would be liable for the $630 difference between the actual amount of the check prior to alteration, $70, and the amount of the check when she transferred it to Ron, i.e. $700. Paula warranted that the check had not been altered when she transferred it to Ron in exchange for his stereo. The warranty against alteration of the instrument was made merely by transferring ownership to the instrument. No words were required to make the implied warranty against alteration.

Dan lost his check book. When Earl found it, he forged Dan's signature and wrote a check to Fred for $390 to purchase tires. Fred endorsed the check and transferred it to Tire Warehouse, Inc. in payment for some inventory he had purchased. When Tire Warehouse Inc. presented the check for payment at the bank, it was discovered that the check had been stolen and that Earl had forged Dan's signature on it. The bank would not pay the check because it lacked an authorized signature. Tire Warehouse, Inc. would have a cause of action against Fred for breach of warranty of genuine signatures. Fred would be liable to Tire Warehouse, and Earl would be liable on the instrument and for fraud. No words were necessary to make the implied warranty of genuine signatures. Fred had made this when he transferred ownership of the instrument to Tire Warehouse. If Fred was required to pay Tire Warehouse, he would be able to sue Earl for reimbursement.

Teri was the maker of a nonnegotiable $200 note payable to bearer after four months. She gave the note to Unis as payment for repairing her kitchen floor because she was short of money when the work was done. Vonny stole the note from Unis and sold it to Big City Finance for $175. When the time had expired, Teri refused to pay Big City because Unis had reported the note stolen. When Big City sued Teri, she successfully defended on the ground that Big City Finance did not have title to the note because it had purchased it from Vonny, a thief. Big City Finance would have an action against Vonny for breach of warranty of good title to the note because Vonny warranted that she had good title by transferring the note to Big City. Vonny made this implied warranty simply by transferring the instrument to Big City Finance.

Essential Vocabulary

1. title
2. transferors' warranties
3. implied warranty of no defenses
4. implied warranty of no alterations
5. implied warranty of genuine signatures
6. implied warranty of good title

VI. PRIMARY LIABILITY UCC 3-410, 3-411, 3-413

The makers of notes and acceptors of drafts have primary liability for payment.

"Primary liability" is unconditional liability. If commercial paper is not paid as promised, all parties with primary liability can be sued. There are only two parties to commercial paper with primary liability: the "makers of notes" and the "acceptors of drafts." The maker of a promissory note is the person signing the note or, if he is an agent, his principal. When a person signs a note as maker, he would have primary liability and could be sued immediately upon default. In cases where an agent properly signs a note for a principal and discloses the identity of the principal, only the principal has primary liability on the note — the agent has no liability.

Sometimes a drawee will accept a draft before it is presented for payment by noting on the back that it has been accepted for payment. When the drawee does this, she becomes an acceptor of the draft. This has the effect of making the drawee primarily liable on the draft. If a seller does not want to accept a buyers check, she may demand that the check be "certified" or accepted for payment by the drawee bank to impose primary liability on the bank. This may be demanded by the seller because the bank is more financially secure than the buyer. If the check is dishonored, the seller can sue both the bank and the drawer. If a check or other draft has not been accepted by the drawee, no party has primary liability. All parties have "secondary liability." Secondary liability is conditional liability and is discussed in the next generalization.

Essential Vocabulary

1. primary liability
2. makers of notes
3. acceptors of drafts
4. certified check or draft
5. secondary liability

VII. SECONDARY LIABILITY UCC 3-414, 3-501, 3-508

Drawers of endorsers have secondary liability for payment and are liable after timely presentment and notice of dishonor.

Only the makers of notes and the acceptors of drafts have primary liability. This means that prior to acceptance by the drawee, no one has primary liability on a draft. All other parties to commercial paper have "secondary liability." Secondary liability can be defined as conditional liability. The liability of the drawer of a draft is conditional upon prompt presentment of the draft to the drawee for payment. The drawer is not liable on the draft if the payee delays in presenting the draft to the drawee for payment. The presentation of a note or draft to the maker or drawee for payment is called "presentment."

When a person signs the back of commercial paper, she becomes an "endorser." A person may be required to endorse commercial paper to transfer ownership or merely to lend credit to the instrument. Endorsers who are not signing to transfer ownership are called "accommodation parties." By endorsing commercial paper, endorsers make the implied warranty that the commercial paper they endorse will be paid when it is properly presented for payment. Parties to commercial paper who endorse commercial paper to transfer ownership are liable for both payment and the transferors' warranties. Accommodation parties are only liable for payment. Endorsers have secondary liability. This means that their liability is conditional upon prompt "presentment" and "notice of dishonor."

Any delay in presentment or giving notice to the endorser that the paper was "dishonored" will end the endorser's liability for payment of the commercial paper. Commercial paper is dishonored when it is not paid according to its terms. The holder of a note or draft must present the paper for payment on or before the due date if the paper is payable on a specific date and within a reasonable time after receiving the paper if it is payable on demand. Notes and drafts that do not specify due dates are payable on demand.

"Notice of dishonor" is notification that the commercial paper has not been paid according to its terms. Notification is usually required to be in writing. Notice must be given promptly and is effective when sent even if it is not received. Endorsers are liable to all of the endorsers who endorsed the instrument after them and anyone who owns the note or draft when it is dishonored. Endorsers' liability for payment is conditional upon the holder promptly presenting the note or draft for payment and giving notice of dishonor by midnight of the third business day after the paper has been dishonored.

Irene signed a draft drawn on Harry and made payable to Julie for $100. She also signed a promissory note payable to Julie for $200. Both the draft and the note were payable on demand. Two years after the instruments were delivered to her, Julie presented both the draft and the note to Irene for payment despite the fact that the draft was drawn on Harry. Irene refused to accept and pay either one of them. Julie sued both Irene and Harry on the draft and Irene alone on the note. By the time she sued, Harry had suffered a financial disaster resulting in his inability to pay what he owed Irene.

Harry had no liability on the draft because it had never been accepted by him for payment. Irene had only secondary liability because her liability on the draft was conditional upon Julie's presenting it to Harry within a reasonable time. Julie's failure to present the draft to Harry for payment within a reasonable time discharged Irene's liability on the draft. Julie will have to suffer the loss resulting from Harry's financial disasters. Julie would have won in the action to collect the amount owing on the promissory note. Irene had primary or unconditional liability on the note so her liability was not discharged by Julie's failure to make presentment within a reasonable time.

Jeff signed a promissory note payable to Kim. Kim endorsed the note and delivered it to Larry. Larry presented the note to Jeff for payment on the due date. Jeff was unable to pay as promised. Larry, therefore, sued both Jeff and Kim. Kim first learned that Jeff had dishonored the note when she received service of process in the lawsuit filed by Larry about twenty days after Jeff had told Larry that he couldn't pay. Kim was probably not liable because, as an endorser, she had only secondary liability for payment. She warranted that Jeff would pay as promised when she endorsed and transferred the note to Larry. However, her liability for payment was conditional upon Larry's sending her notice of Jeff's dishonor by midnight of the third business day after Larry learned that Jeff couldn't pay. Larry could successfully sue only Jeff on the note because Kim's liability was discharged by the delay in giving notice of the dishonor.

Essential Vocabulary

1. secondary liability
2. presentment

3. endorser
4. accommodation party
5. endorsers' liability for payment
6. dishonored commercial paper
7. notice of dishonor

VIII. IMPLIED ENDORSERS' WARRANTIES UCC 3-414, 3-417

Endorsers, other than qualified endorsers, make the implied warranty that the instrument will be paid.

Endorsers of commercial paper make the implied warranty that the instrument will be paid according to its terms and agree to pay it in the event of dishonor. However, endorsers can limit their liability for payment of the instruments they indorse by giving notice future holders of the paper will not have recourse to them for payment in the event of dishonor. This is done by including the words, "without recourse," in the endorsement. Endorsements without recourse are called "qualified endorsements," and endorsers who limit their liability in this way are called "qualified endorsers." Qualified endorsers are not liable for payment of the commercial paper they endorse if the obligated party defaults on the note or draft. They do, however, retain liability if the paper is dishonored due to a defense, alteration, signature that is not genuine, or lack of title. The qualified endorsement does not limit liability for the implied transferors' warranties made when title to paper is transferred to new owners.

Miko endorsed a promissory note by writing the words, "without recourse," above her signature when she sold the note to Nancy. The note was subsequently dishonored because the maker had suffered severe cash flow problems. Miko would not have been liable to Nancy for payment of the note because she was a qualified endorser. However, Miko would have been liable even though she was a qualified endorser if the instrument had not been paid due to the fact that the note had originally been obtained by fraud, or because the note had been altered, or because a necessary signature had been forged, or because the note had been stolen or "converted." Even qualified endorsers make the implied transferors' warranties. Qualified endorsers merely limit their liability in the event the instrument is dishonored due to the obligor's inability to pay.

Essential Vocabulary

1. without recourse
2. qualified endorsement
3. qualified endorsers

IX. NEGOTIABLE INSTRUMENTS UCC 3-104

A negotiable instrument is an unconditional promise or order to pay a sum certain at a time certain to order or bearer.

Commercial paper can be nonnegotiable or negotiable. Before the requirements that a note or draft must meet to be negotiable are presented, the importance of negotiability will be discussed. Ownership of nonnegotiable commercial paper can be transferred by assignment. A person receiving title to a nonnegotiable note or draft is an assignee. As you will recall from the chapter on assignment and delegation of contract rights and duties, an assignee has no better right to collect the benefits assigned than the assignor. For example, if Tom and Sally enter into a contract in which Tom is required to repair Sally's television set for $400 with the repair and payment to take place in one month, Tom can assign his right to collect his $400 fee to Unis right now. However, if Tom fails to repair the television set as agreed, Unis, the assignee, cannot collect the $400 because Tom could not collect due to his breach of contract. Unis' ability to collect the $400 is dependent upon Tom's performance and other factors over which she has no control.

The owners of negotiable notes or drafts are more secure than the owners of nonnegotiable commercial paper. Ownership of negotiable commercial paper is transferred by negotiation. The person receiving title to a negotiable note or draft is a holder in due course. A holder in due course can receive a better right to collect the amount due on the paper than the party who transferred ownership of the instrument. In the example involving the repair of the television set above, Unis could have collected the $400 even though Tom failed to repair the television set if Sally's promise to pay Tom was in the form of a negotiable promissory note.

It is important to note that whether a person who obtains ownership of commercial paper is an assignee or a holder in due course depends upon whether or not the paper was nonnegotiable or negotiable in the first place. In other words, endorsing the back of a draft and delivering it to a new owner is called "assigning" the draft if the draft is nonnegotiable and "negotiating" the draft if the draft is negotiable. Similarly, the person receiving the note is called an "assignee" if the note is nonnegotiable and a "holder in due course" if the note is negotiable. The rights of the transferee of commercial paper depend upon whether or not the note or draft meets the requirements of negotiability.

Notes and drafts are "nonnegotiable commercial paper" if they do not meet the requirements of negotiable commercial paper. "Assignment" is the process of transferring ownership of nonnegotiable commercial paper by delivery and, in the case of order paper, endorsement to a new owner. An "assignee" is the party to whom ownership of nonnegotiable commercial paper is transferred. The assignee is called an "ordinary holder" of the commercial paper. The terms, assignee and ordinary holder, are synonymous.

Notes and drafts are "negotiable commercial paper" if they meet the requirements of negotiable commercial paper set forth in this section's generalization. "Negotiation" is the process of transferring ownership of negotiable commercial paper by delivery and, in the case of order paper, endorsement to a new owner. A "holder in due course" is the party to whom ownership of negotiable commercial paper is transferred. The holder in due course can generally enforce the commercial paper despite the fact a former owner could not enforce the paper due to a defense or discharge. Most defenses and discharges presented in earlier chapters will not prevent a holder in due course from successfully collecting the amount owed on the commercial paper. Mistake, intentional misrepresentation, innocent misrepresentation, undue influence, performance, accord and satisfaction, and impossibility of performance are a few examples of defenses and discharges that are ineffective against a holder in due course. A mere assignee cannot collect anything if there is any defense to the payment of a note or draft.

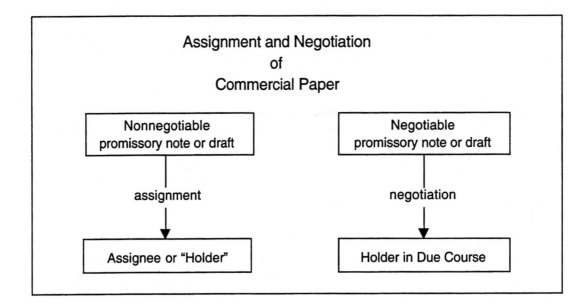

Whether a holder will be a holder in due course immune to personal defenses or merely a holder with only the rights of an assignee depends upon whether the note or draft was negotiable when it was signed. Negotiable commercial paper cannot become nonnegotiable after it has been signed, and nothing can be done to make nonnegotiable paper negotiable. Negotiable commercial paper is actually a "formal contract." A formal contract is a promise that is required by law to take a prescribed form. Negotiable commercial paper must be an unconditional promise or order to pay a sum certain at a time certain to order or bearer. Essentially there are four major requirements regarding the form of negotiable commercial paper. Any failure of the note or draft to meet all four requirements results in the note being nonnegotiable. Negotiable commercial paper must be:

(1) an unconditional promise or order to pay;

(2) a sum certain;

(3) at a time certain;

(4) to order or bearer.

Both nonnegotiable and negotiable commercial paper must be embodied in signed writings. However, the written documents do not necessarily need to be made of paper. They could be written on wood or stone and still be considered commercial paper. The signature required could be a name or a witnessed sign or mark and be written in cursive style or printed as long as the person making the signature intended the marks to constitute a signature.

A negotiable note or draft must contain an "unconditional promise or order" to pay money. A promise to pay is a promissory note while an order to pay is a draft. To be unconditional, the obligation to pay must not be subject to anything happening or not happening. A note with the words, "I promise to pay to bearer $100 on demand," would be negotiable, while a note containing the words, "I promise to pay bearer $100 on demand if Sam delivers topsoil to my home as promised," would not be negotiable because the obligation to pay is conditional upon the delivery of the soil.

Negotiable commercial paper must contain a promise to pay or an order to pay a "sum certain." A "sum" is a sum of money only — nothing else. To be "certain," one must be able to determine the amount due by information to be found within the four corners of the instrument. A note containing the words, "I promise to pay to the order of Andy $400 with interest thereon at the rate of 1% per month from April 1, 1994, and to deliver four watermelons," would not be negotiable because the maker must deliver watermelons in addition to paying money. The note does not merely require the paying of a sum. A note that contains the words, "I promise to pay to the order of Andy $400 with interest thereon at the rate of 1% per month from April 1, 1994," would be negotiable because only money is required to be paid and the interest can be determined by applying the interest rate included in the note.

A note that contains the words, "I promise to pay to the order of Andy $400 with interest thereon from April 1, 1994 at the prime rate being charged at the time of payment by Big Bank of Salt Lake City, Utah," would not be negotiable because the interest cannot be determined from information contained within the four corners of the instrument. Although the instrument requires paying a sum of money only, the sum required is not certain because Big Bank must be consulted regarding their prime rate at the time of payment to determine how much is due. Interestingly, "collection clauses" do not affect the negotiability of commercial paper because they become operative only if the paper is dishonored. A collection clause is a clause in a note or draft that requires a party to pay court costs and attorneys' fees in the event the instrument is not paid according to its terms.

Consider a note containing the words, "I promise to pay to the order of Andy $400 with interest thereon at the rate of 1% per month from April 1, 1994. In the event of default, I agree to pay all costs of collection including court costs and reasonable attorneys' fees." This promissory note would be negotiable despite the presence of the collection clause because the clause would not become operative until default. The amount due on the note can be determined from the instrument itself in the absence of default so it is negotiable. The negotiability of commercial paper is determined at the instant it is signed and cannot be subsequently changed. If an instrument is negotiable when it is signed, it cannot be made nonnegotiable by a subsequent action. Similarly, if commercial paper is nonnegotiable when signed, subsequent events or alterations of the documents cannot make them negotiable.

To be negotiable, an instrument must be payable at a "time certain." A time certain is a time that can be determined to occur with certainty. A note or draft that does not include a provision dealing with time of payment is payable on demand. This meets the time certain requirement because the time the holder demands payment can be determined when it occurs with certainty. Paper payable on a definite date also meets this requirement. Paper payable at times that are ambiguous or that may not occur are nonnegotiable.

For example, a draft drawn on Big City Credit Union containing the words, "Pay to the order of Ben $300," would be negotiable because it is payable on demand. It would also have been payable on demand if it contained the words, "pay on demand," "pay on sight," "pay 10 days after sight," etc. Pay on sight means pay when the instrument is presented for payment, i.e. pay on demand. Since these events will occur and their occurrence can be determined with certainty, the requirement of time certain is met. A draft containing the words, "Pay to the order of Ben $300 on June 1, 1994," would be negotiable because it is payable on a specific date. However, a draft containing the words, "Pay to the order of Ben $300 the second day of the next Winter Olympics," would not be negotiable because it is payable on a date that may not occur if the Olympics are not held as planned. Since the negotiability of a note or draft is determined when it is signed, the draft would not become negotiable even if the Winter Olympics were held as planned prior to the draft becoming due. A note or draft payable on "Easter" would not be negotiable because Easter is celebrated on at least two different dates.

A negotiable note or draft must be payable to "order" or be payable to "bearer." This is the reason that checks have the words, "pay to the order of" printed on them next to the line on which the name of the payee is placed. A note containing the words, "I promise to pay to the order of Irene $600," would be negotiable because it contains the words, "pay to the order of." However, a note containing the words, "I promise to pay Irene $600," would not be negotiable because it is not payable to bearer and does not contain the words, "pay to the order of." It is important to notice that a note or draft can be "order paper" by virtue of naming the payee and still be nonnegotiable because it lacks the words, "pay to the order of." The note, "I promise to pay bearer $600," would be negotiable because it is payable "to bearer." Of course, notes containing the words, "pay to the order of cash," or "pay to the order of bearer," are negotiable because they are payable "to bearer."

Essential Vocabulary

1. nonnegotiable commercial paper
2. assignment
3. assignee or ordinary holder
4. negotiable commercial paper
5. negotiation
6. holder in due course
7. formal contract
8. unconditional promise to pay
9. unconditional order to pay
10. sum certain
11. collection clauses
12. time certain
13. payable to order or bearer

X. NEGOTIATION UCC 3-202

A negotiable instrument is transferred by negotiation to a holder in due course who is immune to personal defenses to payment.

XI. ASSIGNMENT

Nonnegotiable commercial paper is transferred by assignment to an assignee (ordinary holder) who is subject to personal defenses.

Betty induced Charles to issue a signed promissory note to her for $7,000 by telling him that she would deliver a famous painting to him for that amount. In reality, she never had the painting and did not intend to deliver anything for the note. The note was signed by Charles and read as follows: "I promise to pay to bearer $7,000 ten days after sight. If I fail to make payment as agreed, I will pay reasonable costs of collection." Betty later sold the note to Donald for $5,500 by delivering it to him. Donald did not know of Betty's intentional misrepresentation.

To determine whether or not Charles would be liable to Donald on the note, the first step is to determine whether or not the paper was negotiable. This note was negotiable because it was a signed unconditional promise to pay a sum certain at a time certain and was made payable to bearer. Since Donald gave $5,500 for the note in good faith without notice of Betty's misrepresentation, he qualified as a holder in due course. If the paper had been conditional upon delivery of the painting, the note would have been nonnegotiable and Donald would not have been a holder in due course. In that situation, Charles could have raised the defense of misrepresentation since Donald would have only had the rights of an assignee.

Evan signed a promissory note that read as follows: "I promise to pay Frank $200 on demand." When Frank demanded payment, Evan paid him as promised. Frank gave Evan a receipt, but he kept the note. Later, Frank endorsed the note on the back and sold it to Gary. Gary sued Evan on the note, and Evan defended on the ground that he had already paid Frank. To determine the rights and liabilities of the parties, one must first determine whether or not the note was negotiable. Although the note was a signed, unconditional promise to pay a sum certain at a time certain, it was not negotiable because it was not made payable to "order" or to "bearer." Evan would probably not be liable because Gary was only an assignee, and, as such, his claim on the note was discharged by Evan's payment to Frank. Gary would need to collect from Frank for the breach of warranty of payment he made when he endorsed the note and delivered it to Gary.

If the note had contained the words, "pay to the order of Frank," instead of merely "pay Frank," the note would have been negotiable, and Gary would have been a holder in due course. Evan would have been liable to Gary even though he had previously paid Frank because discharge by payment is only a personal defense which is not good against a holder in due course. When a promissory note is paid, it must be returned to the maker. This is especially important when the note is negotiable to prevent further negotiation. If the holder of negotiable commercial paper refuses to return the paper upon payment, the aggrieved party can sue for conversion to recover it.

CHECK YOUR UNDERSTANDING

DIRECTIONS: Read each of the following questions. Choose the best answer and study the discussion of the question.

1. Conan owed George $800. George owed Dragon $500 so George gave Dragon a signed piece of paper reading "Dear Conan, please pay $500 of the money you

owe me to the order of Dragon when he asks you for it. Sincerely yours, George."
Conan is probably:

   a. a drawer.

   b. a drawee.

   c. a payee.

   d. an accommodation party.

   e. a well known barbarian residing in your neighborhood.

DISCUSSION

(b)   The letter written by George and given to Dragon was a draft because it ordered Conan to pay Dragon $500 on demand. Since George signed the draft, he was the drawer. Conan was being ordered to pay the draft so he was the drawee. Dragon was the payee. An accommodation party is a party who endorses commercial paper merely to warrant payment of the instrument rather than to transfer ownership in the instrument. Since there were no endorsers, there were no accommodation parties.

2. Which type of commercial paper can be negotiated by delivery without endorsement?

   a. order paper

   b. bearer paper

   c. qualified paper

   d. demand paper

   e. sight drafts

DISCUSSION

(b)   Only bearer paper can always be negotiated by delivery. Order paper names a payee so it requires an endorsement for negotiation or assignment. There is no commercial paper called qualified paper. Demand paper and sight drafts are commercial paper payable on demand. They may be either bearer or order paper depending on whether or not the payee is named and what type of endorsements are used. Order paper payable on demand or sight cannot be negotiated without endorsement.

3. An endorsement that will change bearer paper to order paper is:

    a. a special endorsement.
    b. a qualified endorsement.
    c. a restrictive endorsement.
    d. a blank endorsement.
    e. an accommodation endorsement.

DISCUSSION

(a)   Special endorsements consisting of words such as "pay to the order of Nancy" or "pay Nancy" change bearer paper to order paper requiring an endorsement for further negotiation or assignment. A qualified endorsement consists of the words, "without recourse." A qualified endorsement does not by itself change order paper to bearer paper or vice versa. However, if a qualified endorser merely signed her name under the words limiting liability for nonpayment, the paper would become bearer paper. For example, an endorsement signed by Alice, "without recourse, *Alice*," would be a blank, qualified endorsement and would change the instrument to bearer paper. The endorsement signed by Alice, "pay to the order of Ben, without recourse, *Alice*," would be a special, qualified endorsement and would change the paper to order paper. Similarly, a restrictive endorsement or an accommodation endorsement would not change bearer paper to order paper if they did not include a special endorsement.

4. Killer bought a negotiable promissory note from Bee which had a large black spot on the back. Unknown to Killer, Bee had blacked out the words "For Deposit Only to the Account of Flower." Flower's signature and Bee's signature were genuine. Killer is probably:

    a. a secured party.
    b. bound by the restrictive endorsement that was covered up.
    c. not responsible for the restrictive endorsement since he did not cover it or know what words had been covered.
    d. an executrix.
    e. a trustee.

DISCUSSION

(b)   Killer would be bound by the restrictive endorsement that had been blacked out. Once an endorsement is on the back of commercial paper, present and future parties are bound regardless of attempts to modify, cancel, or obliterate it. Killer should not have purchased the note when he observed the black spot on the back. No secured transactions are involved in this case so Killer would not be a secured party. An executrix is a female personal representative of a person who died leaving a will. A trustee manages property for the benefit of someone else. Neither an executrix nor a trustee are involved in this question.

5. Ed forged Dan's signature on a check made out to himself and negotiated it to Fred by endorsing the back. Fred negotiated it to Gary by endorsing the back. The bank refused to honor the check when Gary presented it for payment. Gary immediately gave all parties mentioned notice of the dishonor. Fred will probably:

   a. be liable to Gary even though Dan's signature was a forgery.
   b. be liable to Gary only if Gary cannot collect from Ed.
   c. be liable to Dan for negotiating the forged check.
   d. be able to collect from Dan if he's a holder in due course.
   e. not be liable to Gary.

DISCUSSION

(a) Fred will be liable Gary because the check was not paid due to the forged signature. When Fred endorsed the check and transferred it to Gary he made the implied warranties that the check would be paid and the implied transferors' warranties. One of the warranties of transfer is that the signatures are genuine. Since Dan's signature was forged, Fred would be liable. Although Ed is liable to Gary on the check along with Fred, Fred is liable whether or not Gary could collect from Ed. If Gary collects from Fred, Fred can collect from Ed. No one is liable to Dan because Dan has not lost anything. The bank refused to pay the check with his forged signature. Dan could not be a holder in due course or have any liability because he didn't sign the check.

6. Grant issued a draft to Hitch drawn on Credit Union. Hitch negotiated the draft to Iris. Iris presented the draft to Credit Union for payment. Which of the following is correct?

   a. Credit Union will be liable to Iris if it doesn't honor the draft.
   b. Credit Union will be liable to Grant if it honors the draft without Grant's permission because a "two party" draft is involved.
   c. Credit Union will not be liable to Iris if it doesn't honor the draft even if Grant has sufficient funds in his account.
   d. Hitch may be liable to Grant for negotiating the draft without authority.

e. Iris may be liable to Hitch for presenting the draft to Credit Union instead of Grant for payment.

DISCUSSION

(c)   Credit Union is a drawee. Drawees have no liability on drafts until they accept them for payment. Since Credit Union did not accept Grant's draft for payment, it would not be liable to Iris even if Grant had sufficient funds in his account to cover the draft. Credit Union's contract with Grant might make it liable to him for refusing to honor the draft, but the contract between Grant and Credit Union would not give Iris a cause of action. Credit Union would not be liable to Grant if it honored the draft regardless of how many parties were involved as long as none of the signatures were forged. Hitch had the right under the UCC to negotiate the draft to Iris without Grant's permission. Iris presented the draft to Credit Union for payment because Credit Union was the drawee. Presentment of drafts to drawees for payment is a condition of drawers' liability on the draft.

7.   Sam presented a check at Big Store. The clerk refused to take the check because Sam had no guaranty card and the check was for $540. Tom, a well known customer, told the clerk that he would vouch for Sam so the clerk had Tom sign the back of the check. Under Tom's signature, the clerk stamped "For deposit only to the account of Big Store." The bank dishonored the check because Sam did not have sufficient funds in his account, and all parties received notice. Tom is:

a. liable on the check because of his endorsement.
b. liable on the check as an acceptor.
c. not liable on the check because his signature was not an endorsement necessary to the chain of tile.
d. not liable because his guaranty was not in writing.
e. liable only if Big Store cannot collect from Sam.

DISCUSSION

(a)   Tom became an endorser when he signed the back of the check. Endorsers are liable for payment of the instrument in the event it is dishonored. Tom's endorsement was not necessary to transfer ownership of the check to Big Store because he was not a party to it. Endorsers that sign merely to guarantee that an instrument will be paid if it is dishonored are called "accommodation parties." If Tom had to pay Big Store, he could collect from Sam. Tom was not an acceptor because he was not the drawee of the check. Acceptors are drawees who accept drafts for payment. Tom's liability comes from his endorsement. He became liable to Big Store when the check was dishonored. Big Store does not need to attempt collection from Sam before it pursues Tom, but it would probably sue both in the same action.

8. Pepper stole a negotiable draft from Quince. He forged Quince's signature and sold it to Bunny who knew nothing of the theft. When Bunny later found out about the theft, she sold the note to Sid and endorsed the back "Without Recourse, *Bunny*." The note was not honored due to the forged signatures and the theft so Sid gave all endorsers notice of the dishonor. Bunny is:

   a. not liable to Sid because she did not steal the draft.
   b. not liable to Sid because Sid is not liable to Quince for stealing the draft.
   c. not liable to Sid because she is a qualified endorser.
   d. liable to Sid because she warranted genuine signatures.
   e. liable to Sid as an accommodation party.

   DISCUSSION

   (d)   Bunny is liable because she transferred the instrument to Sid. Her endorsement without recourse released her from liability for mere nonpayment of the draft. However, she made the warranties of transfer when she sold the draft to Sid. She warranted that there were no defenses to payment, that the instrument had not been altered, that all signatures were genuine, and that the Sid would receive good title to the instrument. She was liable because there had been forgeries and she did not, therefore, have good title to the draft. Bunny was not an accommodation party because she was an owner of the draft and signed it to transfer ownership to Sid.

9. Abe and Phil entered into a contract in which Abe was required to give Phil a $200 note for Phil's television set. Abe signed a paper that said, "I promise to pay Phil $200 on or before September 1, 1994. This note will bear interest at the rate of 1% per month." Abe delivered the note to Phil who said, "Thanks for the gift — the deal's off." Phil refused to return the note. He later signed the back of the note and delivered it to Bud who paid Phil $100 for it. Bud knew nothing of how Phil got the note and didn't ask. Which of the following is probably true?

   a. Abe is liable to Bud.
   b. Abe is liable to Phil.
   c. The shelter rule applies here.
   d. This note is transferable only by assignment.
   e. Bud is liable to Abe as Phil's accomplice.

DISCUSSION

(d)   The promissory note given by Abe to Phil was not negotiable because it was not made payable to order or bearer. This nonnegotiable note could be transferred only by assignment and anyone who received it would be an assignee subject to all the defenses to which prior holders were subject. Since Phil could not collect on the note because he had converted it and breached his contract with Abe, Bud could not collect anything on the note either. The shelter rule gives everyone who purchases commercial paper the protection of a holder in due course if an earlier holder actually qualified as a holder in due course. This rule is not involved because the note was nonnegotiable. Bud would not be an accomplice to any criminal activity because he was not aware of the facts regarding the conversion of the note.

10.   A negotiable note contained the words, "Pay to the order of Bill." Bill endorsed the note by signing his name on the back. Before he delivered the note to its purchaser, he lost it, and Pinchit found it and sold it to Candace who knew nothing about Bill's losing the note. Candace required Pinchit to endorse the instrument so Pinchit signed the note as "Seeya Later," one of his aliases. Candace is probably:

   a. entitled to nothing on the note because it was not delivered by Bill to Pinchit.
   b. entitled to nothing because Pinchit did not legally endorse the note.
   c. a holder in due course.
   d. protected because the Pinchit did not sign his real name.
   e. an assignee of the note.

DISCUSSION

(c)   Bill changed the negotiable note form order paper to bearer paper by placing a blank endorsement on the back. When Pinchit sold the note to Candace, he negotiated the note, and Candace became a holder in due course. Bill will probably need to pay the note because the defense that the note was stolen would not be effective against a claim made by a holder in due course. The fact that Pinchit did not sign his real name to the note would not have affected the negotiation. Signatures are effective even when aliases are used. Pinchit was the bearer of the note and, as such, could negotiate the draft to a holder in due course even though he could not obtain payment himself on the note because of his conversion.

SECTION VI
MISCELLANEOUS TOPICS

PROPERTY
LIENS
LABOR LAW
CREDIT LAW

Chapter 22
Property

As discussed in previous chapters, title is ownership. Deeds, certificates of title, and other documents are only evidence of title. Anything that is valuable and can be owned is property. Property is usually conceived as something that can be possessed. However, since intangible things that are valuable can be owned, it is more accurate to think of property as a collection of rights in a thing. This chapter presents generalizations that deal with common problems relating to property that arise in business. Most of the generalizations deal with both real and personal property. The first two generalizations deal with the two most common ways both real and personal property can be owned by more than one person or company at a time. Generalizations III-X deal exclusively with real property. The purpose of this introduction to property law is to alert the student to potential problems that can arise and encourage continued study of the law.

Property can be divided into two great classes: real property and personal property. Real property consists of land and things permanently attached to it. Objects that are permanently attached to land are called fixtures. Buildings, trees, sod, and cement work are fixtures. Personal property is all property other than real property. Personal property can be classified as tangible or intangible. Tangible personal property consists of ownership rights in property that is tangible or can be touched. Boots, cars, boats, and pencils are tangible personal property. Contract rights, causes of action, and other rights are classified as intangible personal property because they cannot be touched.

I. TENANCY IN COMMON

Tenants in common share undivided interests in property which will pass to their estates upon their deaths and can be sold to purchasers who become tenants in common.

Two or more people can own property at the same time. Unless otherwise agreed, the property interest that each owns is called a "tenancy in common." The word "tenancy" comes from the Latin word, tenere, which means to hold or possess. A tenancy is common, then, is ownership and possession in common. Each person sharing ownership is a "tenant in common." Each tenant in common shares an "undivided interest" in the property owned. An undivided interest can be loosely defined as the right to use all of the property a fraction of the time or the right to take a fractional share of all of the profits produced by the property.

For example, if three people own equal interests in an airplane as tenants in common, they would each own an undivided one-third interest in the plane. This would mean that they each own the right to use the plane one-third of the time. If the plane is sold, each owner is entitled to one-third of the proceeds of the sale. If a tenant in common dies without a will, his interest passes through his estate to his next of kin. If he has a will, his interest passes to whomever the will names as the grantee. When a tenant in common sells his interest in the property, the new owner becomes a tenant in common with the remaining tenants.

Andy and Bob each paid half the cost of a new boat to become owners as tenants in common. Each became an owner of an undivided one-half interest in the boat. This means that each could use the boat half the time. They would need to agree on how to divide the time since each may want the boat during summer months more than winter months. If they could not agree, they could file an "action for partition." An action for partition is a suit to have the court divide property among the co-owners according to their interests. When the courts cannot physically divide the property between the parties to a partition action without destroying its value, the property is ordered to be sold and the proceeds divided between the parties.

In the case of Andy and Bob, the court would order the boat to be sold and the proceeds to be shared equally between them because the boat would be worthless if it were cut in half. If Andy had died leaving a will that granted the interest in the boat to his daughter, she would become a tenant in common with Bob. If she later decided to sell her interest in the boat, she could do so without Bob's permission or consent and the purchaser would become a tenant in common with Bob.

Essential Vocabulary

1. tenancy
2. tenancy in common
3. tenant in common
4. undivided interest
5. action for partition

II. JOINT TENANCY

Joint tenants share undivided interests in property which will pass to the surviving joint tenants upon death and can be sold to purchasers who become tenants in common.

When two or more people share ownership interests in property, they can agree to create a "joint tenancy." A joint tenancy is similar to a tenancy in common except that when a joint tenant dies her share automatically passes to the surviving joint tenant or tenants rather than to anyone else. Each joint tenant holds two interests — (1) an interest in the possession and use of the property, and (2) a potential interest in the ownership of the remainder of the property that will become actual when another joint tenant dies. The potential right to become the owner of the interests of the other owners when they die is held by all of the joint tenants together, and is called the "right of survivorship." The owners who jointly hold the right of survivorship are called "joint tenants."

A joint tenancy is created when property is purchased by the owners specifying that they are joint tenants or indicating that they shall have rights of survivorship. When this occurs, the owners take the property as joint tenants and not as tenants in common. Joint tenants, like tenants in common, share undivided interests in the property and have the right to use the entire property a fraction of the time or the right to a fractional share of the entire profits produced by the property. However, when a joint tenant dies, her interest passes directly to the surviving joint tenants by virtue of the right of survivorship without passing through the estate of the joint tenant who died. Survivorship is the right to a deceased joint tenant's interest in property. Since the property interest does not pass through the estate, a will would have no effect. Any property held in joint tenancy would pass to the surviving joint tenants even if the deceased left the property to someone else by will.

The right of survivorship places the parties to a joint tenancy in a special relationship arranged by them when they acquired the property. Later purchasers would be strangers to this relationship. The law, therefore, provides that although a joint tenant can sell her joint interest without the permission of any of the other joint tenants, the purchaser becomes a tenant in common with the remaining tenants even though the seller was a joint tenant.

For example, if three sisters purchase a condominium as joint tenants, it would be possible for one of the sisters to sell her interest to a stranger without the permission of the other sisters. However, the purchaser would become a tenant in common with the two sisters who kept their interests. The remaining sisters would still be joint tenants as to each other but they would be tenants in common with the new owner. If one of the two remaining sisters died, her share would pass by survivorship to the living sister who would then own a two-thirds interest in the property while the tenant in common would still own only the one-third interest he purchased. If the tenant in common had died rather than one of the sisters, his interest would have passed to his next of kin. The sisters would continue to own their one-third interests as joint tenants.

Dona, Eva, and Fred were siblings. Each paid one-third of the cost of a cabin which they purchased as joint tenants for recreational use. Each would own an undivided one-third interest the cabin. This means that each could use the cabin one-third of the time. If Fred died leaving a will that gave his interest to his son, his interest in the cabin would nevertheless pass to Donna and Eva by survivorship because he held his interest as a joint tenant. Donna and Eva would then own undivided one-half interests in the cabin as joint tenants. When one of them died, the entire property would then belong to the survivor. If Fred had sold his interest during his lifetime, the new owner would have become a tenant in common with Donna and Eva. Donna and Eva would each have owned undivided one-third interests as joint tenants as to each other and the new owner of Fred's interest would have owned an undivided one-third interest as a tenant in common with them. If the tenant in common died before Fred's sisters, his interest would have passed to his next of kin rather than the sisters.

Essential Vocabulary

1. joint tenancy
2. right of survivorship
3. joint tenants

III. REAL ESTATE SALES CONTRACTS

Real estate sales can be secured by real estate sales contracts in which the seller retains title until payment has been paid.

A contract for the sale of real property requiring the buyer to make payments to the seller can be secured by the seller's retaining title until the buyer has finished making the required payments. Contracts for the sale of real property or any interest in real property are called "real estate sales contracts." Most real estate sales contracts that require the buyer to pay the seller in installments contain a "forfeiture clause." Forfeiture clauses provide that buyers will forfeit to the seller all payments and "equity" that they have in the property if they fail to make the required payments at any time during the course of the contract. Equity is the value of the property in excess of the amount owed on it. Most states will not enforce forfeiture clauses. State statutes or court decisions usually require sellers to terminate, or "foreclose," the buyers' interests in the event of default. Foreclosures are required to be conducted in compliance with state "mortgage foreclosure statutes." Mortgage foreclosure statutes are legislative laws that set forth procedures by which creditors can recover what they are owed by the sale of real property. They also allow buyers to recover any of their equity that exceeds the creditors' damages resulting from the default.

Real estate sales contracts that require the buyer to make installment payments to the seller typically allow the seller to retain legal title to the property during the payment period set forth in the contract. The seller is usually not required to convey "marketable title" to the buyer until the buyer has completely paid for the real property. Marketable title is ownership of the property that is free of plausible and reasonable claims by parties other than the buyer. This creates a risk for the buyer during the payment period because title to the property remains with the seller until the buyer has made all of the required payments. The payment period in which the seller retains title typically continues for a period of many years.

During this time the seller could improperly use the land as security for his own debts, and the seller's creditors could reach the land because legal title remained with him. This could result in the buyer's making payments to the seller over a long period of time only to find that the seller's creditors can take the property leaving the buyer with only an unsecured claim against the seller. To avoid this, the buyer can record a "notice of interest" with the recorder of deeds in the county or other political subdivision where the property is located. The notice of interest is a document that indicates that although legal title to the real estate is in the seller, the buyer claims an equitable interest in the property. The recording of this notice of the buyer's interest is very important because it secures the buyer's interest by preserving it against the claims of the seller's future creditors.

Beverly entered into a written contract with Carl to purchase his house for $40,000. The contract required Beverly to make payments for twenty years to Carl, and, when the house was paid off, Carl was required to convey good and marketable title to Beverly by warranty deed. The contract also provided that if Beverly defaulted on any payment, Carl could declare the entire unpaid balance due, and she would forfeit her equity and vacate the premises. Beverly made payments for 15 years. At that time, Carl needed a loan for one of his business deals. He borrowed $25,000 and used the house as security by mortgaging it. The bank that made the loan had no idea that he had previously entered into a contract to sell the property to Beverly.

Carl defaulted on his loan so the bank moved to take possession of the house and resell it. The bank's interest would be prior to Beverly's because she had not recorded a notice of her interest prior to the bank's recording its mortgage. The house would be sold and the proceeds would be used to pay Carl's debt to the bank first. If anything was left, it would be given to Beverly. Beverly could have protected her interest by having her attorney file a notice of interest with the recorder of deeds. Had she done so prior to the bank's filing its mortgage, she would have had priority over the bank's claims. The bank could not have sold the house to another buyer to cover Carl's debt.

If Beverly had breached her contract to make payments to Carl, the forfeiture clause in her contract would probably not have been enforced. Beverly would not have forfeited her equity to Carl even though she breached the sales contract. Most states will not enforce a forfeiture clause in a real estate sales contract. They require that the buyer's interest be foreclosed in the manner of a mortgage in compliance with the foreclosure statutes which allow buyers to recover their equity to the extent that it exceeds sellers' damages.

Essential Vocabulary

1. real estate sales contracts
2. forfeiture clause
3. equity
4. foreclose
5. mortgage foreclosure statutes
6. marketable title
7. notice of interest

IV. REAL ESTATE MORTGAGES

Real estate sales can be secured by mortgages in which the debtor conveys title to the creditor until payment has been made.

At common law a "mortgage" was a pledge of real property by a debtor to a creditor to secure the debt. This was accomplished by the debtor transferring or "conveying" title which he owned to the creditor on condition that the creditor return title to debtor when the debt was paid. At one time, possession of the property as well as title was sometimes given by the debtor to the creditor as in the case of modern secured transactions called pledges. The document used to conditionally convey title to a creditor when only title was being conveyed was called a "mortgage contract." The owner of the land who conditionally conveyed title to a creditor pursuant to a mortgage was called the "mortgagor." The secured creditor was called the "mortgagee" and became the new owner of the property during the term of the mortgage. Today, most states have adopted the position that a mortgage neither transfers possession of nor title to real property. It only creates a "lien" against the land in favor of the mortgagee. A lien, it will be recalled, is a creditor's right to take possession of a debtor's property and sell it to satisfy a debt. The process of taking the property and selling it is called "foreclosure."

Most mortgage contracts contain an "acceleration clause." An acceleration clause is part of a written contract that provides that a creditor may declare the entire balance owing on the debt due when the debtor defaults in making payments. In a mortgage contract containing an acceleration clause, the mortgagee can declare the entire remaining balance of the debt due on default. To collect, the mortgagee can foreclose the mortgage and have the property subject to the mortgage sold. When the property is sold, the mortgagee is paid the amount owing on the debt and the costs of the foreclosure proceedings. Any proceeds of the sale in excess of the balance owed to the mortgagee are paid to the mortgagor. If the proceeds of the sale are insufficient to cover the mortgagor's debt and the costs of the proceedings, the mortgagee can recover a "deficiency judgment" for the balance due and collect it from the mortgagor. A deficiency judgement is a judgment in the amount of the remaining debt that could not be paid from the proceeds of the sale.

When real property is foreclosed, the mortgagor has, for a limited time, a "right of redemption" in the foreclosed property. The right of redemption is the mortgagor's right to recover the property from the mortgagee or whoever has purchased the property by paying the amount due in full along with the expenses of foreclosure. The right of redemption lasts only for a limited time. It normally extends from the date of the mortgagor's default in making payments to a date shortly after the date of the foreclosure sale.

If Beverly purchased real property from Carl, Beverly's obligation to pay for it could be secured by a mortgage instead of Carl's retention of title during the payment period under the contract. To accomplish this, Carl would convey the property to Beverly by deed pursuant to the contract, and Beverly would sign and deliver a mortgage contract to Carl to secure her obligation to pay for the house. Both the deed conveying title to the land to Beverly and the mortgage in favor of Carl would be filed with the recorder of deeds in the county or other political subdivision in which the land was located. These filings would protect Beverly's title to the land while creating a lien against it in favor of Carl. If, after the recording of the mortgage, Beverly used the land as security for another loan, the lender would not receive anything in the event of default until Carl has been fully paid. Carl would be protected because his mortgage would have been filed earlier than the new creditor's mortgage. In addition, Carl would not have been able to borrow money and use the house as security because Beverly would have been the owner of record when the deed was recorded. If Beverly defaulted, Carl would have needed to follow the statutory procedures for foreclosing his lien. Beverly would have been entitled to any of her equity that exceeded her debt to Carl and the costs of the foreclosure procedure. The following is an example of the contents of a typical mortgage form:

MORTGAGE[1]

_____(name), mortgagor, of _____(place of residence), hereby mortgages to _____(name), mortgagee, of _____ (place of residence), for the sum of _____ dollars, the following de-scribed tract of land in _____ County, Utah, to wit: *(legal description of the property).*

This mortgage is given to secure the following indebtedness *(description of the amount and form of indebtedness, maturity, rate of interest, by and to whom payable and where).*

The mortgagor agrees to pay all taxes and assessments on said premises, and reasonable attorneys' fees and court costs in case of foreclosure.

Witness the hand of said mortgagor this __ day of _____, 19__.

_____
(mortgagor's signature)

Essential Vocabulary

1. mortgage
2. conveying title
3. mortgage contract
4. mortgagor
5. mortgagee
6. lien
7. foreclosure
8. acceleration clause
9. deficiency judgement
10. right of redemption

---

[1]This mortgage form is for illustrative purposes only and should not be used in any actual transaction.

V. REAL ESTATE DEEDS OF TRUST

Real estate sales can be secured by deeds of trust in which the debtor conveys title to a trustee until payment has been made.

A "deed of trust" or "trust deed" can be used in much the same manner as a mortgage to use land as security for performance of contractual obligations. A deed of trust is a document that conveys the title to land to a "trustee" with instructions to reconvey title to the debtor when the debt is paid or, in the event of a default by the debtor, to foreclose the debtor's interest in the manner specified by statute. A trustee is a person or corporation entrusted with title to the land until the contract has been performed or breached. In many cases, a bank or attorney is used as the trustee. As with notices of interest and mortgages, deeds of trust must be recorded by filing them with the recorder's office in the county or other political subdivision where the land is located. The foreclosure of a deed of trust is similar to the foreclosure of a mortgage. However, some creditors prefer deeds of trust to mortgages because foreclosure is less expensive.

In our example above in which Carl sold Beverly his house, Carl could have secured the transaction by using a deed of trust instead of a mortgage. In this situation, he would have conveyed his real property to a trustee rather than to Beverly with instructions to reconvey the property to Beverly if she paid as agreed or, in the event of default, to sell the property pursuant to statutory foreclosure procedures. If this device had been used, neither Beverly nor Carl would have been able to use the land as security for another transaction during the payment period because neither of them would have had title to the property – only the trustee would have had title during the period of the trust deed.

Essential Vocabulary

1. deed of trust or trust deed
2. trustee

VI. ADVERSE POSSESSION

Title to real property can be lost to an adverse possessor who occupies real property and pays taxes for seven years.

It has been the policy of the law to promote the full use of property while protecting the right of ownership. If the owner does not use real property enough to be aware of another's occupancy of it, state statutes allow the occupier to acquire title to it by "adverse possession." Adverse possession of real property is the continuous occupancy of land without the owner's permission for the period of years specified by state statute. The length of the continuous occupancy required by statute varies from state to state. Some states also require that the adverse possessor pay the taxes on the property while occupying it for the statutory period. For convenience in memorization, the period of seven years and the requirement of payment of taxes has been assumed in the generalization for this section. The occupancy must be for one continuous period rather than several unconnected shorter periods that add up to seven years. The occupancy must also be without the owners permission rather than the result of a rental agreement or favor. This generalization, as well as all of the others presented in this text, must be researched in the state in which you are doing business.

Supersonic, Inc. purchased 1,200 acres of desert land for future expansion. Shortly after the purchase, Tara, a homesteader, moved onto a portion of the property that had access to water, fenced off about 200 acres and raised sheep and chickens for a year. After the first year, she built a cabin and called the county assessor to value the structure and the acreage within her fence for tax purposes. The county assessor did so and began to send her tax notices on the property which she paid each year for five years. At the end of that time, a representative of Supersonic, Inc. contacted her and told her that she was living on private property. Supersonic demanded that she vacate the area, but she refused. A little over a year later, Supersonic filed suit to have Tara evicted. By that time, Tara had lived upon the property for a little more than seven years and had paid taxes on the property a little more than six years.

Although she had occupied the land for seven years by the time suit had been filed, Tara would probably have been required to vacate the land because she had paid taxes on the property only for six years. Had she been able to occupy the land and pay taxes for one more year, she would have been able to acquire title to the property in an "action to quiet title." An action to quiet title is a legal action to have the court declare a party to be the owner of a parcel of land. To protect its interest in the land, Supersonic should have monitored its tax notices more carefully and investigated any decrease in taxes. It should also have had someone make a visual inspection of the land at least annually to look for unauthorized occupancy, roads, and other evidence of adverse use by others. Unauthorized uses should be promptly terminated or properly documented to show that the use was with the permission of the owner, i.e. that the use was not adverse.

Essential Vocabulary

1. adverse possession
2. action to quiet title

VII. EASEMENT BY PRESCRIPTION

An easement by prescription can be lost to another property owner that has used real property for nineteen years.

State statutes and court decisions allow a real property owner who uses the real property of another without permission for a continuous and lengthy period of time to acquire the right to use the property forever. The right to use the real property of another acquired by use without permission is an "easement by prescription." The period of time varies from state to state and must be researched in the state in which you are doing business. For convenience in memorization, the period of nineteen years has been assumed in this generalization. The use must be continuous and not interrupted by court action or abandonment during the running of the time period. In addition, the use must be without the permission of the owner. The policy behind this law, as in the case of adverse possession, is to promote the full use of land. If a landowner is unaware or unconcerned with another's use of his land for the prescribed lengthy period of time, the full use of the land will be promoted by giving the user an easement by prescription.

Donna had driven over Sam's property to get to her cabin for 20 years. Sam finally got tired of this and put up a fence. Sam will probably need to remove the obstacle under the doctrine of easement by prescription. Using the generalization above, Donna acquired the right to continue using Sam's real property after nineteen years had expired. During the nineteen year period, she would have needed to be using the access without Sam's permission, i.e. adversely. She also would have needed to use the access continuously over that period. Continuous use is a relative term with a definition that varies depending on the way the property is used. If Donna had used the access once each week on the average, continuous use would mean that she used the property that frequently without substantial interruptions for at least nineteen years. Her use would probably still be considered continuous even though she did not use the access for a period of a month or so during the nineteen year period to go on vacation.

If, instead of crossing Sam's property, she had used other access for a year of so during the period, her use would have been interrupted, and she would not have acquired an easement by prescription. The easement Donna acquired would be limited to the type and frequency of use that occurred during the nineteen year acquisition period. If she had used the access on the average of once each week, she could have continued to use it on the average of once each week for ever once she had acquired the easement by prescription. However, she could not cross the property more often than once each week, expand the number of vehicles crossing the property, or cross the property with objects other than vehicles, e.g. pipes, wires, or cattle.

Essential Vocabulary

1. easement by prescription

VIII. EMINENT DOMAIN

Title to real property can be taken by the government for a public use after reasonably compensating the owner.

The police power of government to take privately owned property for a public use is called "eminent domain." The U.S. Constitution requires that the governmental agency taking the property give the owner "reasonable compensation." Reasonable compensation usually amounts to the fair market value of the property or, in cases where the government does not take the entire property, the amount by which the value of the original property was decreased. Real property can be "taken" by actually taking title to build something on the land such as a road or a school, or rendering it useless for its current purposes as by lowering water tables on a farm by construction of a roadway that is not actually located on the affected property. The only restriction on the government's exercise of its power of eminent domain is that the property must be taken for a public purpose. If property is taken for a public purpose but is later not needed, the governmental entity taking the property can sell it to any purchaser.

Tom owned a farm that had a well from which all water needed for his cattle could be pumped. The State Highway Commission began to construct a large highway and overpass next to his farm. While they were digging footings for the overpass, they had to blast and pour concrete in very deep holes next to the farm. Tom noticed that the well's production of water was affected. Tom filed suit to have the construction of the highway stopped because it was destroying his well and affecting his entire farming operation. Tom also sued for the value of his farming business that he claimed would be destroyed by the project if the court allowed it to proceed. An economist and appraiser estimated the value of Tom's farming business at $2,000,000. The property was worth $1,000,000 with the well but only $300,000 without it.

The court would not enjoin the construction of the highway because the state can take property for a public purpose by its power of eminent domain. The state would, however, be required to compensate Tom for the property it took. In this case, the value of the farm land was decreased by $700,000. The government might not have been required to compensate him for his business unless it had actually made it impossible for him to stay in the business at any location. The government only took his property by reducing its value. It did not take his farming business.

Essential Vocabulary

1. eminent domain
2. reasonable compensation

IX. EVICTION

Tenants of real property can be evicted only through proper notice and legal action.

A person becomes a "tenant" of real property by occupying it. A tenant is a person holding possession of real property. Tenants have property rights in the real property they possess that can be terminated only by voluntary abandonment or legal action. Each state has adopted an "unlawful detainer statute." An unlawful detainer statute is a state law that sets forth the procedures for terminating a tenant's rights to possess real property. These statutes require that a tenant be given a "notice to quit" prior to legal action to terminate the right to possess the premises. A notice to quit is a formal, written notice that advises the tenant that the right to possess the property is being terminated. The courts require strict adherence to statutory provisions regarding the contents and timing of the notices. Any defect usually results in the owner's being required to repeat the procedure while the tenant remains in possession.

Successful legal action results in the court's issuing the owner a "writ of restitution." A writ of restitution is a court order which directs a tenant to vacate real property. The writs can be enforced by the police when a tenant will not voluntarily vacate after being served with an official copy of the writ. Only an "eviction" ordered by a court is lawful. An "eviction" is any act of depriving a tenant of possession of real property. Evictions of tenants that are not ordered by the courts are unlawful and result in the owners' liability to the dispossessed tenants for unlawful eviction. In addition, the police will intervene to keep the peace by preventing an owner from carrying out an unlawful eviction. Incidents in which an owner of real property forces a tenant to vacate the premises by threatening illegal action, by turning off the water, by removing door, etc. will result in civil liability for wrongful eviction. The statutes of unlawful detainer often have differing procedures and notice requirements depending on the types of tenants in possession of real property and the reasons for evicting them. Tenancies in real property may be categorized as follows: (1) tenancy at sufferance; (2) tenancy at will; (3) periodic tenancy; and (4) tenancy for years.

Essential Vocabulary

1.   tenant
2.   unlawful detainer statute
3.   notice to quit
4.   writ of restitution
5.   eviction

X.   TENANCY AT SUFFERANCE

Tenants at sufferance occupy real property without legal right and can be evicted only through notice and legal action.

A "tenant at sufferance" is a tenant who wrongfully occupies real property. "Sufferance" means toleration so essentially a tenant at sufferance is an occupier without right who is merely being tolerated by the owner. Tenants at sufferance are often former legal tenants who wrongfully refuse to vacate the premises after the owner has served them with a proper notice to quit. A squatter can become a tenant at sufferance by occupying land without the owner's permission. To evict a tenant at sufferance, the owner of real property must follow the procedures set forth in the state unlawful detainer statutes or be liable for unlawful eviction.

Donna allowed Hue to move into her cabin. When Donna asked him to leave, he refused and continued to live there. Hue entered into possession of the cabin as a tenant at will because he could vacate the cabin at any time, and Donna could ask him to leave at anytime. However, Hue became a tenant at sufferance when he refused to leave and began to occupy the premises wrongfully. Donna could not use force to remove him from the premises. In addition, the police could not remove him until a competent court had issued a writ of restitution. Donna could not have the locks changed while Hue was away or otherwise interfere with his use and enjoyment of the property until she had complied with state law regarding notice and legal action. In taking action to obtain a writ of restitution, Donna could also obtain a judgement for damages from Hue for his unlawful detainer of her property.

Essential Vocabulary

1.   tenant at sufferance
2.   sufferance

XI. TENANCY AT WILL

Tenants at will occupy real property with the permission of the owner for an indeterminate time.

A "tenant at will" is an occupier of real property who takes possession with the permission of the owner without a fixed term of occupancy. Either the owner or the tenant can terminate the occupancy at any time without the other's consent and without liability. If a tenant at will continues in possession after the owner terminates the tenancy, the tenant at will becomes a tenant at sufferance and the statutory procedures for unlawful detainer must be followed for a legal eviction.

Sandy moved into the Kentucky Hotel. The charge for her rooms was $45 per day with payment due at checkout time or when requested by the management. It was agreed that the arrangement could be terminated by either party at any time. Sandy was a tenant at will and, once the tenancy was terminated, would become a tenant at sufferance. As such, she could only be evicted in strict compliance with the state unlawful detainer statute if she refused to voluntarily vacate the hotel.

Essential Vocabulary

1.   tenant at will

XII. PERIODIC TENANCY

Periodic tenants occupy real property with the permission of the owner for a recurring period of indeterminate length.

A "periodic tenant" occupies land pursuant to a "lease" that expressly or by implication allows for the indefinite renewal for successive periods of the same length as the original. A "lease" is any written or verbal rental contract. A situation in which a tenant rents an apartment from month to month is an example of a periodic tenancy because the agreement is that the tenant will continue in possession paying rent by the month until either the tenant or the landlord gives notice that the occupancy will be terminated. The repeated period could be any length of time although the most common is one month.

When periodic tenants are asked to vacate the premises and refuse, the reason for the termination of the periodic tenancy often affects the required timing of the notice to quit and its contents. Tenants being evicted for "waste", failure to pay rent, or merely because the owner needs to use the property for some other purpose are commonly entitled to different types of notice. Waste is damage to the premises. Failure to strictly follow the statutes can result in serious delays in obtaining court relief when a tenant refuses to leave voluntarily.

Essential Vocabulary

1. periodic tenant
2. lease
3. waste

XIII. TENANCY FOR YEARS

Tenants for years occupy real property with the permission of the owner for a period with a definite ending date.

A "tenant for years" occupies real property pursuant to a lease for a definite period of time that is not expected to be repeated without the specific agreement of the parties. The term, tenancy for years, is a bit misleading because the requirement for a tenancy for years is only that the period of occupancy have a definite ending date. If Paula rented a stable to Quick for three months for $600, Quick would become a tenant for years although the period was three months rather than a year because the rental period had a definite ending date.

If a tenant for years holds over without objection from the owner, the tenancy for years is renewed with the same terms and for the same period as the original period. For example, the tenancy for years just mentioned would be renewed for another three month period if, at the end of three months, Quick remained in possession of the stable with Paula's permission. If Paula no longer wanted to lease the property to Quick, she would need to follow the unlawful detainer statute to seek an eviction through the courts. As with all of the other tenancies discussed in this section, owners of real property leased to a tenant for years must strictly follow statutory procedures to evict tenants who wrongfully hold over after the end of the period of the lease.

Essential Vocabulary

1. tenant for years

XIV. ZONING

Local governments can pass reasonable zoning regulations subject to non-conforming uses and allow reasonable variances.

Local governments such as cities and counties have the responsibility of planning the use of real property within their borders to maintain safety and promote the full use of the land. They accomplish this by adopting a "master plan" for the development of their area which promotes police and fire protection, garbage collection, safety, etc. The master plan divides the city, county or other administrative area into smaller areas, or "zones," that are subject to the same regulations regarding development. The city or county zoning board then passes "zoning ordinances" to compel compliance with the master plan. Zoning ordinances are laws that require owners to comply with the planned restrictions on development and use of real property within the various zones. Owners are required to obtain "building permits" from the city or county before commencing construction of any structure on real property. Building permits are licenses issued by the city or county permitting the construction project. Failure to obtain a building permit can result in fines and the ordered removal of any unauthorized structure. Permits are issued only when planned structures conform to the requirements of the zone. Ultimately, inspectors are sent to verify that completed structures conform to the specifications and limitations of the building permits issued.

When an owner wants to build a structure that does not conform to the zoning regulations for the area where it will be located or use the property for a purpose that violates the zoning ordinances, he can seek a "variance." A variance is permission to build a structure or use property contrary to zoning regulations. Variances may be obtained by applying to the zoning board and requesting a special exception. A variance can be granted if it will benefit the community and does not conflict with the rationale of the master plan. Granting too many variances may result in destroying the integrity of the master plan thereby rendering it arbitrary and capricious. If this occurs, city planners must develop and implement a new master plan.

When zoning ordinances are adopted by local governments, owners within various zones often have structures or uses for the property that do not conform to new zoning restrictions. The mere adoption of a zoning ordinance cannot deprive owners of their nonconforming structures or their rights to continue using their properties in the same ways they were used prior to the adoption of the ordinance. The right to use real property contrary to new zoning ordinance is called a "nonconforming use." A nonconforming use is a property right that cannot be taken by the government without condemning the property pursuant to the government's power of eminent domain and reasonably compensating the owner for its decrease in value. Nonconforming uses "run with the land." This means that, when the owner sells the property subject to the right of a nonconforming use, the new owner becomes the owner of the nonconforming use. Non-conforming uses pass from owner to owner with the real property to which they are attached. Although the government cannot decrease or interfere with an owner's enjoyment of a nonconforming use, the owner cannot expand the use by increasing the size or frequency of its use.

Albert owned a farm on which he raised a small herd of 40 cattle. He had a barn on the premises, but did not raise any other animals. The county adopted a development plan that zoned the area where Albert's farm was located for single family housing without allowing farm animals. Albert decided that he needed a new barn so he tore down the one he had. He planned to build a new barn and a chicken coup and to expand his operations to raise 60 head of cattle and 100 chickens. When he went to the zoning offices to obtain a building permit, the officials would not issue one to him because the property was zoned strictly for single family dwellings.

The county had the right to divide its land into zones for the purpose of implementing its master development plan. It had the right to limit future development within Albert's zone to single family housing consistent with the plan. However, because Albert had used his property for growing cattle prior to the issuance of the zoning ordinance, he owned a nonconforming use that would allow him to continue raising 40 head of cattle. The nonconforming use is a property right that will pass to the new owner of his land when Albert sells it and cannot be taken by the county without its compensating him. Albert is entitled to a building permit to build a barn to house his livestock. However he, cannot expand his use by increasing his herd of cattle to 60 head, building a chicken coup, and raising 100 chickens without obtaining a variance from the county zoning board. The board would be able to grant him a variance only if it would not impair the rationale of the master plan. A variance, unlike a nonconforming use, is not a property right. It is merely a license or permission to use the land contrary to the zoning ordinances at the pleasure of the zoning board.

Essential Vocabulary

1. master plan
2. zones
3. zoning ordinances
4. building permit
5. variance
6. nonconforming use
7. run with the land

XV. RESTRICTIVE COVENANTS

A seller of real property can impose reasonable restrictive covenants enforceable by owners of adjacent property.

Sometimes it is in the interest of an owner of land to control its use after it has been sold. For example, a developer wanting to subdivide a large tract of land and develop it for a housing project may be able to increase the price at which the lots can be sold if the character of the development is controlled by requiring structures to include a specified minimum square footage, a garage, a brick facade, fences, etc. It is possible for private individuals to impose reasonable restrictions on the use of real property and the characteristics of structures by including "restrictive covenants" in the deeds by which title to the property is conveyed. These restrictions can be thought of as private zoning regulations that can be enforced by the original parties and subsequent purchasers.

A restrictive covenant is a promise that restricts the use of land in the future regardless of the owner. These "covenants," or promises, bind the "original parties," their "successors," and "assigns." The original parties are the parties who initially agree to the restrictive covenants. They must be in "privity of estate." Privity of estate is a relationship in which the parties have an interest in the same real property or in which the owner is conveying title to the real property to another. Examples of relationships in which the parties are in privity of estate are the relationships of seller and purchaser, testator and devisee, landlord and tenant, tenants in common, joint tenants, etc. The successors of an original party are the people who inherit title to or possession of the land in the future. The assigns of an original party are the people to whom the property is sold or given in the future. When a restrictive covenant binds both the original parties and all future owners in this manner, the covenant is said to run with the land.

Restrictive covenants must also touch and concern the land to be enforceable. A covenant that prescribes certain building characteristics as described above would touch and concern the land because it has a rational connection to maintaining the property values and ambiance of the subdivision. A repugnant restriction on the race or religion of future owners would not have a rational connection to the land and would not be enforced.

Miko purchased 300 acres of land that she wished to develop into an exclusive housing development for affluent owners. She included provisions in the deeds by which she transferred ownership to individual lots that required the homes built to contain at least 5,000 square feet, to include a garage and fireplace, and to be of brick construction. All construction needed to be approved by the homeowners' association prior to its commencement. The provisions also required the owners to own sports cars. Nancy purchased one of the lots from Miko and later sold it to Oliver. At the time he purchased the lot, he owned a sports car. Later, he sold the sports car and wanted to build a frame house with

1,200 square feet on the property. The homeowners in the subdivision, through their homeowners' association, objected to this and the fact that Oliver no longer owned a sports car so they filed suit to enforce the restrictive covenants. At the time the suit was filed, Miko no longer owned any of the lots. Oliver defended on the ground that the restrictions did not bind him because he had never agreed to them, and, even if he had, only Miko could enforce them. He also argued that the restrictive covenants did not touch or concern the land.

Oliver would be bound by the building restrictions regarding the minimum square footage. This restriction would run with the land because it was created by the deed initially issued by Miko to Nancy. At that time, Miko and Nancy were in privity of estate because Miko was a seller and Nancy was a purchaser of the lot. The restrictive covenant regarding the size of the home and its construction rationally touched and concerned the land by affecting the character of the subdivision. It could be enforced by the other homeowners because they purchased their lots in reliance upon the restrictions. The requirement that Oliver own a sports car would not run with the land and could not be enforced because it did not touch or concern the land.

Essential Vocabulary

1. restrictive covenant
2. covenant
3. original parties to restrictive covenants
4. privity of estate
5. successors
6. assigns

XVI. WARRANTY AND QUITCLAIM DEEDS

Warranty deeds convey title to real property and warrant good title, while quitclaim deeds convey title without warranty.

Title to real property can be conveyed by "warranty deed" or "quitclaim deed." A warranty deed is a document that conveys title to real property and obligates the "grantor," or former owner, to pay damages to the "grantee," or new owner, in the event anyone else claims an interest in the property. A warranty deed is properly used when the grantor wishes to warrant that the grantee will acquire "good title" to the property. Good title is ownership free of any "encumbrance." An encumbrance is any claim against the land such as a mortgage or other lien, an easement, etc. When a warranty deed is used to convey title, the grantor warrants that he owns the property free of encumbrances and has the right to convey ownership to the grantee. If the grantee of a warranty deed is evicted by someone with better title or discovers liens or other encumbrances on the property, the grantor signing a warranty deed will be liable for the purchase price and damages.

A quitclaim deed is a document that conveys only whatever title to real property the grantor happens to have. It does not obligate the grantor to pay damages to the grantee in the event someone else claims an interest in the property. Even if the grantor owns no interest in the property, the grantee gets no interest in the property and has no cause of action against the grantor in the absence of fraud. Each type of deed is appropriate in some circumstances and inappropriate in others. When the grantor is not certain that he has title or the grantor is being ordered by a court to convey only his interest in the property, a quitclaim deed should be used.

Paula wanted to purchase a hotel from Drive Inns, Inc. Drive Inns issued a quitclaim deed to her when she paid the $500,000 purchase price. She later discovered that there was a mortgage on the premises securing an outstanding debt owed by Drive Inns for $100,000. Drive Inns defaulted on the loan so the mortgagee took possession of the hotel and sold it for $500,000. The mortgagee took $125,000 from the proceeds to cover the mortgage and the costs of foreclosure. The remaining $375,000 was given to Paula. Paula sued Drive Inns because it did not convey good title to her when she purchased the hotel.

Drive Inns, Inc., the grantor, would not be liable because it had conveyed the property to Paula, the grantee, by quitclaim deed. The deed conveyed only whatever title Drive Inns held. If a warranty deed had been used, Drive Inns would have been liable to Paula for the value of the hotel and any additional damages she incurred due to the foreclosure action. Paula's interest would have been protected since Drive Inns would have warranted its ownership of the property and the absence of encumbrances.

Alice and her husband, Benny were seeking a divorce. At the end of the divorce proceedings, Alice was ordered to convey her interest in the home of the couple to Benny as part of the property settlement. She was not required to pay off the mortgage or the mechanics liens filed against the property in favor of workmen who had recently repaired the roof of the home without being paid. She used a warranty deed to convey her interest to Benny. When the mortgagor and roofers began to foreclose their liens on the property, Benny made Alice a party by suing her on the warranties against encumbrances made by her warranty deed.

Alice would be liable to Benny even though she had not been ordered by the divorce court to pay the mortgage and the roofers because she used a warranty deed to comply with the property settlement. By using the warranty deed, she agreed to be liable for any encumbrances on the property such as the mortgage and mechanics' liens. She should have used a quitclaim deed because she was not required to pay the mortgagee or the roofers. A quitclaim deed would have conveyed only the interest she had in the property without warranties. A good rule of thumb that warranty deeds should be used when

WARRANTY DEED[2]

_____(name), grantor, of _____(place of residence), hereby conveys and warrants to _____(name), grantee, of _____ (place of residence), for the sum of _____ dollars, the following described tract of land in _____ County, Utah, to wit: (legal description of the property and any exceptions to the covenants of warranty).

Witness the hand of said grantor this _____ day of _____, 19___.

_____
(grantor's signature)

QUITCLAIM DEED[3]

_____(name), grantor, of _____(place of residence), hereby quitclaims to _____(name), grantee, of _____(place of residence), for the sum of _____ dollars, the following described tract of land in _____County, Utah, to wit: (legal description of the property).

Witness the hand of said grantor this _____ day of _____, 19___.

_____
(grantor's signature)

real property is being conveyed pursuant to a typical sale, and quitclaim deeds should be used when title to the property uncertain or the property is being conveyed to settle a dispute.

---

[2]This document should not be used in any actual transaction and is offered here only as an example.

[3]This document should not be used in any actual transaction and is offered here only as an example.

Essential Vocabulary

1. warranty deed
2. grantor
3. grantee
4. good title
5. quitclaim deed

CHECK YOUR UNDERSTANDING

DIRECTIONS: Read each of the following questions. Choose the best answer and study the discussion of the question.

1. Paula owns an undivided 2/3 interest, and Sally owns an undivided 1/3 interest as tenants in common in a condominium near a ski resort. Paula is an avid skier, but Sally rarely skis. Paula probably has a right to:

   a. use 2/3 of the condominium floor space at the same time Sally uses the remaining 1/3 of the space.
   b. use the condominium 2/3 of the time without Sally, but she may need to allow Sally to use it during some of the winter months.
   c. use the condominium during cold months over Sally's objection if Sally could use it for 4 months during warm weather.
   d. use the condominium only when Sally does not want it.
   e. preempt any sale of the property to another by Sally.

DISCUSSION

   (b)   Paula owns an undivided 2/3 and Sally owns an undivided 1/3 interest in the condominium. This means that Paula can use the entire condo 2/3 of the time. They would need to agree on which months they would occupy the property, or seek partition of their interests. If they sought partition, the court may divide the months or weeks up between the parties so that each would have access to the condo during the winter. Although they could agree to use the condominium together, their undivided interests would allow them to use the entire condominium. Either Paula or Sally could sell her interest to another party without permission or consent. The new owner would become a tenant in common with the tenant that did not sell.

2. Jack and Phil each owned an undivided 1/2 interest in a $100,000 certificate of deposit as joint tenants. Jack left his share to his daughter by will and Phil had no will. Jack died first, and Phil died three months later. Which of the following is true?

    a. Phil's estate will receive the certificate.
    b. Each estate will receive 1/2 the proceeds.
    c. Jack's estate will receive the certificate.
    d. Jack's estate will receive 1/2, and Phil's share will be lost to state or federal taxes because he didn't have a will.
    e. Jack's daughter will receive 1/2 the proceeds, and Phil's estate will receive the other 1/2.

DISCUSSION

    (a)   Phil's estate will receive the certificate because Jack's half interest passed to Phil by survivorship when he died despite the provisions of his will. Since Phil had no will, the entire certificate would have passed to his estate. After Phil's creditors had been paid, any remaining proceeds from the certificate would have been passed by the court to his next of kin. Contrary to the impression created by some estate planners, the certificate would not have been taken by the taxing authorities because Phil had no will. If Phil had a very large estate, he may have incurred greater tax liability because of the absence of a good estate plan, but the taxing authorities do not penalize people merely for not having a will.

3. Henry wanted to purchase a home. He wanted to make payments to the seller with the seller obligated to convey good and marketable title to him when he had completely paid for the home. Henry should probably have his attorney:

    a. record a quitclaim deed when he signs the contract.
    b. record a warranty deed when he signs the contract.
    c. record a notice of interest when he signs the contract.
    d. record a trust deed when he finishes paying for the home.
    e. do nothing until he receives legal title to the property.

DISCUSSION

    (c)   Henry would need to protect his interest in the property against the claims of the seller's creditors by having his attorney file a notice of interest with the governmental office charged with recording deeds in the county in which the property is located. It will also be advantageous to have a title search completed prior to signing the contract and recording the notice of interest to make certain that he is aware of all of the claims against the property that would have priority over his claims. It might be safest for Henry to forego the purchase if the title search shows any encumbrances at all prior to recording a notice of interest. Any encumbrances that were recorded prior to Henry's filing would have priority over his interest in the property.

4. Carol lived on Gary's land for ten years with his permission. She:

   a. can be legally evicted by Gary if he uses reasonable force.
   b. can be evicted only through legal action.
   c. acquired the property through adverse possession.
   d. owns an easement by prescription.
   e. has a fee simple defeasible title now.

DISCUSSION

(b)   Carol was a tenant at will until Gary asked her to leave. When she refused to leave, she became a tenant at sufferance. As a tenant at sufferance, she can be legally evicted only by Gary's strict adherence to the procedures set forth in the state's unlawful detainer statute. Legal action will be necessary to evict Carol in the event she will not leave voluntarily. Gary may not use force. Carol would not have acquired the property by adverse possession or acquired an easement by prescription because her possession of the property was not adverse. She possessed it with Gary's permission. A fee simple defeasible is a conditional title to real property and is inapplicable to this question.

5. Lois had used a well for water on Neal's land for 20 years. Neal did not own the water, but he did own the well. Neal decided that he wanted to stop Lois from using the well. Neal can probably:

   a. stop Lois from using the well if he acts soon.
   b. stop Lois from using the well anytime as long as he brings his action before she starts to pay taxes on the water.
   c. stop Lois from using the well anytime before she has adversely possessed it.
   d. not stop Lois because she has acquired the right to use the well under the doctrine of easement by prescription.
   e. not stop Lois from using the well because she has taken the well for a public purpose under the power of eminent domain.

DISCUSSION

(d)   Lois has acquired an easement by prescription that would allow her and subsequent owners of her property to use the well forever. She acquired the easement by her continuous and adverse use of the well for more than nineteen years. Neal lost the ability to stop Lois from using the well when the nineteen-year acquisition period expired. The payment of taxes is not required to acquire an easement by prescription. However, her failure to pay taxes on the well would stop Lois from acquiring a property right in it by adverse possession. Only the government has the power to take private property for a public use by eminent domain.

6. Paula owned a fish hatchery. The school board for her area decided to construct a school on her property. Paula refused to sell the land, so the school board filed suit to condemn the property under the state's power of eminent domain. Paula sued to stop the construction of the school. She will probably:

    a. win an injunction halting the project.
    b. win an injunction halting construction but she will need to find the school board a new location for its school.
    c. lose because you can't fight city hall.
    d. lose because ownership rights in a fish hatchery are not property rights.
    e. lose because the state can take her property by its power of eminent domain; however, the state will need to pay her the reasonable value of the land.

DISCUSSION

(e)   The state can take Paula's property for a public use if it reasonably compensates her. Use of property for public school construction is a public purpose. Reasonable compensation would be the value of the land taken for school construction. Paula would not be able to halt the construction of the school. Ownership interests in fish hatcheries are property rights that cannot be taken by eminent domain without compensation.

7. Donna allowed her son, Mike, and his wife to live in her house with her. She and Mike got into an argument after he had lived there for about a month, and she demanded that he leave. Mike refused to leave and continued to live there despite Donna's demands that he vacate the premises. Donna finally had the locks

changed while Mike and his wife were out one evening. Which of the following is probably true?

a. Mike can probably force Donna to allow him and his wife back into her home.

b. Donna may not change the locks, but the police will take him off the premises because he is now a trespasser.

c. Donna may use reasonable force to evict Mike from the premises if he refuses to leave when he discovers the locks have been changed.

d. Mike may stay, but he will need to pay a reasonable rental.

e. Donna can have the locks changed while Mike is absent from the premises without risk of liability for wrongful eviction.

DISCUSSION

(a)   Mike and his wife were tenants at will until Donna told them to leave. When they refused to vacate the premises they became tenants at sufferance. It would have been necessary for Donna to follow the procedures of the state unlawful detainer statute to evict them. Since she had not done so, her changing the locks amounted to an unlawful eviction. For this reason, Mike and his wife could probably force Donna to allow them back into Donna's home. Donna may also have incurred some liability for unlawful eviction. The police would not assist Donna in unlawfully evicting her "guests."

8. Arnold owned an alligator ranch. When he started the ranch, it was miles from the nearest town. Over the years, however, the city grew to the limits of the ranch and beyond. Eventually, the city zoning board passed a zoning regulation prohibiting property owners from owning more than two animals for pets. Up to that time, it had been Arnold's practice to have approximately 300 alligators on the ranch. The neighbors complained about the ranch, and the city issued Arnold an order to stop raising the alligators. The city filed suit to close Arnold's ranch, and Arnold filed a counterclaim requiring the city to purchase the ranch from him or allow him to continue his activities. Arnold will probably:

a. win because his ranching activities constitute a nonconforming use.

b. win because the city cannot impose zoning regulations that interfere with property used for business purposes.

c. lose because the city can condemn his property without compensating him if his use interferes with the city's master plan.

d. lose because Arnold's ranching activities constitute a variance that can be revoked by the city at any time.

e. lose unless he can obtain the approval of a majority of his neighbors.

DISCUSSION

(a) Arnold owned a nonconforming use when the city zoning board passed the zoning regulations. Although the city has the power to pass the regulations, it must allow him to continue alligator farming or condemn his farm by eminent domain and pay him for it. He does not need to apply for a variance because he owns the nonconforming use with or without the approval of his neighbors.

9. Which of the following relationships would meet the privity of estate requirement for creating a restrictive covenant that would run with the land?

   a. seller-purchaser
   b. principal-agent
   c. parent-child
   d. lawyer-client
   e. any fiduciary relationship

DISCUSSION

(a) To create a restrictive covenant that will run with the land to all future owners, the parties must be in privity of estate. Privity of estate is a relationship in which the parties have an interest in the same real property or in which the owner is conveying title to the real property to another. Only the seller-purchaser relationship fits this requirement. The other relationships are merely fiduciary relationships that do not generate privity of estate. Fiduciary relationships are not relevant to the creation of restrictive covenants that run with the land.

10. Tom was ordered by the court to convey his interest in a home to his ex-wife subject to a mortgage the couple had entered into with a bank to finance one of their vacations. Tom's ex-wife was ordered to pay the mortgage. Which of the following would be properly used to convey Tom's interest in the home to his ex-wife?

   a. a warranty deed
   b. a limited warranty deed
   c. a quickclaim deed
   d. a quitclaim deed
   e. an assignment of contract

DISCUSSION

(d)   Tom should use a quitclaim deed to convey his interest to his ex-wife because he was not ordered to pay the mortgage. If he used a warranty deed, he would be liable to his wife for the balance of the mortgage despite the court's order that the ex-wife pay the mortgage. Limited warranty deeds usually make some but not all of the warranties of title made by a warranty deed. This too would have been the wrong instrument to use because Tom was not ordered to pay any of the encumbrances that may be on the title to the property. "Quickclaim" is merely a mispronunciation of "quitclaim." There was no contract to assign so an assignment of contract would not be appropriate.

Chapter 23
Liens

Liens are commonly used by creditors to secure debts. There are numerous liens created by statute that cannot be covered in this section. However, the generalizations that are presented here will be a valuable aid to further study of the topic and provide a rudimentary understanding of how liens work. Liens are generally created by statute or legal action. The index of the state code will provide a complete list of liens enforceable in the state. After learning the rudiments of lien law, it would be valuable to peruse the liens available in your state code.

I. LIENS

A lien is a creditor's right to take possession of a debtor's property, sell it, and use the proceeds to satisfy the debt.

In the absence of a lien, a creditor has no right to take a debtor's property. Any attempt to do so is actionable by the debtor as conversion. There are numerous liens that are allowed by state and federal statutes. This chapter will discuss only the very most commonly used liens. Liens are either "possessory liens" or "filed liens." A possessory lien requires for its enforceability that the creditor retain possession of the property subject to the lien. No filings are required for possessory liens, and the lien is usually lost if the creditor allows the debtor to recover possession of the property. A filed lien requires filing of some type of notice for its existence or enforceability, and the creditor is not required to retain possession of the property subject to the lien.

As discussed in the chapter on secured transactions, security interests are liens that can be possessory or filed. A security agreement can create a possessory lien when the creditor takes possession of the collateral pursuant to a pledge. Lay-away and pawn contracts are examples of pledges. A security agreement can also lead to a filed lien when the debtor has possession of the collateral. The security interest is perfected by the creditor's filing a financing statement with the state commercial code department. Liens created by mortgages were discussed in the chapter dealing with real property. Mortgages and deeds of trust are types of filed liens enforceable against others when they are appropriately filed in the state office where deeds are recorded. In studying liens, it is important to determine whether a particular lien is possessory or filed since a possessory lien can be lost if the collateral is returned to the debtor, and filed liens can be lost if they are not timely and appropriately filed.

Henry owed Jim $2,000. When Jim found out that Henry had purchased a $2,000 table saw instead of paying him, he went to Henry's shop and took the table saw while Henry was out to lunch. Henry called the police and sued Jim for conversion. Jim will be responsible for both theft and conversion. Henry's indebtedness to Jim did not give him the right to take Henry's property in the absence of a lien.

Essential Vocabulary

1. lien
2. possessory liens
3. filed liens

II. JUDGMENT LIENS

Unpaid judgment creditors have judgment liens on the unexempt real and personal property of judgment debtors.

In the absence of a security interest in collateral or some other lien, a creditor cannot take a debtor's property and sell it to satisfy a debt without suing the debtor and obtaining a "judgment." A judgment is a court order setting forth the official decision of a court upon the respective rights and claims of the parties to an action brought before it. The judgment creates a filed lien called a "judgment lien." A judgment lien gives the creditor the right to take the debtor's property, sell it, and use the proceeds to pay the judgment debt. The judgment is entered on a "judgment docket." A judgment docket is a list of judgments which is open to public inspection and provides official notice of judgment liens. A creditor owning a judgment lien is called a "judgment creditor," and the debtor is called a "judgment debtor."

A judgment places a lien on all of the "unexempt real and personal property" belonging to the judgment debtor. The unexempt real and personal property is the property that the judgment creditor can sell to satisfy the judgment debt. State and federal statutes make certain types of property, such as limited amounts of income, jewelry, clothing, furniture, equity in a home, etc., exempt from sale for humanitarian reasons. These items are referred to as "exempt property." Judgment creditors can enforce a judgment only upon unexempt property by obtaining appropriate writs and orders from the court. The enforcement of a judgment is called the "execution of a judgment."

The main writs for executing a judgment are the "writ of execution," the "writ of garnishment," and the "charging order." The writ of execution directs a constable or police officer to seize the unexempt real and personal property of the judgment debtor, sell it, and pay the proceeds into court where the judgment creditor can take them as needed to satisfy the judgment. The writ of garnishment directs whomever owes the debtor money to pay the money to the court instead of to the debtor for the satisfaction of the judgment. A garnishment is often used to seize the debtor's bank accounts or paycheck. A charging order directs any partnership of which the debtor is an owner to pay the debtor's share of the profits and, in the event of dissolution, his share of the assets to the court for the satisfaction of the judgment.

When a judgment has been executed resulting in the full payment of a judgment creditor, a "satisfaction of judgment" must be filed by the creditor with the court. A satisfaction of judgment is a document that indicates that the judgment has been completely paid and terminates the judgment lien. As is the case of a failure to file a termination statement to terminate a security interest, any failure to file a satisfaction of judgment promptly after the judgment has been satisfied, or paid, is actionable by the debtor.

Essential Vocabulary

1. judgment
2. judgment lien
3. judgment docket
4. judgment creditor
5. judgment debtor
6. unexempt real and personal property
7. exempt property
8. execution of a judgment
9. writ of execution
10. writ of garnishment
11. charging order
12. satisfaction of judgment

III. REPAIRMEN'S LIENS

Unpaid repairmen have a lien on the personal property in their possession that they have repaired.

When a person renders a service to the owner of personal property by repairing or improving the property, she acquires a "repairman's lien" on the property. A repairman's lien is a possessory lien acquired on property for the amount due for the services. Services can be rendered on personal property by dry cleaners, automobile mechanics, watch and television repairmen, etc. The lien arises when the services are rendered while the property is in the possession of the repairman, dry cleaner, shoemaker, etc. The lien is lost when possession of the property is returned to the owner. Sate statutes provide a procedure for notifying the owner of the claimed lien and ultimately foreclosing it. As is the case with most liens, the law typically allows the owner to redeem the property by paying the amount owed prior to its sale. When a lien is foreclosed and the property is not redeemed, it can be sold at a "public sale" or at a "private sale". A public sale is an advertised auction while a private sale is a sale by the lienholder to a buyer without an auction. Regardless of which type of sale is used, it must be conducted in a reasonable manner to ensure fairness to the debtor. This usually means that the debtor must be given notice of the sale and an opportunity to redeem the property.

Ellis, an automobile mechanic, rebuilt the carburetor on Irene's van. He acquired a repairman's lien on the van by working on it that is enforceable as long as the van remains in his possession. It is important to note that Ellis has acquired a "repairman's lien" rather than a "mechanic's lien." If Ellis is not paid, he should contact an attorney to assist him with the foreclosure of his repairman's lien. If he releases the van to Irene without being paid, he will lose his lien and be left with a cause of action against her for breach of her contract. If he prevailed in an action for breach of contract, he would be able to acquire a judgment lien.

Although Ellis can have the van sold after he acquires a judgment lien, the repairman's lien is more desirable because he can retain possession of the van during litigation. This will place considerable pressure on Irene to settle the dispute if she needs the van for daily transportation and decrease the chance that she will not still own the property when the judgment lien is created. If she does not pay Ellis before the lien is foreclosed, she will have an opportunity to redeem the van by payment of Ellis' claims prior to sale. If she cannot arrange financing in time to redeem the van, Ellis can sell it at public or private sale following the foreclosure process.

Essential Vocabulary

1. repairman's lien
2. public sale
3. private sale

IV. MATERIALMEN'S AND MECHANICS' LIENS

Unpaid materialmen and mechanics can file liens on the real property they improved to compel payment by the owner.

"Materialmen" are individuals or companies that furnish materials that are used to improve real property by becoming a part of a building or other structure attached to the land. "Mechanics" are individuals or companies that furnish labor in the improvement of real property. State statutes allow these classes of creditors to file liens on the land on which the improvements are located and sell it to collect their charges. A lien in favor of a company that has supplied material used to improve real property is called a "materialman's lien." A lien in favor of a company or workman that supplied labor used to improve real property is called a "mechanic's lien." These liens are preferable to judgment liens because they can be filed prior to any court action. Both of these liens are filed liens.

Abuse of these liens will result in criminal and civil liability. State law specifies the contents of the lien documents and deadlines for filing. Statutory procedures must be strictly followed or the lien is generally lost. Once a lien is filed with the county recorder for the county in which the real property is located, the owners and general contractors often have serious difficulties in obtaining further advances of funds from the lending institutions financing the project. This sometimes adds to the pressure on the owner and general contractor to settle disputes that can ultimately lead to the filing of liens. Liens can be waived by materialmen and mechanics who have been paid prior to filing. Once a lien has been filed, it can be released by filing a release of lien when the materialman or mechanic has been paid.

While liens protect materialmen and mechanics, they can result in special problems for the owner of the real property. An owner can contract with a general contractor for the construction, pay all charges and still end up with a materialman's lien or mechanic's lien filed against the property. Such contracts typically require the general contractor to pay for the necessary materials and to pay any subcontractors working on the project. The owner is required to pay the general contractor. However, if the general contractor does not pay the material suppliers or the subcontractors who worked on the project, they can file liens on the property to compel the owner to pay them even if he has already paid the general contractor. This can result in the owner paying the costs of the project twice and being left with only a cause of action for breach of contract against the general contractor.

For this reason, an owner of real property is often required by statute to obtain a "payment bond" from the general contractor to insure the proper payment for materials and labor used on the project. A payment bond is a contract between the general contractor and the owner in which the contractor promises to pay materialmen and mechanics.

The owner must require that the payment bond be made with "sufficient sureties." "Sureties" are third parties who guarantee that the contractor will keep his promise to pay the materialmen and mechanics. Sureties are generally insurance companies or other individuals with assets "sufficient" to cover any anticipated liability for materials and labor. Unpaid materialmen and mechanics can sue sureties directly as can the owner if the general contractor breaches his promise to pay. Sureties must be paid for accepting liability on a contractor's payment bond. This results in increased costs for the project to the owner. Most states now have laws protecting the owners of residential property from liens resulting when contractors fail to pay subcontractors even after being paid by the property owner. These laws allow subcontractors to submit claims to a state fund, but they cannot file liens on the residential property. However, materialmen and mechanics are still permitted to file liens on commercial property when they have not been paid.

Dick hired Tracy to repave the parking lot of his business. Tracy hired subcontractors to do the job. The job was completed satisfactorily so Dick paid Tracy. Unfortunately, Tracy did not pay the subcontractors or materialmen so they filed liens on Dick's business property about a week later. Dick will have a cause of action against Tracy, but he will need to pay the subcontractors and materialmen even though he has already paid Tracy. If Dick had been unwilling to take the risk that Tracy might not pay for the labor and materials used to pave the parking lot, he could have paid a higher price for the job and required Tracy to execute a contractor's payment bond. The bond would have required third parties or sureties to guarantee that Tracy would pay the subcontractors and materialmen as promised in the contract. Had this been done, the sureties would have been required to pay for the materials and labor rather than Dick. Of course, they would have had actions against Tracy if they had been required to pay on the bond.

Essential Vocabulary

1. materialmen
2. mechanics
3. materialman's lien
4. mechanic's lien
5. payment bond
6. sufficient sureties

V. LIEN PRIORITIES

Perfected liens have priority over unperfected liens and similar liens have priority in the order in which they attached.

Although state statutes frequently substitute different rules to promote various public policies, similar liens generally follow the rule that liens that attach first must be paid first. When two or more creditors have liens on the same property, the creditor who owns the first lien filed must be paid all that he is due when the property is sold before the second lien holder can be paid anything. The creditor who's lien attached second must be paid in full before the creditor who's lien attached third can be paid anything, etc. Therefore, creditors holding liens in the same property do not share in the proceeds of any foreclosure proceedings equally or pro rata. When the proceeds are not enough to satisfy all of the creditors, the creditors who acquired their liens later will not be paid. If the proceeds of the foreclosure exceed the amounts owed to creditors, the excess is given to the debtor. It rarely happens that there is any excess for the debtor after creditors and costs of foreclosure have been paid.

For example, if a watch repairman repairs a watch that is already subject to a valid and perfected security interest in favor of the seller, the security interest would have priority over the watch repairman's lien because it attached to the watch first. This would mean that in a foreclosure of the watch repairman's lien, the secured party would be entitled to be fully compensated before the watch repairman could receive any proceeds from the sale. If the secured party had failed to perfect his security interest, he may have lost his priority because he failed to take steps to protect himself and others by filing a financing statement. If there had been two holders of perfected security interests in the same watch, the first to file would have had priority. In the case of mortgages on real property, a similar rule is applied. If property subject to two recorded mortgages is sold pursuant to a foreclosure proceeding, the first mortgage recorded would need to paid with the proceeds of the sale before any of the proceeds could be used to pay the amount secured by the second mortgage. Priorities of lien holders are often regulated by statute and exceptions to this section's generalization are frequently made for public policy reasons.

CHECK YOUR UNDERSTANDING

DIRECTIONS: Read each of the following questions. Choose the best answer and study the discussion of the question.

1. A lien:

  a. is a type of tax shelter.
  b. must be filed with the court to be effective.
  c. is a statutory right belonging to certain classes of debtors.
  d. is a creditor's right to have property owned by a debtor sold to satisfy a debt.
  e. will never attach to exempt property as defined by state and federal law.

DISCUSSION

(d)   A lien is a creditor's right to have property owned by a debtor sold to satisfy a debt. A tax shelter is a business tactic designed to minimize taxes and is not relevant here. Not all liens are filed with the court. Mechanic's liens, for example, are filed with the recorder of deeds to real property. While liens are authorized by statute, they belong to creditors rather than debtors. Judgment liens may not attach to a debtor's exempt property. However, most other liens will attach to property exempt from the execution of a judgment lien. For example, a refrigerator is exempt from execution. However, if the owner of the refrigerator uses it as collateral in a secured transaction, the secured creditor receives a security interest in the refrigerator and can take possession of it on default and sell it.

2.   A charging order enables judgment creditors of a partner to:
   a.   execute upon specific partnership property.
   b.   execute upon a partner's partnership interest.
   c.   use partnership assets to the same extent as the partner could prior to issuance of the order.
   d.   become partners in the business until they have been paid.
   e.   reach the personal assets of the other partners for payment of the judgment.

DISCUSSION

(b)   A charging order is a court order that enables a creditor to reach a debtor's interest in a partnership. The order will not allow a creditor to take specific partnership property or force the partnership to dissolve. It will, however, allow a creditor to take the partner's share of the partnership profits. In this respect, a charging order resembles a garnishment more than a writ of execution. The charging order does not allow a creditor to become a partner, use the partnership assets, or reach the personal assets of other partners.

3.   Unis took her automobile to Vern's Auto Repair. She asked Vern to replace the brake shoes on the vehicle, and Vern agreed. They did not discuss the price for these services when she left the car. Vern did the work and gave her a bill for $200. Unis refused to pay the bill. Vern can probably:
   a.   do nothing.
   b.   only sue for damages.
   c.   retain possession of the vehicle if he files a mechanic's lien.

d. retain possession of the vehicle if the police believe his fees are reasonable.

e. retain possession of the vehicle even if the police find the charges to be excessive because he has a repairman's lien.

DISCUSSION

(e)   Vern acquired a repairman's lien on the car by working on it. He will be entitled to the reasonable value of his services in quasi contract even though no contract was formed due to the parties' failure to agree on a price. Vern can retain possession of the car until he has been paid the reasonable value of his services. If Unis does not pay him, he can follow the statutory procedures for foreclosing his lien. The car can be sold, and he can be paid from the proceeds. Unis would be entitled to any amount by which the proceeds exceeded the reasonable value of Vern's services. Vern may be liable for conversion if Unis offers a reasonable amount, but he refuses to release the car unless she pays an unreasonable price. Mechanic's liens are filed by people who work on real property rather than automobile mechanics. The police do not have jurisdiction over a civil matters. They will not intervene merely because they feel the charges are unreasonable. The reasonableness of the charges is an issue for a civil court.

4.   Warren purchased a warehouse and lot from Yaro for $1,500,000. Yaro had not paid City Builders Supply for repairing the roof. After Warren took possession of the warehouse, he was contacted by City Builders when they demanded payment. When he refused to pay for the repairs, City Builders filed a mechanic's lien on the property and filed suit to foreclose it. City Builders will probably:

a. lose because Warren was not a party to its contract with Yaro.

b. lose because Warren had already paid Yaro for the property and the price included payment for the repairs.

c. lose, but it can repossess the materials used in the repair.

d. win only if it can show that Yaro was sued first for the repairs.

e. win even though Warren had paid Yaro for the property.

DISCUSSION

(e)   City Builders Supply acquired a valid mechanic's lien by filing a notice of the lien with the recorder of deeds. This lien attached to the real property and could be enforced by City Builders even though Warren had paid Yaro. City Builders could foreclose its lien and sell Warren's warehouse and lot to cover the debt. Of course, if the property was sold, Warren would be entitled to the difference between the amount of the debt and the amount for which the property was sold. There is no requirement that Yaro be sued first. City Builders could not repossess the materials used in the repair. When the materials were installed, they became part of the real property as fixtures. The repossession of materials or destruction of labor expended on real property is economically wasteful and not allowed by the law. The police will normally stop mechanics and materialmen from damaging real property in attempts to "repossess" their labor or materials. If Warren has to pay City Builders, Yaro may be liable to Warren if he used a warranty deed to transfer title since a mechanic's lien is an encumbrance on the title.

5. National Finance made a business loan to Fred for $75,000 in January. In March, Public Bank loaned him $150,000. Public filed a deed of trust to secure its loan to Fred in April. National had its deed of trust filed in May of the same year. Unfortunately, the property was severely damaged by an earthquake leaving the property worth only $90,000. Fred stopped making payments on both loans and the banks moved to foreclose their deeds of trust. Which of the following is probably correct?

    a. Neither National nor Public Bank can foreclose the trust deeds because they did not file them when the loans were made.
    b. The deeds can be foreclosed, and National and Public Bank will share equally in the proceeds with each receiving $45,00.0
    c. The deeds can be foreclosed, but because Public Bank was owed twice as much as National, Public Bank will receive $60,000 while National receives only $30,000.
    d. The trust deeds can be foreclosed, but Public Bank will receive all of the proceeds because it filed its deed of trust first.
    e. The deeds can be foreclosed, but National will need to be paid first because it made its loan before Public Bank.

DISCUSSION

    (d)   Trust deeds are filed liens that come into existence only when the deed of trust is properly filed. In the absence of a statutory exception to the general rule, the first party to file a lien has priority over those who file later. Public Bank has priority because it filed before National. Public Bank will need to be paid all that it is owed before National would be entitled to anything. Since the value of the property is less than Public Bank's claim, National will probably receive nothing from the sale. When the property is sold pursuant to foreclosure, all liens against it will be terminated. National will need to sue Fred to obtain a judgment lien. Once this is accomplished, the national could pursue the unexempt property belonging to Fred for satisfaction of the judgment.

Chapter 24

Labor Law

The National Labor Relations Act of 1935 was originally known as the Wagner Act. It guaranteed to employees in industries affecting interstate commerce the rights to self-organization, to bargain collectively, and to engage in concerted activities formerly illegal under the Sherman Anti-trust Act of 1890. It was subsequently amended in 1947 by the Labor-Management Relations Act (Taft-Hartley Act) and in 1959 by the Labor-Management Reporting and Disclosure Act (Landrum-Griffin Bill). All of the amending acts have become part of the National Labor Relations Act. The amendments were necessary to balance the power of employers and organized labor while protecting the negotiation process from organized crime. The following generalizations present an introduction to the National Labor Relations Act and modern labor law.

I. NATIONAL LABOR RELATIONS BOARD (NLRB)

The National Labor Relations Board conducts representation elections and adjudicates unfair labor practice charges.

The National Labor Relations Board (NLRB) is a federal administrative agency created by Congress through the National Labor Relations Act to police all aspects of the organization and bargaining process. When employees decide to organize, both unions and employers campaign to influence employee votes. Following the campaign, a "representation election" is held. A representation election is an election in which employees vote by secret ballot to decide whether or not they will organize and which union will represent them. If either management or the union violates the guidelines governing the conduct of the election, employees' rights to organize, or the balance of bargaining power, aggrieved parties can file "unfair labor practice" charges with the NLRB. An unfair labor practice an activity that violates the NLRA or the regulations issued by the NLRB designed to maintain a balance of bargaining power between employers and employees. The NLRB polices the implementation of the NLRA and issues orders requiring violators to cease and desist unlawful activities and correct procedural violations of the law. Unfair labor practice charges must generally be filed with the NLRB for administrative adjudication rather than with a court.

371

While the employees at Fidget, Inc. were considering joining a union, union representatives campaigned in favor of unionization while management campaigned against it. The representation election was conducted by Fidget's management team over the objection of union representatives. When Fidget's managers counted the votes, they announced that the employees had overwhelmingly chosen not to join the union. If the union questions these results, it could file unfair labor practice charges against the company to obtain an order requiring that the election be run again under the supervision of NLRB representatives.

Essential Vocabulary

1. National Labor Relations Act (NLRA)
2. National Labor Relations Board (NLRB)
3. representation election
4. unfair labor practice

II. UNFAIR LABOR PRACTICES OF EMPLOYERS

Employers may not interfere with self-organization, refuse to bargain, contribute to labor organizations, or discriminate against union members.

It is an unfair labor practice for an employer to interfere with the "self-organization" of employees. Self-organization of employees refers to employees engaging in activities aimed at forming or joining an organization for the purpose of bargaining with the employer regarding wages, hours, and working conditions. Interference has taken the form of "blacklisting" and requiring employees to sign "yellow dog contracts" as a condition of employment. Blacklisting is the practice of maintaining a list of employees who are known union supporters or advocates of unionization. The list is shared among employers to prevent union supporters from finding work in the industry. The practice constitutes an unfair labor practice and is usually illegal under state law as well. Yellow dog contracts are employment contracts that make support of union activities or engaging in organizational activities grounds for termination of employment. The colorful name of this practice comes from the perceived cowardly nature of using this means to prevent unionization.

Once employees have organized and chosen their "exclusive bargaining agent," employers are required to bargain with the employees' representatives. The exclusive bargaining agent for organized employees is the representative they choose to bargain on their behalf. The bargaining agent is exclusive in the sense that the employer must bargain only with the employees' chosen representative rather than individual employees or some other union. Any failure to bargain with the employees' bargaining agent is an unfair labor practice.

The employees of Gusher, Inc. voted to be represented by the International Brotherhood of Plumbers (IBP). Gusher refused to recognize the IBP and attend meetings to discuss wages, hours, and working conditions. The IBP can file an unfair labor practice charge with the NLRB to obtain an order compelling Gusher to bargain in good faith. It would also be an unfair labor practice for Gusher to form its own union and require employees to choose it as their representative. Gusher could not contribute financially to IBP and thereby dominate it. Gusher may not discriminate in any way against employees who object to unfair labor practices and file charges with the NLRB.

Essential Vocabulary

1. self-organization
2. blacklisting
3. yellow dog contracts
4. exclusive bargaining agent

III. UNFAIR LABOR PRACTICES OF UNIONS

Unions may not engage in secondary activities or pressure employers to join employer organizations, pay for services not rendered, or cease bargaining with certified unions, or bargain with non-certified unions.

Unions may not engage in "secondary activities." Secondary activities are labor actions designed to pressure employers through other businesses. While a union may use strikes and picketing to pressure the employer of the workers it represents, it is an unfair labor practice to pressure other companies to stop doing business with the primary company during a strike. Unions cannot threaten other companies with strikes or picketing if they transport the primary company's goods. Agreements with unions that a company will not transport a company's goods if it is on strike are illegal, "hot cargo agreements." Union activities aimed at stopping other companies from purchasing goods or services from the primary company during a strike are illegal, "secondary boycotts." It is also an unfair labor practice for unions to pressure employers to agree to "featherbedding contracts." A featherbedding contract is an agreement to pay for services that are not rendered or are not needed.

The NLRA also protects the choice of employees in their union representatives. Once the employees have chosen a union to represent them in negotiations with their employer, other unions may not pressure the employer to stop bargaining with the "certified union." A certified union is a union that has been certified by the NLRB as the exclusive bargaining agent of the employees following an election or voluntary recognition by the employer. It is also an unfair labor practice for a union to pressure an employer to bargain with an "non-certified union." An uncertified union is a union that has not been formally selected by the employees through an election or an authorization card campaign.

The union had organized the workers of Balloon's Etc. and Carl's Trucking during previous organization campaigns. During a strike against Balloon's Etc., the union threatened to picket Carl's Trucking if it picked up or delivered any of Balloon's merchandise. Carl's Trucking could file an unfair labor practice charge against the union because it was pressuring Carl's Trucking to engage in a secondary boycott of Balloon's Etc. Similarly, the union could not attempt to negotiate an agreement with Carl's Trucking in the future in which Carl's Trucking would agree not to transport goods of a company subject to a strike by the union. While strikes, boycotts, and picketing are allowed when aimed at the primary company involved in a labor dispute. Pressure cannot be brought to bear upon or through secondary companies who do business with the primary company.

Essential Vocabulary

1. secondary activities
2. hot cargo agreements
3. secondary boycotts
4. featherbedding contracts
5. certified union
6. non-certified union

IV. CRAFT AND INDUSTRIAL UNIONS

Craft unions represent skilled laborers on a regional basis, and industrial unions represent unskilled laborers on a plant by plant basis.

Craft unions organize workers on a regional basis rather than a plant by plant basis because skilled laborers practice their trades in many industries in the area where they reside. Essentially, tradesmen compete with other laborers with the same skill regardless of the industry in which they work. Skilled laborers tend to shift from company to company within a given geographical area doing the same job. Craft unions work for skilled laborers by protecting their jobs from unskilled laborers and negotiating for improvements in wages, hours, and working conditions. Craft unions formed the American Federation of Labor (AFL) to assist them in uniting to take political action.

Industrial unions represent unskilled laborers in mass production industries. They organize workers on a plant by plant basis because unskilled workers compete with other unskilled laborers for the same jobs in the plant. Industrial unions formed the Congress of Organizations (CIO) to assist them in taking political action. The AFL and CIO have merged to form a single organization, the AFL-CIO, at the national level to represent the interests of organized labor on the political level.

Since unskilled laborers are paid less than skilled laborers, employers sometimes attempt to train unskilled laborers to complete some of the work traditionally completed by tradesmen. This sometimes results in jurisdictional disputes between the craft and industrial unions. The AFL-CIO has helped to resolve such disputes by working with unions on a case by case basis to arrive at voluntary settlements and no-raiding pacts.

Essential Vocabulary

1. craft (trade) unions
2. American Federation of Labor (AFL)
3. industrial unions
4. Congress of Industrial Organizations (CIO)

V. ORGANIZATIONAL CAMPAIGNS

Organizational campaigns may be conducted on company premises by employers anytime and by workers while not on duty, but union representatives may not enter the premises without permission.

"Organizational campaigns" consist of activities engaged in by workers, union representatives, and employers designed to convince workers to vote in favor or against a union. Activities resemble political campaigns in terms of the methods employed to win votes. Typically, management campaigns against unionization of workers while union representatives and employees campaign in favor of it. As is the case with political elections, campaigns may be spirited and dynamic. Promises are made in speeches and literature by both sides until a representation election is held. Due to the importance of access to employees during organizational campaigns, the NLRA sets standards for conducting the campaigns.

Organizational campaigns may generally be conducted on company premises by employers anytime prior to 24 hours before the employees vote. This is allowed because the employer owns the premises and pays the employees' wages whether they are working or attending a meeting scheduled by the employer. Workers may conduct organizational campaigns on company premises as well because they have the employer's permission to be there. However, they are limited to campaigning during their lunch and other breaks to avoid interfering with work of the company. Union representatives may not campaign on company premises without the employer's permission if the company has a blanket no solicitation policy applied equally to all outsiders for safety or other reasons. Union representatives do not have any greater right to enter an employer's premises than other outsiders. Because of this, union organizers may request an "Excelsior List." An Excelsior List is a list of employee names and contact information that union organizers can use to facilitate contacting employees after working hours. The lists are named after the case in which employers were first required to provide them.

The International Brotherhood of Bagel Bakers wanted to urge the employees of Pastry Inc. to join the union. When union representatives entered the plant, they were stopped and escorted out by company security officials who informed the organizers that the company had a no solicitation policy that was applied to all outsiders seeking access to employees on company premises. The union representatives filed an unfair labor practice charge against the company for interfering with their organizational campaign. The NLRB ruled for the company because the organizers were merely trespassers when they entered the premises without the employer's permission. Without the permission, union representatives may only conduct their organizational campaigns through meetings conducted outside of company premises. However, sympathetic employees may recruit co-workers at the plant during their lunch and other breaks because they have the employer's permission to be on the premises.

Essential Vocabulary

1. organizational campaign
2. Excelsior List

VI. BARGINING UNITS

The NLBR will determine the appropriate composition of disputed bargaining units subject to the following: supervisors and managers may not form a unit; professionals may not be included without prior majority consent; plant guards may not be included with other employees; and craft severance is permitted.

When a group of workers decide to organize the question arises regarding which employees the proposed union will represent. For example, would the union represent everyone working for the company or just the assembly line workers? The group of employees to be represented by the union are referred to as the "bargaining unit." The composition of the bargaining unit has important implications for the company and union organizers. Consider for example, a plant that employs one assembly line worker for every two packers, but only the assembly line workers favor unionization. The composition of the bargaining unit is critical the outcome of any representation election. If the bargaining unit includes only assembly line workers, the union will be certified the winner of the election. However, the union will lose the election if the bargaining unit includes both assembly line workers and packers. An employer wishing to avoid unionization and union organizers may have very different views regarding the proper composition of the bargaining unit. When this occurs, the NLRB will determine the proper composition of the bargaining unit subject to the rules listed above in the generalization.

Expanding on the assembly plant example above, suppose that the plant included the following employee groups: assembly line workers, packers, managers, accountants, electricians, and plant guards. Which groups would be properly included in the bargaining unit. Only members of the potential bargaining unit may vote in the representation election. Assembly line workers and packers could be included because they are both composed of unskilled workers. The company managers cannot be included in any unit. The accountants may not be included in the unit unless a majority of them consent because they are considered professionals. Although plant guards may organize, their unit may not include any other employees because they are in charge of plant security during job actions. The electricians may initially be included in the bargaining unit, but they will be allowed to opt out if a majority of them elects not to be part of the unit because they are skilled workers and the unit contains unskilled workers. Skilled workers are sometimes referred to as "craftsmen" or "tradesmen." Severing the ties between bargaining units for unskilled workers and those for skilled workers, i.e. craftsmen, or tradesmen, is referred to as "craft severance."

Essential Vocabulary

1. bargaining unit
2. craftsmen
3. tradesmen
4. craft severance

VII. AUTHORIZATION CARD CAMPAIGNS

If 30% or more workers sign authorization cards, the union may petition the NLRB for a representation election.

In an authorization card campaign, union organizers contact workers and ask them to sign authorization cards. "Authorization cards" are cards indicating that workers authorize the union to act as their exclusive bargaining agent. If at least 30% of the workers sign the cards, the union may petition the NLRB to hold a representation election. If fewer than 30% sign, an election may not be held due to insufficient interest in unionization of the workers.

The International Brotherhood of Chemical Workers conducted an organizational campaign and convinced 20% of the dock workers to sign authorization cards indicating that they authorized the union to act as their exclusive bargaining agent. Although interested employees and union organizers worked together to add workers to their ranks, they were unsuccessful. The employer refused to recognize the union so union organizers filed a petition with the NLRB requesting that it hold a representation election to determine the will of the majority of workers by secret ballot. The NLRB should deny the petition because fewer than 30% of the workers indicated an interest in unionization through signing authorization cards.

Essential Vocabulary

1. authorization card campaign
2. authorization card

VIII. VOLUNTARY EMPLOYER RECOGNITION

If authorization cards are signed by a majority but voluntary employer recognition is denied, the employer can require signatures to be verified by a neutral party, the union can picket for 30 days, and either party can petition for a representation election.

If more than 50% of the employees sign authorization cards, unions typically request "voluntary recognition" from the employer. "Voluntary recognition" is recognition of the union as the exclusive bargaining agent of the employees without an election on the ground that the authorization cards demonstrate that the union would win any election that might be conducted. Employers who refuse to voluntarily recognize unions notwithstanding the fact that a majority have signed authorization cards typically dispute the composition of the bargaining unit or the authenticity of the signatures on the cards. The NLRB can be petitioned to determine the proper composition of the bargaining unit as discussed above. If the employer questions the authenticity of the signatures on the authorization cards, it may require that they be verified by a neutral, third party prior to recognizing the union. If the employer refuses to recognize the union whether or not the signatures are verified, the union may engage in "recognitional picketing" for up to thirty days. Recognitional picketing is picketing designed to pressure an employer to voluntarily recognize the union as the exclusive bargaining agent of the employees. At any time, either the employer or the union may petition the NLRB for a representation election to settle the matter by having the employees vote by secret ballots.

Essential Vocabulary

1. voluntary recognition
2. recognitional picketing

IX. REPRESENTATION ELECTIONS

The NLRB conducts representation elections by secret ballot and certifies the results barring subsequent elections for 1 year or the length of the contract whichever is longer.

Representation elections conducted to determine if employees want to join a union are called "certification elections." The name comes from the fact that a union that wins the right to represent employees in such an election is certified by the NLRB as the exclusive bargaining representative for the employees in the bargaining unit. All representation elections are conducted by secret ballot. If employees that are represented by a union would like to remove the union as their bargaining agent, a "decertification election" must be held. Unions can be removed only through a majority vote of the employees they represent. When a new union campaigns to replace the union that represents employees, the resulting election is referred to as a "raid election." When both the union and the employer consent to the election, an election can be held without the necessity of an order from the NLRB. When only the union or the employer wants the election, the NLRB must be petitioned for an order requiring the election. Once a representation election is held, no subsequent elections may he held for one year or the length of the contract between the employees and the employer, whichever is longer. This is called the "one year rule." Restrictions on subsequent elections are necessary to control the frequency of disruption caused by the employer and union campaigns.

The International Brotherhood of Robot Assemblers (IBRA) campaigned with employees of Dan's Robots, Inc. to convince them to replace their current union, The National Mechanical Assemblers Union (NMAU). After a bitter campaign, IBRA managed to obtain the signatures of 32% of the employees on their authorization cards. Neither the NMAU nor the employer would consent to a representation election to determine the will of the employees. In this situation, the IBRA can petition the NLRB to order a representation election. This type of election is a raid election.

Essential Vocabulary

1. certification election
2. decertification election
3. raid election
4. one year rule

X. CAMPAIGN TACTICS OF EMPLOYERS

The NLRB may order employers to cease and desist, rerun elections, or bargain for threatening plant closures, unilaterally making concessions, or holding captive audience presentations within 24 hours of elections.

Although union representatives may generally speculate regarding the benefits of union representation, employers' campaign tactics are subject to significant regulation. The NLRB may order employers to cease and desist practices held to be unfair campaign tactics if the campaign is still in progress. If the campaign has been concluded and unfair employer campaign tactics are likely to have influenced the outcome of the representation election, the NLRB may order the election to be rerun. In severe cases of employers using unfair campaign tactics, the NLRB may issue an order to bargain requiring the employer to recognize the union regardless of the outcome of the representation election.

Employers may not threat plant closures to discourage employees from voting in favor of unionization. Employers also may not attempt to make issues that form the basis of union campaigns moot by simply giving employees the benefit promised by the union before the election is held. In addition, employers may not require employees to attend their presentation against the union within 24 hours of the election. Employers have the privilege of being able to speak with workers during working hours while union representatives generally do not. If employers make presentations within 24 hours of the election, union representatives would be unable to schedule an after-hours meeting with employees to respond to the employers' statements. This limitation on employers' right to hold captive audience presentation during working hours is referred to as the "24 hour rule."

During a bitter organizational campaign, union representatives consistently claimed that their representation would result in significant improvements in wages despite employer claims and "proof" that this was not economically feasible. To combat this rhetoric, the employer held a meeting on the day of the representation election to present its financial records and explanations of the economic realities faced by the company. When the election was held, a majority of employees voted against unionization. If the union representatives file an unfair labor practice charge against the employer, the NLRB may issue an order requiring the election to be rerun. The employer violated the 24 hour rule to influence employee voting. This deprived union representatives of an opportunity to respond to the claims of the employer. If the election were run again, union representatives would have an equal opportunity to address issues with the employees.

Essential Vocabulary

1. 24 hour rule

CHECK YOUR UNDERSTANDING

DIRECTIONS: Read each of the following questions. Choose the best answer and study the discussion of the question.

1. In a situation in which an employer feels that the union representatives have engaged in an unfair labor practice, the employer should:?

    a. file unfair labor practice charges with the union.
    b. file unfair labor practice charges with the NLRB.
    c. file charges with the Industrial Commission.
    d. file suit in court.
    e. file suit in federal court.

DISCUSSION

  (b)   An employer may file an unfair labor practice charge with the National Labor Relations Board any time. The Board will hear and determine the charges. If the Board finds that either the employer or the union representatives have engaged in unfair labor practices, it may issue cease and desist orders, orders to rerun the election, or an order to bargain depending upon which side violated the rules and procedures dictated by the act and regulations. Since the employer is accusing union representatives, the Board is likely to issue a cease and desist if the election has not already been held and an order to rerun the election if employees have already voted. Charges are not filed with the union or the employer because they are not neutral parties. The Industrial Commission is a state agency charged with policing employee wage and injury claims as well as various other state employee protection laws. Suit may not be filed in a state or federal court until all administrative remedies have been exhausted. Since the NLRB is a federal administrative agency, charges must be filed with it first.

2. The board of directors decided that it was not in the best interest of the corporation to negotiate with it's employees' union representatives. The board, therefore, required all new employees to sign a contract in which they agreed not to join or support any collective bargaining organization. Violation of this agreement would constitute grounds for termination of employment. This practice is:

    a. legal unless state law prohibits it.
    b. legal under the Employment at Will Doctrine.
    c. illegal under the Sherman Anti-trust Act of 1890.
    d. an illegal yellow dog contract.
    e. an illegal secondary boycott.

DISCUSSION

(d) Contracts threatening termination of employment for union activities are illegal under the NLRA. The term "yellow dog contract" is a derisive term coined by proponents of organized labor who felt requiring employees to agree not to organize was a cowardly practice. Since the NLRA is a federal statute, conflicting state law and the Employment at Will Doctrine would not be controlling under the Doctrine of Federal Supremacy. The Sherman Anti-trust Act has been supplanted by the NLRA and does not apply to organized labor. Secondary boycotts are unfair labor practices sometimes committed by unions and are not applicable to this situation.

3. An employment contract in which an employer agrees that employees can refuse to handle goods shipped from a plant in which other employees are on strike is:

    a. an illegal trusteeship.
    b. a legal union shop agreement.
    c. a closed shop provision.
    d. a hot cargo agreement.
    e. a featherbedding contract.

DISCUSSION

(d) Agreements not to handle goods produced by companies being struck are called "hot cargo" agreements. They are a form of secondary boycott that is prohibited by the NLRA. Closed shop and union shop provisions are two types of union security clauses. Closed shop provisions required prospective employees to join the union before they could be hired and are illegal under the NLRA. Union shop provisions require employees to join the union as a condition of continued employment and are legal in states without state "Right to Work" legislation. Featherbedding contracts refer to contracts negotiated by unions in which an employer is required to pay for unnecessary work. This practice is also prohibited under the NLRA.

4. Which of the following unions would generally be best for welders who are hired for specific jobs and then move to new employers frequently?.

   a. The American Federation of Labor
   b. The Congress of Industrial Organizations
   c. The AFL-CIO
   d. an industrial union
   e. a craft union

DISCUSSION

(e)   Craft unions represent skilled workers on a regional basis because they tend to be hired for specific jobs and then move to new employers when the job has been completed. Industrial unions represent unskilled workers and organize them on a plant by plant basis because they tend to remain with the same employer. The American Federation of Labor and the Congress of Industrial Organizations merged to form the AFL-CIO. This national organization is the political arm of organized labor unions and does not represent workers on the local level.

5. Some of the employees of Fat Chicken, Inc. wanted to form a unit for collective bargaining. They started to meet with their fellow employees during lunch and breaks in the company cafeteria to discuss organizing. Eventually, they contacted a union and asked for an organizer employed by the union to help them recruit employees. 'When Sal Monella, the company manager, found out what was going on, he issued an order stopping employees and union organizers from speaking with employees on company premises. In doing this, he cited the company policy that prohibited all solicitation on the premises. Sal's order is probably an unfair labor practice when applied to:

   a. skilled workers.
   b. unskilled or semiskilled workers.
   c. anyone trying to organize the employees of Fat Chicken.

d.   the employees of Fat Chicken but not the union organizer.

e.   the union organizer but not the employees.

DISCUSSION

(d)   Employees may campaign for organization on company premises when they are on break or at lunch. However, outsiders may not solicit employees if the company has a blanket no-solicitation policy. Since Fat Chicken will not allow any organizations to solicit on company premises, union organizers may not do so either.

6.   During an authorization card campaign to organize 100 employees at Doughnuts Galore, Inc., union organizers obtained 26 signatures from employees authorizing the Brotherhood of Doughnut Hole Cutters to represent them. The union can probably:

a.   demand employer recognition of the union.

b.   petition the NLRB for a representation election.

c.   do nothing because there is not a substantial interest in organizing.

d.   strike for up to 30 days to obtain employer recognition.

e.   stop unionized firms from dealing with Doughnuts Galore.

DISCUSSION

(c)   The organizers cannot proceed because they do not have at least 30% of the employees signing authorization cards. Organizers may petition the NLRB for a representation election only the 30% requirement has been met. Organizers may demand employer recognition of the union only if more than half of the employees have signed authorization cards. In this situation, the union may petition the NLRB for an election or picket for up to 30 days. Striking without begin organized and stopping other unionized firms from dealing with the company would constitute unfair labor practices on the part of the union.

7.   Sixty percent of the employees at General Appliance signed authorization cards designating the International Brotherhood of Appliance Workers as their collective bargaining representative. The employees consisted of production line workers, licensed electricians, office clerks, and accountants. Which of the following workers cannot be included in the bargaining unit without their separate, majority consent?

a.   production line workers

b.   licensed electricians

    c. office clerks

    d. accountants

    e. all of the above.

DISCUSSION

    (d) Professionals may not be included in a collective bargaining unit without approval by a majority. Since accountants are professionals, they may not be included in the unit without their separate, majority consent. The other employee classes listed may be included from the outset. However, the licensed electricians may exercise their right of craft severance to be released from the unit after they are included because they are skilled workers.

8. If an employer refuses to recognize a union when the union announces that a majority of employees have signed authorization cards, which of the following is correct?

    a. The NLRB will order the company to recognize the union as the bargaining agent if an arbitrator verifies the signatures.

    b. The union can picket the employer or petition the NLRB for a representation election.

    c. the union can picket customers to pressure the company for recognition.

    d. The union can require the company to petition for an election.

    e. The company can replace the employees who signed authorization cards.

DISCUSSION

    (b) If a majority of the employees in the proposed bargaining unit have signed authorization cards, the organizers may request voluntary employer recognition of the union as the exclusive bargaining agent of the employees. If the employer refuses voluntary recognition, the union may offer to have an independent third party verify signatures. If the employer refuses even this, the union may picket for recognition for up to 30 days. At any time, the union or the employer may petition the NLRB for a representation election. Picketing customers would constitute an unfair labor practice. The union may not force the employer to petition for an election, and the company may not take action against employees that support the union.

9. Before a representation election is held, unions are generally entitled to:

    a. recruit employees on the business premises.

    b. meet with employees during working hours if the employer does so.

    c. an Excelsior List

    d. preliminary recognition if only one union is attempting to organize the employees.

    e. use company property for meetings after regular working hours.

DISCUSSION

(c)   Prior to representation elections both the union organizers and the employers may campaign to influence employee votes. Since union organizers are often not permitted access to employees on the premises, they must provide organizers with an Excelsior List containing the names and contact information on all employees working in the proposed bargaining unit. Unions may not generally campaign on the business premises or meet with employees during working hours. Unions are not entitled to preliminary recognition under the NLRA.

10. Yellow Dog Biscuits, Inc. campaigned earnestly against the union during the organization campaign. It successfully defeated the union's organizing campaign by threatening to close the plant if the union was successful and by giving the employees a raise without consulting the union. The union can probably:

    a. do nothing for one year because it lost the representation election.

    b. immediately mount another authorization card campaign.

    c. obtain a bargaining order from the NLRB.

    d. require the company to pay for an arbitrator to recount the ballots.

    e. obtain a judgment against the company for its expenses in opposing the company propaganda.

DISCUSSION

(c)   Employers may not unfairly interfere with organization through unfair labor practices during the campaign. Employers may not threaten plant closures or make unilateral concessions to employees during the campaign. When this occurs, the NLRB may order the election to be run again or simply order the employer to recognize the union as the exclusive bargaining agent for the employees.

Chapter 25
Credit Law

The rights of debtors and creditors have evolved considerably in modern times. Much of the law delimiting their relative rights and responsibilities is governed by state and federal statutes. This section will summarize the most important concepts and form a good foundation for students of business and management.

I. CREDITORS' REMEDIES

Creditors may obtain writs of garnishment and attachment prior to judgment and writs of garnishment and execution after judgment.

Creditors are provided with protections from debtors who attempt to hide or damage their assets once suit has been filed against them. In an appropriate situation, a creditor may petition the court for a "writ of garnishment" or a "writ of attachment" before judgment has been entered. A "writ of garnishment" is a court order requiring third parties holding funds belonging to the debtor to pay them into court. A "writ of attachment" is a court order requiring the debtor or third parties in possession of the debtor's property to deliver the assets to the sheriff or constable for safe storage until judgment has been entered. If a creditor can show that a debtor is attempting to hide property that could be used to satisfy the debt, the creditor may post a bond to obtain the appropriate writs from the court. The bond is usually required to be in an amount of twice the value of the property to be seized. After judgment has been rendered in favor of a creditor, the creditor may obtain a writ of execution requiring the judgment debtor to deliver his "non-exempt property" to the sheriff or constable for sale to produce funds to satisfy the judgment debt. No bond is required for the issuance of a writ of execution or garnishment issued after a judgment has been entered by the court. Nonexempt property is property owned by a debtor that can be seized by a creditor holding a judgment. Certain property is declared exempt from execution by state and federal statutes for humanitarian reasons. "Exempt property" usually consists of basic necessities, e.g. furniture in use, personal clothing, etc.

Arnold sued Bill for breach of contract. After the suit was filed, but before trial, Arnold learned that Bill was preparing to send his personal property to relatives living in different states and empty his bank accounts to hamper collection of any judgment that might be rendered against him. Arnold could petition the court for a pre-judgment writ of attachment to have the sheriff or constable seize Bill's nonexempt personal property. If necessary, Arnold could obtain a pre-judgment writ of garnishment to seize Bill's bank accounts. Before the writs could be issued, Arnold would be required by the court to post a bond in an amount equal to twice the value of the property and funds to be seized. If Arnold's claims were later found to be illegitimate, the bond would ensure funds to cover any damages awarded to Bill against Arnold.

Essential Vocabulary

1. writ of attachment
   writ of garnishment
   nonexempt property
   exempt property

II. FRAUDULENT TRANSFERS

Fraudulent transfers in which debtors hinder collection by passing property to third parties without full consideration will be set aside.

Creditors may only attach and execute upon property to which the debtor has title. If the debtor no longer has title to property once owned, it is not subject to seizure and sale. In light of this, debtors sometimes attempt to hinder collection through fraudulent transfers in which they give assets to others in an attempt to separate themselves from title. A "fraudulent transfer" is a transfer of assets owned by a debtor to another for less than full consideration. In theory, creditors still have access to the proceeds of assets sold for full consideration so sales in good faith are not considered fraudulent. However, a transfer for less than full consideration such as a gift passes title without producing funds accessible by creditors. Fraudulent transfers are typically indicated by secrecy or the retention by the debtor of possession or the right to use or obtain the return of the property at a later date. Fraudulent transfers may be set aside in actions by creditors against third parties holding assets formerly held by debtors.

Charlene was found liable in the amount of $25,000 in an action for breach of contract brought by Dynamo, Inc. To stop Dynamo from seizing her home entertainment center and having it sold, she gave it to her sister, Ellen. When Dynamo discovered this and demanded that Ellen deliver the property to the constable for sale, she refused to cooperate. Dynamo can sue Ellen to have the court set aside the fraudulent transfer. Once the transfer is set aside, Dynamo can proceed to execute the judgment.

Essential Vocabulary

1. fraudulent transfer

III. ASSIGNMENTS FOR THE BENEFIT OF CREDITORS

Assignments for the benefit of creditors transfer nonexempt assets to trustees for liquidation and stay execution without discharge of indebtedness.

Debtors can agree with creditors to an "assignment for the benefit of creditors." An assignment for the benefit of creditors is an arrangement in which the debtor assigns title to his property to a trustee for the benefit of creditors. Once the property has been sold by the trustee and expenses have been paid, the proceeds of the sale are distributed to participating creditors. These assignments are binding only on participating creditors who agree to the "stay of execution" on their judgments. A stay of execution is a cessation of all attempts to collect from a debtor. Once the proceeds of the trustee's sale have been distributed, creditors may resume collection efforts because the assignment does not discharge their claims.

Edwin owed three creditors a significant amount of money. Each of the creditors sued him and required his presence in court during their collection efforts. Edwin agreed he owed the debts, but did not have sufficient property to satisfy them. To provide relief from continual collection efforts, Edwin could contact his creditors and arrange for an assignment for the benefit of creditors in which he would deliver his nonexempt property to a trustee for sale. If the creditors agreed, they would cease to attempt to collect from Edwin during the assignment. The assignment would provide Edwin with at least temporary relief from his creditors' collection efforts.

Essential Vocabulary

1. assignment for the benefit of creditors
2. stay of execution

IV. COMPOSITION AGREEMENTS

Composition agreements allow debtors to discharge the debts of participating creditors through partial payment.

State statutes allow debtors to enter into agreements with some or all of their creditors to pay a portion of each creditor's claim in full satisfaction of the debt. These agreements, called "composition agreements," are binding only upon participating creditors. The consideration supporting a creditor's agreement to a composition is the discharge of the debtor's debts by the other creditors. The advantage of these agreements is that debtors can obtain relief from harassment by their creditors without the necessity of filing for bankruptcy while creditors obtain at least partial settlement of their claims. Compositions are frequently associated with assignments for the benefit of creditors.

Francis was generally able to pay her debts, but she owed a doctor and a hospital many thousands of dollars due to a recent medical crisis for which she was uninsured. She had few assets and her earned income was insufficient to pay the debts. Unfortunately, she was frequently contacted regarding payment by her medical creditors. Francis may be able to meet with her medical creditors or their representatives to disclose her financial situation and arrange for partial payment to discharge her obligations through a composition agreement under state law.

Essential Vocabulary

1. composition agreement

V. EXTENSION AGREEMENTS

Extension agreements allow debtors to extend the time for payment of their debts.

State statutes allow debtors to enter into agreements with some or all of their creditors allowing them to extend the time for payment. These agreements, called "extension agreements," are binding only upon participating creditors. The consideration supporting a creditor's agreement to an extension is the agreement to an extension by other participating creditors. While extension agreements require the debtor to pay the entire obligation, creditors do not disturb the debtor during the extended payoff period. The advantage of these agreements is that debtors can obtain relief from harassment by their creditors without the necessity of filing for bankruptcy while they pay their creditors. Often, debtors are able to arrange for both compositions and extensions with their creditors in appropriate situations.

Although Gerald was generally able to pay his debts, he suddenly became unable to pay them as they became due because of a serious financial setback. To avoid being sued and increasing his costs due to litigation, Gerald may be able to meet with his creditors or their representatives to disclose his financial situation and arrange for additional time to pay through an extension agreement under state law.

Essential Vocabulary

1. extension agreement

VI. CHAPTER 7 LIQUIDATION (STRAIGHT BANKRUPTCY)

A petition in Chapter 7 requests the debtor be allowed to obtain discharge through liquidation of nonexempt property and partial payment to creditors.

A "voluntary petition" in bankruptcy may be filed by any debtor other than a decedent's estate, trust, stockbroker, railroad, insurance company, lending institution, or governmental agency. Voluntary petitions are filed by the debtor to obtain relief from creditors' collection activities. Voluntary petitions may be filed as frequently as once every six years. In addition to voluntary petitions, creditors may file "involuntary petitions" against debtors that are not paying their debts as they become due. Involuntary petitions are involuntary in the sense that creditors are requiring a debtor to submit to the provisions of the bankruptcy law. Involuntary petitions may only be filed under chapters 7 and 11 of the Federal Bankruptcy Act. Federal law provides that involuntary petitions may be filed by one or more creditors if there are fewer than 12 creditors. If there are more than twelve creditors, involuntary petitions may be filed by three or more creditors. Creditors filing involuntary petitions against debtors must together have at least $5,000 in unsecured claims. Petitions in bankruptcy may be filed under several different chapters of the Federal Bankruptcy Act. Each chapter takes a different approach to providing debtors with relief from creditors' attempts to collect their debts and providing creditor's with a fair opportunity to collect a portion of their claims.

A bankruptcy filed under Chapter 7 of the Federal Bankruptcy Act is referred to as a "liquidation" or "straight bankruptcy." In a liquidation or straight bankruptcy, the debtor's nonexempt property is liquidated or sold and any proceeds are distributed to creditors in total satisfaction of their claims against the debtor. The filing of a petition results in the imposition by the court of an "automatic stay." An automatic stay is a court order prohibiting creditors from pursuing any further actions to sue or collect from the debtor during the bankruptcy proceedings. All pending litigation, garnishments, writs of execution, etc. must be immediately discontinued once the petition is filed. Since the bankruptcy law and the courts that administrate it are federal, they override state legislation and court orders under the Doctrine of Federal Supremacy.

Once the petition has been filed, a meeting of creditors is scheduled and a "bankruptcy trustee" is appointed by the court. The bankruptcy trustee can be any person with appropriate experience and expertise who is charged with gathering the debtor's nonexempt property and selling it on behalf of the creditors. During the first meeting of creditors, the debtor is examined regarding his assets. The trustee will seize all nonexempt assets and sell them for the benefit of the creditors. The proceeds from the sale are first used to pay the trustee and other administrative costs of the proceedings. Any funds remaining are applied to the claims of creditors. Payments are made to creditors by the bankruptcy trustee based upon the size of their claims compared to the total claims of all creditors, e.g. available funds may only allow 10% of claims to be paid. The debtor's nonexempt assets include gifts, inheritance, and insurance settlements paid to the debtor within 180 days of filing the petition for relief in bankruptcy.

The bankruptcy proceeding usually results in a "discharge." A discharge is a federal court order discharging the debtor from further liability on the debts listed in the petition. However, debts arising from unpaid taxes, criminal actions, intentional torts, and family support obligations cannot be discharged in bankruptcy. Family support obligations include debts arising from separate maintenance agreements or orders, alimony, and child support. In addition, debts arising from "reaffirmation agreements" not rescinded prior to issuance of the discharge order are not discharged. Reaffirmation agreements are agreements between the debtor and secured creditors in which the debtor agrees to repay the debts notwithstanding any discharge in bankruptcy. Occasionally, debtors enter into such agreements to avoid having creditors exercise their rights to take possession of or sell specific property held by the debtor subject to security agreements, mortgages, deeds of trust, etc.

Helen does not make enough money to pay her debts. Creditors are constantly suing her and requiring her presence in court to answer questions regarding her property. Despite the fact that it is illegal, her employer is threatening to fire her because garnishments are repeatedly filed against her wages. If Helen files a petition in bankruptcy under Chapter 7, she will need to declare her nonexempt assets and deliver them to the trustee for sale. Once the petition is filed, the automatic stay will prevent her creditors from further harassing her for payment. Following the sale of her assets and distribution of the proceeds to her creditors her debts will be discharged and her former creditors will no longer be able to pursue their claims.

Essential Vocabulary

1. voluntary petition
2. involuntary petition
3. liquidation

4. straight bankruptcy
5. automatic stay
6. bankruptcy trustee
7. discharge
8. reaffirmation agreements

VII. CHAPTER 11 REORGANIZATION

A petition in Chapter 11 requests that the debtor be allowed to obtain discharge through the reorganization of the business under a plan providing for extended, partial payment of debts.

A voluntary or involuntary petition for bankruptcy under Chapter 11 of the Federal Bankruptcy Act requests that the court appoint a committee of unsecured creditors to assist the business in "reorganization." A reorganization may include restructuring of debt and equity within the company, renegotiating contracts with third parties, renegotiating collective bargaining agreements with unions, and arranging for extensions and partial payments of company debts. Once the petition is filed, an automatic stay goes into effect protecting the company from further actions by its creditors.

A creditors' committee is appointed by the court consisting of unsecured creditors to assist in the formulation of a plan for reorganization that will allow the business to continue in operation while addressing its obligations to its creditors. The object of the plan is to preserve the business while providing creditors with at least partial payment of their claims. Once the committee of creditors approves a plan, the court will appoint a trustee to implement it. Plans typically provide for extended, partial payment of debts while the debtor remains in business. Plans often provide for division of the equity in the company between the original owners and creditors. If secured creditors are provided with adequate security under the plan, the court may require them to participate by not exercising their rights to seize specific company property. Once the plan has been fully, and successfully implemented, the remainder of the listed debts of the company are discharged.

Intrepid Airlines has not been profitable due to a downturn in the economy and the cost of complying with federal regulations to prevent terrorism. Its collective bargaining agreement with employees will not expire for another year. Intrepid owes a significant amount of money to a jet manufacturer for planes recently purchased. If the manufacturer repossesses the planes, the Airline will lose so much of its business that it will not longer be viable. Intrepid can file petition in Chapter 11 and request that the airline be reorganized to allow it to continue in operation. Once the petition is filed, an automatic stay goes into effect stopping all creditors from pursuing their claims against Intrepid during the proceedings. A committee of creditors may adopt a plan providing for the transfer of an ownership to the manufacturer and allowing the business to continue in operation. The collective bargaining agreement may be replaced immediately with an employee compensation package approved by the committee and employee representatives to prevent the total loss of the business. If the plan is successfully implemented, the airline may be able to continue in operation indefinitely despite its temporary financial problems.

Essential Vocabulary

1.   reorganization

VIII. CHAPTER 13 WAGE EARNERS' PLANS

A voluntary petition in Chapter 13 requests that the debtor be allowed to obtain discharge through the execution of a plan for extended, partial payment of debts.

Petitions under Chapter 13 may only be voluntarily filed by debtors. To qualify for relief, debtors must have regular income with less than $250,000 in unsecured debts and less than $750,000 in secured debts. Along with the petition, the debtor must file a plan to make partial payments to his creditors over an extended period of time. If the plan is approved by the court, a trustee is appointed to administer it. The restrictions on the characteristics of debtors that may file have earned Chapter 13 bankruptcies the nickname, "wage earners' plans." When the debtor has successfully implemented the plan and made the appropriate partial payments of his debts, the court will issue a discharge forever barring creditors claims against the debtor on the listed debts.

Jared is not able to make payments on his debts as they come due. Although he is working, creditors are constantly interfering with his employment by taking action against him to collect their debts. Jared may file a petition under Chapter 13 requesting that he be allowed to additional time to repay his debts and that his debts be discharged before he makes full payment. Once the petition is filed, the automatic stay would prevent his creditors from taking further action against him and his property. A trustee would be appointed to supervise his compliance with the plan's provisions until it has been successfully executed. Once the plan has been performed, all remaining claims against him would be discharged.

Essential Vocabulary

1.   wage earners' plans

IX. PREFERENTIAL TRANSFERS

A trustee in bankruptcy may have the court set aside preferential transfers and liens made by the debtor.

One of the primary purposes of the bankruptcy laws is to protect the claims of creditors. This can be accomplished only if all creditors with the same class of claims are provided with an equal opportunity to obtain payment on their claim. If debtors are allowed to pay some creditors to the exclusion of others, this objective cannot be obtained. Consequently, trustees in bankruptcy are allowed to have "preferential transfers" to creditors set aside by the court. A preferential transfer is a payment or transfer of property to "insiders" within the year preceding the filing of the bankruptcy petition that would result in the creditors receiving a greater proportion of their claims against the debtor than other creditors. Insiders are relatives and others with whom the debtor has a close relationship. Transfers to creditors who are not insiders within 90 days of filing the petition are also deemed preferential if the creditors receive a larger proportionate share of their claims than other creditors due to the transfers.

Payments on consumer debts less than $600 and payments to secured creditors are exempted from the preferential transfer rules. The exemption for consumer debts is necessary to limit the burden on the courts and trustees to examine the small and frequently occurring transactions ordinary consumers would be expected to have. The exemption for payments to secured creditors is necessary to address the reality that they would execute on the collateral or real property securing their claims if they were not paid. Payments to secured creditors increases the debtors equity in the property securing the debts. Because a debtor's equity in nonexempt property can later be accessed in appropriate situations by the trustee, other creditors are not disadvantaged by such payments. When preferential payments or transfers are set aside by the court, the creditors receiving them are ordered to return the payments or property to the trustee for proportional distribution to the entire group of creditors.

Karen could not make payments on her debts as they became due. When creditors began to threaten legal action, she gave her car, worth $50,000, to her brother in full satisfaction of her $55,000 debt to him. Six months later, she filed for relief in bankruptcy. Because the car was her only significant asset, her other creditors would essentially receive nothing pursuant to the bankruptcy proceedings. The trustee could petition the court to set aside the transfer as a preferential transfer. Karen's brother would be required to return the car or the proceeds from its sale to the court for distribution pursuant to the proceedings. Karen's brother would be entitled to only a proportional share of the proceeds from the sale of the car along with the other creditors.

Essential Vocabulary

1. preferential transfer

X. PRIORITIES IN BANKRUPTCY

Secured debts, administrative expenses, middle debts, employee benefits, consumer deposits, alimony, support, and taxes must be paid before general unsecured debts. (SAME CAST)

Once nonexempt property has been sold pursuant to a petition in bankruptcy, the trustee must arrange for distribution of the proceed to creditors. Certain classes of debts are entitled to priority under the Federal Bankruptcy Act due to considerations of policy and practicality. Debts entitled to priority must be completely paid before any funds can be distributed to creditors with unsecured claims. "Secured debts," "administrative expenses," "middle debts," "employee benefits," "consumer deposits," "alimony and support obligations," and taxes must be paid before general, unsecured creditors.

Secured debts are debts secured with liens on personal or real property. They must be in full before general debts because the creditors have the right to repossess and resell the property securing their claims if they are not paid. However, secured creditors are only entitled to priority up to the value of the property securing their claims. Any amounts in excess of this are considered general, unsecured claims and are not entitled to priority. Administrative expenses are expenses resulting from conducting the bankruptcy proceedings. They are given priority in an effort to use the debtors' assets to pay the costs of the proceedings. Middle debts are debts incurred during the bankruptcy proceedings. It is necessary to provide for priority satisfaction of middle debts or third parties would refuse to do business with bankruptcy trustees and debtors attempting to satisfy their obligations according to plans approved by the court. Employee benefits consist primarily of insurance and retirement benefits payable to employees. They are accorded priority pursuant to public policy attempting to protect wage earners and prevent them from becoming wards of the state. Consumer deposits are typically down payments made by consumers on consumer goods. Priority is accorded for these claims based upon the widely applied policy of consumer protection. Consumer deposit claims are often so small that it is not cost effective for consumers to protect their own interests in the bankruptcy proceedings. Alimony and support obligations imposed by state law requiring family members to provide for each other both during marriage and after separation or divorce. This priority is consistent with a policy against placing debtors' current and former family members in a position where they will become wards of the state. Of course, taxes are entitled to priority satisfaction due to the fact that they represent the debtor's obligations to society.

Essential Vocabulary

1. secured debts
2. administrative expenses
3. middle debts
4. employee benefits
5. consumer deposits
6. alimony and support obligations

CHECK YOUR UNDERSTANDING

DIRECTIONS: Read each of the following questions. Choose the best answer and study the discussion of the question.

1. Andrew owes Baker $35,000. When Baker files suit to collect the debt, Andrew begins to make preparations to give his motor home to his sister as a birthday gift. If Andrew learns of this, he:

    a. can seize the motor home, sell it, and keep the proceeds in full satisfaction of Baker's debt.
    b. can seize the motor home, sell it, and pay the proceeds to the clerk of the court for safe keeping.
    c. can prevent the transfer by posting bond and obtaining a prejudgment writ of attachment against the motor home.
    d. can do nothing to stop the transfer which will result in placing the property beyond the reach of the judgment lien.
    e. can do nothing to stop the transfer, but he would be able to have the transfer set aside as a fraud against creditors if he wins a judgment.

DISCUSSION

(c)   Baker can petition the court for a prejudgment writ of attachment to prevent the transfer. The court would require him to post a bond in twice the value of the property. The bond would be used to ensure that funds would be available to satisfy any claims that Andrew may have against Baker if Baker lost the lawsuit. Property cannot be seized and sold prior to judgment because the rights of the parties have not been adjudicated.

2. Charlene won a judgment against Diane for $3,000. Diane's only asset was her stereo. To avoid losing the stereo, Diane gave it to her husband as a birthday gift. When Charlene attempted to execute on the stereo, Diane's husband claimed he owned it. Which of the following statements is correct?

    a. Charlene can have this transfer set aside by a court and sell the stereo to obtain funds to satisfy the judgment.
    b. Charlene cannot have the transfer set aside because Diane no longer has title.
    c. Charlene can prosecute Diane's husband for theft.
    d. Charlene can take possession of the stereo through a writ of garnishment.
    e. Charlene can take possession of the stereo only if Diane's husband was living with her at the time of transfer.

DISCUSSION

(a)   Because the transfer from Diane to her husband was a gift, it was a fraudulent transfer that will be set aside by the court. The fact that she still had access to the stereo by virtue of giving it to her husband would be evidence of a fraudulent transfer but it not required to maintain the action. When the court sets this fraudulent transfer aside, title will return to Diane making the property subject to execution on the judgment.

3. EFG Corporation owes three creditors $6,000. The corporation is no longer a viable company, and its only asset is a large rock crusher. To avoid the expense of filing a petition in bankruptcy, EFG can:

    a. sell the crusher and distribute the proceeds to shareholders.
    b. assign the rock crusher to a trustee to sell it for the benefit of the creditors.
    c. give the rock crusher to it's largest creditor in an attempt to pay at least one of the creditors.
    d. file a petition for a state bankruptcy.
    e. sell the crusher if each creditor receives the same amount of money from the sale.

DISCUSSION

(b)   An assignment for the benefit of creditors makes the most sense in this situation because the shareholders are not liable for the debts of EFG. The assignment would save much in expenses that would eventually be paid to the creditors based upon the proportion of their debt compared to the debts of all three creditors. Assume that the crusher were sold for $3,000, and EFG owed creditors the following amounts: A – $1,000, B – $2,000, and C – $3,000. A would receive one-sixth of the proceeds or $500 because his claim was one-sixth of the total amount of claims. B would receive $1,000, and C would receive $1,500. Although their claims for the remainder would not be barred by the assignment for the benefit of creditors, they would be unable to collect the remainder of their claims because the corporation had no additional assets.

4. In a composition of creditors under state law, which of the following is correct?
   a. Creditors will retain the right to collect the remainder of their claims against the debtor.
   b. Creditors will waive the right to collect the remainder of their claims against the debtor.
   c. Creditors will waive the right to collect the remainder of their claims until the debtor files for bankruptcy.
   d. Creditors will not waive the right to collect the remainder of their claims unless assets are assigned to a trustee for sale.
   e. Creditors must participate in a composition under state law.

DISCUSSION

(b) Creditors waive the right to collect the remainder of their claims against the debtor when they enter into a composition agreement under state law. Creditors are not required to participate and those that elect not to participate are free to continue to pursue their claims against the debtor. Trustees may or may not be involved in a composition. Typically, the debtor makes agreed partial payments to creditors in complete satisfaction of his debts without the necessity of filing for bankruptcy.

5. In an extension agreement under state law:
   a. Creditors can be required to participate.
   b. Debtors can choose the amount they would like to pay to their creditors under the agreement.
   c. Debtors can require creditors to participate in the agreement.
   d. Creditors agree to allow the debtor to make smaller payments over a longer period of time.
   e. Creditors require the debtor to make payments over a longer period of time.

DISCUSSION

(d) Creditors agree to allow the debtor more time to make payments. These agreements are typically used in conjunction with composition agreements to avoid the necessity of filing for bankruptcy. Participation by creditors is optional, and all parties must agree to the amount of the payments and the extension of time allowed to the debtor.

6. Harold filed a suit against a customer who owed him $42,000 and won a judgment. The customer filed for bankruptcy and notified Harold. Which of the following statements is correct?

   a. Harold can execute on property owned by the customer prior to filing the bankruptcy action.
   b. Harold may seek relief under the state statute dealing with composition agreements.
   c. Harold's right to collect on his judgment is not affected by the bankruptcy.
   d. Harold cannot collect on his judgment but he can file another action to collect the $42,000.
   e. Harold cannot collect on his judgment beyond making a claim in the bankruptcy action.

DISCUSSION

(e) Harold cannot pursue the collection of his judgment due to the imposition of the automatic stay when the bankruptcy petition was filed by the customer. His only remedy will be to file a claim as a creditor in the bankruptcy action. The stay will prevent him from seeking any relief whatsoever under state law. The doctrine of res judicata will prevent him from filing another action against the customer after the bankruptcy has been concluded. Harold may only file for relief as a creditor in the bankruptcy action.

7. Peters Printing, Inc. cannot make the payment on a new printing press it purchased. Peters' creditors are preparing to execute on the assets despite the fact that the business is a going concern. Although some creditors are willing to discuss an extension and composition, others are not. If Peters would like to continue operating the business, it should:

   a. file for relief under Chapter 7 of the Bankruptcy Act.
   b. file for relief under Chapter 11 of the Bankruptcy Act.

   c. file for relief under Chapter 13 of the Bankruptcy Act.

   d. pursue a state court order for a composition of creditors.

   e. pursue a state court order for an extension of time for payment.

DISCUSSION

(b) Peters must file under Chapter 11 for a reorganization. A liquidation under Chapter 7 would result in the sale of all business assets. Chapter 13 is primarily for wage earners rather than businesses. Compositions and extensions under state law are voluntary and creditors cannot be compelled to participate. If the creditors that would not be likely to participate held significant claims against Peters, a bankruptcy petition would be the best remedy for Peters.

8. Rene had incurred significant debts due to being out of work. Finally, she obtained a job. Unfortunately, her automobile would be required for transportation to and from work. Her creditors routinely summoned her to court to disclose her assets and threatened garnishment and execution on her automobile. Despite her attempts to reach an agreement with her creditors, they continue to attempt to collect. If Rene would like to pay her creditors while retaining possession of the automobile, she should:

   a. file for relief under Chapter 7 of the Bankruptcy Act.

   b. file for relief under Chapter 11 of the Bankruptcy Act.

   c. file for relief under Chapter 13 of the Bankruptcy Act.

   d. pursue a state court order for a composition of creditors.

   e. pursue a state court order for an extension of time for payment.

DISCUSSION

(c) Rene should file under Chapter 13. A liquidation under Chapter 7 would result in the sale of all nonexempt assets and could result in the loss of her automobile. Chapter 11 is primarily for businesses. Compositions and extensions under state law are voluntary and creditors cannot be compelled to participate. A bankruptcy petition filed under Chapter 13 would be the best remedy for Rene because creditors could be compelled to cease their attempts at collection during her execution of her repayment plan. The plan could include provisions for both an extension of time, reduction of payments, and, ultimately, discharge of her remaining debts by partial payment.

9. A significant payment to a creditor which unfairly compromises the pool of assets available to pay other creditors, is:

a. a preferential transfer that may be set aside.
b. a preferential transfer that may not be set aside if it was made to satisfy a legitimate debt.
c. a preferential transfer that may only be set aside if it was made without adequate consideration.
d. a transfer in fraud of creditors.
e. a tortious transfer.

DISCUSSION

(a) Preferential transfers may be set aside whether or not they were intended to be fraudulent and whether or not the debt was legitimate. These transfers are made on antecedent debts rather than as part of a purchase. When transfers are made to pay for a current purchase, creditors are not harmed because they would have access to the property purchased. Transfers in fraud of creditors are usually made for little or no consideration in an effort to hide property from creditors. They may be set aside in state and federal actions to set aside fraudulent transfers and conveyances. Preferential transfers do not normally give rise to actions in tort.

10. Which of the following obligations would be entitled to priority in an a bankruptcy proceeding?

a. past due child support
b. past due education loans
c. past due utility bills
d. past due charitable contributions
e. past due rent

DISCUSSION

(a) Past due child support is a family support obligation given priority under public policy. The other obligations are only general in nature and would be paid, if at all, as general claims in bankruptcy.

Index